FIGHTING AND WRITING

Luise White

FIGHTING AND WRITING

THE RHODESIAN ARMY AT WAR AND POSTWAR

DUKE UNIVERSITY PRESS | *Durham and London* | 2021

© 2021 Duke University Press
All rights reserved

Designed by Matthew Tauch
Typeset in Minion Pro by Westchester Publishing Services

Library of Congress Cataloging-in-Publication Data
Names: White, Luise, author.
Title: Fighting and writing : the Rhodesian army at war and postwar / Luise White.
Description: Durham : Duke University Press, 2021. | Includes bibliographical references and index.
Identifiers: LCCN 2020022213 (print) |
LCCN 2020022214 (ebook) |
ISBN 9781478010623 (hardcover) |
ISBN 9781478011729 (paperback) |
ISBN 9781478021285 (ebook)
Subjects: LCSH: Southern Rhodesia. Army. Selous Scouts. | Whites—Zimbabwe—History. | Whites—Race identity—Zimbabwe. | Zimbabwe—Race relations—History. | Zimbabwe—History—1965–1980. | Zimbabwe—History—Chimurenga War, 1966–1980.
Classification: LCC DT2988 .W45 2021 (print) |
LCC DT2988 (ebook) | DDC 968.91/04—dc23
LC record available at https://lccn.loc.gov/2020022213
LC ebook record available at https://lccn.loc.gov/2020022214

Cover art: Eleven Troop 3 Commandos at Deka on the Zambezi, 1978. Photograph by Tom Argyle. Courtesy of Chris Cocks.

CONTENTS

vii		*Acknowledgments*
xi		*Place-Names, Currency, and Acronyms*
1	**1**	Zimbabwe's Liberation Struggle and Rhodesia's Bush War: Locating Its History
31	**2**	"Blood and Ink": Memoirs, Authors, Histories
59	**3**	"Your Shona Is Better Than Mine!": Pseudo Gangs, Blacking Up, and the Pleasures of Counterinsurgency
83	**4**	"Each Footprint Tells a Story": Tracking and Poaching in the Rhodesian Army
109	**5**	"There Is No Copyright on Facts": Ron Reid-Daly, Authorship, and the Transkei Defence Force
121	**6**	"Every Self-Respecting Terrorist Has an AK-47": Guerrilla Weapons and Rhodesian Imaginations
141	**7**	"A Plastic Bag full of Cholera": Rhodesia and Chemical and Biological Weapons
167	**8**	"Will Travel Worldwide. You Pay Expenses": Foreign Soldiers in the Rhodesian Army
197	**9**	"What Interests Do You Have?": Security Force Auxiliaries and the Limits of Counterinsurgency
222		Conclusions
227		*Notes*
261		*Bibliography*
281		*Index*

ACKNOWLEDGMENTS

My published scholarship has gone from a history of prostitution to a study of rumors to a book about an assassination in Zimbabwe's liberation movement to this, a book about white soldiers fighting against African nationalism in the 1970s. This trajectory makes perfect sense to me. With the exception of *The Comforts of Home*, which began life as my dissertation, these studies did not begin with questions about a specific past or place but with my nearly obsessive interest in a body of evidence, oral or written, that I sought to write with and about. What that has meant in practice was that that "big picture" that everyone but historians demands was sometimes absent but most often came late to the table. This book is no different: I had found the memoirs of former Rhodesian soldiers and the contests around their publication and reception fertile subject matter: I was less interested in adjudicating who won and who lost this war and why than I was in studying how soldiers understood the war and their place in its conduct. As someone schooled in the importance of microhistory, I believed that the small was important in and of itself; it might offer insights into other places and other times, but the joy and despair and ambivalence soldiers found in this conflict offered me a critical way to understand this war. It was only after I began to think about these memoirs critically and in a broader context that I began to answer questions about who won and who lost this war and why.

This has been a slow journey. I first went to Zimbabwe in the mid-1990s with a very different project. I was fortunate to have financial support from the Social Science Research Council and the Wenner-Gren Foundation for Anthropological Research and intellectual support from the Department of Economic History at the University of Zimbabwe and from my township-savvy assistants, Joseph Seda and the late Simba Handesani. My first serious engagement with these war memoirs was when I was a fellow at the Center for African Studies at the University of Kyoto in 2000, where Esei Kurimoto and Matoji Matsuda were especially thoughtful interlocutors. I wrote most of the manuscript when I was a fellow at the National Humanities

Center in 2016–17. I had been there before, in the early 1990s, largely due to the great generosity of Kent Mullikin, so it was a special honor to return to the Center as the Kent Mullikin Fellow. I was thrilled to be there, to talk and think out loud with my fellow fellows, and to be pampered by the extraordinary librarians. Brooke Andrade and Sarah Hughes laughed at me when I said that I thought finding a complete run of *Soldier of Fortune* might be a challenge. In between those fellowships there were research trips, and I am grateful to the friends who sheltered me in different countries. For decades Helen and Robert Irwin have put me up in London, and Murray McCartney and Irene Staunton have been a refuge and a home in Harare since the last century. In other places and at other times I have been the fortunate houseguest of Diana Jeater in Wick, Megan Vaughan in Oxford, Judy Butterman and Roger Tangri in Gaborone, the late and sorely missed Bill Freund in Durban, Anne Mager in Cape Town, and Jon Hyslop, Isabel Hofmeyr, and David Moore in Johannesburg. Jon was my companion in Johannesburg's wide range of secondhand bookstores, where I first discovered the density of Rhodesian soldiers' memoirs.

The rest of my source material came from archives and libraries. I had the good fortune to do research in the Rhodesian Army Association papers—barely cataloged and arranged in the order in which they were put in storage lockers in South Africa in February 1980—at the British Empire and Commonwealth Museum in Bristol before it closed in 2011. The staff was unfailingly accommodating during my several visits. Jennifer Betts of the Hay Library at Brown University helped me get the most out of a short stay, and Dorothy Woodson was an enthusiastic host during my visit to the Zimbabwe Collection at the Sterling Memorial Library at Yale University. David Easterbrook welcomed me to the Africana collection at Northwestern University many times. Without fail, archivists and librarians have been exceptionally helpful throughout this research, but none so much as Ivan Murambiwa in the National Archives of Zimbabwe and Dan Reboussin at the University of Florida. For more than twenty years UF has been my home, and a good one from which to write. As I began to think about writing this book, chairs and associate chairs in the Department of History encouraged me to teach courses about war and war memoirs. The university's Center for African Studies (CAS) has been one of those charmed spaces that every academic should experience. It has and has had a wide, interdisciplinary group of scholars who like each other, who care deeply about the future of the continent we study, and who respect each other's intellectual traditions: we know how to publish, and we know how to party. I am grateful to the directors who supported this project with goodwill and even better humor—Michael Chege, Leonardo Villalon, Abe Goldman, and Brenda Chalfin—and to the associate director, Todd Leedy. The Center allowed me to organize a large conference on war in Africa at UF in 2005 and provided the bulk of funds for a 2013 conference I organized with Miles Larmer at Sheffield University. The papers and discussions from both events have informed this book. The Center for Humanities and the Public Sphere of the College of Liberal Arts and Sciences at UF funded a workshop I organized with Alioune Sow on the production of memoirs in Africa, and its Rothman Endowment provided a generous subvention for the publication of this book.

Three scholars deserve special thanks. I first got to know Len Smith when we were both fellows at the National Humanities Center in 1993–94. I'm not sure I would have even contemplated writing about soldiers had it not been for his example of what kind of history a history of a military could be. Over the years he has been patient with my questions while proving beyond the shadow of a doubt that you could write about armies and still be one of the cool kids. Steve Davis began the doctoral program at the at the University of Florida in 2003. The very fact that this book exists owes a great deal to working with him on his dissertation (now a book) about Umkhonto wa Sizwe in South Africa. I like to joke that we grew up together as military historians of the region, but the fact is he matured much faster than I did. In 2011 I moved offices in the Center for African Studies and found myself next door to Alioune Sow, a scholar of Francophone African literature. As our daily greetings and gossip turned to our research, I became fascinated by his work on prison memoirs in Mali and his attention to their publication. When I began this book, I realized that those casual conversations made for more careful writing about memoirs.

My fellow Zimbabwe scholars have been generous with references, newspaper clippings, encouragement, and really, really good company. Historians of Uganda in the 1970s went beyond the call of collegiality when I was trying to find out about Zimbabwe guerrillas trained in Idi Amin's Uganda in the late 1970s. I am grateful for the help and enthusiasm and not infrequent legwork of Alicia Decker, Mark Leopold, Derek Peterson, and Edgar Taylor. Chris Cocks and Chas Lotter were exceptionally generous with photographs. Jacob Dlamini helped me track down court transcripts and judgments. Greg Mann has routinely asked the kinds of questions that helped me keep my feet on the ground, and Patricia Hayes is perhaps the only person I know who was truly happy to spend hours talking about pseudo gangs with me. Over many years many former combatants from all the armies in this war have been willing to spend time with me, answer my questions, and offer suggestions and reading lists and photographs. As with my previous books about this period, I have not named informants but cited my field notes because these were conversations, often casual, that at the time I did think would become a book. Once again let me thank the men and women who were not cited. They will see their impact on my thinking, if not their names.

At Duke University Press, Elizabeth Ault's enthusiasm was infectious: it got me to finish this book. Before I was done, however, friends and colleagues read all or various chapters: Jeffrey Adler, Jocelyn Alexander, Gary Baines, Mathew Booker, Brian Child, Samuel Fury Childs Daly, Steve Davis, Michael Hagermann, Douglas Howland, Nancy Rose Hunt, Jon Hyslop, Benjy Kahan, Corrine Kratz, Greg Mann, Fiona McLaughlin, Dee Mortensen, Francis Musoni, Steven Pierce, Tim Scarnecchia, Leonard Smith, and Alioune Sow. I am grateful for the careful and critical readings they gave my work. I hope I didn't let them down.

I started working in Zimbabwe in 1995. My visits there have coincided with what is euphemistically known as Zimbabwe's "decline." Talk about this war and its heroes and villains has accompanied this decline. I do not intend this book to change the importance of this war or to claim that various heroes and villains have been mislabeled, but I hope that it will occasion another way to think about the war and the meaning of its conduct.

PLACE-NAMES, CURRENCY, AND ACRONYMS

The convention of historical writing of the country this book is about is to include a list of place-names in the front matter, with Rhodesian names on one side and the Zimbabwean names on the other. I will not do that here. The country I write about had four names between 1960 and 1980; what these were and how they changed are discussed at the start of the first chapter. I avoid such lists because of my concerns about a notion of before-and-after in history: a list of place-names and their changes suggests a too pat transformation from colony to nation, from bad to good, from minority to majority rule. Such a list also suggests that transitions are instantaneous, that a threshold has been crossed. For the record, however, Rhodesia became Southern Rhodesia from mid-December 1979 to April 1980, when it became Zimbabwe. Salisbury, the capital, became Harare only in 1982. More common and never part of any list has been the tendency to use "Rhodesian" to mean white and "Zimbabwean" to mean African. I have tried to avoid this as often as I could throughout this book.

With the breakup of the Central African Federation, Rhodesia named its currency the pound (£). Cast out of the sterling zone shortly after the Unilateral Declaration of Independence (UDI), Rhodesia valued its pound at US$2. In 1970, Rhodesia adopted the dollar as its currency. It was designed to be valued at half a British pound and between 1970 and 1980 hovered at about US$1.50. This currency—most often written as R$—was not convertible outside of Rhodesia, however, so most foreign trade took place in South African rand (ZAR) or European or African currencies.

It also is a convention of Zimbabwean historiography to provide a list of acronyms at the start of the book. Parties and armies and factions and policies are often known by their initials, which take on a life of their own in politics and academic studies. I have avoided listing these acronyms in my other work: doing so gives all organizations an equivalency that they did not have. Such lists are also not very helpful. They obscure the ways that white political parties changed their names because they were very fluid coalitions and African political parties changed their names because they had been banned and had to create a new one. Thus, the Zimbabwe African People's Union (ZAPU) was the new name for the banned National Democratic Party (NDP), which itself was the new name for the banned Southern Rhodesia African National Congress (SRANC). In 1963 the Zimbabwe African National Union (ZANU) was formed by dissidents in ZAPU. A list of acronyms and what each one stands for does not do justice to the complexities of party names. In 1976, for example, ZANU and ZAPU formed a united front with which to negotiate at all-party conferences. This was the Patriotic Front that negotiated both at Geneva in 1976 and at Lancaster House in 1979. In preparation for the 1980 elections, ZANU left the Patriotic Front but kept the name in parentheses. This may have been a convenience for the ballot, so as to distinguish itself from the ZANU led by Ndabaningini Sithole, which had been part of the internal settlement. The party is still known as ZANU(PF). ZAPU was left with the name Patriotic Front under which it contested the election. After the election it returned to ZAPU. The following list is of the acronyms I use in this book:

ANC	African National Congress (South Africa and Northern Rhodesia)
ANC	African National Council (in Rhodesia)
AP	Associated Press
ARC	Armored Car Regiment
BSAC	British South Africa Company
BSAP	British South African Police
CIA	Central Intelligence Agency (US)
CID	Criminal Investigation Department (of BSAP)
CIO	Central Intelligence Office (Rhodesia)
FNLA	Frente Nacional de Libertação de Angola
FRELIMO	Frente de Libertação Moçambique
FROLIZI	Front for the Liberation of Zimbabwe
IDAF	International Defence and Aid Fund
INTAF	Internal Affairs
JOC	Joint Operations Command
MPLA	Movimento Popular de Libertação de Angola
NDP	National Democratic Party
OAU	Organization of African Unity
OCC	Operations Coordinating Council
PAC	Pan African Congress (South Africa)

PATU	Police Anti-Terrorist Unit
PCC	People's Caretaker Council
PLO	Palestine Liberation Organization
PsyAc	Psychological Action
RAF	Royal Air Force
RAR	Rhodesian African Rifles
RDR	Rhodesian Defence Regiment
RENAMO	Resistência Nacional Moçambicana
RF	Rhodesian Front
RhAF	Rhodesian Air Force
RLI	Rhodesian Light Infantry
RR	Rhodesia Regiment
SADF	South Africa Defence Force
SAP	South African Police
SAS	Special Air Services
SASOL	South Africa Synthetic Oil Ltd.
SFA	Security Force Auxiliaries
SRANC	Southern Rhodesia African National Congress
SRP	Safe Return Program
UANC	United African National Council
UDI	Unilateral Declaration of Independence
UNHCR	United Nations High Commission on Refugees
UNITA	União Nacional para a Independência Total de Angola
ZANLA	Zimbabwe African National Liberation Army
ZANU	Zimbabwe African National Union
ZAPU	Zimbabwe African People's Union
ZIPA	Zimbabwe People's Army
ZIPRA	Zimbabwe People's Revolutionary Army
ZUPO	Zimbabwe United People's Organization

1 ZIMBABWE'S LIBERATION STRUGGLE AND RHODESIA'S BUSH WAR

Locating Its History

Naming the past is a way to talk about the present; it signals a position. In this case it proves either one's support or disdain for self-determination and African nationalism. How does one name the past I write about? Between 1898 and 1980 the country that is now Zimbabwe had four names: Southern Rhodesia (1898–1964, but as Southern Rhodesia part of the Central African Federation from 1953 to 1963), Rhodesia (1964–79), Zimbabwe-Rhodesia (1979), and Zimbabwe (1980–). This has made for unwieldy chronologies and awkward historiography, to the point that it has been commonplace to reduce the four names to two, Rhodesia and Zimbabwe. These in turn became a shorthand for race that created a series of either/or scenarios that omitted too much. The two names and all they embody have allowed for some self-serving discursive flourishes in which authors vow never to return to Rhodesia only to arrive in Zimbabwe at the start of the next chapter.[1] But this has reduced a complicated history to a progression from one separate and distinct country to another, from minority-ruled Rhodesia to majority-ruled Zimbabwe.

In most of these histories, Rhodesia was a placeholder, an aberration in the postcolonial world that delayed African rule in a country that had another name. There is a large body of scholarly literature that uses the term "colonial Zimbabwe" for the period before 1980 even though neither Southern Rhodesia nor Rhodesia was a colony; other literature calls Rhodesia Southern Rhodesia as if its period of renegade independence should not be named. I argue that the Rhodesia-to-Zimbabwe story is too limited to fully describe its fractured and sometimes bewildering history. The war about which I write was an enormous part of that history, and what an author calls that war literally stakes out a political position. Zimbabwe's

Map 1.1 Rhodesia, 1964–1979.

liberation struggle is enshrined in nationalist historiography. However nuanced and critical an analysis is, this was the story of guerrilla armies defeating minority rule in Southern Africa years after the era of decolonization. What Rhodesians—even after there was no country of Rhodesia—called the bush war has another meaning. At its best it is the story of brave white men defending their land, and at worst it removes the struggle from a political context: it describes where white men patrolled and fought; it reveals nothing about what they fought for.

How, then, do I write the history of a war, or any part of that war, when the most basic vocabulary with which to describe the conflict—the names of the country—carries so much content that it can overwhelm analysis? Are white soldiers fighting for an independent white-ruled Rhodesia Africans or just whites? There's the additional problem that this book is about a war in a country that no longer exists. Did this mean that Rhodesia could be whatever authors wanted it to be? Was it the place where white men did what needed to be done, where they said, "So far and no further"?[2] Rhodesia became a locus for like-minded men, fictional Americans who "felt like" Rhodesians or fictional white Kenyans for whom fighting African guerrillas elsewhere was "personal" (see chapter 8). Or was it the more prosaic place where this imaginary never fully took hold nor did it fully overlap with white supremacy (see chapters 3 and 4)? How did former soldiers, whatever their nationality or wherever they thought they belonged, write about this war after 1980? That question troubled me for many years, but I seem to have worried too much. Rhodesian soldiers were not alone in writing about countries that no longer existed: the Confederacy or the Boer Republics of South Africa all had national narratives that came after the nation was lost in a war. These former soldiers replaced a war of weapons with a war of words, as Bill Nasson put it. Nasson describes postwar Boer writing—"Afrikaaner" was not in common use before 1920—in terms of its materiality. The South African war left a "residue." It cast "a long shadow" because the meaning of its history was concrete in the sense that it was the opposite of transparent: it began Boer history anew; it prevented a critical look at what went before the war. Afrikaaner nationalism was thus built on the victories and defeats and agonies and attacks of the war.[3] Much of this can be said about the Confederacy and to a lesser extent about Biafra—a favorite Rhodesian example of British perfidy—where the short-lived nation became more popular as a lost cause than it had been as a cause.[4] In contrast, Rhodesian writing about the bush war did not create a unified wartime experience (see chapter 2). Soldiers' war of words was not so much about Rhodesian nationalism—which I have argued was never a straightforward project—as it was about the confusion and contradictions of the war itself. There was nothing concrete in its imagery; it was a literature that struggled over what being a white Rhodesian meant, and what pasts and futures soldiers brought to the war.

Some History

There are basic histories needed to understand this war. In 1896–97, when the country was under the rule of Cecil Rhodes's British South Africa Company, adventurer administrators organized a disastrous invasion of the Transvaal. Almost at once there was an uprising in the country. Many European settlers were killed, and the repression was brutal. Moreover, the repression brought bushcraft to the fore: hunters and trackers used their knowledge of the wild to hunt and track Africans. Whether the rising was a war of clans and spirit mediums who attacked white settlers or an anticolonial revolt organized by clans and spirit mediums does not matter for this book, at least not as much as the extent to which the fear of another uprising became a staple of white popular culture in the country.[5] Almost sixty years later there was the creation and demise of the Central African Federation (1953–63). An amalgamation of Southern Rhodesia, Northern Rhodesia, and Nyasaland had been proposed for years.[6] It only came about after the decolonizations of the late 1940s—in India especially but also Cyprus and Israel—when the Colonial Office sought new territorial forms, not simply to rule but to end its rule. African opposition was intense from the start, but the colonial overreaction during the Nyasaland Emergency of 1959 led to commissions that recommended it be dissolved. The issue was not just British and Southern Rhodesian soldiers firing on unarmed protesters; the issue was that this took place in 1959, when most of Anglophone Africa was preparing for independence.[7]

Southern Rhodesia did not prepare for independence, or at least not independence with majority rule. In 1961, as the federation was understood to be failing, Southern Rhodesia produced a new constitution. It was considered a masterful document that Africans had a hand, albeit a small one, in crafting. It promised Africans equal representation in parliament in an unrealistic fifteen years. The constitution was at first accepted by African nationalists, including Joshua Nkomo and Robert Mugabe, then of the National Democratic Party (NDP), and then rejected by them, creating two linked narratives that would last twenty years, that whites offered too little, too late and that Africans were intransigent, rejecting all incremental improvements.[8] The NDP was not the only political party opposing the new constitution, however. In 1962 the Rhodesian Front (RF), led by Ian Smith and supported by far-right segregationist parties, won a narrow victory proposing independence instead of decolonization. Although Britain opposed this, most of the war matériel belonging to the federation and the entirety of its air force were returned to Southern Rhodesia in 1963. The official rationale is that these forces began there and should be returned, but throughout the continent it was understood that the country was given the military capacity to withstand an invasion. In 1964, when Northern Rhodesia became independent as Zambia and Southern Rhodesia changed its name to Rhodesia, the RF was elected by a landslide and began acrimonious negotiations with Britain over its future. In November 1965, a week after the British governor had extended the state of emergency, Rhodesia made a Unilateral Declaration of Independence. This was UDI, an acronym used to describe the act and the period of Rhodesia's independence.⁹

The NDP had been banned before the 1961 constitution was in place. It then became the People's Caretaker Council (PCC) before it was banned again when it became the Zimbabwe African People's Union (ZAPU) in exile. It was led by Nkomo, whom many members considered increasingly autocratic. In 1963, when he proposed to make ZAPU a government in exile so that he could negotiate with Britain as head of government, many party members left ZAPU to form the Zimbabwe African National Union (ZANU). Years later this was explained by several binaries, that the split was between Shona and Ndebele peoples or between Soviet and Chinese clients. Both explanations are woefully inadequate. While the leaders of ZANU—especially Rev. Ndabaningini Sithole, Robert Mugabe, and Herbert Chitepo—were indeed Shona speakers, they had all once been connected to liberal, multiracial political parties.[10] ZAPU had regular contacts with the USSR since the early 1960s; by the 1970s it had secure lines of East European funding; Rhodesians insisted that there was rarely, if ever, a shortage of weapons (see chapter 6). In its early years, ZANU was not regarded as a serious rival to ZAPU by its East European donors. Chinese support for ZANU only became noteworthy after the Sino-Soviet split; between 1963 and 1966, ZANU was closer to Kwame Nkrumah's Ghana and its particular vision of Pan-Africanism than it was to any Cold War ideology. The party had no real benefactor in its early years, with the bulk of its weapons coming from guns purchased from the black markets of Congo by its representative in Zambia. At least as important as ethnicity or Cold War politics, however, were contemporary, continent-wide events: ZANU grew up, as it were, with the Organization of African Unity (OAU), also founded in 1963.[11] Both ZANU and the PCC were banned in Rhodesia in 1964, and Nkomo, Mugabe, and Sithole spent the next ten years in detention. These detentions meant that African politics took place increasingly in Rhodesia's prisons.

In December 1965 the foreign ministers of the OAU countries declared war on Rhodesia; they set up a Liberation Committee, based in Dar es Salaam because several liberation movements had camps in Tanzania, which would channel East European funds to guerrilla armies. The OAU regarded ZAPU as the legitimate guerrilla army struggling to liberate Zimbabwe. In 1966 ZANU's national chairman, Herbert Chitepo, left Tanzania, where he had been director of public prosecutions, for Lusaka, where he became the head of ZANU's external wing. He was to organize ZANU's armed struggle from there, which meant he sought East European funding for weapons and uniforms. Neither ZANU nor ZAPU had anything resembling an army, however. Both had youth wings that had honed their skills in township violence—a tendency in ZAPU thought this would encourage Rhodesia to negotiate majority rule—and many of these men went to Tanzania or Zambia to train as guerrillas. Starting in 1963, perhaps one hundred young ZAPU were sent to the USSR, China, North Korea, and Cuba for training. When they returned to Zambia, they were tasked with training ZAPU's military wing. ZAPU's joint operations with South Africa's African National Congress—a well-established favorite of Soviet support—in 1967 and 1968 gave it revolutionary credentials above and beyond the failed infiltration. ZANU's first incursions into Rhodesia were even less successful. Most of the cadres who were deployed were untrained and unarmed; many had been in exile so long that they were confused by new landmarks of tarmacked roads and plowed fields. ZANU's army became the Zimbabwe African National Liberation Army (ZANLA) in 1965; in 1966, when ZANU had men in training camps, the OAU recognized it as a legitimate liberation movement.[12]

As more and more men were trained by ZANU and ZAPU in the camps of Tanzania, there were more and more debates about how the armed struggle should be fought. Life in the camps was often tense. Even press-ganged men seemed to want to fight, and to fight with guns (see chapter 6). There were mutinies. The March 11 Movement in ZAPU in 1971 and the Nhari Rebellion in ZANLA in 1975 were not solely about ideology or ethnicity, as many authors have argued, but about strategy, training, and most of all favoritism and corruption in senior staff. Many March 11 rebels were deported to Rhodesia, where several were tried for treason and hanged, but those who remained in Zambia encouraged a debate within the army about discipline and favoritism. ZAPU then re-created its army as the Zimbabwe People's Revolutionary Army (the acronym of which was written as it was pronounced, ZIPRA) but not before a large number of guerrillas—ZANLA claimed one-third of ZAPU's fighting force—crossed over to ZANLA in Zambia and in Kongwa camp in Tanzania. Another protest against the conduct of both armies was the creation of a new party in 1971, the Front for the Liberation of Zimbabwe (FROLIZI). Its only army was made up of defectors; its main source of support was from Zimbabwean exiles abroad. After six months of claiming to be an army rather than a political party, it was given funds by the Liberation Committee. The physical and rhetorical struggles between ZANU and ZAPU in early 1970s Tanzania and Zambia had been barely manageable: a new political unit, whether it was a party or an army, was intolerable. ZANU and ZAPU formed a joint military command that paid lip service to a unified liberation movement, but its goal was to strengthen both parties' claim to OAU funds.

The Nhari mutiny and its repression changed the history of ZANLA, in part because they coincided with an attempt to negotiate an end to the war. This was the détente promoted by Henry Kissinger of the United States, several multinational corporations, and South Africa, and intensified by the Carnation Revolution in Portugal in 1974 and the pending independence of Angola and Mozambique. The presidents of the frontline states—Tanzania, Botswana, and Mozambique—met with Nkomo and Sithole, who were released from detention to attend the meeting in Lusaka in November 1974. After three weeks of tense meetings, a declaration of unity was signed by the leaders of ZANU, ZAPU, and FROLIZI to join forces under the label of Bishop Abel Muzorewa's enlarged African National Council (ANC), which had mobilized ZAPU in Rhodesia to a oppose a settlement plan in 1972 but was fully compromised by Rhodesia's Special Branch in 1973. Two long-serving ZANU foot soldiers, Thomas Nhari and Dakari Badza, led a group from a camp in Mozambique to Lusaka, where they killed and kidnapped several ZANU. By the time the mutineers returned to Mozambique, ZANLA had sent cadres chosen from men from camps in Tanzania, where I was told they had more experience with guns, to hunt them down. Perhaps 150 of Nhari mutineers were executed there. Three months later, Chitepo, who signed the execution orders, was killed by a car bomb in Lusaka. Within a week, fifty-seven ZANU members and ZANLA officials were arrested and 1,300 ZANLA were detained in their camps in Zambia. Who killed Chitepo—still the subject of great debate—is less germane for this history than is the imprisonment of so many senior ZANLA at the same time guerrillas were supposed to fight under the umbrella of the ANC, which created almost eighteen months of disarray in the armed struggle.[13] Cadres complained that they did not know who they were fighting for, although ZIPRA was able to establish itself in camps in Zambia during this time. (By the late 1970s, ZAPU had a larger army in Zambia than Zambia did.) Rhodesian forces held their ground during these months of confusion in guerrilla armies but did not manage anything resembling a decisive victory. In May 1976 senior officers from ZANLA and ZIPRA founded the Zimbabwe People's Army (made into the word ZIPA). Based in Mozambique and aggressively presenting itself as a revolutionary force capable of invading Rhodesia, they denounced negotiations as unnecessary.

They did not receive OAU funds, although they controlled ZANLA's camps in Mozambique, but received monies from Olusegun Obasanjo in Nigeria and blessings from Samora Machel in Mozambique, who introduced them to the Scandinavian embassies that might support them. In recent years ZIPA has been infused with nostalgia, the democratic alternative that never reached fruition, but whatever its promise, ZIPA's most important accomplishment was to put ZANLA and ZIPRA on notice: if they weren't going to actively fight a war, someone else would.[14]

By 1976 both armies had more recruits than they could usefully train, and by 1977, when both ZANLA and ZIPRA regrouped it was to fight a Rhodesia that had lurched from one botched attempt at settlement to another. Pressured by skilled and heavy-handed British and American diplomats, keenly aware of South Africa's near exasperation with the Rhodesian project, Smith and the Rhodesian Front agreed to the internal settlement of 1978.[15] The settlement was between the RF and several domesticated African political parties: Muzorewa's newly renamed United African National Congress (UANC); Ndabaningini Sithole's ZANU, which he hoped would have some legitimacy after he was ousted as party leader by Mugabe, who now headed ZANU(PF); and Chief Jeremiah Chirau's Zimbabwe United People's Organization (ZUPO), which had almost no credibility outside of white political circles. ZANU and ZAPU had formed the Patriotic Front (PF) in order to appear unified at the conference in Geneva in 1976. There was no real unity, but ZANU created a new acronym, ZANU(PF). The 1978 settlement allowed for very close to one man, one vote elections the following year. Both Sithole and Muzorewa claimed to have surrendered guerrillas on their side (see chapter 9), and as Rhodesia planned an election—one the Patriotic Front boycotted—during a war, the Rhodesian security forces sought a way to retrain and deploy these former guerrillas. Many were not guerrillas and were press-ganged at least as much as early ZANLA and ZIPRA had been; many of the men who trained them thought many were unemployed urban youth or petty thieves seeking a way to hone their skills. Starting in 1978, ZIPRA brought thousands of soldiers from Angola and Zambia who had been trained in conventional warfare; their deployment changed the war dramatically, as ZANLA began to infiltrate more and more guerrillas over a wider area.

Muzorewa won the election of March 1979. Depending on who one believes, he won 43 percent of the vote or 69 percent in an election declared free and fair by the official British observers. Rhodesia became Zimbabwe-Rhodesia, which was called "Rhobabwe" almost at once. It had an African head of state and Africans in its cabinet. Muzorewa was considered "weak" by the Rhodesian military. The former generals I have spoken to said he did whatever whites told him to do, which was to exert a level of force, especially airpower, that previously had not been deployed.[16] The years 1978 and 1979 were a period of cross-border bombing raids, sometimes in retaliation for an attack, as in the bombing of Westlands and Mkushi camps in Zambia in 1978, and sometimes as bold strategy as in attacks on various camps in Mozambique. Guerrilla forces tended to see airborne attacks as Rhodesia's desperation and, indeed, planes were shot down, men were killed, and key targets escaped capture as the number of increasingly well-armed ZIPRA and ZANLA increased. At the same time, the number and arms of soldiers loyal to Muzorewa grew. They were funded primarily by South Africa and soon became a private army—Pfumo reVanhu, spear of the people—as did Sithole's more problematic cadres (see chapter 9).

The bombing raids into Zambia and Mozambique changed the course of the war and shaped how it would end. Although Kenneth Kaunda and Samora Machel, along with every other African leader, denounced Muzorewa and his election as illegitimate, they knew that even 40-odd percent of the vote was proof of some popularity, and if his regime could survive it might eventually be recognized as legitimate. In August 1979 the Commonwealth Heads of State met in Lusaka, where, after private conversations with almost every African head of state, a version of the Anglo-American proposals of 1977 was made into a formal recommendation for the end of the war. Britain then invited the PF, Muzorewa's government, and the RF to a meeting in London at Lancaster House. Both Nkomo and Mugabe denounced the proposals and the meetings, at least in public. In private they were lectured by Machel—and possibly cautioned by Kaunda—who told them that if there was a way to end the war through negotiations the PF should take it. The negotiations at Lancaster House took three contentious months, but in the end a cease-fire was put in place and elections scheduled for late February 1980.[17] As we shall see, Rhodesians loved to say they won every battle and lost at the negotiating table (see chapter 2). That's wrong: white-ruled Rhodesia did very well in the constitution written in London; it was Zimbabwe-Rhodesia that was all but erased. Zimbabwe-Rhodesia was to become Southern Rhodesia until the election; it was for the first time under direct British control. Muzorewa and his supporters and donors were left struggling for his political life, and his army became more aggressive and violent than ever before.

Manpower and War Power

This history is essential, but it omits one salient point that informed this war and informs this book, that neither Southern Rhodesia nor Rhodesia ever had a sizable or a stable white population. From the conventional founding moment of the seven-hundred-strong Pioneer Column arriving in 1890 to 1980, the white population was transient in the extreme. Rhodesia was a land of opportunity; when it was not, men and women moved on. Southern Rhodesia became one of many sites in the circular migration of skilled and semiskilled white men in the industries of central Africa. White population growth was through immigration, not births, but two-thirds of the white immigrants who came between 1921 and 1964 left the country. The emigration was intensified by war. By the 1970s, the Rhodesian press disparaged the men and women who came and went, calling them "good time Charlies" and "rainbow boys."[18] Even so, the idea of those early pioneers—men and women who coaxed wealth from inhospitable land and who put down an uprising—lasted for decades. In 1966, a cartoon history of the first year of UDI featured one frame in which a white farmer is interviewed for radio. "My opinion on orderly hand-over? Tell them that after a lifetime of hacking a farm from the tough African bush I hand over nothing—orderly or disorderly."[19] Belonging was not a matter of personal history; it was an imaginative project, one that gave whites a claim to African soil.[20]

The question of who should fight this war, and what skin color they should fight in, informs this book (see chapters 3, 8, and 9). There were certainly not enough whites to fight a prolonged war. Southern Rhodesia's white soldiers were known, if they were known at all, for fighting somewhere else. Ian Smith had been a fighter pilot during World War II. He had trained in Southern Rhodesia, was shot down in Italy, and had fought with Italian partisans there. Several whites fought as volunteers in Malaya in 1951; the Malaya Scouts were loosely affiliated with C Squadron Special Air Services (SAS); these men served in the Rhodesia Regiment (RR), which had fought with the British Army in the Boer War, World War I, and World War II. It was part of the federal army that served in Nyasaland in 1959. In 1961—beginning an era that saw the greatest increase in white immigration—Southern Rhodesia raised an all-white infantry unit, the Rhodesian Light Infantry (RLI), which was to become the largest regiment of the war. As the federation's weapons of war were transferred to Southern Rhodesia, officers commanding African troops asked for two battalions of the African infantry unit, the Rhodesian African Rifles (RAR). The RAR was originally the Rhodesia Native Regiment, formed in 1916; it became the RAR in 1940. It was one of the African regiments that liberated Southeast Asia in World War II. It was an askari regiment, African soldiers commanded by white officers—a commonplace colonial regiment often called "rifles"—that was by far the most experienced infantry unit in the country, and by many reckonings the most effective in the late 1970s. In 1963 the RF refused another African battalion: I have been told the party feared African soldiers, but that the army did not. By the end of the war, the army had won: there were three RAR battalions, a depot, and a jazz band.[21]

In the last years of the Central African Federation, conscription was considered necessary to address the new contingencies of African nationalism. In 1960, Southern Rhodesia introduced a superficial conscription of four months for young men—white, Coloured, and Indian—who had resided in the country for two years or more. Coloured was a legal category referring to people of mixed race. The Rhodesian Army had an acronym for nonwhite troops, CAE, for Coloured, Asian (meaning Indian), and Eurasian. Coloureds and Indians served in two units, eventually combined into the Rhodesian Defence Regiment, which primarily provided transport and supply. In 1960, the first conscripts were sent to the border Northern Rhodesia shared with the newly independent Congo, where young white Southern Rhodesians were said to have watched in horror as Belgians fled for their lives.[22] At the time of UDI—when the OAU declared war on Rhodesia—national service for whites, Indians, and Coloureds was increased to four and a half months. In 1970, South Africa rotated between one thousand and fifteen hundred policemen in and out of Rhodesia; there is a body of literature that regards this as the essence of white supremacy, as the ultimate linkage between the apartheid and Rhodesian governments. Some of the most prominent murderers of the South African state served in Rhodesia and credited their time there with how they learned to fight terrorism.[23] Rhodesian Army documents and my own conversations have suggested something very different, however: they were poorly trained and had almost no success in operational areas. I have been told that these were urban policemen incapable of life in the bush; they were bad shots and not disciplined. They could not hold their own with those white Rhodesians who knew the land.[24]

Once the guerrilla war began, and certainly by 1972, conscription of white Rhodesian youths intensified, but by then Rhodesia was a republic and could only call up citizens, rather than residents. This was finessed somewhat with practices that would not have withstood the scrutiny of international law, but by 1972 whites were leaving Rhodesia in record numbers, while other immigrant families were reluctant to apply for citizenship. Foreign soldiers arrived—for many, Rhodesia was the last stand of empire at least in an English-speaking country—but the importance of these men resonated outside the country, not within its armed forces (see chapter 8).

The basic outlines of national service are that by 1972, all white males aged eighteen to twenty-five were required to undertake nine months of "service training" in the army or the police. After their initial service, these men could then be called up over the next three years to serve in the Territorial Army, a force made up of civilians who had completed their military training commanded by regular officers. In mid-1975, national service was extended to one year, and all white males aged twenty-five to thirty were liable to call-ups for fifty-nine days each year; this was extended to eighty-four days almost at once. Men aged thirty to thirty-eight were liable to call-ups for shorter periods. In 1976 conscription was first increased to a year, and then to eighteen months by the year's end; the age limit was raised from thirty to thirty-four.[25] Men aged eighteen to thirty-four who had fulfilled their national service obligation were now placed on "continuous call-up" for the Territorial Army: they could be redeployed for unspecified intervals. This was so disastrous for morale and administration that the army sought ways to get men to stay longer, such as bonuses for enlisting for an extra year. By 1977, however, the call-up was a nightmare to run. Officers routinely complained that they spent more time administering call-ups than they did fighting. Equipment was always in short supply. In 1977, for example, the British South African Police (BSAP) only had radios for half the men it called up each year.[26] Starting in 1978, territorials and police reservists under thirty-eight were required to serve a maximum of 190 days per year, although half the younger group did not report for duty. Men aged thirty-eight to forty-nine were called up for ten weeks in periods of two to four weeks at a time, but only the most experienced soldiers in that age-group were placed on active duty. By then the RF was desperate enough to entertain ideas about how to abolish the call-up altogether, but by January 1979 this was impossible. In preparation for the April election, the manpower requirements were such that men fifty to sixty years old were called up to serve as guards in urban areas. The army had hoped to find those former regular soldiers who had avoided call-ups since their retirements, but only 20 percent of the men called up came forward.[27]

Given Rhodesia's white population, even if every man called up served, there were still not a lot of soldiers with whom to fight a war. What this meant in practice was that the army in particular favored small groups that were tracking units that combined idealized rural boyhoods in which white youths learned the ways of the wild—the "bush" in "bush war"—with twentieth-century counterinsurgency tactics (see chapters 3 and 4). These groups were tasked with gathering intelligence and identifying guerrilla bands so that larger units could capture and perhaps kill them, although kills were detrimental to the process of finding out who and where guerrillas were. "Turning" was an obsession for these small groups, the practice by which guerrillas could be made to change sides and return to their groups to gather intelligence (see chapters 3 and 4). There were to be carefully crafted stories to explain turned guerrillas or white men masquerading as guerrillas to guerrilla gangs. These practices suggest that counterinsurgency may be a misnomer; it was not always clear, as Nicky Rousseau has argued, that the insurgents' insurgency came first.[28] By the last years of the war, the creation of Security Force Auxiliaries (SFAS) was the opposite of the ideal of small groups of soldiers and the intelligence they gathered through clever strategies and deceptions; it was also a way to deal directly with the manpower shortages that plagued the security forces. Indeed, the creation of SFAS gave the lie to many Rhodesian military tactics. However they were trained and whatever they did in the countryside, their numbers undermined the notion of small groups and subterfuge: the widespread assertions that many camps and patrols of SFAS were killed by security forces suggest that the difficulty of telling who was friend and who was foe had become as insurmountable as it was perhaps irrelevant, even as foes had changed their tactics (see chapter 9).

African studies have tended to study wars and soldiers in Africa as something separate and distinct from wars and soldiers elsewhere. This war in particular tends to stand alone; when it has been studied, it has been shown to have had guerrillas guided by spirit mediums. If white soldiers are discussed at all, they are usually folded into South Africa's border wars.[29] There is a literature known as Rhodesiana, which includes the memoirs I frequently cite, that insists on a Rhodesian exceptionalism—the land was theirs, whenever they arrived in the country, and they had every right to fight for it. Rhodesian-born authors were scathing about this, but they understood that if recent immigrants from Britain wanted "a pool and servants . . . to cut the grass you never had in the UK," they would be willing to pay the price of "burning down the odd village."[30] This was Rhodesian exceptionalism, a history of something imagined as "responsible government" that entitled a defense of minority rule. This book argues against this. There was nothing exceptional in the Rhodesian project, but there was a specificity that shaped much of the conduct of this war: the landscape was critical to this, but so were the youths, whenever they arrived in the country, and their understanding of history. This was a war in a very particular place.

War-in-the-Place

Do men go to war for a place, a landscape? Is a new home or a fatherland the reason men are willing to risk life and limb? In his study of Anglo-American war memoirs, Samuel Hynes argues that men go to war because they have a "war-in-the-head," that an older generation's experience of war shapes what a younger generation hopes to find in battle.[31] Thus, the British volunteers of World War I believed in the romance of the late nineteenth-century wars of conquest. In Rhodesia, no single war seemed to take hold in the minds of young soldiers, and no single conflict seemed to provide a singular imaginary. World War II was always present; members of the Rhodesian Front—the name itself recalled the National Front in Britain—routinely called decolonization "appeasement" and spoke of Munich often. Smith's war service was invariably mentioned by foreign journalists but was of no real interest to national servicemen. As a war-in-the-head World War II was distinctly personal. The travel writer Jan Morris met a law professor in 1977, "soft spoken, learned and anything but racialist," who spent one week each month flying troops to remote operational areas. It was invigorating, he said, a reprise of his time in the Royal Air Force (RAF) during World War II.[32] By the early 1970s, however, generals had tethered the conduct of the 1970s war to that of 1897. The two new units formed to meet the demands of guerrilla warfare were given the names of the heroes of the repression of the rising. Courtney Selous, hunter of animals who became a hunter of men, was resuscitated in the Selous Scouts, a fabled pseudo-gang unit (see chapters 3, 4, and 5). Rhodesia's mounted regiment, formed in 1975, was called Grey's Scouts after George Grey, captain of the Bulawayo Field Force of 1896 (see chapter 8). The original police force that could not contain the rebellion, the British South Africa Company Police, became the British South African Police, which kept the name until 1980. Two end-of-empire conflicts—Malaya and Mau Mau in Kenya—may have helped shape Rhodesian strategies, in which white men masqueraded as black men or brown men to win a war, but they were never wars-in-the-head.

Young soldiers did not seem have their parents' or officers' wars in their heads. The American volunteers who gave interviews made ominous references to Angola or Vietnam (see chapter 8), but these were more about the political outcomes than anything to do with the way these wars were fought. The war-in-the-head for many young (and not so young) soldiers came from popular culture, not anyone's experience. Dennis Croukamp was a Rhodesian regular soldier who joined the army in 1964. Describing his second confirmed kill in the eastern highlands in 1970, he recalled, "It felt really good taking a life in this way. The Hollywood syndrome of holding one's heart and saying, 'Help me, I have killed someone' is a load of crap, it feels good, really good."[33] Dick Gledhill, an RLI commando born in Kenya and resident in Australia, was told to release the safety on his gun as soon as his parachute hit the ground: "It could mean the difference between who shoots first. Remember, it's not your job to die for your country. Your job is to make the other fucker die for his."[34] Did Gledhill paraphrase General Patton's speech to the Third Army that serves as the beginning of the 1970 movie and pass it off as his commanding officer's words, or did the officer paraphrase the speech? This book puts the war-in-the-head in its place. I argue that the location of this war—the bush war—became how and where it was imagined by Rhodesian soldiers. The landscape shaped their fighting, the hunting and tracking and sheer danger of rocks and rivers.

Peace-in-the-Head

Whatever wars were in their heads, what did Rhodesians see as an end of this war?[35] No one—not even the far-right segregationists—assumed that a total military victory was possible or even what that might mean. Was it routing every insurgent, in and out of the country? Was it unconditional surrender, in which guerrilla commanders handed over their automatic weapons in solemn defeat? Such futures were rarely voiced, if they were imagined at all. Writing about a very different African war, Isabel Hull has argued that the Germans' near extinction of noncombatants in their repression of the Herero revolt was the only kind of complete victory that was possible under military protocols. If there were to be no negotiations—or any kind of civilian end to the conflict—then the military conquest by a superior force required wider and wider bands of destruction.[36] Rhodesia, almost seventy-five years later, is the opposite case. The war was never fought for total victory, whatever that might have meant, and there was never an imagined surrender of all guerrilla forces. The security forces did not have the ear of government until the election of 1979 and did not exert control over the government until after the Lancaster House agreement had been signed in December 1979.[37] Even then, Rhodesian security forces had little power. Operation Quartz had been promised in the event of a Mugabe victory; Rhodesian forces would take over the country and attack ZANLA in their assembly points. It never happened. "All day long," a BSAP wrote, "we cleaned our weapons and waited for the code word 'quartz' to be transmitted on the radio," but in vain. Instead, General Peter Walls, commander of the army, wrote a whiny letter to Margaret Thatcher asking her to void the election results and threatening a coup if she did not. She made him wait three days for a reply, delivered orally by the governor's deputy.[38]

Instead, the peace Rhodesian officials imagined was one that included enough Africans so as to prevent future war. In this way Walls was perhaps happier with Zimbabwe-Rhodesia than anyone else was. It was a government of African figureheads, willing to do what the military asked. Zimbabwe-Rhodesia might have been the best thing for the military, but starting in the early 1970s, before the guerrilla war intensified, officials and most officers understood that the peace had to be a negotiated settlement that would include Africans. Almost everyone agreed. Many of the memoirs I cite contain formulaic scenes in which the young men who want to leave the country when they are called up are lectured by their fathers: the job of a Rhodesian soldier, they were told, was to hold the line so that the government could have a strong position from which to negotiate.[39]

Did young soldiers want more? Did they want a war in which Rhodesia would be victorious? In May 1976 military intelligence officers came to the university to examine slogans painted on the wall. "Let RLI loose, we'll clean the country" and "We want control, let us loose, RLI."[40] A year later—two years after mass conscription was in place and six months after majority rule was on the table—the army's counterintelligence unit commissioned a survey of soldiers' morale. Almost all soldiers complained about a lack of aggression: "Why do we only react?" All national servicemen—and the report capitalized "all"—worried about their ability to get good jobs when their national service was over, especially since they were liable to call-ups with territorial units. Many civilian firms now employed white women or Africans because they were not called up. There was "considerable bitterness" over university students being released early to begin their studies. The majority of men surveyed asked, "What are we fighting for if there is going to be majority rule?" Almost everyone insisted that call-ups be extended to Africans. Many said they would not accept a black government, and many more said they would not serve in the military of an African-ruled government. Everyone complained that they did not have "sufficient information" about government plans for the future.[41]

Soldiers' specific comments showed contempt for strategies. Complaints about the lack of aggression became complaints about policies: "We should dominate the borders, but our orders allow Zambians to do so instead"; "The longer we hang back the more difficult it will be to knock out the terr bases"; "We can win this war so there is no point to any negotiations at this stage." Some soldiers demanded that patrols be allowed to "eliminate" villages that willingly sheltered guerrillas.[42] Most units complained that they were understrength in the field; military personnel were wasted in the rear ("too much cocktail party life" at the senior ranks). Almost everyone complained that the call-up needed to be rationalized. Too many units were understaffed and without trained specialists. To get units to full strength, many of those interviewed said they would be willing to serve with Coloured troops even though the "discipline of Coloured persons left much to be desired," but almost all would be happy to serve with the RAR. An army at full strength, without favoritism, would allow the police to return to police work and reservists to "get into the army to be real soldiers." At the moment, however, "this war is being fought as a no-win war."[43]

None of this is to suggest that soldiers wanted a complete military victory and officers and government officials wanted a negotiated settlement, but there was no fixed, shared vision of what peace would look like. Even if the Rhodesian Army had wanted to act on the bravado of the young men who demanded of army researchers that they be allowed to eliminate villages that sheltered guerrillas or to attack guerrilla bases across the border, they could not. Rhodesian security forces were not fully in control and sometimes not fully aware of government policies and strategies. What I want to argue from these examples—and what is critical to this book—is that almost no one believed that Rhodesia was trying to win the war.

Why Did They Fight?

Given all this, why did young white men fight in this war? For all the years I've been working on this project and for all the years I've written with and about oral history, I've never asked a former Rhodesian soldier why he fought. It is hard for me to imagine that any answer would not be overdetermined. If men had said they fought against communism or for responsible government, they would not have explained their own motivation. Besides, had I asked that question, I would have done so in the early twenty-first century, years of Zimbabwe's precipitous decline and renewed antiwhite rhetoric and farm invasions. What would have been the right answer then? Sue Onslow and Annie Berry conducted ninety-three interviews with former Rhodesian soldiers in 2009–10. Although their questions and concerns are very different from my own, one example should make my point. When they asked, "Was it worth it?" a common reply was, "We were fighting to stop what has happened *now*." But the now of 2010 was different from that of 1983, or even 1990, when white farmers often remarked that they had never had it so good.[44] What would they have said then? Men might have believed that guerrillas were a communist threat—hard as it would be to credit from twenty-first-century policies—or because they believed Africans could not govern the country, but what young men believed and why they served and answered repeated call-ups are, I think, different issues. Instead of asking why men fought, I want to look at white soldiers' morale, and ask why they continued to fight, even as victory was not the goal.

Why did white Rhodesian men fight? Most of the Rhodesian security forces were men who served because they were legally required to do so. Memoirs and novels describe young men who served without enthusiasm because they were called up. Some were proud to do their duty, to be with their friends who were going to war, or thought it "cowardly not to defend one's country."[45] National service, however, was adjusted for those men accepted to universities abroad: men going to university in Britain were released early to do so, and intake periods were changed to coincide with the South African academic calendar. Young men served—at least until their degree programs started—with varying degrees of desire and commitment. Desertion remained punishable by death, but there was no formal mechanism to track down deserters or even the men who did not respond to their call-up papers.[46] Men did desert, or simply evaded national service for many years, but most army officers did not consider this a problem. In 1977, for example, the BSAP discovered that the army had no list of men who left their units never to return.[47]

What, then, did it mean to stay in one's unit, to fight in this war? Jan Morris, for example, could not "imagine these people fighting to the last man, sacrificing their farms and factories, their very identity as a nation, rather than submit."[48] Dan Wylie, an RAR officer in the first months of

Zimbabwe-Rhodesia, wrote in his diary that he would serve in the army of an African government: "Personally, I'm fighting for a standard of life, if the government starts wrecking those standards, I'll fight the government. Or go to Spain. Or something."[49] Several of the chapters that follow argue that many soldiers continued to fight a war the conduct of which was not shaped by the military: these men organized their operations so they could poach elephants, or deployed a futile violence in gathering intelligence and then checking the intelligence held by other units (see chapters 4, 7, and 9). Other men who continued to fight either changed affiliations (rather than sides) or continued to fight for the same cause in another country (see chapters 4, 8, and 9).[50]

How Did They Fight?

For the many years I was researching this book, I assumed it was impossible to fight a guerrilla war with an army of conscripts. I probably thought this because I am an American who came of age during the Vietnam War, which was fought with conscripts, but I had been repeating it until I had dinner with the founder of Rhodesia's first tracking combat unit, who said, "You've been talking to too many regular soldiers." Rhodesian conscripts, he insisted, brought skills to the army beyond those basic training could offer—these men were carpenters, apprentice electricians, mechanics, and hunters. They could follow spoor and shoot, and they could fix cars and dress wounds. These skills could translate into effective soldiering without much effort, although the skills of being a good shot or clever with machinery did not mean anyone wanted to be an effective soldier, or even shared commanders' vision of what effective soldiering might be. Moreover, in many memoirs and novels, young national servicemen claimed they arrived in basic training already skilled. This is probably a common enough boast of young men in war, but in this case many national servicemen who had learned to shoot as teenagers did so at gun clubs with "jungle lanes," which were so well known that I've only read one text that explains them. These lanes were narrow paths in which cardboard human figures (of no given color) popped up or descended from trees, so that youths could practice shooting them.[51] Many men, especially those bought up on farms, knew how to track and shoot at least as well as their instructors; some of them trained their comrades on patrol (see chapter 4).

Did this mean that white soldiers arrived in depot already able to shoot and kill? And, if they did, did this mean they were willing to do so? Thinking of a group of people as so different that they are "less than human" has been thought to make killing easier.[52] Did the young men who used racial epithets, told racist jokes, and believed in white rule want to eliminate the Africans who opposed them? Was their violence toward Africans arbitrary and extreme? Did they see Africans as less than human, like beasts or vermin, easily subject to the most extreme and arbitrary violence? There is ample evidence of Rhodesian soldiers animalizing Africans, especially Africans in the army's employ. Africans were "natural" trackers, with preternatural hearing and sense of smell, who were able to see things in the wild that white men did not notice at all (see chapter 4). There were other African qualities—how they walked, how they stood still—that white soldiers were expected to mimic, however briefly, in pseudo gangs (see chapters 3 and 4). How do these practices and ideas fit with those of dehumanizing an enemy to make killing him easier? And what do these practices and ideas mean for my ability to locate the conduct of this war in broader histories of soldiering in the twentieth century?

In 1999 Joanna Bourke argued that soldiers describe killing not as a task they were forced to perform in wartime but as a source of joy and pride. Using evidence from twentieth-century wars, she claimed that men go to war in order to kill.[53] This book asks two questions of Bourke. First, is all talk of killing about killing? And, second, is killing the most important thing that goes on in a war? What would she make of Siegfried Sassoon's account of going to his officers training course in France in 1916? On his way to lectures given "with homicidal eloquence," he was keenly aware of the fine mornings and their fresh air. "I was like a boy going to school early, except no bell was ringing and, instead of carrying Virgil and Thucydides, I carried a gun. Forgetting, for a moment, that I was at the Front to be shot at, I could almost congratulate myself on having a holiday in France without paying for it."[54] How does wanting to kill describe the 10 percent of the men of Reserve Battalion 101 in 1943 Poland who asked to be relieved of their orders to shoot Jews and load them onto transport trains instead? In 1943 they could have had no doubt about what would happen to these people when the trains reached their destinations, but they themselves did not want to kill them.[55] How does a desire to kill help us understand what Danny Hoffman calls "the dangerous terrain of conversation" he came to expect with every new group of *kamajors* he encountered in war-torn Sierra Leone and Liberia? The young men suggested anointing him with magic water that would protect him from bullets; they would fire automatic weapons at him to prove it. An older man suggested boiling him for two days or smoking him for seven.[56]

Do these examples mean that soldiers want to kill or that they don't want to kill? Stories of killing or boasts about wanting to kill may not actually be about killing. Hoffman, for example, did not think he was being threatened so much as he was being used as an example, a coded way to talk about ritual practices that served as lessons of their efficacy. The magic that gave these youths their power—the correct application of water or smoke—could only be disclosed in cryptic, allegorical terms: too much description gave away too many secrets. The conversations themselves were "a test of male bravado" for the kamajors and for Hoffman, but within that bravado are lessons, and how young men learn them, not wholly dissimilar to Sassoon's. Indeed, the fact of killing may not be what a soldier finds compelling about dead insurgents. When Chris Cocks, RLI, saw a guerrilla corpse for the first time, he wondered if dead soldiers from his regiment would look the same. He was shocked to see the more experienced soldiers on his patrol searched the bodies "like common thieves!" But when they found cash on a body—there were fabulous stories of finding thousands of dollars on the corpse of a guerrilla paymaster—it was divided equally among the patrol.[57]

But what of men who speak of killing with pride? I quoted Dennis Croukamp earlier. He believed that professional soldiers want to face their enemies. Even so, he had his second confirmed kill in 1970. (A confirmed kill was one in which the source of the fire could be identified, hardly a straightforward task when artillery or automatic weapons are in use [see chapter 6]). He did not feel damaged by killing, but killing people in wartime changed his thinking about "shooting helpless wild animals. I never again shot another wild creature just for sport." Croukamp insisted that the men who turned to drink or violence after a war would have done so without the war.[58]

Is feeling good about killing after one has killed the same thing as wanting to kill? There is a conspicuous absence of trauma in the memoirs I cite in this book. This may be a convention of a specific genre (although I doubt it). It is entirely possible that the authors I cite saw the violence of wartime—especially the violence meted out toward Africans—as permissible and not worth commentary, or that automatic weapons and bombs made it easy to avoid thinking about having killed. It is equally possible that the absence of trauma may have been a more mundane example of what Kenneth MacLeish discovered in his interviews with American veterans of multiple deployments in Afghanistan and Iraq. These soldiers resented the assumption of guilt and trauma. As wartime practices were increasingly medicalized, soldiers complained about the mental health assessments that followed their deployments. One soldier was asked if he dreamed of shooting people. "You don't have to dream when you do it in real life," he answered. What was traumatic, one retired veteran told MacLeish, was to be told by a social worker that he had done terrible things in combat and should feel guilty about them.[59] When men did experience postwar guilt, was it about killing in wartime or about postwar events witnessed in peacetime—the "what is happening *now*" Onslow and Berry heard so much about? White veterans of South Africa's war in Namibia did not claim to be distressed by having killed, but by seeing the enemy they considered inferior now lauded as freedom fighters and elected to parliament.[60]

Is it that soldiers want to have their actions judged on their own terms? Did they understand killing as a learned skill, a capability soldiers are trained to use wisely and well? The Scot Peter McAleese had been SAS, a perpetrator of domestic violence, and a mercenary before he joined the Rhodesian Army; he devoted a third of a chapter to a description of his first kill, when he served in Aden. "I felt good, I felt fit, I felt hard. This was the first time I had been in a contact and killed anyone. The euphoria was nothing to do with ending another person's life. I felt good because I had not panicked, I had not let down my friends. I had reacted as a professional soldier trained by professional soldiers." Competence, as in lessons learned, may be more important than the fact of killing. Still, the firefight was as exciting as anything he had ever done, he wrote, but then he was "a very aggressive young man."[61]

What about men who shot but had no idea if their fire was lethal or even hit the mark? This is the terrain of confirmed kills. There is ample evidence, above and beyond S. L. A. Marshall's classic *Men against Fire*, that not all soldiers shoot, even when ordered to do so. However contested the history of the text, and whatever methodological problems there were with Marshall's research—published in 1947, the same year the Kalashnikov went into production—the book transformed infantry training. Men were trained to shoot on reflex; they were trained in conditions similar to those they would encounter in battle so that the sights and sounds of battlefield carnage would not distract a man from the task at hand. They were trained as McAleese was, to react, to shoot without panicking, to fire as a professional would. Training for battle, especially battle with automatic weapons, was not so much about training to kill but about inculcating in a body of knowledge that defined soldiers; it was to give men self-confidence in battle. Men who trained and deployed in small groups would be cohesive and loyal to each other. Tactics and weapons were to become instinctive reactions to sights and sounds. Camaraderie was a huge issue for Marshall, as it was for McAleese. Training was for not getting killed and not doing anything that might get a comrade killed.[62]

Popular versions of this have emphasized killing, however, but perhaps incorrectly. The drills that supposedly "desensitized"—a term that sounds quaint in the twenty-first century—men to violence were also the drills that combated boredom. Bayonet practice and demonstrations of knife fighting were, in the training camps of Tanzania, designed to keep men engaged when there were no weapons to practice with.[63] Rhodesian military training did not seem focused on killing, however racist young white men were. The RLI, the largest and whitest infantry unit in the country that after 1976 had the largest intake of men, had seventeen weeks of basic training, including hours spent leopard crawling. Many recruits did not think they were learning skills needed in a guerrilla war; they found bayonet training embarrassing. National servicemen joked that they were learning "how to shoot, how to guard bridges, how to jump out of helicopters, really useful things like that." Parachute instruction for commando units was described as "screaming, shouting, hitting, kicking." Counterinsurgency training was essentially training in bushcraft: men had to learn how to survive in the wild for a week or more while tracking a guerrilla band. It was a few days of lectures about which berries were edible, which plants quenched thirst, and how to snare small animals. Specialized units like the Selous Scouts and the SAS had specialized selection courses and specialized training in isolated places—the Selous Scouts selection course was the ultimate version of this—but for national servicemen it seemed ridiculous. "What kind of army has to resort to that kind of bullshit?"[64]

Let me return to Reserve Battalion 101, which shot past the men they were instructed to kill. Was this because they were uneasy about killing or because they were incompetent shots?[65] If men are trained to kill—however general or specific that training is—does not killing or not shooting accurately mean they were badly trained or that they were disobedient? For all his aggression, McAleese, then in the SAS, refused to kill an unarmed man who had wandered by his patrol as it prepared an ambush. The corporal ordered McAleese to shoot the man; he had seen the patrol laying antipersonnel mines. He refused, saying, "If you want to kill him, do it yourself." The corporal repeated the order, and McAleese fired deliberately wide; the man ran off, and the gunshot compromised the ambush as much as the man would have done. McAleese did not think himself disobedient but professional and prudent: "I am keen to be the first to kill the enemy, especially in a fire fight but I have never been someone who could kill a civilian in cold blood."[66] Was this a question of context rather than one of desire? In 1978 a group of ZANLA fired on an RAR patrol outside Mount Selinda mission on a Saturday night. Because it was well known that ZANLA frequented the girls' dormitories there, the patrol did not return fire for fear of shooting young civilians. Would unwillingness to kill an unarmed civilian apply to an armed civilian? A. J. Balaam led a Selous Scouts patrol into Mozambique in 1976, hoping to gather intelligence on guerrilla movements. They identified a man who could help them, but they could neither coax nor coerce him to leave his homestead. When the man picked up a fallen branch and attacked the African Selous Scouts, the patrol responded with bayonets and guns. The man ran off. Balaam hoped he survived, not because he did not want a civilian killed by his patrol but because "he was a brave man and deserved to live."[67]

Who deserves to live and who deserves to die? There were worthy foes, of course (see chapter 6), but there were also automatic weapons and bombing raids that made it impossible to see how any foe died or who killed him. Leonard Smith has argued that novels rather than memoirs contain stories of killing. The displacements of the third person and fiction allow for easier descriptions.[68] This war may be different precisely because of the landscape. ZIPRA recruits from the western part of the country had to cross the Zambezi River for training in Zambia, and ZIPRA guerrillas had to cross the river again to infiltrate Rhodesia: they called it "the first enemy," as they risked rapids and attacks by crocodiles.[69] Indeed, Rhodesian war novels contain powerful scenes of death by nature. In one novel, a seriously wounded guerrilla calls out that he wants to surrender, that he has information for Special Branch, but he is killed and eaten by a hyena.[70] In another, a Rhodesian soldier turned poacher is attacked by a buffalo. The game ranger hero saves him but is himself killed by a bull elephant he has distracted from charging the industrialist who wants to flood the game park.[71] In another novel a crocodile emerges from the Zambezi to kill the guerrilla about to shoot a case-hardened Special Branch. "This is Zimbabwe," the guerrilla says. "Rhodesia is dead." At the end of the novel the Special Branch chases a guerrilla leader to Victoria Falls, where the man desperately clings to the rock face only to be swept away by the raging Zambezi River. The questions of context and desire troubled the Special Branch: "I knew I didn't want him to die . . . this way. A quick bullet, a rope, these he deserved."[72]

I argue that when the landscape kills, soldiering—at least soldiering in the head—is situated in place. Knowledge of flora and fauna and river currents was the time-honored means of warfare in the country; it may have been more important than accurate fire or obedience. The specificity and power of place—and the knowledges that Africans could impart to whites about that place—shaped the history of the conduct of this war. I do not mean that this war should be studied in isolation from other wars, especially since guerrilla armies were keenly aware of nationalist struggles elsewhere, but I will argue that knowledge of place, of plants and animals and rivers and gorges, is critical to the study of counterinsurgency.

Discipline and Morale

Many national servicemen's memoirs describe incident after incident of disobedience and distrust. Was this because they were well trained but rebellious, poorly trained, or just disobedient? In the years of massive conscription and the years of fighting a no-win war, it may have been hard to tell and harder to discipline. There were men who never learned to shoot well and did not show up for extra target practice, and there were men who mocked military protocol: they wore their own shoes on patrol, they did not wear their uniforms when it was required, they sunbathed when they were ordered to keep all their clothes on, or they wore regimental insignia to thumb their noses at regulations. There were reservists who did not care enough about a patrol or the war to show up, and there were memoirists who celebrated their casual disobedience. It is possible to read some of the following chapters as portraying youthful exuberance and embodied, adolescent humor. It is also possible to read this material as accounts by men who were actively disobedient and who destroyed equipment. In 1974, for example, the armorer for the Tenth Rhodesia Regiment threatened to report men if they continued to use the magazines on their automatic weapons to open bottles.[73] At the end of 1976 the minister of defence came to announce the extension of national service to eighteen months to a Rhodesia Regiment platoon that was about to stand down. The men shouted obscenities as he spoke. That evening, after prodigious drinking during which one of

1.1 Recce patrol, Kayemba, 1978. Courtesy of Chas Lotter.

them acquired a handgun—no one remembered how—a few of the men approached the minister in a nearby hotel in a way that made his bodyguards draw their weapons. They were not disciplined.[74] After General Walls announced the internal settlement to an RLI barracks, a MAG gunner removed the strap of his 20-kg belted machine gun and threw it at the general's feet. "If you're going to give it to the kaffirs, sir, you can get a kaffir to carry this." Walls murmured that he understood.[75] In the last years of the war, young RAR officers complained about how often they were sent on patrol with faulty intelligence; they had to rewrite their orders into something more pragmatic and tactical.[76] In a photograph of a recce patrol—men skilled in tracking and counterinsurgency—from Kanyemba on the border with Mozambique in 1978, one can see the uniforms, the deadpan expressions, and two men standing in the middle of the group. One is barefoot and holds a beer bottle, and the man next to him is exposing himself: camaraderie, disobedience, and morale in a single image.

Did anyone object or complain about such behavior? I have been told by several former officers that by the late 1970s there were many regiments "doing their own thing," which I have taken to mean that centralized command structures were weak. This suggests that the power of various regiments and individual patrols and even of soldiers was easily amplified. The

the Selous Scouts, for example, overruled Special Branch interrogators as to which guerrilla was turned, and many of the auxiliaries trained by Special Branch were killed by regular army (see chapters 3 and 9). Did anyone call such actions inefficient?

Writing of World War I, Leonard Smith has argued that command is an inadequate way to think about military orders: rank-and-file soldiers have the power to obey or disobey. They negotiate: the orders they follow and which ones they ignore are decided by consent and consensus, not command.[77] I do not want to draw a straight line between a French battalion in World War I and Rhodesian conscripts sixty years later, but this may clarify much of what is included in this book. If the overall strategy of the war was to allow Rhodesia a strong bargaining position in an eventual negotiated settlement, was there any reason to discipline reservists changing their orders? Did anyone complain about drunken threats, or Selous Scouts declaring large areas off-limits to other security forces? None of this is resistance—and certainly not resistance as most African historians understand the term—but is whatever happens when a stonemason, finished with his national service and on his third tour of reserve duty, assumes he can write orders as well as his officers did, or when the leader of a pseudo gang takes a prisoner on patrol against the orders of his interrogators. This isn't exactly disinterest, but it's not an interest in fighting the war either. The disobedience was casual. There were no mutinies beyond Coloured, Asian, and Eurasian (CAE) soldiers refusing to parade at depot in 1973; they demanded equal pay with white soldiers.[78] There was virtually no fragging—and that was something I have asked about. In 1979 a white officer was killed by hastily trained African volunteers and a 2RAR officer was "accidentally" shot dead when he staggered back to camp after an afternoon of drinking. But to repeat a question I asked earlier in this section, was this an accident, disobedience, or the result of too many beers?[79] My point here is that if the war was fought as a holding action, did soldiers, on the ground, do more? I am not saying that Rhodesian security forces fought badly: they rarely lost a contact, and they fought well, with great skill and camaraderie. But they did not win, even in the years when ZANLA and ZIPRA were in turmoil.

The frequent militarization of urban spaces in wartime was hardly unique to Rhodesia, however; elsewhere, this militarization has been shown to change the gender dynamics of city life.[80] But in Rhodesia it was further proof of the idea of disillusioned, violent soldiers fighting everyone but guerrillas, an idea that took hold by 1979. David Caute visited Rhodesia frequently while writing for the *New Statesman* and *The Observer*. He was an astute and eloquent observer, and I cite him often, but his description of young soldiers' indiscipline and fury in the last year of the war both defies credibility and reveals a popular sense of soldiers out of control. He called the violence of young servicemen "endemic." A bar manager and British Army veteran claimed he had been all over the world and never saw "behavior like this." Caute claimed, incorrectly, that Salisbury bars closed on Saturday afternoon and that bars had hotlines direct to the military police: "Calling the civilian police wasn't much use: the psychotic servicemen merely took them on."[81]

Bar manager veterans notwithstanding, none of this was true. Bars did indeed close every afternoon but reopened a few hours later; if men still had drinks on their tables, they were not asked to leave while the bar was closed. The "civilian police" was made up of as many national servicemen as the army was. I am not concerned with the accuracy of this story as much as I am about why it was told in mid-1979. Minority rule was over and done with, whatever the outcome of the war. Many memoirs from 1978 and 1979 describe the futility of continued patrols and the exhaustion of young men. Did stories of drunken soldiers attacking police and civilians and each other take hold in 1979 to show that they understood how pointless the war was? "The lads," a young soldier in the army's psychological action (PsyAc) unit told Caute as he held his palm level with his nose, "have had it up to here."[82]

This War, This Book

In an effort to make sure no soldier inadvertently revealed sensitive information, PsyAc issued graffiti-style stickers to be placed in urinals in towns and operational areas. There were sixty different messages, including the drop-shaped "Are you having a security leak?" There was the mouth-shaped "Don't give lip service to terrorism" and the lip-shaped "Women's lib is one thing, women's lip another." A few skirted homosexual desire: "Have you got a Mao Tse Tongue?" "Your tongue could pull a trigger." "An open mouth makes a big target."[83]

This is not a book about the multiple meanings of stickers found in toilets, although it is worth asking how PsyAc arrived at these phrases, but it does seek to acknowledge the military's commentaries on soldiers and their soldiering. I also look to soldiers' memoirs to provide commentaries on soldiers and their soldiering. I have often asked former soldiers what makes this or that memoir ring true. Sometimes I was told it was the description of tracking or shooting, but most often it was the description of practical jokes: "We were great pranksters."[84] It was a war of young, white men together in the intimate spaces of barracks and patrols in a countryside that was now dangerous. There were what I think were typical references to private fantasies—the woman who played soldiers' requests on the Rhodesian radio talked of the damage the war was doing to their right hands—but the social life of the war was homosocial. It was also young, at least for national servicemen, and the clever ideas from PsyAc and the war memoirs I cite are sometimes painfully adolescent.[85] It was a war of some fighting, to be sure, but also a war of pranks and jokes performed for an audience of like-minded young men.

This book has two entangled narrative arcs. These are a history of counterinsurgency strategies and practices in the Rhodesian forces, and the writings of former Rhodesian soldiers. The history of counterinsurgency practices is broadly chronological; the history of war memoirs has an unstable chronology, as a great many of these memoirs reflect and engage with other soldiers' memoirs while a few publish revised memoirs (see chapter 2). As chapters 2 and 3 show, counterinsurgency practices were most often imaginaries of hearth and home, and how desirable it was to bring Africans into those spaces, preferably as servants. Chapters 3, 4, and 5 are about counterinsurgency and the reverence accorded pseudo gangs and white men masquerading as Africans. These practices are those of intimacy, of white operatives dependent on Africans to teach them to walk and talk like Africans: their description in memoirs celebrated the fictions of no one really knowing who was who. The idea of successful masquerade and crossing boundaries seeped into questions of how authorship was determined and the conventions by which copyright was to be allocated. Chapters 6 and 7 are about weapons and how they were imagined both by the Rhodesian war project and by the Rhodesian war memoir project. Guns were symbolic of and in the struggle—see any number of images of a silhouetted AK-47—and Rhodesians followed the genealogy of weapons with great care and admiration during the war. Insurgents had insisted for years that they were poisoned by security forces—in their food, in their drink, and in their shoes—but biological and chemical weapons are commonplace only in memoirs and postwar writing. Were these practices so secret that they could only be revealed after Rhodesia ceased to exist, or was there a merging of the idioms of African ideas about harming and Rhodesian ideas about the ingenuity and courage of their war effort? Chapters 8 and 9 return to the linked issues of manpower and counterinsurgency. If pseudo gangs and tracking units required specific Rhodesian skills, a knowledge of a specific wild learned from Africans, foreign soldiers who came to defend white men or prevent another Vietnam undermined this. Whatever Rhodesians imagined about Cubans or Russians poised to invade, foreign soldiers in the Rhodesian Army made this war more ambiguous, less about a specific place and its people and more about its slogans. Chapter 9 describes the last years of the war and the last years of trying to find enough men to fight it. As coups and countercoups shaped ZIPRA and ZANLA and as Zimbabwe-Rhodesia took shape, special forces trained security force auxiliaries. Some were former guerrillas, some were trained in other countries, and some had no political or military interests whatsoever. Large groups of soldiers did not enhance the war effort, however. They were considered liabilities, too incompetent or too violent to continue fighting, so that in the last months of the war they were killed off, frequently by the same small group units they were designed to replace.

My use of memoirs and other published material in this book is messy, not because of a sloppy method on my part but because these memoirs have untidy provenances and muddled reliabilities. Are the stories written by former soldiers and officials true or false? Were they someone else's story passed off as one's own? Were they stories told and retold in countless bars before a final version was committed to paper? Given the number of memoirs I use in this book, and the more than thirty-year span in which they were published, I suggest these questions do not matter. Instead, I want readers to understand these stories as those former Rhodesian soldiers believed they should tell them: these are stories, taken together, that debate and disagree about what it was like to fight this war.

2 "BLOOD AND INK"

Memoirs, Authors, Histories

One of the primary sources with which this book is written is memoirs by former Rhodesian soldiers. I do not mean primary as most historians understand the term, as contemporary, eyewitness accounts. Instead I mean primary as in primarily: a large proportion of the evidence in various chapters comes from memoirs. What does this mean for me as a historian? I would only call these memoirs reliable evidence insofar as I have relied on them: they are, like other memoirs, filled with exaggerations and embellishments and many, many untruths. This is of course also true of archives and interviews, but we as readers and scholars tend to make demands of memoirs that we don't make of, say, annual reports or interview transcripts. I don't want to hide behind these generalizations, however: I am not using memoirs here because they are as flawed as other sources are, although it is useful to keep that in mind, but because for the history of this war they are the most detailed and analytical sources I have found. Taken together they do not tell an operational history of the war, or its politics and resistances, but they do tell me something about its conduct. These memoirs reveal soldiers' ideas about and analyses of wartime practices.

Who wrote these memoirs? The most straightforward answer would be to say men who served in the Rhodesian security forces between 1960 (when the army was part of that of the Central African Federation) and 1980, when Rhodesia became Zimbabwe. This only explains why these particular memoirs tell a story of decolonization and insurgency and counterinsurgency; who these authors were and when they wrote are more complicated. Some authors constructed their subject positions carefully; others wrote in response to what other authors wrote. These authors tell war stories after the end of the war but also after the end of the country they fought to defend. They tell their stories to each other. Some have published with commercial presses and sought audiences outside of Africa. Many publish with vanity presses or self-publish. Several publish with a specialized press, in which case specialized editors make their presence known. These authors have been to war movies. They read each other and they read historical writings about the war. (One book quotes me.) Some write sequels to their memoirs, and others publish revised versions of their memoirs years later. All this means that these authors do not fit neatly into any category that makes an author's individual contribution singular and noteworthy; there is no way I can identify "the-man-and-his-work" as one unique entity. They are authors in what Michel Foucault called a classical sense of authors, historical figures "at the crossroads" of specific events. In this case, following Foucault, their presence at the crossroads suggests their texts may include voices other than their own, as it should be: these men fought in armies and regiments, not as individuals, even though as individuals they revised or expanded their accounts of wartime experiences. But the crowded crossroads has meant these authors remained separate from their texts, to the point that the system of ownership of their published work—copyright, plagiarism, rights of reproduction—has been so haphazardly acknowledged that they were subject to multiple lawsuits. These memoirs do not embody their authors, but instead are texts in which authors describe and debate the conduct of this war.[1] The texts, then, are part of this history. Indeed, I take the title of this chapter from a phrase from a soldier, born in Northern Rhodesia in 1953, who served in the South African army, not the Rhodesian one. Eeben Barlow is best known as the founder of a private security firm, Executive Outcomes, which employed a number of Rhodesian bush war veterans. In his memoir he complained that Executive Outcomes was falsely accused of a botched coup attempt in Equatorial Guinea. Rumors and accusations could not hurt them, he wrote. The history of Executive Outcomes "was written in blood and ink."[2]

African Memoirs, African Wars, and African Authors

Not every Rhodesian veteran wrote a memoir, of course, but by the early twenty-first century some regiments were dense with memoir writers, either because of the number of educated young men conscripted into them or because the regiment was well practiced in self-promotion. As a result, this book lists toward two regiments. By the mid-1970s the RLI took the largest number of national servicemen and seems to have generated the most memoirs. The Selous Scouts was a counter-gang unit founded in the early 1970s. Originally small, biracial, and "top secret," it managed to publicize itself so much that it became a publishing bonanza after the war.

These memoirs were published after the war, which means they were published after Rhodesia ceased to exist. In April 1980 the country changed both its government and its name. The fact of the transition—called independence with no irony at all—has been considered a definitive break, enshrined in books about Zimbabwe with a before-and-after list of place-names in the front matter. The question of how memoirists write about a national army when the nation for which it fought no longer exists may not be an important one, however; it is, after all, the history of many armies in nineteenth- and twentieth-century Europe. My questions are somewhat more contained. In recuperating the experience of war, do memoir-writers also recuperate the nation, or do the security forces stand alone? Does the reimagining of the white-ruled nation require support for minority rule, or can these authors manage to portray their experiences on the ground as something that is not about race? My answers require a circuitous route.

Memoirs about Africa—being African, growing up in Africa, being in jail in Africa, fighting for or against African nationalism—are texts that are expected to (and are marketed as being able to) "say something" about Africa to readers who may know very little about the continent. In 1991 Kwame Anthony Appiah wrote that ways of presenting African artistic production to an international audience were shaped by broader ways of thinking about Africa. Was something "genuinely" African, "traditional," and thus free of the taint of colonialism and Western influences, or was it "universal," a condition achieved through colonialism and European influences?[3] This may be a useful way to approach African war memoirs. For example, Emmanuel Jal was a child soldier in Sudan. In the first ten pages of his memoir we learn that his father was a policeman and his mother a nurse and devout churchgoer. Yet when he is rescued by a white aid worker and taken to Kenya, he claims soap was so alien to him that its sweet smell makes him put it in his mouth as if it were fruit.[4] In *Scribbling the Cat*, K, the former RLI befriended by Alexandra Fuller, uses the slang "china" for friend. This term comes from Cockney rhyming slang, "my mate/china plate," and made its way into Southern African English through post-1945 British immigration and the pidgin languages of command in the mining industries of the region. Fuller, however, glosses "china" as a term for friend because of "china crockery, something precious."⁵ The middle ground may not be much better. In 1963 Margery Perham wrote a foreword to J. M. Kariuki's *"Mau Mau" Detainee* that lectured readers as to why an African political memoir would be worth reading. Kariuki's text might disturb Britons, she wrote, but it also shows the author's "attitude of mind," shared with "thousands" of other Africans, who "are likely to play an active part in the future of Kenya."⁶ It was a good idea to read an African—or at least this African—because his book offered a political blueprint.

Who decides what an African says about Africa in his or her memoir? Was it the men who stood at the crossroads with the author or men he encountered later? The copious body of memoirs of the Mau Mau revolt in central Kenya in the 1950s offers me a way to answer these questions. Several chapters in this book are framed by other kinds of memoirs, including those about the Mau Mau revolt, which was a favored Rhodesian example of just how "berserk and bloodstained" Africans could be and why European control was needed.⁷ That it didn't end well for Kenya's whites made it yet another example of Britain's perfidy, but one to be used with great caution. (By the late 1960s Rhodesians had Biafra as an example of British hypocrisy.) Nevertheless, between Africans becoming barbarians and decolonization, Mau Mau became a war that Britain could be said to have won, or at least an insurgency Britain defeated by the clever tactics of brave white men. Rhodesian officials sometimes claimed that Ian Henderson, Kenya Special Branch hero, advised this or that branch of the Rhodesian government about the war over some vague period of time. None of the men I write about read the copious number of memoirs former Mau Mau produced, but these memoirs and the questions of who wrote them and how great an impact that writing had on the text and the history gleaned from that text set the stage for questions about authorship and audience that are critical to this book.

Kariuki is a case in point. He was a literate activist who had smuggled 12,000 shillings into detention, money he used to bribe guards to send his letters to the governor of Kenya, to MPs in Britain, and to the International Red Cross. As he was transferred from camp to camp, his reputation as a camp spokesman grew. He had been educated in an independent school system that was very attentive to students passing the Cambridge Certificate exam: he would have had good English-language skills before he was detained, and he honed these by writing letters. But in the preface to his memoir he mentions that he had "assistance with the grammar" from Clyde Sanger, a Canadian journalist who spent much of the 1960s and

1970s reporting from Africa and who would have been very sympathetic to Kariuki. What assistance did Sanger give? Did he tighten sentences or restructure paragraphs? It is unlikely that Sanger would have impacted the content of the work—and Kariuki the letter writer would have had a draft in mind—but did he write or revise any of it or suggest some parts be expanded and others omitted?

Did it matter? A few years earlier, Donald Barnett, a young doctoral candidate from UCLA, had met Karari Njama, who had been Dedan Kimathi's secretary in the forest, where he claimed to be the only man with a secondary school education. (Although Barnett interviewed one of the other secondary school graduates in the forest, he never corrected Njama in print.) Njama told Barnett he had wanted to write his account of Mau Mau for some time, and Barnett offered to help him record it. When they realized this would take longer than they initially thought, Njama resigned his teaching position and came to Nairobi to live with Barnett and his family. After six months of living and working together, they produced a text. Barnett was soppy about their "understanding and friendship" and "the mutual trust and understanding we achieved," but Njama did not comment on their relationship. In the text Barnett was at pains to write the history of the Movement (his capital letter) and framed each chapter with an introduction to provide context and to remind readers that this was a Movement. These frames were based on his other, but often uncited, interviews with former Mau Mau. Njama, however, used the text to write a history of Mau Mau that enshrined Dedan Kimathi as the legitimate commander of guerrilla forces. Njama is not inattentive to Barnett's "Movement"—he describes in great detail the debates about how to redistribute which land to whom—but he was perhaps at his most eloquent when he chronicled the disarray in the forest after 1956 and the misery of the forest fighters. *Mau Mau from Within* is less of a collaboration than it is two books, or one book (Njama's) and fragments of another (Barnett's), but the circumstances of its production and its content should remind us that not all the forms of ghosting and collaboration, or help and assistance with grammar, influence the final text.[8]

What about ghostwriters who really write stories, or editors or writers who take unvarnished truths and varnish them? John Okello was one of the leaders of the Zanzibar revolution. He could neither read nor write English; he was at best barely literate in Swahili, but his account of the events leading up to the January revolution was published as *Revolution in Zanzibar* in 1967.[9] It is commonly said to have been written by David Koff, an American graduate student, and edited by Sanger.[10] Koff also "helped" Waruhiu Itote prepare his manuscript, *"Mau Mau" General*. Did "prepare" mean typing, editing, or putting a story in chronological order? Could it mean all of those things? And what if it did? Must a memoir contain only one person's experiences, one person's memories, and one person's words? Oginga Odinga, leader of the opposition party in Kenya in the 1960s, thanked Ruth First, "who has not only edited the manuscript but who has also given it shape."[11] What shape emerged from the editing of a Kenyan nationalist sidelined in the first years of independence by a South African communist in exile in Britain? If an editor provides context or comprehension, is it different from what a comrade might have done in the heady days of nationalist struggle? Was Odinga's memoir more Marxist or more cosmopolitan for First's editing? Nelson Mandela's *No Easy Walk to Freedom* was written, according to the men who had been on Robben Island with him, "on a conveyer belt."[12] Did the men who shared Mandela's trials and imprisonment add ideas and events that made the text more or less accurate than it would have been if they had never seen it? The answer to this question does not lie in the definition of memoirs, but in a definition of the author. Authorship is usually messy; even the least messy memoir can contain many voices and may have been shaped by many hands. In his book on memoirs Thomas Couser uses the term "self-life writing" to describe those texts that focus on a discrete part of a person's life.[13] How, then, do we understand the self-life writing when the author revises his memoir? And what if there are many selves involved in the life writing? What if there is an author, a ghostwriter, and the comrades from whom both author and ghost sought corroboration? What if a ghostwritten book was revised by the author and not the ghost? Who is the author then?

My question is, So what? What difference does it make if one person wrote about his experiences in colonial jails or if two people did? What does it matter if several detainees weighed in on the experience of Robben Island, rather than just one famous one? If as historians we are interested in the text, in descriptions of prison cells and late night meetings, does it matter who is speaking, as Foucault asks?[14] Does it matter if the description of prison cells and the political analyses were shared and honed in exchanges in and out of jail? When I ask what difference does it make, I am not throwing up my hands in frustration; I am being literal: What actual difference does it make if there is one author or three or four? Marshall Clough wrote an excellent history of Mau Mau that is both about these memoirs and written with them. Clough was not concerned about authorship—he sees far less ghosting than I do, for example—and as a result he produced what I think of as a history without worries, a reconstruction of events and ideas from the texts at hand. This is not to say that Clough takes authors at their word. He reassured his readers that he tended to doubt passages written with the hyperbole of revolutionary zeal, or ones that claimed Mau Mau had hundreds of guns to shoot down British planes.[15] But why? Mau Mau gangs probably did not have hundreds of guns total, let alone any with the range to shoot at British aircraft, but why discount the Marxist rhetoric or revolutionary zeal that may have been added later, because of an interlocutor's reflection or reading? If we allow for a notion of experience that may be outside an author's everyday vocabulary, or even if we embrace the fog of war for small wars, then why is a phrase or a slogan added years after the event not credible?

In his doubts, Clough is firmly within the disciplinary boundaries of African history. Historians of Africa are often wary of questions of mediation, or the public acknowledgment thereof, in large part because we have invested mightily in the authenticity of African accounts, of Africans "speaking for themselves." But, again, are selves singular? Is there a kind of speech or words that is not inflected and influenced by others? Two of the memoirs I rely on were written by journalists; two others were written by professors of literature. Did these men construct their memoirs as they would have done their other published work?

Memoir Wars

Is all speaking for oneself true? But what about when an author—whoever or how many he or she might be—dissembles? What do we do when an author lies, or hides an event or birthplace or parentage, or makes claims that are false—do these things invalidate a text? In the last twenty years there have been debates and controversies about the truth of some canonized memoirs that became so nasty and painful to read that the questions that created the controversy have been obscured. These are questions that anyone who has written with and about oral history for thirty-odd years would find risible: that storytellers often embellish their life stories to the point of making things up; that they tell other peoples' stories as their own; and that what people say about their birthplace, their parents' birthplace, or critical events depends on who is asking, who else is in the room, and what they think an answer will achieve. When informants give contradictory information about parentage, birthplace, or residence, these are not problems to be resolved but windows into the complexities of belonging.[16]

The debate over the authenticity of the canonical slave autobiography *The Interesting Narrative of the Life of Olaudah Equiano, or Gustavus Vassa the African: Written by Himself* may be the best-documented case of memoir skepticism. In an article and subsequent book, Vincent Carretta, a scholar of eighteenth-century English literature, challenged critical facts about Equiano: using a ship's muster roll and a baptismal record, produced years apart, Carretta claimed that Equiano was born not in Africa but in South Carolina; he could not be an "Eboe" who endured the Middle Passage. By stressing Equiano's Britishness, Carretta suggested that the text be read as the work of a passionate abolitionist and innovative storyteller and not that of an African who based his abolitionism on experience.[17] Two responses to Carretta argued that the presentation of two separate birthplaces made Equiano's story more credible rather than less; it located him firmly in the eighteenth-century Atlantic world, where birthplace was less of a marker of ethnicity and nationality than it was to become. Alexander Byrd argued that "Eboe" was itself a category created in the African diaspora of the eighteenth century, an identity that was more concrete in London or South Carolina than it was in what is today Nigeria. James Sweet took the point further: scholars might insist that Equiano be either African or American, but he himself would have been both Igbo and Carolinian, depending on who was asking and what he wanted an assertion of belonging to achieve.[18]

The debates around Equiano were struggles about the life and work of a long-dead author. Everyone who participated was an academic, and while they might have fought bitterly, they used the same tools. The other two controversies had the quality of a free-for-all as one pitted an activist against an academic and the other pitted an author claiming to be a recovering drug addict against Oprah Winfrey's engine of popular culture. Rigoberta Menchú Tum was an exceptionally articulate spokeswoman for the Popular Front that was decimated by Guatemalan troops in the early 1980s. She was awarded the Nobel Peace Prize for her advocacy in 1992. Her story was a testimonial, a genre of Latin American radical politics in which a subaltern spoke for herself and her compatriots to a worldwide audience: testimonies are narratives that seek to make a difference. (We will see this term again in chapter 8, referring to exposure.) It was recorded by the Venezuelan anthropologist Elisabeth Burgos-Debray—who had been looking for a young woman activist to interview—in her Paris home. The circumstances of the interview and the production of the subsequent text raised a number of questions. Menchú knew only rudimentary Spanish at the time, and there has been intense disagreement about who translated the questions asked in Spanish into the Quiché Maya in which she answered. These were in part questions about who was present during the interviews, who transcribed them, who edited them, and which political party vetted the manuscript. There were assertions that Menchú repeated party dogma or presented others' memories as her own, and that Burgos-Debray had interviewed other Guatemalan exiles and used parts of their stories in Rigoberta's testimony for dramatic effect. This troubled the idea of a single author, as did the question of who held the copyright, who received royalties on which edition, and who received the prize money.[19]

Almost ten years after the English-language edition of *I, Rigoberta Menchú* was published, the anthropologist David Stoll researched and published an ethnography of local politics in Guatemala's Mayan villages, including Menchú's home. His research coincided with a period in which Mayan activists formed umbrella groups to participate in civil society; Stoll argued that the Popular Front Menchú described had limited peasant support and that many of the army's atrocities were the result of guerrilla adventurism and internecine rivalries.[20] The people Stoll interviewed doubted that Menchú had witnessed every execution—in one case, of her brother—she said she saw, and they recounted different versions of a massacre in which her father was killed. In the siege of the occupied Spanish embassy in Guatemala City in early 1980, thirty-six or thirty-seven indigenous revolutionaries were killed in a mysterious fire. Like the massacres described in chapter 9, the issue of how people were killed by whose hand or hands is not wholly clear. Menchú said it was the army's chemical weapon; those who escaped were gunned down. Stoll did not think the army set the fire, but that it was either a strategic failure or the revolutionaries' attempt at martyrdom.[21]

Burgos-Debray joined forces with Stoll in 2008, brandishing her radical credentials, which made the controversy even more unpleasant and intense than it had been.[22] Battle lines were drawn. Supporting Stoll in any way was tantamount to attacking the cause of indigenous rights: "Is the suffering of Mayan Indians less painful because Rigoberta embellished her life story? . . . To say that she lied means that no genocide ever occurred in Guatemala."[23] A few years later, Couser insisted there should be no controversy at all. No one should hold Menchú to the standards of other memoirists. In Latin America testimonies were collective and communal; authors of testimonials spoke for larger communities, not themselves.[24] When Menchú defended herself, however, she upheld her right to tell the story ("Should I beg forgiveness because they killed my father?"). She clearly understood the complexities of authorship in ways her defenders did not: The story "of my community is also my story. I am not from the air, I am not a little bird who came alone from the mountains. . . . I am the product of a community, and not only the Guatemalan community." When asked if she should return her Nobel Prize, she noted that the "Nobel Peace Prize is not the Nobel Prize for Literature. That one they give to someone who writes books."[25]

In 2005 James Frey published his memoir of addiction and recovery, *A Million Little Pieces*. Six weeks later, Oprah Winfrey praised the book on her television show, guaranteeing a larger readership than Frey's publisher could have predicted. Two weeks later an investigative website reported that parts of the book were exaggerated and others were fabricated: it was not that Frey made up altercations with police or jail time or his addicted girlfriend's suicide, but that he created a persona of a violent drug addict, rehabilitated by friends and family, which was not true. Frey, however, had first offered the text to Random House as a novel; it was the publisher who asked him to rewrite it as a memoir because it would sell better. He did exactly that, and the book became a best seller, but the fact that he wrote and published a story that was not his own as his own became all that mattered. His deception was market driven. His previously loyal readers claimed they were lied to and defrauded by the experience of reading the book as a memoir. What was as important as the nature of the text was the denunciation of it. Winfrey's televised, public censure of Frey was heralded as a much-needed moment when someone stood up for truth. Her demand for authorial honesty was held up as a reprieve in an era characterized by lies about weapons of mass destruction in Iraq and the cover-up of pedophile priests.[26]

The meaning attached to exposing Frey was out of proportion to what was made up in the text, and as such it neglected a key point about how former drunks or addicts might tell their life stories. Why would we think anyone who spent years inebriated or stoned would be able to chronicle those or later years with anything resembling accuracy? Wouldn't he or she have to fall back on well-known circulating stories, like those Frey told? Drunks and addicts have and probably shared many ideas about what to tell lawyers and judges and social workers to prove they want to get help or at least a lenient sentence. They may exaggerate their wrongs so as to make the desire to right them more compelling. And for people in treatment or seeking treatment as a way to avoid jail time, isn't the challenge one of storytelling: How do you tell the lawyer or the judge or the social worker a story that is not so clichéd as to be unbelievable but is also not so different from other peoples' stories that it might not be believed? For drug addicts or anyone entangled in the legal system or recovery industry, is the narrative that gets you the best treatment a true one or a tried-and-true one? Why would we think writing would be different? The exposure of Frey's untruths ignored these questions and instead demarcated a clear line between true and false that could and should be policed.[27]

War Memoirs

No one really worries if war memoirs are true or false, however. We take war memoirs at face value because of the extraordinary authority that comes from having been in war. War memoirs are read as true stories, Samuel Hynes reminds us at the start of his classic study, "*because*"—the italics are his, not mine—the author was there, in the battle or the trenches or on patrol.[28] Even when we understand, as Leonard Smith argues we should, that the experience of battle or patrol has been constituted through language and the structures of narration, scholars of war tend to use war memoirs as hard evidence. Yes, Smith notes, "the line between fiction and nonfiction remains stubbornly unclear," but this has not troubled historians very much: it was difficult to write with these sources but not as difficult as it was to write without them.[29] If we write history from war memoirs, how can we be sure it will be accurate? That may not be possible. Paul Fussell wrote that a "memoir is a kind of fiction" that differs from first-person novels in that the author constantly implies he or she is telling the truth because much of the memoir is linked to historical facts.[30] Tim O'Brien did not believe a true war story could or should be a coherent narrative. However true a story might be, "it's difficult to separate what happened from what seemed to happen." What seemed to happen becomes an event that requires detailed description.[31] War memoirs written as fiction, as with Siegfried Sassoon or Tim O'Brien, are neither controversial nor in need of correction. No one really demands a complete truth from war memoirs; there is Lord Wellington's caution that a battle is like a ball—participants can only accurately describe what went on in their corner of it—or the pre-O'Brien fog of war, but most of all there is the sheer power of experience, however experience was constituted: soldiers were there, historians were not.

But—and this is a big but—historians have other sources for these wars. Samuel Hynes provides an impressive list of major British authors who were at the Battle of the Somme.[32] But no one reads Robert Graves or Siegfried Sassoon to learn what happened there, nor do we read Tim O'Brien or Ron Kovic to learn about US tactics and triumphs in Vietnam. These are personal stories, most commonly framed, Smith reminds us, as stories of baptism, of personal transformation, most often read as telling us what happened to men in war rather than about the conduct of a war itself.[33] I want to do something different here, however: I want to read Rhodesian war memoirs as a body of work that allows for an interrogation of the conduct and complications of the war these men fought.

So far, so good: war memoirs are a genre in which gray areas are tolerated, sometimes even celebrated, and they give us experience and emotion in what would otherwise be the history of how one side won and how the other lost. But what do war memoirs tell us about wars that have no established operational history beyond the jingoistic, in which there were no decisive battles or bombing raids? War memoirs are national and specific to wars. I don't want to make too much of writing about an army of a country that no longer exists, but it is worth asking if there is anything Rhodesian about Rhodesian war memoirs. Almost all white Rhodesians, after all, were immigrants, some quite recent and some eager to leave as soon as their sons completed national service. So who were Rhodesians, however many or few there were? The Rhodesian project, indistinct as it was, did not produce a singular notion of nationality. There was the myth that was articulated late in the war by the South African–born minister of defence—Rhodesians were a "breed of men" whose example will "go some way towards redeeming the squalid and shameful times in which we live"—and there were the men Rhodesian-born soldiers believed would happily burn down a village so they could have a servant cut the grass they never had in Britain. There were the men who left the country as soon as they finished high school.[34]

However complicated white Rhodesian belonging was (or is), wars are national, whether liberating the nation or defending it, and the men who write about their wartime service write in national languages and national idioms. These idioms changed with each war. The war memoirs of the Great War of 1914–18 established the genre of war memoirs. *Good-*

Bye to All That, Memoirs of an Infantry Officer, Storm of Steel, along with the novels *All Quiet on the Western Front* and *Farewell to Arms*, were the work of well-educated, middle-class men who volunteered for war. Hence the issue of consent, and authors' ambivalence about having agreed to risk their lives, undergirds their stories.[35] If there was romance to that war, it took place outside of Europe, in the story crafted in the desert by T. E. Lawrence.[36] Writing about World War II memoirs, Samuel Hynes suggests that the liberation of concentration camps in April 1945, more than the liberation of Japanese prisoner of war camps, gave them their tone: *this* was what the enemy had been all along. And this seems to have helped to generate a more embodied set of memoirs, in which soldiers focused on scared faces and disfigured corpses.[37] Writing about Americans in Vietnam—a war with massive conscription and educated young men—Hynes was lyrical about the relationship between combat, vocabulary, and prose. There was a level of profanity that was not present in earlier Anglo-American war memoirs; the absence of any clear victories or lines of battle seemed to produce memoirs that were disconnected stories, as in Tim O'Brien's war story. Vietnam was a war without a front, a war without direction, told in stories without plots.[38] Gary Baines has argued that memoirs of South Africa's Border War of the 1970s and 1980s modeled themselves on Vietnam memoirs as they sought to reclaim this last venture of South African imperialism as conscripts' experiences.[39] In contrast, Rhodesia's war was one in which the country was the front, a war in which soldiers were not fighting on foreign soil but on a land they claimed as their own, protecting it from invading nationals. Moreover, the continuous call-ups of the mid- and late 1970s blurred any line between soldier and civilian. This raises serious questions about the glossaries I will discuss later in this chapter; it may explain why these memoirs fight so openly with each other over who did what during this war.

I cannot make this point too forcefully. In the chapters that follow, authors argue with, criticize, and disparage other former soldiers, many of whom are also authors. Sometimes they just write about an offense without naming the offender, but most often they name names and circumstances. In dozens of conversations with former Rhodesian soldiers, they disparaged South African police, told me that a famous lieutenant had once shot a woman with a child on her back in Nyasaland in 1959, that another resigned his commission rather than be charged with stealing mess funds, that this one was a poacher, and that this or that officer "was the biggest liar of them all." This is categorically different from what other

Southern African memoirists have done. Eugene de Kock was arguably the most famous apartheid era assassin. In his as-told-to memoir he described his nine tours of duty in Rhodesia between 1968 and 1975. He had nothing but praise for the RAR, and he was grateful for the "basic bush principles" he learned that would be so useful later in his career, as when he formed the biracial counter-gang, Koevoet, in the Border War. After that he ran South Africa's assassination squad in the 1980s and early 1990s. In his dictated memoirs and books based on interviews with him, he was critical of the conduct of his fellows, but that outrage was general. He was being charged with the murder and mayhem that he was ordered to do; it was the state that was the criminal, not him alone or his fellows in general.[40] The distinction is an important one: Rhodesian war memoirs did not debate the legality or morality of the war, but they were very concerned with the propriety with which individual soldiers executed it.

War memoirs are not only national but also temporal. They are written and published at specific times, and as much as they reflect national wartime issues and narrative practices, they affirm the times in which they are published. Thus French memoirs and novels of World War I were published years after the war, not just because of the distance a self might have required to write about such sacrifice and carnage, but because 1920 through 1939 were the years of what Leonard Smith has called the "relentless commemoration" of the war and its dead.[41] The period between 11 September 2001 and the US invasion of Iraq eighteen months later generated a series of memoirs by Muslim women, some fabricated and some written by women who left the Middle East when they were six or seven, which revealed the damning oppression of Islamic societies.[42] A few years later there was an obsession with child soldiers in Africa. Ishmael Beah's *Long Way Gone* was published in 2007; Emmanuel Jal's *War Child*, coauthored by a British journalist, was published in 2009. Fantasies about the persecution of Muslim women or concerns about child soldiers did not disappear, of course, but their power to claim transnational markets and respectable publishing houses did.

I will discuss Rhodesian war memoirs' early history in the next section, but it was only when Zimbabwe began its precipitous decline in the late 1990s that they were published in rapid succession. Once the farm invasions began in 2000, when the question of race was reworked into national politics and the liberation struggle became one of many failed promises, the number of war memoirs increased exponentially. These works are of a moment, perhaps one that the individual authors are only vaguely aware of.

Authors (and publishers) were clearly impressed by the commercial successes of Peter Godwin's *Mukiwa* or Alexandra Fuller's *Let's Not Go to the Dogs Tonight*, but there was something else at work; the idea of wartime white experiences in Rhodesia offered a way to make politics personal, to tell individual stories to a transnational audience so that they could learn various truths about abuses of power. Christina Lamb is a foreign affairs correspondent for the *Sunday Times*. In 2002 she published *The Sewing Circles of Herat*, the story of her search for a young Kabul diarist.[43] She first went to Zimbabwe in 1999 and continued to visit there during the most aggressive attacks on white-owned farms. In 2007 she published *House of Stone: The True Story of a Family Divided in War-Torn Zimbabwe*.[44] Thus, my question is not just what is Rhodesian about Rhodesian war memoirs, but what about them is thought to appeal to a wider audience, and what conventions and narrative strategies do Rhodesian authors deploy at which times to reach that audience?

Rhodesians' War Memoirs

What happens to memoirs that are not only postwar but postnational? Do national idioms and conventions outlive the nation, or are they produced and policed by its demise? What happens to authorship, and the authority thereof? On the face of it, it would seem that these memoirists would go the way of Fuller and Jal: they could write whatever they thought was appropriate because there was no one in their audience to keep them honest. But the opposite seems to have happened; memoirs of the Rhodesian war became a profoundly careful kind of memoir writing; they became a genre that was concerned with what was true and what was false and policed that boundary with great conviction and occasional outrage. There were conventions governing the publication of names and images in the now-it-can-be-told books, for example: names in many texts of the 1980s were changed so as to protect a former soldier from reprisals but were kept close enough to the original that a man could recognize himself. Photos of soldiers were printed with a black bar over the upper part of the face, so as to render them unrecognizable. And photos were not the only things that were deliberately blurred. In one publication, a Rhodesian assassin told a story, and two years later the memoirs of the head of Rhodesia's CIO cast doubt on it. What do we see if we read these in sequence, as corrections of some versions and warnings about revealing others?[45]

Many of these authors published revised memoirs, sometimes adding material to the first one and sometimes continuing the story. Chris Cocks, an author and publisher, wrote two memoirs, the first about his time in the Rhodesian Light Infantry and the second about his years in various reserve units. In the first he told a story of planning to leave the country when he received his call-up papers: he would go to Mozambique, and from there he would become a merchant seaman and see the world. His sisters talked him out of this; the issue was not one of patriotism but of not leaving his parents embarrassed and ashamed.[46] One year and a hundred pages later, Cocks signed up as a regular, and we learn for the first time that he had been accepted to a university in England; his reenlisting not only shocked his parents but would delay his admission to university for a year.[47] Cocks published his second memoir about his time as a reservist. In this memoir, like the first, he planned to leave the country when he got his call-up papers, but in this text he had already been accepted to the Sorbonne, to study law. He still contemplated going to sea to escape the draft, but he thought better of it and reported for duty.[48] Is this just another example of the kind of scrutiny that the James Frey memoirs of the world cannot withstand? Are two universities the equivalent of two birthplaces? Did Cocks fail the Equiano test?

I think not. As with Equiano's birthplaces, the several universities reveal something about the author's world. Cocks had applied to several universities in the United Kingdom and France; he was admitted to universities in Paris and Exeter and to Cardiff to study law.[49] He did not, however, write about these applications as part of his autobiography, but with an offhand reference in his first memoir and a more detailed, perhaps even fanciful, reference in *Survival Course*. Is this a problem in and of itself? If we read one text at a time, we get one university, but if we read them as a body of material we get two. Does this mean that the Equiano test is not one a memoir needs to pass to be true, but that different universities or birthplaces are to be read in sequence, as an elaboration, a reflection on the options and exaggerations available to young white men at a specific time?

Rhodesian war memoirs, especially conscription memoirs, contain powerful if formulaic scenes of young men accepted to prestigious British universities. The young men want to leave the country, their parents want them to stay: the young men serve—thus making the story part of a war memoir—and Rhodesian manpower boards rework their release dates so they can arrive in Britain or South Africa for the start of term.[50] Did Cocks's revelations about different universities at different times represent an unfolding, a gradual deployment of the names of schools and courses of study in moments when audience trumped experience? Authors pick and choose what they write about and what they omit, especially if they are writing about their own lives; that is what makes them so useful as commentaries about what it meant to fight in this war. Bruce Moore-King, for example, wrote a part memoir, part meditation on the war, touting his own experience in various units. He was on the Grey's Scouts patrol that took the American photojournalist Ross Baughman with them, only to have Baughman's prize-winning photographs embarrass the Rhodesian military and perhaps cause Moore-King's commanding officer, an American professional soldier, to resign (see chapter 8). Moore-King described a Grey's Scouts interrogation and his British commanding officer with contempt, but he did not describe being on that patrol, with that commander, although the story was well known years before he published his book.[51] Was he dissembling or protecting himself, or did he not think that patrol was any more important than the one he described? And was Moore-King's omission the reason Baughman mentioned him in his memoir published decades later?[52]

These authors write to each other; they discipline each other's fabrications. Before he came to Rhodesia, Peter McAleese spent an unhappy time fighting with Holden Roberto's FNLA in Angola. When he first arrived in Africa, his group of mercenaries had only just left Kinshasa airport when they were stopped by a roadblock. An experienced soldier, McAleese was relieved when an interpreter sorted things out. "Others have written about this incident as taking place inside Angola, which doubtless looks better on their combat CV," he wrote.[53] Not every author was so discreet. As we will see in chapters 4 and 5, some memoirists named names when accusing this or that soldier of wrongdoing, great and small, while others gave enough detail regarding rank so that anyone who cared to could figure out who was being written about. Rhodesian war memoirs of the late 1990s and beyond borrow from each other, criticize each other, and bring secondary materials into the text; they generate and respond to their own controversies. The struggles in these memoirs are not against ZANLA's or ZIPRA's version of events, about which many authors are remarkably ignorant, but are struggles within and about the Rhodesian forces. Thus, this literature is self-referential and intertextual in the extreme; sometimes evidence seems up for grabs, and sometimes evidence circles back on itself. For example, an American serving in the Rhodesian Army had been warned by Special Branch that the painkillers he was about to take from a ZANLA infirmary were poisoned. He did not take the pills, but he was not sure if this was not a cruel joke. Years later, when he read a dissertation about Rhodesia's chemical warfare program, he believed it. When he self-published a book about his wartime experiences, he cited the dissertation as hard evidence.[54] A few years later, when the dissertation was published as a book, this story appeared as an example of the Rhodesian chemical weapons program. Many of the stories and events in these memoirs are not true, or at least not wholly accurate. Some stories and events are denounced overtly, and some are denounced with careful subtlety; others generated lawsuits (see chapter 5): these memoir wars are not between scholars and authors but between authors. Both as war memoirs and as struggles over how this war should be chronicled, these texts, taken together, give us a history of the war and the contests around it that is unlike any other material available at this time.

Let me give one more example, one that shows the extent of these contests and the place of memoirs therein. These are memoirs and books based on interviews that not only are about who did or did not do what, but that take on some of the defining events of the last years of this war. The Viscount tragedies—Viscount was the make of the aircraft—of 1978 and 1979 are a case in point. In September 1978 a civilian aircraft was shot down after taking off from the resort of Kariba; in February 1979 a second Viscount was shot down. There were fifteen survivors of the first crash who were shot by anxious young ZIPRA; there were no survivors of the second. It was taken as a given that the planes were shot down by ZIPRA using Soviet-made surface-to-air missiles. ZIPRA was known to have such weapons, young ZIPRA were the first on the scene, and Joshua Nkomo all but admitted it. Indeed, Rhodesia responded to the September 1978 crash with bombing raids on ZIPRA camps in Zambia.[55] The crash of February 1979 was somewhat more problematic. By then, Rhodesian authorities required all planes leaving Kariba to gain altitude over the lake so as to be out of missile range when flying over Rhodesia. The pilot did not do this; he may have been making up for a late departure, or he may have been one of the many pilots who ignored these instructions, as his copilot had complained the week before. But if many pilots did this, why was this plane shot down? At the time many journalists and later ZAPU claimed that General Peter Walls was scheduled to be that flight. ZIPRA intelligence had learned he was traveling to and from Kariba on a civilian aircraft, having addressed a passing-out parade. ZIPRA operatives had seen him at the airport. When the flight was delayed, he and a few other passengers were chosen at random to take another flight. Walls did not object or pull rank; as David Caute wrote, "Rhodesia was an egalitarian society." Did Walls know of the attack and arrange to be put on a later flight, and if so, was the attack a failure of ZAPU intelligence or a success of Rhodesia's?⁵⁶

No one questioned that ZAPU ordered these attacks, but there were questions and recriminations about how well the attacks were executed. Over the years there have been specific accusations, sermons, memorials, monographs, and a novel (see the last paragraph of this chapter) about the attacks and the Rhodesian response. Keith Nell, SAS and a man I quote in this book, published a memoir about tracking the ZIPRA gang that shot down the first plane. He was aided by Martin, a would-be guerrilla who provided critical information to Special Branch and then helped Nell train a group of auxiliaries to gather intelligence in the region south of Kariba. The information paid off: Nell's men and a few SAS were ready for the ZIPRA gang when they returned from Zambia. Within a year or two, Nell was attacked in print and in social media: he made it all up, his auxiliaries had been nowhere near where he said they were, and his SAS comrades denied capturing the gang in question. Darrell Watt, SAS (see chapter 4), told his interlocutor that Nell had learned about the group from a disgruntled headman eager to save his daughters from the ZIPRA gang. Watt noted that his account differed so much from Nell's that it had occasioned "a bitter debate."⁵⁷ A few years later, in 2019, Geoffrey Alp, a forensic auditor, wrote a book inspired by the questions that Nell's book left unanswered. Using investigators' reports of the crashed planes and running several computer simulations taking altitude and range into account, Alp did not believe a surface-to-air-missile could have been involved: there were only a limited number of places from which a Strela-7 could have been launched, and it could only hit targets below a certain altitude. When all the numbers were crunched, guerrillas would have had a twelve-second window in which to arm and fire a missile. More important for Alp was that the damage to the plane was consistent with that caused by a bomb placed either in the wheel bay or the air intake valve. Alp left it to the reader to make up her mind, but he asked, if it was sabotage, was it the work of a ZAPU sympathizer or a white technician unhappy with a shift toward majority rule?⁵⁸

Curfew Breakers and Chairman Mau

If memoirs of African wars, like any other kind of African memoir, are tasked with telling readers outside the continent something about Africa, who decides what readers need to learn from an African war memoir? And how much of that decision is based on the place of publication and who the readers are imagined to be? Is the presentation of Africa outside of Africa to be constrained or exaggerated? Peter Godwin was an established journalist when he published *Mukiwa*, a childhood and war memoir, in 1996. It was published in Britain and the United States and was widely read in Southern Africa. My evidence for this is anecdotal: when I sat reading the book in the garden of a Harare hotel in an unseasonably warm July, several men, black and white, came up to me to tell what a good book it was. When I spoke to former Rhodesian soldiers, however, they too liked the book but were dismayed that Godwin repeated the wartime story of the curfew breaker, a tale heard by almost every national serviceman on his first day in depot. Godwin did not claim to witness the story he repeated in great detail. In areas under martial law, curfew breakers were to be shot on sight. A young sergeant saw an old man furiously pedaling his bicycle to get back to the protected village before curfew, but the sergeant shot him, saying he would not have made it back by six. No one bothered to report him because nothing would come of it.[59] I have not found this story in a locally published memoir.[60] Is this because authors wanted to make their fellow soldiers appear to be gentler than they were, or because they assumed no one would believe it? What, then, were the urban legends that appeared in locally published war memoirs? As a national serviceman and aspiring journalist, Angus Shaw wrote down rumors, stories, and jokes as he heard them. He repeated the story of a white homeowner just returned from reserve duty who watched his gardener repair a lawnmower. The gardener removed the cylinder and laid out each part on the grass in sequence, exactly as someone would clean a weapon. Did this mean his gardener was a guerrilla, a sleeper? The homeowner called the police, the gardener was interrogated and confessed, and an AK-47 and stash of ammunition were found nearby.[61] I don't want to make too much of these examples; they don't necessarily prove anything about wartime Rhodesia, but they show affect, intent, and whom an author thinks he's writing to.

There have been a very few commercial successes of Rhodesian war memoirs published in Britain or the United States; Godwin's first book is one of them. Most of the memoirs I cite here were published in Africa, years after the war. In this they are typical of war memoirs as a body of literature, but the histories of these publications are more complicated and more political than the fact of an author having established a distance from a remembered self.[62] The structuring of Rhodesian war memoirs began shortly after the war. Peter Stiff's publishing house, Galago, did much—if not all—to shape postwar Rhodesian memory. Indeed, these texts often repeat the phrase first coined—at least in print—by Stiff, that Rhodesia won every battle but lost at the negotiating table.[63] The phrase is wrong. First, there weren't really any battles, and second, while Rhodesian soldiers were not routed anywhere, they did not win any decisive victories either, especially during the mid-1970s when guerrilla forces were in disarray. In terms of strategy in the middle and late 1970s, it is not altogether clear that the Rhodesian state wanted victory more than it wanted a strong position from which to negotiate some kind of transition to majority rule. But the sentiment and the idea of a brave and almost invincible fighting force took hold.

The formal publication of Rhodesian war memoirs began in earnest with Ron Reid-Daly's account of Rhodesia's famous counter-gang regiment, the Selous Scouts, published by Galago in 1982. It is not a canonical memoir, but it was presented as a first-person account of events, written as if it were told to a neutral interlocutor. It also generated the publication of other Rhodesian war memoirs. The text has a convoluted and contested authorship and authorial afterlife, as we shall see in chapter 5. In the midst of lawsuits, new war memoirs were published, possibly encouraged by the financial success of *Selous Scouts Top Secret War*. Many were self-published, and many were written by one author. Those that were not made a clear distinction between the man whose story it was and the man to whom it was told; a 2009 memoir has two separate acknowledgment pages for the author and the man whose story it was.[64] And whose stories were these? Did editors intervene? Chris Cocks, the man of two universities, was the sole author of *Fireforce*, which was published by Galago. Would a more engaged editor have limited him to one university per call-up notice? In the Galago edition, Peter Stiff made changes that he considered important. He told me that he removed all the references to drugs in *Fireforce*. He thought the RLI should be seen as heroes, not druggies. A few years later he gave materials on chemical warfare, brought to him by a Rhodesian chemist, to Jim Parker for *Assignment Selous Scouts*.[65]

Again, we have the issue that one narrator may actually be two narrators, two selves, either the author and the as-told-to person or just an editor with heavy-handed concerns. I think it is useful to read revisions that become inventions (assuming they were not inventions all along) and editorial desires that overshadow authorial recollection as additional layers of history and meanings added by authors and editors who stood at already crowded crossroads. There are also many Rhodesian war memoirs that have no editorial oversight. Many authors published their memoirs themselves with vanity presses or vanity desktops or electronic editions. These self-published memoirs have singular authorship, virtually no editing, and no fixed audience. There is no discernible mediation and no copyediting, as in a "knew African day."[66] Barry Stranack, growing up in Malawi, "had heard of Mau Mau and I had even heard of Chairman Mau, but I didn't know whether those two were connected. I guessed he was the leader of the band."[67]

Beyond spelling, the sources I use are flawed, but those flaws, taken together, reveal another layer of conduct and of debate and contest. They tell a story of poaching by special forces at a level of specificity that exists nowhere else (see chapter 4). They reveal more about the cultural content of the war effort than an accurate description of a patrol might have done. In these memoirs, there is an obsession with domesticating Africans, and there is a fascination with Africans relieving themselves told with all the subtlety of twelve-year-olds.

Domesticity and domestic service have a rich and theoretically dense literature in African studies.[68] Although much of that literature focused on women, it showed how domesticity was the opposite of savagery in Western eyes: Africans could be made less wild by taking care of a Western hearth and home, what Nancy Rose Hunt has called "the knife and fork doctrine." But domestic service was about transformations—and making men into boys—and the intimacy of bringing Africans into the private spaces of a home.[69] Turning Africans, usually but not always insurgents, into domestics happens often in these war memoirs. *Top Secret War* used metaphors of kitchen and bath to describe the making of pseudo gangs: there was to be the right "recipe" for race relations, blacked-up white men wore makeup that always left a ring in the bathtub, and in Rhodesia and Rhodesia alone guerrillas who came on side were called "tame terrorists." The taming was so important that in his revised memoirs Reid-Daly called these men "tame insurgents," as if "terrorist" was the term that would offend readers in 1999. But that taming, whether in the war or postwar, was not necessarily about subduing the savage African but about bringing these men into intimate contact with white soldiers. In one of the chapters added to the second version of his memoirs, Reid-Daly wrote of drinking in his quarters with General Fritz Loos, commander of South African Special Forces. When Reid-Daly sent Chigango, his majordomo, to get more ice, Loos asked, "Do you really trust these black soldiers of yours?" Reid-Daly was astonished. "Fritz," he said, "that man who has gone to get the ice is not a soldier, he was an insurgent, and a high ranking one at that. He is now my butler and could off me at any time if he chose to do so. If I can trust him I sure as hell can trust my own soldiers."[70] There was another Chigango, an aged villager who was supposed to lead a pseudo gang to guerrillas. He refused to believe that the pseudos were white soldiers; surely they were Indian members of ZANLA. After the ambush Chigango helped set up failed, the unit took him with them, making him their cook.[71] In the winter of 1976, Chris Cocks's RLI patrol captured a young guerrilla. He was fourteen or fifteen and was terrified he would be shot; when he was not, he volunteered useful information, which he quickly realized meant he could not return to his gang. As Cocks wrote, "Thus it was that a young guerrilla became our faithful and likeable batman for the rest of the patrol." He not only fetched water but became "adept" at making tea. When it was time for the patrol to return to the base camp, "it seemed natural" that the youth should come too, and within a short time "he was happily integrated into the kitchen staff."[72] It was not only guerrillas who were brought into the intimate spaces of white folks' food and drink. In 1979 Graham Atkins was called up to the Rhodesia Regiment, which had begun taking African volunteers a year earlier. White society, he lamented, had not caught up to the Rhodesian Army. When he and his mates—six whites and one African—went out one Sunday in jackets and ties, they decided to crash a wedding reception, but they knew that their African comrade, Moses, could not be smuggled in unnoticed. Moses was willing to stay outside, but Atkins had a solution. He grabbed a silver tray and linen napkin and asked Moses to impersonate a waiter. He entered by the back door and became "invisible" at once. His comrades helped him out by calling out, "Hey, waiter. Six beers please. *Checha!* Quick!"[73]

Less commonplace than writing of domesticating African men were discussions and descriptions of Africans' urine. Urine and the smell thereof were an important part of tracking (see chapter 4) and thus were occasionally significant. Anthony Trethowan led a police patrol in Filubisi in 1977 tracking on a rocky ground. He thought they had lost the spoor until he saw a large, still-wet stain where a man had only recently urinated on a rock. "The terrs were in the saddle!"[74] Tony Ballinger, conscripted into the Rhodesia Regiment late in the war, when he was painfully aware of the futility of his patrols, wrote that the "rules of engagement stated that we mustn't ambush closer than 50 metres to a hut" because African huts rarely had latrines and that anyone seen within that radius of a hut was assumed to be a civilian. Beyond fifty meters, the man or woman was an insurgent.[75] None of this would be noteworthy—indeed, I probably wouldn't have noticed it—if not for two descriptions of African women urinating published thirty-three years apart. *Top Secret War* repeats a story that two Selous Scouts were said to have told everyone. In 1979 a car had stalled near a Selous Scouts ambush site. As the men in the car busied themselves with repairs, a large African woman walked off the road. Much was made of her size and gait relative to those of large herbivores; she stopped within two meters of where the men lay in ambush. They were surprised she did not see them, and when one raised his head "he watched in total fascination as she relieved herself, like a horse in a stable," and then walked back to the road.[76] Ballinger told a story from 1977. His patrol was waiting in ambush by a beer hall when two large African women walked toward a nearby path. They did not take the path, however, but stopped abruptly, turned their backs to the patrol, and hoisted up their dresses and began to pee. Ballinger was two feet away, wearing camo cream. "Buckets of hot piss shot out of them like a waterfall—splashing and bubbling all over the flash finder of my rifle. The stench of fermented urine was overpowering."[77] Was this kind of thing common during ambushes? Or did Ballinger hear the original story over the years and remake it as his own? If he did, why did he choose to paraphrase this particular story from the widely read *Top Secret War*? Why was this a story worth repeating?

To be fair, there is something very adolescent about these memoirs: after all, this was largely a young man's war, fought by national servicemen just out of secondary school. If nothing else, this may explain the Selous Scouts, on a mission to destroy a ZANLA camp in Mozambique, shouting "Viva your bloody arse" at the FRELIMO troops they passed.[78] There was the Rhodesian Light Infantry, an all-white regiment formed in 1960, and called "the Incredibles" long before they saw action. The RLI took a great number of national servicemen, many of whom wrote about being in it or being on operations with it. There were soldiers who considered the regiment cannon fodder and those who considered it the best of the forces; many members of other branches of the service considered them inept, high on drugs, or both.[79] When Peter Godwin, BSAP, realized the villagers' cooperation he had nurtured for months had been demolished by an RLI search-and-destroy operation, he played off their nickname, "the Incredibles": "You're incredible, alright. Incredibly fucking stupid."[80]

Words of War

Almost all these memoirs have glossaries, some of soldiers' argot, some of military acronyms, and some of commonly used terms, however defined. Armies, navies, and wars generate specific vocabularies. Most of these remain specific to armies, navies, and wars, although a few have entered ordinary speech quickly. Until 1918, for example, a trench coat was known by the brand of raincoat (Burberry). Most war memoirs—of armies, navies, and specific wars—do not have glossaries. The 1985 edition of Robert Graves's *Good-Bye to All That* has a glossary "for non-British readers" defining words like "don" and "spanner," but as a rule wartime slang is not glossed in most war memoirs.[81] There are no glossaries in the World War II memoirs of E. B. Sledge or Guy Sager for example. And why should there be? A critical point of war memoirs is the fact that the author was at war and has special knowledge from that war: he may write about it, but he does not need to explain it. Books about Africa may be somewhat different; publishers who seek readers outside the continent might want to gloss terms and phrases. Doris Lessing's account of her four visits to independent Zimbabwe has one that categorizes words by their origin: Portuguese, Afrikaans, and "indigenous languages."[82] Peter Godwin's three books, the first of which was published only a few years later, do not, nor do Ishmael Beah's and Emmanuel Jal's.

Why then do Rhodesian war memoirs have glossaries? And why do almost all self-published books have glossaries? Are glossaries part of a national idiom, one of things that was Rhodesian about Rhodesian war memoirs? Did former soldiers need to identify which words were used and explain where they came from? Rhodesia's was a war in which the entire country was a front, a war in which soldiers were fighting not on foreign soil but on a land they claimed as their own, protecting it from invading nationals. Moreover, the continuous call-ups of the mid- and late 1970s blurred any line between civilian and soldier. This might explain why these texts argue so openly with each other, but it raises even more questions about the glossaries. If most of these books were written by former Rhodesian soldiers for other former Rhodesian soldiers, why explain what certain words mean?

Why indeed? These glossaries do not gloss every alien term. Rhodesian English contained several words that came from African languages almost fully formed, a borrowing that did not happen to the same extent in other settler societies. White people routinely called cattle "mombies," an Anglicized plural of the Shona *mombe*, or if they refer to traditional healers at all they call them "nangas," after the Shona *nganga*. The racial epithet "munt" comes from the Bantu root word for person, -*muntu*. However rare this kind of seepage is, these words do not appear in these glossaries. What did get included was Taal (from Afrikaans, "talk"), the argot of the RLI.

Taal was celebrated in a wartime regimental history as "the innovation of regular soldiers," and although its development was stifled by the influx of national servicemen, it was in widespread use by the end of the war. The author provides a glossary as well as examples of the "highly stylized patters," He offers imaginary scenarios for the use of Taal, such as troopers watching television, or a machine gunner recalling an effective contact, or a soldier asking for a ride back to barracks, saying "catch me a glide."[83] In one wartime novel a couple dining out reads a poem in Taal on the back of a menu. "They've got a language of their own, those guys," the man explains.[84] Taal was another order of seepage, however. It was the argot of the Coloured community in Salisbury, and while it was appropriated and embellished by each new intake of RLI, it became fixed in novels.[85]

Other words, specific to the war, are not included in any glossaries I've seen. These glossaries do not explain the diminutives with which the war was conducted, a war in which "troopies" fought "terrs." In its canonical form, troopies were RLI, but the term was used more broadly as the war went on. Terrs were always terrs. "Tame" terrorist and its acronym, TT, do not appear in these glossaries, but CT, for "communist terrorist," does. The phrases "taking the gap" or "gapping it," both of which mean leaving the country, often upon receipt of call-up papers, do not appear in any glossary I have seen. The terms are from rugby: "taking the gap" describes taking the ball into a space between tacklers, but "gapping it" is disreputable; it is selfish and refers to keeping the ball when it should be passed to teammates.[86]

Which words are in these glossaries? There are many Afrikaans words, especially those used in Taal, and some Shona words specific to the war: *pungwe* for guerrillas' all-night meetings, and *masoja* for Rhodesian soldiers. There is Rhodesian slang, as in "goffel" or "goffle" for Coloured, for example, and there are terms specific to the war. "Fred" for FRELIMO and "floppy" for an African killed in a contact; the term derived from how men fell when hit with automatic rifle fire. "Frantan" was the term for locally manufactured napalm, derived from the frangible (domed) tanks with which it was shipped to the airplanes that dropped it.[87] "Gook" was used as a synonym for guerrilla and insurgent in Rhodesia and Rhodesia only. Glossaries define it as "guerrilla" or "enemy"; they give its derivation from American English. The word is in fact a semantic field, first used by Americans in the Philippines during the Spanish-American War: "gugus" was a corruption of Tagalog, the language. It may have been one of several terms; "goo-goo" was another. In its American usage, "gook" suggested a degree of disorientation and passivity: Japanese captives during World War II were said to have "goo-goo" eyes, and shell-shocked American soldiers in the Pacific and in Korea were said to have "gone Asiatic." During the Korean War it was used to mean any Asian, friendly or unfriendly, military or civilian. (Whatever the word had meant to Americans before, the term sounds very similar to the Korean *kuk*, used as a suffix to denote a foreigner.) The term was clearly a derogatory word for Vietnamese in Southeast Asia in the 1960s and 1970s, but by the time it was in widespread use in the Rhodesian Army, it was a synonym for insurgents. In any number of conversations, former Rhodesian soldiers have used "gook" as a term that was more polite than "terrorist." White and African Rhodesian (and Zimbabwean) soldiers used the term as if it did not have a history as a racial epithet.[88]

Why does a usage as specific as "floppy" appear in these glossaries but not "gook" or "gapping it"? Is it because any former soldier would know some of these terms but might need to be reminded of others? Are these glossaries postwar sharing, the offering up of words and their meaning so as to bond readers to authors? Do glossaries allow authors—however many people an author might be—to own their wartime experiences, by showing the words that they know and readers may not? Or are these glossaries a narrative convention, a literary practice that makes these texts different from the war memoirs of middle-class Englishmen, that shows not only the experience of war but also a mastery of African words? As the next chapter shows, the mastery of African words and gestures, and much else, shaped how Rhodesia promoted its war effort.

How Texts Matter

As we will see, books about Rhodesia's war effort mattered. The chapters that follow detail the many borrowings and copyright infringements and arguments based on a close reading of these texts. This is largely a postwar phenomenon, as was the construction of the Rhodesian Army as an extraordinary fighting force. Chapter 8 describes the two or three dozen Americans who became interested in fighting for Rhodesia from reading articles in *Soldier of Fortune*. Such claims were promoted by *Soldier of Fortune*, of course, but the idea of war described in books and articles is critical to this book. Hynes's war-in-the-head doesn't fit neatly here. Previous conflicts in Africa and the decolonizing world were occasionally offered as examples, but overall the practice of Rhodesian counterinsurgency remained distinctly local.[89] Toward the end of the war, David Caute wrote about Angus Neal of the SAS, the regiment credited for being better than Selous Scouts and not boasting about it. On a weekend leave at his parents' club, Caute admires how quiet and self-contained he is, a muscular young man who wants to study chemistry at Newcastle University. He patiently explains to Caute why there are no Africans in the SAS: "Because even after you make the grade you can be weeded out. Blacks would take umbrage." He hopes for European intervention in the war. The war needed more offensive action, and it is "time Europe looked after Europeans—it's the white man who is getting a raw deal throughout the world."[90]

We will hear this again in subsequent chapters. What made Neal different was his weekend reading, *Operation Zambezi*, the fictionalized account of the retaliation for a civilian aircraft brought down by ZIPRA. Caute calls them "super-Aryan Commando raids" into Zambia, made famous by the insolent message to the Lusaka control tower demanding that the Zambian air force stay on the ground, or else. (It was, however, given after the raid, which Caute knew, but the arrogance was still there, however misplaced.) For Caute, "It's odd—or is it?—that the genuine article, the real SAS commando, should want to soak up a mythological version of his own exploits."[91] Caute goes on to imagine Neal the killer, but I want readers of this book to focus on Neal the reader, the man who wants to read about the conduct of war he is part of to appreciate and understand it. War-in-the-place, indeed.

3 "YOUR SHONA IS BETTER THAN MINE!"

Pseudo Gangs, Blacking Up, and the Pleasures of Counterinsurgency

In pseudo operations, security forces and loyal local people, some of whom may have been former insurgents, track down gangs of real insurgents and capture or kill them. In so doing, pseudos earn great praise for their subterfuge and daring. Pseudos are said to be the creation of young, forward-thinking men; once in place, they demonstrate the capacity of militaries to innovate and adapt to changing conditions on the ground in a way that conventional armies could not. Pseudo gangs are credited with having defeated insurgents in Malaya and Kenya. They offered imperial powers the kind of low-intensity (and inexpensive) warfare that involved local populations (or a proportion thereof) and allowed for the orderly transfer of power at the end of empire, not the messy ends of empire of the British in Palestine, the French in Algeria, or the French and the United States in Vietnam.

I am not concerned with whether or not this is true as much as I want to show that the Rhodesian Army, aware that the country had too small a white population to have a large military, saw in special forces and pseudo gangs a kind of warfare that was neither too white nor too violent: the favored term was "minimum force." Indigenous people could provide local knowledge and do some of the work of repression, and what pseudo operations failed to provide in intelligence they made up for in courage and cunning. Counterinsurgency campaigns in Malaya, Vietnam, and sometimes Rhodesia have generated a body of literature—often cast as "lessons from"—that argues that the institutional practices of armies were at odds with effective counterinsurgency. Armies are too often hostile to change from below. They have to be weaned from their preference for technology-driven, expensive, conventional warfare in order to see the potential of low-intensity operations, which were far less expensive to fight. On the whole, this literature saw intelligence as a strategy critical to the defeat of an insurgency. There is also a literature that has scoffed at the merits of counterinsurgency tactics; it has located the genealogy of pseudo gangs in the self-promotions of their architects rather than innovative armies.[1]

Whether they are praised or condemned, pseudo operations are understood to involve pretending, masquerade, and crossing boundaries thought to be concrete. Guerrillas might turn, but the men who authorize the turning must pretend to be guerrillas, if only for a short time. In the "lessons from" literature, "posing as insurgents" requires no interrogation whatsoever.[2] As a way of looking more critically at posing, I have turned to transgender memoirs. I don't want to push this analogy too far, and I most certainly don't want to compare a temporary and strategic transformation to a long-desired permanent one, but there are discursive similarities. The lessons from counterinsurgency literature and transgender memoirs describe struggles with established authorities, the ability to pass in a masquerade, and no small amount of smug satisfaction at having done so. For all the Rhodesian Army complaints about counterinsurgency units, the security forces were proud of their pseudos. Their model was decidedly British—the first incarnations were militarized police units, run by Special Branch, that followed the wholly unsuccessful British counterinsurgency in Palestine—inspired by the repression of Mau Mau in Kenya. Even Selous Scouts who had fought in Malaya recalled visits to Kenya as formative; those who did not recalled reading accounts of pseudo gangs from Kenya.[3] Again, I am not concerned that this might be an incomplete history of counterinsurgency. Instead, I want to point out a critical similarity in the Kenyan and Rhodesian pseudo operations: counter-gangs infiltrated real gangs by virtue of the stories they told them.

Nowhere is this clearer than in Frank Kitson's book *Low Intensity Operations* (1971). Kitson developed pseudo gangs in Kenya, after which he went on to Malaya, where he expanded their use by incorporating regular soldiers in pseudo gangs. After Malaya he served in Cyprus and Northern Ireland. Before taking up his command in Belfast, he spent a year at Oxford, where he wrote a book about how insurgencies could be defeated. Kitson insisted that local politics was at the center of any insurgency: no insurgency would succeed without wide popular appeal. This was a young man's insight, according to the later literature that specialized in lessons from various counterinsurgencies.[4] An older generation demanded major operations—the war in their heads was World War II in Europe—that were dismal failures. Kitson—at twenty-six the oldest of the field intelligence officers he commanded in Kenya—believed in the power of narratives. Gathering intelligence was cumulative. The interrogation of captured insurgents was useful to a point, but many such men had to be captured before interrogators could compare and assess information. Insurgents, however, could prepare for this and change tactics shortly after a capture. More useful, and more difficult, was turning captured insurgents against their comrades, but a turned insurgent required a story that explained his return to his former comrades. The intelligence such stories required was learned and deployed in a sequence: the original background information from a captured guerrilla was used to create a successful cover story; this would lead to even more information, often of a specific nature, such as which group would be where at a given time. This alone would have enabled a small patrol of turned insurgents and security forces to destroy a group of insurgents, or perhaps learn information that would lead to the capture of more important insurgents. In most cases the pseudo patrol would alert a larger, better-armed patrol to the insurgents' location, and their better-armed colleagues could kill or capture the insurgents. If the pseudos were not able to capture or kill insurgents, they would need a story that could allow them to escape quickly. In *Low Intensity Operations*, Kitson imagined this scenario working perfectly in densely forested areas, Malaya, or Norway.[5] Beyond the Norwegian forests, British soldiers might need to masquerade as insurgents, which meant that their cover stories were even more important in their masquerade.

Mau Mau for Rhodesians

The Mau Mau revolt in Kenya lasted from 1952 to 1958, overlapping with the first years of the Central African Federation, and had a powerful meaning in Rhodesia. It was a rebellion that showed how truly barbaric Africans could be and how victorious the British could be when they tried. The idea of Mau Mau justified the federation and its empty rhetoric of partnership: "Trying to stop it going black like Ghana, trying to stop it going berserk and bloodstained like Kenya."[6] There is a fantasy here, to say the least. Even if Ghana wasn't black before and after independence, nothing about Mau Mau ended well for Kenya's whites, but that made it an even better fit for the rhetoric of Rhodesian independence, at the end of federation, that Britain was dishonest, hypocritical, and pandering to African nationalists. Not only did Kenya become independent only a few years after Tanganyika, which had no revolt, but the man accused, almost certainly wrongly, of organizing the rebellion and "leading Kenya to darkness and death" became its first president.

Individual Rhodesian authors celebrated the savagery of Mau Mau, with scenes of rapes and murders of white mothers and grandmothers.[7] Rhodesian officials as a whole were enamored with the defeat of Mau Mau: even though its expense in money and manpower strengthened the case for decolonization, nothing quite equaled the romance of white men in blackface going into the forest and capturing the traumatized fighters still there. Although several Rhodesian officers, including Ron Reid-Daly and John Hickman, had served in Malaya, it was the practice of pseudo gangs in Kenya that made them call Kitson and Ian Henderson "masters of irregular warfare."[8] This became an embodied romance after UDI. It was said that the person, not the persona, of Ian Henderson, the Kenya Special Branch who led the pseudo team that captured Dedan Kimathi, was in Rhodesia, as an adviser. Ken Flower, head of Rhodesia's Central Intelligence Organization who then served as head of Zimbabwe's CIO, wrote a now-it-can-be-told memoir that, along with *Top Secret War*, portrayed Rhodesia as powerful and popular. He was besotted with Mau Mau. He visited Kenya before the state of emergency was declared in 1952, and five years later wrote a note on the glories of pseudo gangs. They were "incredible—Europeans blackened up and disguised as Mau Mau wearing clothes or skins—even lice— . . . Achieved WONDERFUL SUCCESS." Flower insisted that Henderson actively supported the Rhodesian cause. "From outside our borders we attracted a number of experts who had served in other theatres of conflict, including Ian Henderson from Kenya who worked with us for years, unobserved in the Prime Minister's Office."[9] Henderson's departure from Kenya has its own contested history, but this particular twist to his story seems unlikely.[10] Not only were there only a few years between Henderson's leaving Kenya and his taking charge of security in Bahrain in 1967, but he never mentioned being in Rhodesia, and no one—not a soldier, not a fellow policeman, not a journalist—ever wrote about meeting him.

Why Henderson? No one who had been or continued to serve in the British Army—Kitson especially—would have come to Rhodesia, even in an official's fantasy, but Kitson's book about defeating Mau Mau was available for anyone to read. I suggest that there was something homespun about Henderson. He was a Scotsman brought up in Kenya, son of a farm manager, a man who learned an African language from his childhood playmates, so that his practice of being a pseudo represented a plausible ideal. Whatever advice he was supposed to provide is beside the point; he was a man with the requisite skills to pass as African.

Turning Mau Mau

In their canonical 1950s form, pseudo gangs were aptly named. They were false gangs, patrols of security forces that pretend to be insurgents both to gather intelligence and to eliminate the other, real gang. Thus "counter-gang" is a reasonable but not wholly accurate synonym. In its ideal form a pseudo gang requires at least one turned guerrilla who now willingly fights for the government. Such a man with the right story could easily present himself to the actual guerrillas without arousing suspicion. Turned guerrillas could also instruct ordinary soldiers and police in the ways of insurgency so they too could pass as insurgents. Because of issues of leadership and authority, pseudo gangs would have at least one white soldier, and how he might be disguised so as to maintain the charade was to shape much of the mythology of pseudo operations. A successful pseudo gang would contain two pretenses: African guerrillas who had changed their political identities completely and white men who changed their racial identities for a few days.

In the first years of Mau Mau the issue for the young Britons and younger white Kenyans was how to gather intelligence from captured insurgents. The most effective interrogations, Kitson wrote, were those in which interrogators asked questions to which they knew the answers; it was a quick way to tell if a prisoner was lying. When a prisoner tripped up or was corrected, he often began giving truthful answers, and then an interrogator asked the questions he wanted answered truthfully.[11] In the spring of 1954 one interrogation allowed for a radical shift in how information was gathered. As he questioned the captured Mau Mau called James in *Gangs and Counter-Gangs* and George in *Bunch of Five* (as in two birthplaces), Kitson realized he needed the notebook of a dead gang leader. He called out to a clerk who was working unnoticed in a corner of the large room; the clerk tossed him the notebook. Kitson believed James (or George) was so impressed by seeing the book arrive from a darkened corner of the room in response to an English word he did not understand that James (or George) believed Kitson had magical powers. He began to talk without hesitation. He answered questions without evasion and soon wanted to work for Kitson and against his former comrades.

At first James (or George) was able to show soldiers where a gang was so they too could be captured. Later he was allowed to join a Mau Mau gang that did not know he had been captured. He was then able to give concrete information about where the gang was and what it planned to do. Back at camp he taught Kitson's men Mau Mau ways, their slang, their handshakes, and their signs. Soldiers began wearing their belts upside down, with the buckle inverted. "They had suddenly become Mau Mau—what a laugh!" Equally amusing were the incidents of patrols of Africans led by one white man encountering Mau Mau. There was nowhere to run, so the white officer hid behind a bush. No one noticed because the gang did not expect to see a white man. Indeed, Mau Mau gangs seemed willing to chat with anyone who "appeared to be a Kikuyu and a friend." Kitson soon realized that James (or George) had the time of his life impersonating senior Mau Mau. Why not get James (or George) to teach African soldiers to impersonate gangsters as a regular means of getting information?[12]

A true pseudo operator had to be up-to-date on the slang and handshakes of Mau Mau gangs so James (or George) soon outlived his usefulness. Ian Henderson thought pseudos had a short shelf life: they were the men who surrendered because they were "less tough, less primitive" than the men still in the forest. They wanted good food and warm clothes and "a feeling of security," and they soon became too comfortable to effectively go back into the forest and gather intelligence.[13] It also became necessary to turn men from as many different gangs as possible. But who could be turned? Kitson soon realized it made no sense to try to turn the men who were intensely political, and instead he concentrated on the young men, like James, who had joined the gangs "in the spirit of adventure." They were tired of their "drab lives" in the reserves or on a white-owned farm; they thought it would be "fun" to be in a gang and carry a pistol. This made them like "young men of spirit" everywhere; as prisoners they were "the easiest to handle because they were the easiest to satisfy." At first it took several days of interrogation and discussions with other turned prisoners before they were selected for pseudo work, but as the number of counter-gangs grew, African members became adept at identifying such young men. After all, a former white pseudo wrote, these men knew the fears and deprivations of guerrillas, how fearful they were of security forces and wild animals, how weak and exhausted they were from lack of sleep. Often, turned Mau Mau could gradually get new captives to turn simply by engaging them in everyday gossip of the struggle: after they had revealed more information than they intended, there was nothing else for them to do. Years later Kitson recalled how much stock he put in these youths' stories about why they joined Mau Mau and why they turned: some, like James, liked the excitement of carrying a weapon in a gang of any sort, so long as they could loot. Some would follow any cause that was in front of them, while others like Kamau—Kitson's "closest friend and associate"—knew they could avoid being hanged by working as pseudos.[14]

Ian Henderson described turning as a process of indoctrination: prisoners were given hours of lectures on the futility of their struggle and the malevolence of their leaders. They were made to confront how unprepared they were for war. They were taken to shoot at targets on rifle ranges, so that their poor marksmanship was obvious to all, and they were taken in helicopters for heart-stopping rides. The men being encouraged to turn were treated with kindness, allowed to carry their guns in the camp, risky as that might seem, so that the pseudo gang could be assured of their loyalty on maneuvers. If the process worked, it took nine or ten days, during which time these men were not allowed to bathe or to remove the clothes they were captured in.[15] For Kitson, the process of turning took place in three stages. The first was harsh: prisoners were chained, fed poorly, and interrogated. Kitson said this was to make sure they understood they were not heroes, but this was the time when they told their stories. Should they be chosen for pseudo work, they would be unchained and put to work. In this second stage there would be no discussion of pseudo work, but gradually they would have more freedom in the camp. Once a prisoner was deemed satisfactory for the third stage, everything changed: the prisoner was allowed to carry arms; he slept with other prisoners. When they went out on patrol, he was given a pistol to make him realize "he was absolutely one of the team."[16]

The Selous Scouts

The first Rhodesian pseudo gang did not have a name. It was organized out of the Combat Tracking Wing by a noncommissioned officer, Andre Rabie, who was known for speaking several African "dialects" so well that he often corrected African soldiers when they were "sloppy" with the grammar of their native languages. Joined by "Stretch" Franklin from the Rhodesia Regiment, Peter Stanton from the Special Branch Terrorist Desk, and several RARs and a few former guerrillas vetted by Special Branch, they were drilled on how to pass as guerrillas. They were given identities based sometimes on the serial number on an AK-47: they were from this or that village, they were trained in Tanzania, and they had almost been captured in this or that contact. The first pseudo operations gave Rhodesia detailed information about who the ZANLA sympathizers were, who the men who served as go-betweens for guerrillas and locals were—all "the chitter-chatter . . . that soldiers normally despise as useless," Reid-Daly wrote. In September 1973 Rabie was killed in what was later called a map-reading accident. Having sighted guerrillas, his group called in an RLI patrol. Rabie's group stayed out, hoping to find another guerrilla gang. His reading of the map placed the RLI ten kilometers away. Several African soldiers disagreed, but he overruled them, only to be shot by the RLI a few hours later.[17]

It was Rabie's unit that Ron Reid-Daly, already planning his retirement, was asked to take over. He had grave misgivings. How could soldiers, even soldiers who were former guerrillas, tolerate "the enormous strain of adopting a dual personality . . . living a lie in a twilight world out in the bush in the most precarious of conditions" and being "a normal soldier" when the patrol returned to town? As far as he could tell, they all looked like guerrillas: they were bearded, with long matted hair, and seemed on edge and wild, their eyes constantly checking their surroundings. Reid-Daly understood that this came from "the state of limbo" in which they operated in the bush, but he found it disconcerting. He worried that these men would end up drained and distracted, "bush-happy." At the same time, he was impressed by the "immensely close sense of comradeship" between the European and African soldiers. "There was no racial discrimination whatsoever." Indeed, it was obvious that these men had great respect for and trust in each other whatever their race. Reid-Daly was determined that this had to continue in the Selous Scouts, "where men were men and neither race nor colour made a jot of difference."[18]

The Selous Scouts were an intelligence-gathering and tracking unit; contacts—in which there was an exchange of fire—were few and far between. Once a patrol had sighted guerrillas, they were to alert an infantry unit, usually RLI fire force—the descriptive term for helicopter-borne commandos who were "talked on" their target. Tracking and the dark phase lectures that assigned guerrilla identities and stories that had to be learned to the letter were exciting, but giving verbal instructions to a fire force call sign was tedious. The talking on target effectively gave another regiment the action so many Selous Scouts craved, and it seemed to have made many of them impatient. It required setting up a radio and looking up the codes, of making sure of the guerrillas' position, and of unpacking and unfolding the

3.1 First Selous Scouts instructional team, 1975. Courtesy of Chris Cocks.

dayglow orange panels to mark a perimeter. In 1977 Reid-Daly complained about fire force pilots. The men on the ground were the most knowledgeable, and pilots had to listen to them. But they had to remember that most Selous Scouts were Africans, so it was "essential that speech is slow and clear." If airborne personnel became frustrated and angry, this would only confuse African soldiers.[19] Laying out dayglow panels and speaking slowly made for dull soldiering, however. Dennis Croukamp was thrilled by his first year in the Selous Scouts, to be able to meet and talk with guerrilla gangs, to have guerrillas believe you were one of them, but it did not provide the kind of action he sought as a soldier.[20] That action was available to Selous Scouts on external operations, but it was the action of dangerous subterfuge and the pain and exhaustion of walking miles on infected blisters, and of being elated that FRELIMO believed the pseudo gang's story that they were ZANLA heading back to Mozambique.[21]

But whatever the attitudes of white soldiers or the English-language skills of African soldiers in the Selous Scouts, was Mau Mau a useful model for the repression of ZIPRA and ZANLA? Mau Mau, whatever its claims and whatever rank the men in the forest claimed, was not a regular army. There were many World War II veterans in it, but these men did not seem to dominate the leadership positions. The men in the forest did not undergo any military training; there was never a unified command structure or anything that could really be called a unified guerrilla army. Mau Mau was not well armed; most of its weapons were obtained in raids on police stations: Mau Mau's widespread use of the *pangas* (Anglicized Swahili for "machete") was because they were poor, not because they were bloodthirsty.[22] Mau Mau was decidedly local. Beyond land grievances, it is not wholly clear if there were unified Mau Mau goals, nor is it clear that the name "Land and Freedom Army" was in widespread use in the forest. The names generals took for themselves—General China, General Burundi, General Tanganyika—were chosen in an imaginary in which those countries would come to the aid of freedom fighters. Rhodesian insurgents were regular armies, trained in Eastern Europe and other African countries, provided with uniforms, weapons, and lectures on ideology and tactics. It was a liberation army, funded by a subcommittee of the Organization of African Unity that allocated East European funds; they demanded a new nation—hence the Zimbabwe in the names of the two armies. Both armies had intelligence officers, some of whom had trained in the USSR and a few who had defected from Special Branch, who sought to root out informers and send undisciplined men away (see chapter 9). Although not all cadres were allowed to carry guns all the time, when they did, they were well-armed—depending on who was writing for what purpose, insurgents' weapons were newer or better or worse than those available to Rhodesian forces (see chapter 6). Almost all authors agreed guerrillas had the best webbing, however. Given this, was the turning of a Mau Mau equivalent in any way to the turning of a ZANLA or ZIPRA? Reid-Daly did not in fact use the term "turned" beyond turning. Guerrillas who had changed sides were called "*tame* terrorists" in *Top Secret War* and "tame insurgents" in *Pamwe Chete*. I have long thought this was another example of the domestication we saw in the previous chapter, but it is possible that Selous Scouts' use of the term also revealed how unlike Kitson's pseudos Rhodesia's may have been.

"Taming" Guerrillas

Rhodesian Special Branch interrogation of captured guerrillas followed the protocols that had been developed years earlier. Interrogations yielded background information—for example, where did the men come from, where were they trained, and what routes did they take when they entered

Rhodesia? The Selous Scouts promoted themselves as a regiment that would circumvent such conservative methods of policing and soldiering.[23] Their task was not just to find guerrilla gangs but to infiltrate them; they only needed to know where a man trained or how he entered Rhodesia to construct a cover story: they made up the background themselves. Thus, every captured insurgent offered "a whole gallery" of possible scenarios. If all but two members of a guerrilla patrol were killed, could the surviving two be turned to create another pseudo gang? Could a turned guerrilla lead a pseudo gang into an area in which he was not known, saying they had just crossed the border from Mozambique? Could that gang then intercept new gangs infiltrating the area? If a turned guerrilla was compromised, or well-known, could he serve as an instructor, teaching hand signals and code words? Could he help identify locals who would want to help guerrillas new to the area? Given all these possibilities, Reid-Daly described the process by which ZANLA and ZIPRA would be so effectively turned as streamlined to the point of being abbreviated. First, captured guerrillas were looked after with great care, constantly reminded that they had been spared. Those who were injured were given medical treatment at once. When they were interrogated by African and European Special Branch attached to the Selous Scouts, it "was the perfect moment," and in almost nine cases out of ten they offered information to their captors. After that it was "a fairly simple matter" to recruit a man for pseudo work.[24]

How simple was it? A turned guerrilla would visit the captive and recount the hardships of the struggle, the loss of life and limb under fire as their leaders lived well in Zambia and Mozambique, squandering the money that could have been used to buy arms for the cadres. The turned guerrilla would remind the captive that he had been spared. Often Reid-Daly would come himself: he was, in his own words, "the man the terrorists feared more than anyone," so the captive would be impressed to find him such a "friendly chap." Should the captive join the Selous Scouts, he would be given amnesty for the crimes he had committed as a guerrilla, all of which were capital offenses, but before he could become a member of the regiment he had to be deployed with a call sign in which he made every effort to prove his trustworthiness. This meant "showing the good faith of setting up his friends and former terrorist comrades for the capture or the kill." Although some men were overzealous in setting up old comrades, and others were overly aggressive with security forces, turned Selous Scouts were imagined to be without political loyalties.[25] In passages that seem to have been written entirely by Peter Stiff, no captive was ever asked if he supported Mugabe or Nkomo. Why not? Because out in the bush each man's life depended on his fellows. Besides, these men had given up the guerrilla cause for "something irresistible . . . for a band of brothers and comrades known as a regiment."[26]

Were guerrillas really turned in such a gentle way? "No one was ever beaten up by his Special Branch interrogators," Reid-Daly wrote, because it was "vital" to establish a trusting relationship quickly.[27] Were captured guerrillas really so transformed? Would they accept a "tamed" status in exchange for settling scores with some of their old comrades? The confidence that guerrillas would do just that may have been specific to the Selous Scouts, or at least to readers of Reid-Daly's histories of them. A SAS tracking manual from 1977 warned soldiers that turned guerrillas had already proved themselves disloyal once and should not be trusted.[28] Beyond the SAS, however, the process described by Reid-Daly found its way into literature. In a 1997 war novel a captured guerrilla meets a former guerrilla commander, now a sergeant in the Selous Scouts, who tells him that he must make the "same choices I faced when I was sitting in a cell nursing my wounds." He should come on side; "everybody in the country is at war." He should "fight on the side that has the upper hand." After all, "to fight like a soldier—any soldier—is better than the hangman's noose."[29] The author had been an officer in the Rhodesian African Rifles; was he describing something he heard about in wartime or something he read about in peacetime? Keith Samler was Special Branch seconded to the Selous Scouts. Interviewed for a 2012 book, he said it was imperative to treat a captive well. He conducted interrogations in the Selous Scouts "fort" at the end of the airstrip at Rusape. A wounded captive would be seen by an army medic and given a saline injection ("They loved injections"). Samler would offer the captive a cigarette. If the man was well enough to eat, "a white waiter would appear with the biggest plate of food imaginable and a Coke." Samler began questioning the captive a few minutes later: "The answers flowed like a torrent."[30]

Is this the full story that Reid-Daly collapsed in *Top Secret War*, or was it a story expanded in thirty years of recollection and retelling? My point is not that Reid-Daly's original version is right or wrong, but that the 1982 publication offered a template for a specific kind of war memory, a way of expertise and mastery and of thinking about one's place in the conflict. In practice the techniques by which Selous Scouts proved their legitimacy seemed considerably more complicated. Jim Parker, Special Branch seconded to the Selous Scouts in 1977, was informed that Selous Scouts could allay the suspicions of actual guerrillas by using small arms to attack an internal affairs base in a protected village, or, once they were encamped on high ground, they would ask that a Rhodesian fixed-wing aircraft fly overhead at a safe distance and then open fire on the craft as if they were trying to shoot it down.[31] When an attack on an INTAF base or isolated homestead was more successful than had been planned, newly turned guerrillas were most often blamed.[32]

Reid-Daly promoted the idea of turned guerrillas. One of his regimental innovations was promoting the unit as more international and more representative of global trends than it would have been had it been composed of white Rhodesians. The Selous Scouts were the only regiment in the Rhodesian Army whose soldiers not only were trained in Rhodesia "but who'd undergone training courses in Russia, Cuba, China, and Bulgaria as well." Turning, he argued, brought about a complete transformation. *Top Secret War* is filled with stories of the bonds between black and white Selous Scouts or turned guerrillas in new, intimate hierarchies of domestic service for men like himself (see chapter 2).[33]

Turning is thus the unmarked category of pseudo work. The fact of turning, as absolute and as out of character as it may seem for some insurgents, has not been subjected to much analysis beyond the stories Frank Kitson heard in 1955. Turning was a means to an end; the end was important, not why someone changed sides so dramatically, nor why they turned back after a while. Scholars of The Troubles in Northern Ireland debate whether or not Belfast pseudos, originally organized by Frank Kitson, were effective. Some insist that the IRA was able to win back the loyalty of men who betrayed them, and this compromised pseudo operations, while others argued that the brutality with which informers were punished made pseudos unwilling to reveal what they had become.[34] This debate suggests that turning is a permanent decision, a life change, a break that exchanged one community and commitment for another. This was certainly the Reid-Daly/Peter Stiff position. Yet for all photographic conventions of *Top Secret War*, in which African Selous Scouts' faces were covered over so as to prevent reprisals, Jacob Dlamini describes how South African police informers, including those who worked for death squads, retired to quiet, cautious lives in the townships in which they grew up.[35] As the following pages show, turning was often a strategy, a flexible, temporary status that allowed a guerrilla both to turn and to return. The Shona nickname for the regiment was *skuz'apo*, a hybrid Shona-English term meaning "excuse me here" or "excuse me for what I have done." Reid-Daly insisted that skuz'apo described the arrogance of the pickpocket who apologized for brushing against you as he took your wallet, but the term may well have had multiple audiences and described the moral complexities of turning.[36]

Turning and Returning Guerrillas

Four years after Reid-Daly's death, former Selous Scouts began to cast doubt on the entire enterprise of turning. They told stories of men based in Zambia or Mozambique who used the status of turned to get back there. Kevin Thomas wrote of several turned guerrillas for whom turning was a way to give themselves time to strategize how to stay alive until they could escape across the border. Andrew was a turned ZIPRA who provided background information to Selous Scouts. He was taken on a Selous Scouts patrol in Zambia during which he deserted. Martin Chikondo had been trained in the USSR; he had agreed to serve in the Selous Scouts to avoid hanging. No one believed the background information he provided as he made it clear he was biding his time until a guerrilla victory. Turnings were not always better when Special Branch had done its homework. Captain Morrison was a ZANLA who deserted a battle; he returned to Salisbury, where he found a job at a tent-making company. Special Branch found him and offered him prison or the Selous Scouts. He joined the Selous Scouts and was tasked with leading them to a guerrilla gang to prove his sincerity. He led them into Mozambique, where he arranged a meeting with a ZANLA gang. The gang's leader, Comrade Billiards, seemed to know the group was Selous Scouts and opened fire on the pseudos. It took several weeks for the Selous Scouts to realize that Morrison had not turned at all. He told newly captured ZANLA that they should kill the pseudo gang they were with and cross the border. The unit learned about this from newly captured guerrillas who may not have had a change of loyalty but who saw such information as being potentially advantageous.[37]

Ed Bird, a Special Branch officer seconded to the Selous Scouts from 1974 to 1976, took issue with Reid-Daly's description of turning guerrillas after he read *Pamwe Chete*. Bird had interrogated the captured ZANLA Habakuku Gumbo and declared him a security risk; Reid-Daly ordered him deployed against Bird's recommendation. On patrol a few weeks later, Gumbo shot the rest of the pseudo gang as they slept and took the group of just-captured ZANLA across the border to Mozambique. Reid-Daly made sure there was no public acknowledgment of these deaths, and he never admitted that it was his own adventurism that sent Gumbo on patrol. Indeed, Reid-Daly's version of events was a complete fabrication. He wrote that Gumbo was slow to agree to join the regiment, which made African Selous Scouts uneasy. Bird was outraged by this. A captured guerrilla was never given time to decide if he would join the Selous Scouts or any other unit. After interrogation the Special Branch liaison officer would recommend if he was suitable or not. If a guerrilla was found to be unsuitable—which was rare—he would not be handed over to a court because any legal proceedings would have compromised the secrecy of pseudo operations. Instead, he would be said to have "gone mining," shot without ceremony and his body dumped in an abandoned mine shaft. Reid-Daly wrote that Gumbo returned to Rhodesia to fight, but that too was a lie. Bird made it a point to ask about Gumbo in subsequent interrogations, and he was always told Gumbo was in Mozambique.[38]

Another Special Branch seconded to the Selous Scouts, Jim Parker, took pride in having been able to compromise even the most opportunistic guerrilla. When John Chakarakata—a chimurenga (war) name that was onomatopoetic for machine gun fire—realized he had been captured by Selous Scouts, he was elated to see two of the men he had trained with in Tanzania. He immediately offered to join them. Within a few hours Chakarakata was given a story and sent out on a patrol, although the firing pin had been removed from his AK as a precaution. The patrol soon met a guerrilla group; the commander was immediately suspicious because he thought Chakarakata had been killed. The Selous Scouts could not risk exposure and attacked. Chakarakata, unable to fire his weapon, grabbed a guerrilla's gun and shot him. Terrified that he was now compromised, Chakarakata ran away. Parker found him hiding nearby and told him "not to be silly," after which he worked with Parker planning pseudo operations.[39]

Did Reid-Daly and Stiff dissemble about turning, or did everyone else? The answer is yes, but a sequence of turnings from mid-1979 allow me to compare descriptions of turning and what turned guerrillas then did. In March 1979 Rhodesia held its first one-man, one-vote elections. These were boycotted by ZANU and ZAPU, but turnout was not insignificant, and a black president, albeit a figurehead one, was installed. Guerrillas who surrendered were given a vague amnesty (see chapter 9). Even if Abel Muzorewa had been a skilled politician, it is not clear this would have mattered, but he was not, and he gave in to the military, which began bombing external bases with a special vigor that brought the exiled nationalists to a constitutional conference in September of that year. What this meant for both guerrillas and the security forces is that the present was as unstable as the future appeared to be.

Shortly before the 1979 elections a Selous Scouts patrol set off a land mine under a vehicle they believed belonged to Dumiso Dabengwa, arguably the highest-ranking ZIPRA in the country and a veteran of the Wankie campaign. The passenger was not Dabengwa, however, but Elliot Sibanda, senior intelligence officer for ZIPRA's southern front. Sibanda was seriously injured; according to Reid-Daly's account, Sibanda offered to "tell you everything you want to know" in exchange for immediate medical care. He was somewhat pleased the Selous Scouts knew his chimurenga name, which they translated as "Black Swine." Sibanda was "the most important prisoner of the whole war." He was taken to the hospital at the Selous Scouts fort in Bulawayo, where he had surgery. Relieved to be alive and full in the knowledge that he could be executed, he told Special Branch everything they wanted to know. Sibanda told them that the senior leadership of ZIPRA's southern front command lived in the same building in Francistown. Intelligence met boastful good fortune as the Selous Scouts also learned that the British government had given the Botswana Defence Force an armored Land Rover, designed for use in Northern Ireland. This vehicle could easily be copied by army mechanics and could then be used as a decoy in a daring raid in Francistown, Operation Turrets. Indeed, Selous Scouts arrived at the ZIPRA house in Francistown in two modified Land Rovers claiming to be the Botswana Defense Force in search of a cadre who had shot a Botswana soldier. Once inside they handcuffed all seventeen residents and gathered "a huge quantity" of documents. As the two vehicles returned to Rhodesia, the ZIPRA realized they were now "prisoners of their most feared enemies . . . the Selous Scouts."[40]

Because he was an officer in ZIPRA, Sibanda was interviewed in early 1980 by the London-based International Defence and Aid Fund for a book on political prisoners that was never published. His version was very different. Once he was well enough, Special Branch interrogated him mainly about where ZIPRA had cached arms in Rhodesia. African interrogators threatened him with death, after which Special Branch came in and reprimanded the Africans. Sibanda understood this performance to mean he would be killed for not cooperating. He was too seriously injured to fight again—however unlikely that was for a senior intelligence officer—and he realized the government's amnesty program was a farce: for men like himself, captured and turned, it would mean being taken to a nearby battle camp to train security force auxiliaries, so Sibanda cooperated with the Selous Scouts. This meant living in a house in a Bulawayo township and going to "beerhalls, cocktail bars, and hotels" to identity ZAPU who might be there. He complied because, as his handler reminded him, "he had sold the party out." Within a few months there was a cease-fire and talk of the war's end. The morale of Rhodesian security forces was deteriorating rapidly. They had lost the battle, Sibanda said; captured comrades assured him that in some sections of the country no one had seen a Rhodesian soldier for six months. "The black detectives I was with were . . . asking me such questions as 'Do you think ZAPU is going to tolerate our presence?'"[41] There is another version, of course. A 2018 self-published book on the SAS repeatedly refers to intelligence about ZIPRA activities in Zambia provided by "the swine" but without any explanation of who the swine might be or why he was providing information.[42] Was this intelligence provided by Sibanda during the war or attributed to him or someone known as "the swine" years later? Another turned ZIPRA was Martin Gutu, who went to work for Special Branch rather than be handed over to the courts. Interviewed by IDAF, Gutu was keen to differentiate himself from his comrades who had joined "the other side," who were now Selous Scouts. He never doubted that the liberation struggle was right, and whenever he was alone with other captured comrades, they would discuss how they could help ZAPU.[43]

Blacking Up

If insurgents could act as security forces, even for a short while, could the white soldiers who went out with pseudo gangs act like African insurgents? Could they appear to be Africans? For how long? In *Gangs and Counter-Gangs*, Kitson described the lucky accident by which six-foot-tall, blue-eyed Eric was thought to be in a Mau Mau gang. When the gang came upon a nighttime patrol of pseudos before Eric could get away, James (or George) saved the day. Before the gang saw Eric, James (or George) told them he was the bodyguard of an Indian who was a senior Mau Mau commander. The gang members, like all the mid-1950s Mau Mau Kitson had encountered, were very conscious of rank, and they became somewhat agitated to be in the presence of someone so important. James knew the fiction wouldn't last and managed to arrest the gang, but for ten minutes a white man had passed as an African insurgent. How was this possible, Kitson asked? Even if they believed there was an Indian commander in Mau Mau, were there Indian commanders that were tall, with blue eyes and fair hair?

Eric was philosophical: because the gang had been told there was an Indian present, they expected to see one. They did not expect to see a white man, so when they saw him "they took me for what they expected." No one had ever heard of an Indian Mau Mau, Eric reasoned, but if the gang took him for an Indian without any disguise at all, why couldn't he disguise himself as an African Mau Mau, with "the right clothes" and a wig and his face and arms blackened? No one would look twice at an African Mau Mau.[44]

This foundational moment, this mixing and matching of racial and political categories, made an Indian Mau Mau commander from a tall white man. Whether the crossing was temporary or permanent, whether it was desired or accidental, did not matter as much as did the act of passing, as being seen as who and what you are not. This is what Rogers Brubaker has called "a position in a space of possibilities," one that can be freighted with authority.[45] This moment has been articulated by transgender memoirs and accounts of pseudo operations in almost identical terms. It was about the ability to cross, to move between the two groups, to be a soldier and a guerrilla, to be a man and a woman. This is more than not being found out, but of mobilizing both spaces for specific kinds of knowledge. Kitson was on patrol with a pseudo gang that sang Mau Mau songs as they had done before they turned. As they sang, Kitson began to believe that "we should rise up and kill the whites." How, then, is the boundary crossed? This was a simple matter in wartime novels, where one fictional white Scout told his wife, "It was possible for a white to have an injection which changed the colour of his skin, enabling him to live undetected in enemy territory."[46] In counterinsurgency, the boundary was always crossed at night; in daylight it was too easy to recognize a white soldier, however well blackened up and costumed he was. Jan Morris said as much about her life in Oxford before her gender reassignment surgery. She had a "double life" in central Oxford, "supposedly male in one place, presumably female in another." As she told more and more people about her transition, they began to see her as female: "People see in you what they expect to see."[47] This was true of pseudos as well, albeit in different ways. A few street-smart Special Branch wore "Afro wigs" and carried guerrilla weapons, especially AK-47s with their distinctive shape, so as to disguise their silhouettes rather than their skin. The various blackening-up creams were difficult to get off.[48] Some regiments made jokes about the creams. They were called "a concession to majority rule" by officers in the 2RAR and "black is beautiful" by many special forces, but Reid-Daly insisted that the Selous Scouts take blacking up and the creams with which they did so very seriously.[49]

For men who were not pseudos or who were only rarely blacked up, the boundary could not be crossed. They suspected that whites could never understand African ways of war. On an overnight patrol, Kitson slept between a turned pseudo and a blacked-up white Kenyan; he realized the gulf between his life as commander of an intelligence-gathering unit and his present place in the forest. It was the gap that separated the British Army from Mau Mau. "No wonder we found it so hard to keep up with them," he wrote.[50] When Peter Godwin, BSAP, was seconded to the RAR, he was in awe of an African soldier's ability to realize a homestead was harboring guerrillas. How could he be so sure, asks Godwin? Because nine people live there and they are cooking food for many more; when the girls take the pots to the stream to be washed, they have food in them, as he can tell by how the girls walk. "I know their life. It is the same as my life. So I can tell when something is wrong." And at that moment, Godwin realized that "white soldiers could never win a war in Africa because of our obsession with kill-ratios and fire forces and all the rest of it. Basically, we were fighting blind, absolutely blind." Godwin had been brought up in a rural area, and he had been in this area for a year, "but I could never hope to pick up all the subtleties that were so obvious to this corporal."[51] Godwin's insights did not come from pretending to be African but from understanding the limits of being white: useful intelligence comes not from makeup but from life experience.

There were never more than eighteen hundred Selous Scouts in the entire regiment, however, and of those one-fourth were white in the mid-1970s and one-sixth were white in 1978; most of the officers were white in the first years of the regiment, although that was to change dramatically by the late 1970s. All pseudo operations had to be "fronted by Africans," Reid-Daly wrote, but whites still had to perform a "successful masquerade" in the field. In Reid-Daly's memoirs, however, changing one's skin color was not so easy, as the African gaze was not to be trifled with. Blackening up involved great cognizance of, and respect for, what Africans looked like beyond "the obvious difference of skin color, hair and eye color." Scouts had to be attentive to the subtle differences as well: the shape of the face, "particularly the lips and nose," and the "mannerisms, method of movement, shape of hips . . . and so on." Selous Scouts availed themselves of the "amazing variety of blackening substances" provided for them, including burnt cork, theatrical makeup, and concoctions made for them by the police forensic scientists. White Scouts were also encouraged to wear floppy bush hats and beards, "the bigger and bushier the beard the better, because they served to break up racially characteristic features—at least when seen at a distance." Nothing worked well enough to be called completely satisfactory, however, and blackened-up white Scouts had to rely on Africans to make sure they stayed black. White Scouts "needed to stay black for weeks at a time," so a man could not afford to have "streaks of white becoming visible once he started sweating. This meant that the Africans in a group had to keep a constant, critical eye on their white comrades." A few white Selous Scouts wanted to do this for themselves and "tried everything possible to make them black and keep them black, to increase the effectiveness of their cover, and make their job in the bush easier." Reid-Daly told the laughable story of one white Scout, "although illustrious in history" who "gamely submerged himself in a bath of water liberally spiced with gentian violet." The pain in his urethra was too great, however, and he leaped from the bath because of the "burning agony . . . in the centre facet of the most valued of his family jewels."[52]

However badly Selous Scouts wanted to become black, it was not so easy to become all white again. The "unblackening process" was a constant challenge, wrote Reid-Daly. Men had to subject themselves to "long and often agonizing scrubbing sessions," but no matter how much they scrubbed, they left traces in their ears and hairlines.[53] It does not seem that Reid-Daly ever blacked up; A. J. Balaam complained he always dressed as if on parade. The fantasy of African Scouts helping their white comrades look like them was not shared by everyone. Balaam found the cream heavy and foul-smelling; it ran when he sweated and burned his eyes. On operations on summer nights he had to reapply it often, always aware when the cream ran. Paul French left the regiment after two years because being continually blacked up caused him skin problems.[54]

Passing

Passing as a guerrilla was more than a matter of skin color, however. There also was gait—which many pseudos said was the hardest thing for whites to mimic—and body language. It was possible that anyone taking a close look would notice a mannerism that was out of place. Stories that could explain motions and gestures were part of the narratives that made pseudos seem authentic. The wigs and dirty clothes of Mau Mau were discarded by Rhodesians who favored lectures about communist tactics, weapons, and what guerrillas wore on which infiltration route. This was "dark phase" training; men were supposed to think like insurgents and answer only to their chimurenga names. It included updates on guerrilla hand signals, slang, and what gangs ate in the bush. There was a famously intense course in bush living and a much more embodied course in living like an African. There was a seventy-page, mimeographed *Handbook of Shona Customs* given to soldiers that included the correct forms of deference and address when entering a village, how to locate holy places, and what to call in-laws. It included helpful phrases and stern advice: "Show respect even if you do not feel it" and "Avoid being over-assertive."[55] There were stories to learn and tell. Turned guerrillas drilled white and black Selous Scouts on the routes they took into Rhodesia from Mozambique, commanders' names and attributes, and the name of the nurse in the ZANLA hospital in Maputo where they recuperated from an injury.[56] Was this enough? Did turned guerrillas teach white and black Selous Scouts guerrilla stereotypes? Did they oversimplify African patterns of speech and movement? Were the slogans and commanders' attributes up-to-date or clichés, caricatures of armed struggle? Kevin Thomas wrote that by the end of the war ZANLA countertactics changed so quickly and were so decentralized that it was impossible for pseudo gangs to operate effectively.[57]

Did the lectures and stories and creams work? Those who claimed they did and those who claimed they did not understood the great possibilities and the grave risks of the space of masquerade. This was what Jan Morris, taking hormones but before her surgery, called "a precarious condition," of listening carefully to hear if she would be addressed as "sir" or "ma'am."[58] It was even more precarious for Jake Harper-Ronald, on a Selous Scouts mission in the Zambezi Valley in early 1978: his patrol was "vulnerable," he complained, because they wore the Stetson hats favored by ZIPRA and dressed like guerrillas and carried guerrilla weapons. Indeed, one blacked-up white Selous Scout was shot by an SAS team in the area, and a Rhodesia Regiment patrol feared it had fired on a Selous Scouts or SAS gang there as well. But a few months later his anxiety gave way to bravado. Most of the traits that distinguished black from white were not obvious when men were in vehicles, he had learned. "And there we were, driving into a capital city looking for all the world like a bunch of ZIPRA commandos on a raid. . . . We weren't stopped once or challenged on the 270 kilometer journey from the border."[59]

This, I submit, is the resolution of the moment of trans, the point at which the possibilities have been realized and perfected in an imaginary of flawless transformation. The myth of pseudo operations was that white

Selous Scouts not only managed to look like Africans, but no one believed they were really white men. Two stories from the first years of the Selous Scouts make this point. Kevin Thomas, who cited Frank Kitson in his discussion of pseudo work, told of an old man who volunteered detailed information about a ZANLA camp on a mountain in Nyanga. The pseudo gang decided to "lift" the old man back to their position so they could call in an air strike. When they told the man he was in their custody and they were indeed Selous Scouts, he laughed: they were lying, he said. The white Selous Scouts removed their hats and showed their blacked-up features. The old man laughed even more loudly: he had heard there were Indians who had crossed the sea to fight for ZANLA. Nothing seemed to convince him otherwise.[60] Another pseudo group infiltrated the area north of Mount Darwin where a ZANLA gang had long harassed security forces. A pseudo group made contact with the aged, local go-between. In a remote clearing on a moonlit night after many polite exchanges about cattle and crops "as African manners and custom demanded," the pseudos identified themselves as the dreaded skuz'apo. The man was terrified. "I'll tell you another secret," said the patrol's commander, Basil Moss. "I'm not even an African.... I'm a white man." The contact man refused to believe it. "You, a European... your Shona is better than mine!" As the African Scouts hid in the rocks, trying not to laugh out loud, Moss turned to his fellow Selous Scout and said, "Take off your hat, Winston, and Winston Hart's blonde hair showed in the moonlight.[61]

Fighting

There are several questions here—not the least of which is, Why dye one's penis but not one's hair?—but the one I want to ask is, Was this a winning military strategy? Sixty-eight percent of all guerrillas killed in internal operations in 1978 were "officially credited" to the Selous Scouts, although the figure was quickly applied to the entire war.[62] What does such a number mean, even if it refers to one year or many years or the areas in which only Selous Scouts gangs operated? Does it mean that the Selous Scouts killed 68 percent of all dead guerrillas themselves or that their intelligence led to 68 percent of all deaths? If it is the latter, how much time can elapse between the intelligence and the lethal contact for Selous Scouts to be given credit? If the guerrillas were sighted by another branch of the service after the Selous Scouts found them, did the Selous Scouts still get the credit? There are many ways to parse this figure, but however it is analyzed it seems so large as to be meaningless. Besides, how accurate were Rhodesian statistics on guerrillas killed? Selous Scouts were paid R$100 for every guerrilla killed or captured with his weapons. This increased to R$150 for ten or more guerrillas. A. J. Balaam thought these bonuses were a way of keeping turned guerrillas turned. According to Paul French, rewards were based on weapons collected, not a body count. Reid-Daly insisted that every man be paid immediately upon his return from an operation, whatever the hour, which may have allowed for exaggerated numbers to go unchecked.[63] Weapons not counted could be sold, possibly for more than the reward. Some of these weapons may have been sold to South African special forces who needed guerrilla weapons, and there was a rumor that Reid-Daly sold AKs to an American pharmaceuticals salesman who shipped them to the United States. Special Branch was charged with taking all captured weapons but allowed the Selous Scouts to keep a great many of them. The AKs—especially those with slogans carved on the stock—could help pseudos look like authentic guerrillas.[64]

As we will see in the next chapter, Rhodesian military intelligence did not think the unit was very effective and did not always get reliable intelligence. So what did the Selous Scouts do? Chapter 4 offers another history of their internal operations. The Reid-Daly version of successful turnings suggests a kinship with Kitson's years in Kenya, but almost all other Selous Scouts told a different story. Turned insurgents were a good strategy not just for counterinsurgency but also for insurgency. Turned men could bide their time, or have reasonably safe passage to the border. The intelligence they provided security forces might have been equaled by the intelligence they gave their old comrades.

But was military victory the goal of the Selous Scouts, or even the goal of their official mythmaking? Before Peter Stiff claimed Rhodesians "won every battle," Reid-Daly's imaginary was a kind of military nonracialism, a fanciful meritocracy based on respect and mutual dependence. This wasn't necessarily Reid-Daly's ideology; it was his discovery. For twenty years, Reid-Daly recalled, he had been evaluated as "not suitable for service with African troops." He had never questioned it; but after commanding the Scouts he realized that this had nothing to do with his qualities or those of African soldiers—for whom he now had the utmost respect—but with "the word of the *experts*" in the regular army who had been unable to see the potential of African soldiers. Using vocabularies of hearth and home, Reid-Daly "wanted to amalgamate the best of the African customs and the best of the European customs, and once we had found the right recipe and blended the ingredients together, we'd have a very special sort of relationship between the races, of a type . . . unknown in the Rhodesian Army." For Reid-Daly, being as at ease in Africa as Africans meant becoming at ease with and dependent on Africans: it was a fantasy of what white rule meant, and it was a powerful and long-lasting one. White pseudos learned what constituted racial differences, and how important such differences actually were—all learned from Africans. This was in part about masquerading as Africans and in part about working with Africans. Take the case of Chris Schollenberg, a South African tracker working for the Selous Scouts. He was a man of such idiosyncratic dress and demeanor that Reid-Daly once thought of telling a visiting South African general that Shulie was going undercover as a hippy. When he first began to do reconnaissance for the Selous Scouts, he refused to work with Africans: he thought they were fine soldiers, he said, he just didn't like them. A few months later, he returned to Reid-Daly to ask for an African partner. "There's a tremendous potential for black soldiers in reconnaissance work," he said, "because they can go where a white man can't."[65] Shulie learned to work with Africans. When he and the African Selous Scout with whom he tracked were separated, each feared the other had been killed. When they found each other, white soldiers nearby were moved "almost to tears" at the sight of "a big and well-muscled black Matabele and a big and well-muscled white South African hugging each other emotionally . . . in absolute relief in discovering the other had survived."[66]

These were the pleasures of the counterinsurgency of this chapter's subtitle. It is the imaginary of a common cause, a way to belong if only for a moment, and a way to displace repression onto the actions of local people, whatever their politics. The turning and the skuz'apo and the "better" Shona are more than the smug satisfaction of successful passing; it is that the passing itself reveals that the two sides are not so far apart after all, that they can be bridged in ways that military might alone cannot do. And as the next chapter shows, military might was not always the sole goal of Rhodesian special forces.

4 "EACH FOOTPRINT TOLD A STORY"

Tracking and Poaching in the Rhodesian Army

What made the war-in-the-place concrete were the skills of bushcraft—tracking and hunting, knowledge of flora and fauna, and men on the march. This knowledge was social; it was not something white men could master on their own: they needed African friends or at least African trackers and guides to do so. White Rhodesians tended to be trained so that what they thought was natural to Africans became second nature to them: bushcraft was learned. During the war, ideas about nature were bundled into ideas about which branches of the security forces were best suited to counter nationalist incursions.

In the late 1960s, the repression of Zimbabwe's liberation struggle and the conduct of Rhodesia's bush war were considered a police matter, questions to be answered and problems to be solved by investigation and intelligence. Much of the intelligence came from police involvement in rural areas. Policemen went to kraals to ask families to help them find out if a certain young man had been trained in Cuba, for example. Did anyone recall receiving mail from Cuba, or did they know when their son was out of the country?[1] Guerrilla actions required not military reactions but skillful investigation and skilled African trackers. A 1969 novel by Daniel Carney, formerly of the BSAP, makes this clear. The wife of the policeman hero is killed by a guerrilla gang led by an albino called Whispering Death, who leads his followers chanting, "Who do we hate? The Europeans." The hero's superior officer orders him to stand down. He must not hunt Whispering Death and his gang because that's what "they" want: for whites to lose control, to go into the reserves "blasting away at anything you see," and to abandon the rule of law and lose African support. The hero nevertheless seeks revenge and sets off with his faithful constable, Katchemu, to track

Whispering Death. Katchemu is old and infirm, but he is a great tracker. Watching flies swarm, he goes off the trail, and on his hands and knees scoops away the earth near an anthill, uncovering blood-soaked bandages over a pile of dung. He examines the dried blood: "This one will die soon." He then interrogates the dung: "He unlaced his boots and buried his toes in it, feelings its warmth. 'Maybe two hours in front,' he said. 'That's all.'"[2]

Katchemu not only tracks with great intelligence but does so with animal-like qualities. He may not get down on all fours to sniff the excrement, but later in the novel he smells the dried blood that he separated from the dust as he squatted beside footprints.[3] Is Katchemu an embodiment of Carlo Ginzburg's ideas about the relationship between clues and evidence? Ginzburg argued that the skills of tracking were hardwired: "In the course of countless chases," a hunter "learned to reconstruct the shapes and movements of his invisible prey from tracks on the ground, broken branches, excrement, tufts of hair, entangled feathers, stagnating odors." Humans learned "to sniff out, to record, interpret and classify such infinitesimal traces as trails of spittle" and interpret the evidence therein to make narratives.[4] Clapperton Mavhunga carried this point further, arguing that even as children Africans learned to read footprints to ascertain motive and intent. Their study of footprints was the way to learn the animal's goals and thinking: "What was it thinking as it moved, why was it taking each step in the way it was doing" in a particular direction or path? A well-trained African tracker observed and interpreted every sign and drew conclusions on the spot.[5]

Where does this leave Katchemu? Was he a skilled tracker who could read time and space and movement because he had learned the ways of the wild—bushcraft—because he himself was of the wild, if not kind of wild? He was not subject to the normal frailties of aging, of a dulled sense of smell and declining vision.[6] Even in Rhodesian nonfiction African trackers were presented as innocent and instinctive: men who had no real need for speech. See, for example, Maplanka, a "wizened old Bushman," perhaps five feet tall, who tracked for the BSAP in Matabeleland in the mid-1970s. He never spoke to the two policemen who flanked him as bodyguards when he followed spoor, but he would stop suddenly and point toward the bush and immediately "lie down on his stomach with his face buried in the sand" to hide from the firefight that would begin in a few seconds.[7]

The imaginary that African trackers, however old and infirm, could find their prey and predict a firefight had a long shelf life, as Maplanka shows.[8] But it was an imaginary. African trackers learned to track through practice and, according to a tracker with the South African Defence Force (SADF), teenage boredom. Growing up in a kraal in Namibia, the youth learned to read distinctive patterns in hoofprints so as to find out which cow belonged to which owner. He then learned how to read human footprints, the differences between those of young men and old men, between men's and women's prints, and between those of a small man and a large woman. He was able to study such things because "there was no television or any other Western distraction.... We were so at one with the environment that we could see things others could not."[9] But could those others learn to see these things? ZANLA commander Agrippah Mutambara trained carefully selected recruits to learn to track. He did not assume they already had the skills of reading footprints and disturbances on the ground. He taught them to examine broken branches or trampled grass to see if they had been disturbed by humans or animals. He taught them the sounds of birds and animals. Most of all, he taught how not to be tracked: there was crawling sideways propelled by their left leg, and, most important of all, not to litter. The most severe fine for trainees was for leaving a ration tin or a bullet casing or a piece of paper on the ground.[10]

White men could also learn the ways of the bush, and when they did, their intimacy with fauna was as striking as it was intimate. One of the most powerful examples I know of comes from a 1967 novel in which this scene is one of many tangents: a district commissioner takes a young white man out on a boat on the Zambezi. The young man is collecting snakes and finds a "beauty" swimming in the river. He jumps into the water, catches it, and brings it back onto the boat, holding the black snake's head between his thumb and forefinger. But as the young man attempts to force the snake into his specimen bag, the snake spirals up his arm and sinks its jaws into the man's lower lip. While the black snake clings to the young man's mouth, to the horror of everyone else on board, the young man calmly forces the snake's jaws open and "thrusts" it into the bag. "Snakebite serum!" the district commissioner shouts. "Forget it," says the young man. "It's the black-fanged variety and they don't shoot their poison until they have a real good grip. He only just got me.... I hope I didn't damage his jaws," he mused. "He's a beauty."[11]

Did this bush-savvy white scientist pass the Ginzburg-Mavhunga test? Did the zoologist turned game ranger who told the young recruit Nick Tredger that if guerrillas were lying in wait for an ambush there would be no baboons nearby?[12] I submit these men failed the test. They could not read the future as Katchemu and Maplanka did. They knew the ways of animals without knowing their motives. For Rhodesian security forces, this kind of knowledge was insufficient to track guerrillas. By the late 1960s, when training trackers began in earnest, there was no obvious way to do so. Ethnic stereotypes did not pan out: there were frequent complaints about Shangaan trackers and their ability to shoot.[13] Some RAR companies were skilled at tracking, while others failed to follow basic protocols for tracking wounded men.[14] Security forces insisted that their African enemies were brilliant trackers, however. An SAS patrol tracked locals, thinking this would lead them to a guerrilla camp; they led the patrol to an ambush instead. "Another example," noted the brigade commander, "of FRELIMO's ability because of their deep knowledge of the area and their screen of locals."[15] There were constant worries that African trackers were not loyal. Even when they were loyal, they were not necessarily skilled or energetic trackers. Whatever the problems with African trackers employed by the Rhodesian security forces, they were preferred to white trackers, who were paid more per day, much to the resentment—and possibly lackadaisical tracking—of African trackers.[16] The question became, Could white men learn to track as well as Africans were imagined to? And if white men did become expert in bushcraft, how could they be sure the Africans who tracked with them were loyal? This question was to take on new prominence in the late 1970s, as we shall see, but it obscured another question altogether.

Can White Men Learn to Track?

How were white soldiers to be taught to track? The young white men brought up on farms or in the countryside learned to track as children. They boasted about how well they knew the bush. A. J. Balaam grew up poor on the northern shore of the Zambezi. He and his black friend Robert fished without rod or reel and captured baby crocodiles with ease because they knew the ways of the river and its predators. Dennis Croukamp was tracking and hunting at age nine. Ivan Smith grew up on a white-owned farm, speaking Shona: "bare foot and in the bush hunting, tracking was as easy as riding a bicycle." Kevin Thomas grew up near the Sabi River; with his "young black companions" he fished and explored the shallows and islands. Barry Stranack was able to complete the Selous Scouts' selection course because he remembered that an African childhood friend in Malawi had told him he could quench his thirst by stripping a branch of a mopane tree and chewing the membrane found beneath the bark. Andre Scheepers, who joined the SAS in 1974, grew up on a farm where "some of his best times were with my African friends" with whom he hunted and collected snakes, crows, and eagles.[17] These were not memories of feral childhoods or of learning bushcraft in and of itself; they were ways of laying claim to belonging in Africa, to have acquired knowledge of the wild in childhood, from Africans and from being with Africans.[18] Tom Fuller believed he would be an excellent RAR officer because he had African friends, he spoke a bit of Shona and Ndebele, and he knew local customs: he could get "more out of them" than other whites could.[19] White youths claimed to know the ways of the bush and the ways of the bush war. Dan Wylie grew up in the Vumba hills. On patrol with African soldiers forcing African farmers into protected villages, he saw the landscape with greater clarity than his African gunner did. "Don't shoot," said Mbiti, "it is cows only." But Wylie knew it was more than cows. Looking between the cows' legs, he saw two men, dressed in the "classic dark denims" of ZANLA.[20]

These were the white youths who were willing to train other white soldiers. They knew the landscape and how to read it. Stu Taylor's schoolwork deteriorated when his family moved to the eastern highlands to run a hotel: he spent his weekends and holidays exploring every inch of high ground, both in Rhodesia and across the border in Mozambique.[21] Tracking was an acquired skill, one best practiced by staying upright so as to read shadows. There was CJ Skeepers ("I grew up on my father's farm.... The bush was my life"), one of the army's finest trackers. His father had told him the army would need men like him to track guerrillas, so he enlisted as soon as he was old enough. He could tell how many men were in a group, how fast they were going, and what they were carrying. Skeepers studied tracks by using the shadow cast by the slanting angle of the sun. "Each footprint told a story" with which he could assess the men who made them and how far ahead they were.[22] Anthony Trethowan, BSAP, learned to track from another white policeman. The best time to track was when the sun was low on the horizon "because of shadows that revealed every minute indentation." Trethowan started off looking at his own spoor, to learn the characteristics of footprints, and later followed his constables as they studied tracks, learning how to see who was running and who was dragging his feet. It was African constables who taught him how to cast for spoor on rocky ground.[23] In Wankie Game Preserve it was African game scouts who found a discarded sugar packet with Cyrillic writing on it.[24] Experienced hunters and trackers, like the farmer Faan Martin, were skeptical about white soldiers' tracking skills, as when another white reservist told him guerrillas were near. He had not seen any tracks for a while, but his colleague bent down and picked up a small piece of sugarcane that was still wet with saliva.[25] The tracking recalled in memoirs was a matter of looking down.

However capable white trackers were was irrelevant to the Rhodesian Army of the 1960s; it favored local trackers. In Central Africa in the 1960s, local meant African. Several commanders and generals had been in Malaya, and many more had known of the success of Rhodesian volunteers there; they all praised the good work the best local trackers had done. For men trained in conventional warfare these trackers seemed almost magical: their ability to turn sounds and smells and broken branches into evidence inspired awe and fueled descriptions of the likes of Katchemu and Maplanka. But trackers in Malaya, like trackers in most places, were best at tracking in the environment in which they grew up.[26] Once Rhodesia was preparing for war—even before 1965—there were concerns about whether or not to have a specialized tracking unit. Major John Anderson, before he was forced out, opposed the idea; it was too much like having a private army within the army. He—and others after he resigned—was content to let the police run tracking operations.

By 1967, however, interservice squabbles and genuine disagreements between the police and army over the kind of war this was to be led the army to hire its own trackers. Following the practice in Malaya, the army hired trackers from their own area, paid by the day. But locals didn't always know the technologies of tracking—especially how to avoid ambush—or how soldiers should follow the tracker. Allan Savory, in and out of the Rhodesian Army from 1958 and with the game department until 1964, proposed a course to train trackers, white men who could eventually go on covert operations.[27] They would be trained in what he called "aggressive bushcraft," which was distinct from the "Boy Scout or Army type bushcraft." He was not impressed with the trackers of the parks department, which, next to professional hunters, was probably the largest employer of trackers, although he recruited a few men from there. Instead, Savory offered to recruit from European units, regular and territorial: "Africans are no more suited for this role than they are for SAS selection." Besides, he had found African game trackers reluctant to close in on rogue elephants and man-eating lions. A School of Bush Warfare would be inexpensive to run as it would have a movable site and no permanent buildings beyond an administrative hut: "Instructors and students would live in the open at all times in all weather." Such training would keep Tracker Combat Teams at peak readiness and make use of the periodic lulls in guerrilla activity. Instructors could be on rotation from normal SAS duties. Aggressive bushcraft, Savory wrote, is perhaps the most important requirement for soldiers facing guerrilla armies, but there was no training given for it. Indeed, the recruits he trained the previous year were so "raw" that in a contact they would have been slaughtered by guerrillas.[28]

After a brief debate the army agreed on the number of men in each team (Savory wanted three, the SAS four) and where and for how long the refresher course might take place (a week in the Zambezi Valley or a week in Wankie). The army informed the game department that during training it might be necessary to snare or kill small animals so that students could survive. Instructors should be SAS, but Savory would give lectures for a day or two. The first course, held in February 1968, was rigorous in the extreme.[29] In a detailed description of his course published in 2015, Savory recalled his years in the Territorial Army and the difficulties of getting young, skilled, but arrogant national servicemen to take tracking seriously. He was finally able to train a mixed-race Guerrilla Anti-Terrorist Unit (GATU). When it was dissolved, he was given permission to recruit territorials for his vision of bushcraft into a Tracker Combat Unit (TCU). These men were trained in four-man teams; each man was a tracker. The lead tracker was followed by the controller of the team (he carried a radio) and two flankers who stayed well ahead of the lead tracker and to his side. The flankers had two tasks: to detect ambushes and to pick up tracks that deviated to the side. If a flanker picked up a new direction of the track, he signaled to the others and immediately became the lead tracker. Trackers did not walk in a line but in a wide column so as to see the most territory: they looked at an area perhaps twenty to thirty yards wide. They did not just look down, but up: Were there broken branches, spiderwebs, and birds' nests? A support troop followed the trackers, although Savory tried to do without them. When he had to have support troops, he insisted that they stay far behind and not use radios until the tracking team contacted them; otherwise, they made too much noise.

Savory's tracking was pure Ginzburg. It was a matter of interpretation, but the interpretations had to be reasonable. How fast were men going, where were they going, were they tired or limping, or were they rested from a camp nearby? Branches could answer those questions: tired men or men carrying heavy packs do not duck; tired or injured or limping men grasp branches as they walk, breaking them. Tracking, Savory told me, was like war college in reverse; solders had to figure out what the enemy would do.

Instead of making plans to try to defeat Mugabe or Tongogara, soldiers had to ask what were Mugabe's or Tongogara's immediate goals. Trackers were tasked to read the landscape from a guerrilla point of view. Once that was done, trackers realized that there were only two or three courses of action open to them.[30]

Savory firmly believed white male adults could learn to track. He began with the basic tracking, footprints. The edge of any shoe is revealed by shadows. These are fairly easy to interpret if men are walking in a straight line. Trackers can tell where they are going, whether they were walking at a steady pace or stopping every few feet, how much they are carrying. He did not believe—as the Rhodesian Army was soon to promote—that knowing the pattern on the sole of a shoe was key to much of anything. The edge of a shoe yielded information, not the sole. The figure-eights and other patterns on the bottom of shoes and boots donated from Eastern Europe were easy to discern if someone was walking on moist sand, but otherwise the information from the sole was useless. Whatever is on the sole of a shoe leaves no imprint on grass or rocky ground. Savory was more concerned with the operation of a tracking team than he was with styles of guerrilla footwear. He was "ruthless" about silence: it was trackers' greatest security, and it gave them the element of surprise. For that reason he decided against the use of dogs—they not only made noise in dense bush, but those bred to follow scent were not hardy and did not follow spoor on hot ground. He did not allow men to wear any covering on their legs as it might scrape against bushes; they could not wear webbing for the same reason or anything that protruded from their bodies. "Even if a slight noise could not be heard by the enemy, it could be heard by the trackers and flankers and was thus distracting." To communicate, teams used hand signals or a dog whistle tuned to the hearing of the man with the lowest tonal range. Savory had a cast-iron rule about water bottles: they had to be either empty or completely full. There were two reasons for this. First, a half-full water bottle made a constant, regular noise that was easily detected as human presence. Second, trackers were often thirsty or short of water, and hearing water sloshing in a bottle was distracting and took trackers' minds off their jobs. Savory did not believe in using sentries: "It prevented men from getting enough sleep if a small team had to post sentries." His teams scattered and slept in the bush and met at a prearranged site in the morning.[31]

When I asked Savory about antitracking—disguising or covering tracks—he almost laughed: antitracking slows men down, he said. Walking backward over tracks or running from tree to tree or bending branches backward took too much time. Walking on tiptoes or the sides of one's feet left a deeper impression than walking normally would have done, so why bother? Trackers know the signs of antitracking. The best way to avoid being tracked was to move rapidly over difficult terrain.[32] It was essential to move in the daytime; moving at night simply disturbed too much. I asked about guerrilla antitracking. When guerrillas entered a kraal, they often ran cattle over their tracks, but the best trackers understood this and could figure out where a guerrilla gang was. Trackers had to think like guerrillas and ask if the signs they left revealed the direction of travel or masked the direction of travel. Trackers had to think like guerrillas: Where are they going? Are they in a hurry, or do they have the time to hide their destination? This was not always a matter of reading spoor but of looking around.

Savory believed in the Territorial Army as few Rhodesian regular soldiers did: these men, or their parents, had voted for the Rhodesian Front, they supported the war, and were willing to fight for it. These men were electricians and mechanics and farmers who brought any number of skills to the army, and Savory wanted to access their range of talents and experiences. Nevertheless, his first recruits for the Tracking Combat Unit were all white, professional hunters and game wardens from the parks department, and a territorial officer seconded from the SAS. Not all of them grew up on farms. He also recruited men he knew personally—Paul Coetzee, Malcolm King, Bruce Cook, and Darrell Watt.

Savory created the TCU to be lean and mean, to use only what was essential. The men worked in shorts and tennis shoes, two pairs for each man. The army paid for one pair and Savory bought the other. The expense was worth it because any additional equipment slowed trackers down. He told his men that whenever they entered a ZANLA camp to steal everything they could. Trackers had no camps; there was no place to return to and thus no paths followed: TCU slept hidden in the bush. In between tracking exercises Savory lectured on bush survival skills, which plants were edible and which were not, how to find water or at least get something liquid, and which snakes were poisonous and which were not. This was the bush-savvy science that appeared in fiction at almost the same time. Col. D. H. Grainger, SAS, took Savory's course and used the notes to write a book, *Don't Die in the Bundu*, which contained information about finding food and shelter, and first aid for a wide range of injuries and exposure to poisonous plants. Grainger's book—and not Savory's course—formed the literal basis of Ron Reid-Daly's *Staying Alive: A Southern African Survival Handbook*, published in 1990. Written for soldiers, plane crash survivors, and hunters and hikers who lost their way, the advice about flora and fauna was broader than that provided by Grainger.³³

The TCU was called out frequently after 1969: their task was to track, not to fight. They were deployed to find guerrillas before and after contacts. After a contact they were often called in to track wounded guerrillas.³⁴ In 1970 Savory was elected to parliament. Three years later he reformed the Rhodesia Party with the support of the federation's prime minister, Sir Roy Welensky. By then, however, Savory's open disgust at the conduct of the war made him a pariah in military circles, which may have been why the TCU was recast and handed over to the School of Infantry. By 1970 there were enough officers who had been trained by Savory to give lectures and instruction. National servicemen were sent to training areas to practice tracking for a day or two but without much enthusiasm or success.³⁵

The war entered a new phase in 1973. An increase in guerrilla incursions caused the army to reconsider tracking. For reasons shrouded in mythmaking, Gen. Peter Walls recruited an old comrade from Malaya, Lt. Ron Reid-Daly, to form an elite, secret tracking unit that would double—the pun is intentional—as pseudo gangs. These were the Selous Scouts, named for another famous tracker who fought against Africans in another insurgency. These pseudo gangs were African soldiers and a few white men who had blackened their skin with various creams and cosmetics. The Selous Scouts were based on the conceit that this was not difficult for white men. They could blacken their skin, they could disguise their features with beards and floppy bush hats, and if they spoke at all, they spoke in the Shona or Sindebele they learned as children. Some of the most subtle racially specific characteristics vanished when men rode on vehicles. They would wear uniforms taken from dead guerrillas and carry AK-47s or occasionally rocket-propelled grenades of Soviet manufacture. The fiction was that the masquerade was complete, that no one could tell who was a real guerrilla and who was not. Indeed, the story of the first such gang, the Tracker Combat Wing, started by Paul Clemence (RLI) and Andre Rabie (SAS), was that the blacked-up Rabie was killed when he gave his own position incorrectly and was thought to be a guerrilla by an RLI patrol.³⁶ Although everyone was quick to point out that Rabie's death was due to his own mistake (see chapter 3), it generated a number of stories about the risks faced by blacked-up white men from security forces while on operations. The fact and the fiction gave rise to "frozen areas" in which the Selous Scouts were operating and in which no other branch of the security forces was allowed. This was not only to protect white Selous Scouts but to give them time to establish themselves in an area.[37]

Because the Selous Scouts were to be multiracial, the question of who acquired whose skills was thick with meaning. I have read the sections on the formation of the Selous Scouts in both versions of Reid-Daly's memoirs many times, but each time I am struck by the extent of the transformation he proposes. The goal of the unit was to turn Europeans into Africans (there are two versions of that), to give them a natural lore of the bush, and to make African soldiers better at being Africans. Given the mimicry required by pseudo gangs, this made perfect sense, but it also pushed aside all those men who loved the wild and knew the bush because they learned from their African playmates—men who based their claim to belong in Africa on the intimacies of growing up with Africans. In the Selous Scouts white men could learn to track, but they could not learn to do it as white men. What was natural for Africans could not become natural to white men so long as they remained white. Thus the Selous Scouts selection course was "mainly concerned with turning a European into an African. . . . It ignored the African's natural advantage . . . he already was one." In 1999 Reid-Daly added "as was the enemy." African soldiers were younger, only slightly less animalized versions of Katchemu and Mpalanka: they had "phenomenal physical endurance and . . . an almost uncanny ability to move and see at night." They had an "incredible" sense of direction and a "keen sense of observation" coupled with the power to memorize. The problem was they were afraid of heights and had a "distinct lack of aggression." For these reasons Reid-Daly did not want to try to make Africans "European-type soldiers" but to make "very good African soldiers out of them." Where such men would be so trained was another question altogether. Reid-Daly was given a lease on a wide area of land touching Lake Kariba. This was Wafa Wafa, which normally was translated by Selous Scouts as "you die, you die" but in fact is the Shona third-person singular for "he died." When doubled, however, the term is both intensified and given a more colloquial translation, "whoever dies, dies" or sometimes paraphrased as "survival of the fittest."[38] Wafa Wafa was to be their base. Selous Scouts were not allowed into the township because men had to "get back to nature" to learn real bushcraft. Reid-Daly amended this explanation at length in 1999, noting that nature was neutral; it would neither help nor hinder Selous Scouts, but "if they know the bush, and know it well, it will help them in countless ways . . . and put them well ahead of their enemies."[39]

4.1 Swimming at Wafa Wafa. Photograph by Ron Reid-Daly, courtesy of Chris Cocks.

Was the bush to be mastered or learned? The question is confusing. But then, the whole idea of the Selous Scouts was supposed to be confusing—perhaps ZANLA gangs believed all sorts of reasonable but unsubstantiated stories, perhaps contact men refused to believe blacked-up white men weren't guerrillas, perhaps everyone believed that guerrillas turned forever—but this is something else, that there can be a one-to-one correlation of tracking skills with race, and then with only one race. Being a barefoot white child in the bush as so many young soldiers claimed to have been was not enough; Selous Scouts were not to be with Africans, whatever their self-presentation claimed, but like Africans.

Nevertheless, much in the selection and promotion of the regiment did the opposite. On the advanced training course in 1978, Barry Stranack learned three levels of tracking: simple (following spoor), systematic (following spoor and looking at vegetation), and speculative ("working out a theory" based on where "an indigenous person" would go in an area). Having grown up hunting with African playmates was of no use "because there are distinct differences in behavior in the bush by Africans of European descent and indigenous Africans."[40] A. J. Balaam described some of these differences. The selection course included an exercise involving loading and unloading boats on the shore of Lake Kariba. Whites did this very well because they knew how to swim and had no fear of wading out into the lake; Africans did not do this well because so many of them did not know how to swim. Halfway through the course, recruits were offered cold beers if they would sing and dance. Africans got most of the beers because "Blacks are natural singers and dancers," while whites were terrible at both.[41] What all this seems to have meant on patrol, however, was that white Selous Scouts hung back: however well blacked-up they were, there were simply too many other factors at play—gait, shape of the head, eye color, body language—that revealed white men as white. White Selous Scouts were required to grow beards—also dyed black—and wear wide-brimmed floppy hats that hid what Reid-Daly call "racially characteristic features."[42] Did it work? Many white Selous Scouts doubted that it did. "Blacks cannot pass themselves off as white and vice-versa," wrote Kevin Thomas. The operational Selous Scouts were all African.[43] Black and white Selous Scouts moved mainly at night, thereby ignoring Savory's tracking principles.[44]

Did White Men Learn to Track?

In the mid-1970s Selous Scouts and SAS tracking followed the contours and the spirit of Savory's original training program most of the time. Darrell Watt, one of the original members of Savory's team, described an SAS operation in Mozambique in 1975. The patrol's first task was to dull everything metal. Otherwise the glint of sunlight on an insignia or gun barrel would give them away. He tried to keep men from smoking because the smell carried a long way. He made his men listen to birds: "Their calls changed when they were surprised. This almost always meant someone was coming and gave us time to get ready." The bigger problems were the sounds of men snoring at night and water. Snoring men could be awakened at once, but water was a constant problem and men had to be very careful to ration their intake of water. No one was required to carry an empty water bottle; instead, men were encouraged to share what they had until the bottle was empty.[45] In practice, the mechanics of tracking could overwhelm common sense. In 1975, when Timothy Bax was a Selous Scout, he led a group in the "easy" tracking of a wounded guerrilla. The man left a trail of blood in bush so thick that trackers had to walk single file. Bax knew they were approaching a village by the smell of wood smoke, but they only saw the village when the men followed the spoor around a bend, where they were shot at.[46] Barry Stranack was a firm believer in the superior tracking skills of African Selous Scouts. On one patrol an African Scout fell into an ant hole. He was not injured, but everyone stopped until he recovered. When the patrol resumed tracking and camped for the night, they realized they had been observed for hours.[47] At other times expediency could overwhelm the mechanics of tracking. Paul French, a Briton in the Selous Scouts, tracked a gang of twenty ZANLA in 1976. He and four trackers followed spoor that included the drag marks from a recoilless rifle, until the guerrillas had scattered for antitracking. French's group was stymied until a Rhodesian motorcycle unit came by and gave them rides. They soon found the spoor, which led them to a village that had been abandoned only a few hours earlier. "This job," French wrote, "was a bit of a 'lemon.'"[48]

Outside of special forces it is not clear that Rhodesian commanders made much fuss about tracking. In theory it was the Selous Scouts who were supposed to track guerrillas and call in fire force or whomever, so that officers in the RLI or RAR needed to be familiar with the principles of tracking; their soldiers did not need to learn to track. Whether young national servicemen celebrated their ignorance or their disobedience I cannot say, but memoir after memoir describes young men ignoring every conceivable protocol of stealth and silence. Toc Walsh was a national serviceman with the 1 Independent Company, Rhodesia Regiment, in 1974. His first patrol was on a sandy road in the summer. According to the map there was a pump somewhere on the road. Walsh was sent to find the pump and return to lead his comrades to it. He asked if he could just fire a shot to let them know he had found water.[49] Angus Shaw was the section leader for a patrol tasked with tracking a guerrilla band to a stand of trees on a riverbank, where they would be cornered by the patrol and easily attacked by fire force. The patrol tracked over rocky ground; stones crunched beneath the men's boots. When they finally reached the riverbank, Shaw spent an hour trying to find trees for cover. Instead, he led his men to an abandoned kraal, probably used by guerrillas. As the sun rose, fire force shot at Shaw's patrol.[50]

Antitracking measures had a folklore all their own, sometimes specific to a unit or a group of men. Before any deployment in the countryside, one RLI patrol would sit in the billowing smoke of a fire stoked with newly chopped wood, wearing their gear. Their skin and clothes would become impregnated with the odor of burning wood, a "natural smell of the bush," which would disguise their "human smell" from animals and locals. According to RLI lore, Africans could smell a European body two hundred yards away but "not if it's disguised by the smell of woodsmoke."[51] Ross Baughman met an RLI stick leader who claimed his sense of smell was his best weapon. Campfires and the smell of cooked food made trails in the breeze, and he had learned to recognize the sweat of frightened Africans. To make sure he did not give off any artificial scent himself, he didn't use soap for weeks at a time and made sure that his uniform was washed only in river water or rainwater.[52] Other soldiers thought antitracking was a matter of tracks. Whenever Darrell Watt's patrols rested, they would walk past the point where they would stop and then double back and cover their incoming tracks. Thus, anyone tracking them would follow the spoor past their position and be visible.[53] When Kevin Thomas was with the Selous Scouts, he insisted that antitracking was what any man with "sound bush lore" would do as a matter of course: stay on rocky ground or boulders because the years of accumulated leaf litter and dead grasses would cascade downward and cover his tracks. The man in front constantly walked through spiderwebs but these were made by wagon wheel spiders, which could re-spin a web in a few hours. He also believed it was all but impossible to fool local people. Pseudos often walked barefoot when nearing a village, hoping that their footprints would be lost in local foot traffic, especially where so few Africans wore shoes. But villagers had a thorough knowledge of where they lived, and anything untoward aroused their suspicions. On many mornings Thomas's party hid on a well-watered hillside and watched villagers lingering over the spoor of their passage from the night before.[54]

By 1977, the regular army seemed to de-skill tracking. By then, of course, the war had been going on for years and enough guerrillas had been captured to provide the army with wide-ranging if out-of-date intelligence. The CIO and various branches of the security forces published handbooks of "terrorist tactics" on which countless lectures were based. These pamphlets and lectures explained that guerrilla groups of ten to fifteen walked single file, carrying their own weapons and provisions. There was a list of current hand signals: a clenched fist with the thumb down meant the enemy had been sighted; a raised rifle meant there was something suspicious ahead and everyone should sit while someone went to investigate. There were a range of hand signals to indicate what was ahead and, if necessary, which weapons to bring forward. According to a captured guerrilla, gangs walk normally until they reach cattle tracks. Then they walk on tiptoe, swinging left to right to make their footprints look like those of cattle. Two pages were devoted to guerrilla clothes and shoes: guerrillas had formerly worn

Eastern Bloc boots with a figure eight on the sole, but more recently they preferred Super Pro-Basketball shoes, a Bata-made shoe also preferred by the SAS.[55] The handbooks and the cumulative wisdom of captured guerrillas informed the lectures given to national servicemen. Michael Isemonger, of the BSAP, told a group of RLI that captured guerrillas recognized security forces by their uniforms and by their silhouettes. Captured guerrillas had their own ratings of Rhodesian security forces in terms of their "aggressiveness." Rhodesian forces' fitness was not all their commanders wanted, whereas guerrillas underwent "brutal" training and were then "hunted" in most operational areas and thus remained fit. Captured guerrillas continually commented on how easy it was to spot security forces: metallic badges reflected in the sunlight, cigarette smoke carried for hundreds of meters, and white skin was visible for as much as a kilometer. Troops were advised to keep their clothes on at all times, however hot it was.[56]

Nevertheless, men sunbathed, smoked, and refused to blacken their regimental insignia. Before the war intensified in 1976, the RLI was given to "flamboyant individualism." Men cut up their hats to make them easier to wear in dense bush or just to look better. They rarely wore long camouflage trousers. By 1978 commando units of the RLI began to wear their green berets in combat. Ordered to blacken the beret's silver badge—which would reflect light on a sunny day—men refused: that would be desecrating battalion colors. Until 1977 RLI wore a variety of shoes that left a variety of prints. Most of them wore their own shoes or sneakers, a few wore standard combat boots, and a few wore veldskoens. In 1977 the army introduced "clandestine" takkies, sneakers with no tread. They also had no grip, so men wearing them tried to walk on level, soft ground on which they left a clear impression. Many soldiers recalled how lightweight and comfortable these shoes were, but Chris Cocks was not alone in thinking they were ridiculous: "Whenever I saw treadless footprints, I knew Security Forces were in the area, as the enemy would presumably know also."[57]

The years 1976 and 1977 were a watershed in the conduct of the war. The August 1976 raid on Nyadzonya camp in Mozambique was one of the great successes of the Selous Scouts. Captured guerrillas had told Rhodesian forces that this was the transit camp for a regrouped ZANLA infiltrating Rhodesia, and they described the camp in considerable detail. The Rhodesian government could not be seen to orchestrate cross-border raids, but a mixed-race unit like the Selous Scouts could execute one—indeed, far better than the all-white SAS could, Reid-Daly noted. Pseudo operatives masqueraded as FRELIMO. They drove onto the parade grounds singing revolutionary songs in Portuguese and started shooting. It was a bloodbath by all accounts, in which seventy-two, or seventy-five, or eighty Selous Scouts killed and wounded well over a thousand ZANLA, without losing a single man. Surveying the carnage, Reid-Daly said he couldn't tell if there were one hundred dead or nine hundred dead (see chapter 9), but later he wrote that "it was the classic operation of the whole war."[58] It was also the operation that gave Reid-Daly a new credibility in the security forces.[59]

A few months later a fraught unity gave ZANLA and ZIPRA and their donors a renewed commitment to guerrilla war. In Rhodesia, call-ups intensified, more and more demands were placed on more and more Territorials, and the army became concerned about soldiers' morale. The 1977 survey conducted by the army's counterintelligence unit revealed a broad and growing frustration with the Selous Scouts. The unit seemed to answer to no one and was often incompetent. "They may well be doing a good job somewhere," said an officer in the Armored Car Regiment, "but we only see their undisciplined arrogance when they come to us to demand help or equipment."[60] Indeed, by 1977 the Selous Scouts had grown from 400 to 1,200 to 1,800 men. The unit had expanded to include dogs, horses, signals, and more and more soldiers. In its first years the unit had grown from 120 to 400 and then to 1,200, but by the time it was composed of 1,800 men it was markedly inefficient. "People started doing their own thing," I was told many times. A. J. Balaam joined the Selous Scouts in early 1975. A few years later "the floodgates opened" and "riff-raff" came in.[61] In 1976, Stu Taylor left the Selous Scouts to return to the RLI; he was contemptuous of the expanded regiment. Perfectly ordinary soldiers "bullshitted" their way into the mushrooming unit, where they could get better kit, better equipment, and better bonuses. There was "a lot of confusion over who was who" because of the number of turned guerrillas: "in retrospect I reckon most of them hoodwinked us."[62]

In 1977, at least, Reid-Daly seemed oblivious to all this. He had recruited a pilot—a Bulawayo businessman, Peter Scales, who had his own plane—to fly him to operational areas. He keenly believed in the image of the Selous Scouts and the power of having Africans in his regiment. Writing of that year, Reid-Daly noted that the Rhodesian public was fed a diet of "wildly improbable rumors" about the Selous Scouts' real or imagined exploits and "built a myth about us until we were thought of as akin to supermen." In the wider world, however, Selous Scouts were demonized and even blamed for the "terrorist created holocausts" that were a frequent occurrence in rural areas. This made the local press suspicious and led many African

Selous Scouts to consider leaving the regiment. In 1977 Reid-Daly decided to show off the multiracial quality of the Selous Scouts so the regiment would earn the journalistic respect it deserved; he invited newspapermen to Inkomo Barracks to meet the regiment. He was keen to show the kind of African soldiers he had constructed. The press—including reporters from South Africa and Britain—was impressed by the "genuine multiracial mess" for everyone below the rank of sergeant. The African Selous Scouts literally sang for their supper—"as only Africans can"—as the "spellbound" journalists peppered them with questions in broken English and sign language. The soldiers responded in "monosyllabic Shona" even though most of them spoke English fluently.[63]

Singing still marked African Selous Scouts; tracking did not. The Selous Scouts 1977 tracking manual was a far cry from Savory's original vision. It began by reminding trainee trackers that the best they could expect from a manual was basic knowledge, to become "bush minded," but "no amount of theorizing" was a substitute for practice. It listed techniques—estimate the number of guerrillas, the age of their spoor, and the direction they traveled—and warnings not to disturb the spoor trackers found, but there was nothing about guerrilla motivations or how guerrillas might have been thinking about the landscape. The closest the manual came to guerrilla thinking was to remind trackers to backtrack when they found fresh tracks in the morning as they might well lead to a camp. The twelve recommended antitracking measures were the most obvious ones: move in the rain whenever possible, try to find types of ground that are difficult to track in, walk on the sides of the foot or wear smooth-soled shoes that leave a "less distinctive" print or go barefoot or wear sandals with tire treads. Men were instructed to "be careful" with fires, tobacco, and soap and to be aware of bird and animal alarms as well as frog and insect silences.[64] The SAS, in contrast, had a much shorter section on tracking that was introduced by comments not on the nature of tracking but on the nature of guerrillas, turned and unturned. Believing that African units might not need specialized trackers, all others should have civilians or African soldiers attached for tracking duties. Guerrillas, however, were masters of bushcraft: not only did their superior abilities allow them to see farther and walk farther than security forces could, but their "ability to track and read tracks naturally will make them more proficient in hiding their own." For this reason, there had to be Rhodesian expert trackers or units that were able "to work with and understand loyal African trackers." The disloyal ones, turned guerrillas, should only be deployed with caution. The fact that they have surrendered and led security forces to "a good kill" does not prove they had come on side; instead, it proves how disloyal they could be. They should, however, be used when necessary, but they should also be regularly reminded how fortunate they are not to have been shot before their surrender, that they are now on probation and they "have a score which can only be settled by continuous and satisfactory service." Security forces should take extreme precautions that these men are not leading them into an ambush.[65]

Did Tracking Matter?

Was it a problem that tracking was less of a skill for whites in the late 1970s than it had been in the late 1960s, and that by then fewer and fewer special forces trusted turned guerrillas? One of the questions surrounding the Selous Scouts was what exactly they did on operations. The Rhodesian Intelligence Corps, consisting of wildlife biologists and doctoral students on reserve duty, was tasked with reading and analyzing situation reports to ascertain how effective various units were. It was discovered that the Selous Scouts were effective for the first six days on any operation: they had six days of gathering good intelligence, and after that they spent thirty-six days "wasting their time sitting on hilltops." Why? Was there an inherent limit to how much good intelligence can be learned in one sitting, were they compromised, or were their operations about other things? By the late 1970s many generals in the Rhodesian security forces thought the Selous Scouts were more concerned with ivory poaching than they were with gathering intelligence. Frozen areas were for moving ivory and hides, not for winning a war.[66]

Poaching rhinoceros horns, elephant tusks, and hides has a deep history in southern African insurgencies and counterinsurgencies. As early as 1968 Kevin Thomas, then of the game department, wrote that the biggest problem protecting Wankie Game Reserve was that black rhino were shot by the South African Police (SAP) sent there to strengthen Rhodesian forces. Although several of his colleagues thought some of the rhino might have been killed by Rhodesian patrols, the area was covered in FN 7,62 casings, and there were boot and sole patterns consistent with SAP issue. More to the point, four rhino horns were found in SAP footlockers in their barrack tents. Thomas did not know how these horns traveled from northwest Rhodesia to Hong Kong or mainland China or Yemen, where they were used as dagger handles.[67] Jan Breytenbach, arriving in the Caprivi

Strip in 1970, found well-established networks that moved tusks and skins from the western Caprivi to Windhoek to Johannesburg to Hong Kong; rhino horns from Wankie could have been taken to Caprivi easily or sold to traders in Johannesburg if someone had the right contacts. The slaughter of elephants was so widespread that many white soldiers returned to South Africa from the border with a pair of tusks. Breytenbach was more distressed by UNITA's role in this, however. Well before South Africa's largesse, Jonas Savimbi's party had relied on Portuguese criminal networks. UNITA killed elephants and stockpiled their tusks for eventual shipment to Chinese agents in Pretoria in order to fund itself.[68] Keith Meadows may have referenced Savimbi's poaching in a novel that describes a Rhodesian special forces operative—probably a Selous Scout—who organizes ZIPRA's "Ivory Section." Despite the risk guerrillas faced by drawing attention to themselves, the ivory section killed elephants with the automatic weapons provided by East European and Soviet allies and sold their tusks abroad so as to lessen ZAPU's dependence on those very backers: "Our leaders worry when the Russians or others threaten to stop supplies."[69]

Most units of the Rhodesian Army had shot animals for food, even protected species. When Kevin Thomas was a game ranger, he often shot kudu for men on patrol. Stu Taylor recalled that one RLI shot a nyala thinking it was a kudu, and that two separate patrols deliberately shot two kudu, which they then had to butcher right away.[70] With the exception of shooting the rare nyala, this was all routine and reported as anecdote, not scandal. The accounts of the Selous Scouts' poaching were reported as scandal. The motives seemed to be entirely personal and monetary: for that reason, perhaps, the former game rangers among them were appalled not just by the slaughter of elephants and big cats but by the degree to which superior officers protected poachers. Moreover, frozen areas—in which Selous Scouts were on their own with no surveillance whatsoever—were defined specifically for hunting elephants and big game. Sometimes Selous Scouts went so far as to use RhAF helicopters to shoot elephants from the air.[71] Everyone I spoke to about this, however, referred me to one of the two published accounts of Selous Scout poaching, one by Dennis Croukamp and the other by Kevin Thomas.

Croukamp was an experienced hunter and regular soldier who was one of the first Selous Scouts Major John Redfern (of Army Intelligence) spoke to about stories of poaching in 1978. Throughout an interview that lasted several hours Croukamp admitted that while he heard talk of poaching and ivory tusks almost all the time from rank-and-file Selous Scouts, he had no personal firsthand knowledge of poaching. Thomas was later to dispute this, writing that Croukamp, like everyone else, had seen the boxes of hides and ivory. Croukamp was more specific in his memoir, writing that he had never seen any "haphazard or organized poaching," but he, like everyone else, knew about the out of bounds quarry just outside the training area in which crocodile eggs were covered with river sand. Once they hatched, they would be killed and mounted and sold. He never saw a leopard trapped and shot, but a Territorial told him that leopards were trapped in cages and then shot in the head with a .22 caliber rifle so as not to damage the skin. Elephants and leopards were killed at Wafa Wafa, and their hides were cured and tusks cut and marketed from Selous Scout Training Troop. This was less than a kilometer from Inkomo Barracks with its incomparable singing; it was the site of the graveyard where African Selous Scouts were buried. Training Troop was far enough from the comings and goings of regular Selous Scouts as to give the training officer relatively free rein; Reid-Daly was the only regular visitor. The shipping of boxes of animal products and the sale of ivory went on in full view of the men being trained or training Selous Scouts: the office was often called the "Curio Shop." Both Croukamp and Thomas had seen several boxes of ivory cut from tusks, mounted baby crocodiles, elephant feet, dozens of elephant hair bracelets, and boxes of hides there. None of this was hidden, although there was enough anxiety about poaching that when Thomas joined the unit in late 1974 he was repeatedly asked if he was a "national parks plant."[72]

Croukamp's memoir is especially interesting because he gave the manuscript to Reid-Daly for his comments, which were then published in the text. Many of Reid-Daly's comments defend the expansion of the regiment—that most Rhodesian generals had no vision or imagination and that the SAS was all white and hated the Selous Scouts—but he did address the poaching issue head on. First of all, James Anthony (called Ant by everyone) White had a taxidermy license; he had had one for years. Indeed, when he was sent to Zambia to assassinate Joshua Nkomo, his cover story was that he was a taxidermist from Kenya scouting business opportunities in Zambia. He had forged papers from Kenya and a "wealth of knowledge on bush craft and wild animals" he had gained when he was an instructor at Wafa Wafa, although he did not manage to kill Nkomo.[73] By the time he headed Training Troop, army headquarters had given him permission to pursue his hobby, and he had received permission from the game department to use the head and skin of any animal the Selous Scouts were allowed to shoot. Reid-Daly allowed White and a Territorial who also had a taxidermy license to run a business out of Training Troop. He could not see any reason why "any Selous Scout could not make extra pocket money to supplement his miserable Army salary—provided it was legal." Wafa Wafa was too important as a training facility for anyone to jeopardize it by poaching animals. Besides, there were at least twenty Special Branch attached to the Selous Scouts on a permanent basis. If there was poaching of game going on anywhere, wouldn't Special Branch have figured it out? Reid-Daly never listened to gossip, he wrote. He doubted the stories of poaching because he knew that they were started by some malcontent with an ax to grind against someone. Contradicting many accounts, he wrote back to Croukamp that he had heard only one official complaint about poaching. An officer found a steel box filled with ivory tusks at Chiredzi Fort. When Reid-Daly sent someone to investigate, he learned that the steel box belonged to a Special Branch officer: "Ironical, isn't it?" Reid-Daly wrote.[74]

Kevin Thomas had heard the ongoing rumors of poaching and wanted to ignore them. He had enlisted in the Selous Scouts after considerable soul-searching about how best to defend Rhodesia; he did not want to rock the pseudo gang boat in any way. But he had heard stories about Ant White's poaching when White was in the RLI and Thomas was in the game department: now that he was a Selous Scout, he noticed that whenever White's name came up at Wafa Wafa, conversation changed to his ivory dealings. Thomas heard that leopards were being trapped and killed during selection courses at Wafa Wafa, and he had seen the body of a mature male leopard handed over to White. He saw a 210-liter drum full of dead crocodile hatchlings in formalin; he assumed these would be mounted as curios and sold. White told Thomas that these hatchlings came from a nearby crocodile farm, but there were constant whispers that they were pulled out of Lake Kariba at night using a spotlight to dazzle them: it was so simple "even a twelve year old can do it," just as A. J. Balaam had noted. Once an NCO found a dead and decomposing elephant in the training area. He removed the very substantial tusks and gave them to the park warden. When White learned of this he was livid and Thomas was alarmed: he knew as a former game ranger that when poachers did not feel any threat from authorities they would leave the tusks in the skulls of elephants they killed because they were much "easier to remove . . . after decomposition."[75]

John Maltas, a young Territorial who some believed was planted in the unit by John Redfern, made a formal complaint to Army Counter Intelligence: he said he saw dust from cut ivory piling up outside White's closed garage door. Because White had a taxidermy license, this was not technically illegal, but it did require an investigation by the army. The police became involved as well; this made many in the Rhodesian Army uneasy, as they believed that Special Branch was involved in poaching and selling ivory as well. Several officers insisted that Don Stannard, of Salisbury Special Branch, from which he was said to play many sides (see chapter 8), told Reid-Daly he was under investigation. When Reid-Daly asked that the police visit to Training Troop be delayed a day, the CID was only too willing to comply. When the police arrived, no ivory or hide or crocodile hatchling could be found anywhere. CID concluded that there were no illegal activities. White and Patrick Mavros (the Selous Scout who made the jewelry) both had taxidermy licenses and permission to export game products. Men like Thomas seethed: these licenses did not give White and Mavros permission to kill game illegally or indiscriminately. If White was a "true taxidermist," practicing a demanding and creative profession, "he would not have had any time to soldier." Every NCO had to know that Training Troop was a conduit for raw wildlife products, almost all of which were protected by international convention. Everyone talked about this among themselves but did not believe a case could be made against the poachers.[76]

My argument here is not about the demise of the Selous Scouts or the story of a good regiment gone bad, or even that an evil regiment proved to be worse than anyone thought. Instead, it is about the persistence of bushcraft and knowledge of the wild in the Selous Scouts poaching operations, even as the unit expanded. Knowledge of crocodile hatchlings—how to capture them and how to incubate them—determined one of the Selous Scouts' illicit products. Hunters' knowledge came to the fore here in ways that tracking manuals never approached. Thomas was disgusted when he realized why a dead elephant had been left to decompose: it was how he could be absolutely sure that this elephant had been shot for ivory. Such knowledge meets the Ginzburg-Mavhunga test; these men knew the ways of animals and the wild in which they lived and died, and knew what stories emerged from the conditions of death. But such knowledge inverted what I call the Savory test: instead of thinking like guerrillas, these men thought like poachers, and the motivations they understood were those of the game department and the networks that exported animal products. The narratives they constructed were not about what guerrillas would do but what various generals and departments would believe. The bridge too far, for Thomas at least, was not bushcraft but its opposite. When Thomas asked Reid-Daly why an eighteen-year-old who failed the selection course was nevertheless admitted to the regiment, he was told that some men had other skills the unit needed. Thomas doubted this: the selection course in Wafa Wafa was central to the publicity machine that was the Selous Scouts, so what were the skills an eighteen-year-old might have that made passing the course irrelevant? One evening over drinks Thomas's fellow Selous Scouts laughed at his misgivings. This eighteen-year-old was the son of the man who provided the equipment to cut tusks.[77]

I conclude this chapter with two stories and a reprise. Ant White and Ron Reid-Daly had much in common—both left the country, both were involved in militarizing Southern Africa, and both sued their critics—as they revealed markedly different relationships to landscape and tracking therein. White had been one of several Selous Scouts who went to Chipinge, on the border with Mozambique, to train RENAMO soldiers in the late 1970s. In addition to whatever training he did, White set up networks and routes so that RENAMO could purchase arms; these networks and routes were also useful for the sale of rhinoceros horn and ivory. White used these routes for his own trade starting in 1980, which he did under various code names (Snow White, Ivory White, etc.). Was setting up trade routes for the sale of rhinoceros horn and ivory incidental to training RENAMO, or was training RENAMO the cover for running ivory? In the early 1980s White left Zimbabwe for Mozambique, where he was involved in ivory sales from the port of Beira. In 1986 he joined Long Reach, a private intelligence-gathering firm funded by South African military intelligence, headed by Craig Williamson. The members of the board of directors were all military men, including White. White remained in Beira but was said to have begun running guns; he may have shipped weapons to Natal to precipitate anti-ANC violence there. Years later he was accused—by Dirk Coetzee and Eugene de Kock—of having assassinated Olaf Palme, the prime minister of Sweden, on Williamson's orders. In 1999 White sued two Swedish newspapers for claiming he shot Palme and that he and Williamson were responsible for the near extinction of elephants in Mozambique. He claimed the editors were responsible for gross defamation of White and his family. In February 2000 the European Court of Human Rights ruled that the lawsuit was inadmissible.[78]

Reid-Daly's story was only somewhat different, and it will shape the following chapter. In the hope of finding evidence of poaching, military intelligence tapped his phone in January 1979, but apparently not very well: it is not clear that the bug worked or produced any evidence at all. Reid-Daly clearly thought it did and insisted that it compromised his spies in Zambia.

Whether it worked or not, the genealogies of the Selous Scouts and the support the regiment received from Peter Walls were such that no action was taken against Training Troop. Reid-Daly became increasingly emotional, however. Although he was to write that he simply stated the facts about his phone being tapped, he seems to have lost control at a dinner celebrating the anniversary of the founding of the RLI: he accosted Major John Hickman, commander of the Rhodesian Army.[79] Some dinner guests said Reid-Daly punched him, others said they shouted at each other, but Hickman demanded that Reid-Daly be arrested for insubordination. He was not arrested, but a day or two later Reid-Daly was court-martialed on the decision of anonymous senior officers. The proceedings were secret, but it was soon well known that Reid-Daly was given a reprimand, a humiliation for a senior officer and one that would end his career. Reid-Daly appealed the court-martial but lost that case in December 1979—one day after the Lancaster House agreement had been signed—after which he resigned from the Selous Scouts. By then many in the Rhodesian forces were happy to see him leave. Reid-Daly then made a civil suit demanding R$20,000 in damages from Hickman, R$10,000 from Redfern, and R$5,000 each from Des Fountain, director of military intelligence, and John Maltas. That application to sue was denied, but he appealed.[80] The appeal was heard in Zimbabwe in December 1980 by three judges, two of whom had ruled years before in the key cases by which Rhodesia claimed and maintained legitimacy. In the appeal Reid-Daly singled out Hickman, who had "wrongfully and unlawfully" recorded his personal and official phone calls, as well as taking and copying personal and official documents from his office. This was an invasion of his privacy and an attack on his dignity and reputation, "both personally and as a solider," which "lowered him in the esteem of others." Three judges held that no case could be brought against a commanding officer for an action taken in the course of his duties, even if it was done without probable cause. They dismissed out of hand Reid-Daly's claim that there was an internal directive that the Selous Scouts were "immune from investigation." But in a civil court, prosecuted as a civil matter, the case could go forward as one of trespass. The judges denied Reid-Daly's request that Hickman pay the costs of the appeal. If the case was not brought to trial, there would be no costs. If it went to trial, costs and the amount paid for damages, should such an award be made, would be determined by the court.[81] Reid-Daly dropped the case but insisted his reasons were not about money or court costs. It was because he had moved to South Africa: "I was forced by the circumstance of no longer being resident in the country of my birth."[82] In South Africa, however, Reid-Daly had other career options. He was to command the Transkei Defence Force, at the rank of general, and he was to try his hand at writing.

In this, White passed the Ginzburg-Mavhunga test with flying colors. He read the landscape for its large mammals, for the routes they took and the routes he could use to export their tusks and horns; he knew how war changed these routes. He knew the wild without respect for borders and boundaries. He may not have been at one with the wild, but he was at one—or at least at ease—with the technologies of war, so he could read the landscape to include war-torn areas and mined paths. As for Reid-Daly, for all his boasts about turning white soldiers into African trackers, he did not even have the Ginzburg-Mavhunga test in his line of sight. For Reid-Daly the knowledge of the wild that could be was secondary to his belief in his men—at least the white men under his command.[83] He took pride in who could catch baby crocodiles and who knew where to shoot a leopard with what kind of bullet so the skin would not be damaged, and who could provide the equipment that could cut a tusk most effectively. Bushcraft was less important for fighting, to be sure, but it was his soldiers who knew the wild that was more important to him than the wild itself.

5 "THERE IS NO COPYRIGHT ON FACTS"

Ron Reid-Daly, Authorship, and the Transkei Defence Force

Why were the Selous Scouts so good for postwar reading? I argue that the regiment was a fabled counter-gang in large part because it wrote its own fables. The memoirs of its founder, Ron Reid-Daly, came to be promoted as what was unique and powerful about Rhodesian forces, but depending on how I evaluate the material that follows, they were either "his" memoirs or his "memoirs." The history of the histories of the Selous Scouts is at least as interesting and important as their exploits. *Top Secret War* is not only the first Rhodesian personal narrative about the war written during the postwar period but also perhaps the most plastic of historical sources. It shows the clever genius of Rhodesian counterinsurgency operations to white nationalists and the cynical cruelty of Rhodesian counterinsurgency to black nationalists. Beyond various nationalisms, and beyond the romance of the idea of pseudo gangs, stood Reid-Daly, a man who seemed to have loved litigation.

Who Is an Author?

Reid-Daly went to South Africa at the end of 1979, abandoning his lawsuits but taking with him a number of documents, including operational plans and debriefing reports. Shortly after he arrived there, he was given financial assistance to write a book about the Selous Scouts. The assistance came from a small group of men, called "the syndicate" in legal documents, which included Peter Stiff and Gideon Henry Erasmus, a friend of Reid-Daly's who had served with him in the RLI, where he was once the heavyweight boxing champion. Using the documents he brought with him and his own knowledge, Reid-Daly wrote a manuscript of 357 pages—he said it was typed; Stiff told me it was handwritten—in four months.[1] When Reid-Daly completed his manuscript, the syndicate hired a ghostwriter—Christopher Munnion, formerly Africa correspondent for the *Daily Telegraph* and known to be sympathetic to Rhodesia—to put the narrative into publishable form. The first lawsuit between Reid-Daly and Stiff's publishing company, Galago, said this worked out; the second said it did not.[2] The syndicate then offered the work to various publishers overseas, none of which were interested. Eventually Reid-Daly went to Stiff, whose publishing house was relatively new and very small. Stiff read the manuscript and concluded that it did not do justice to the story and suggested that he be allowed to rewrite it. Reid-Daly agreed, and his group of benefactors—one of whom was Stiff—commissioned Stiff to rewrite the book and publish it. Reid-Daly gave him the manuscript and many of the documents he had brought with him. Stiff used the manuscript as a starting point; the book he published was based on various documents, conversations with Reid-Daly, and interviews with other former Selous Scouts.

As he was writing the book, Reid-Daly had taken up command of the Transkei Defence Force (TDF); he may have had limited opportunities to edit the text. Stiff wrote as much in a 2001 book, when he claimed he was the author. Referring to himself in the third person, he wrote that the details of Reid-Daly's lucrative contract "were confirmed to the author during March, April and May 1981 when he was writing the book *Selous Scouts: Top Secret War* in association with Ron Reid-Daly, Erasmus, and former Selous Scout captain Chris Gough."[3] Nevertheless, *Selous Scouts: Top Secret War* was published as by Ron Reid-Daly "as told to" Peter Stiff. Neither Galago nor Reid-Daly held the copyright, however; that was held by Gideon Henry Erasmus. Stiff's wife, Frances Lategan, made the maps and retained copyright on them. First published in 1982, *Selous Scouts: Top Secret War* went through several editions, including a 1983 paperback, and sold more than 135,000 copies, earning Galago substantial profits and Erasmus substantial royalties. According to Stiff, Reid-Daly "never got over" Stiff being called the author of the text.[4]

Once he finished the draft manuscript, Reid-Daly's first months in South Africa were identical to those of many Rhodesian ex-combatants who had come south in late 1979 and early 1980. What makes his South African itinerary different is that the authors who have written about his activities there were all sued by Reid-Daly: Peter Stiff was sued several times, and *Scope* magazine was threatened with a lawsuit only once. *Scope* was a

South African publication largely for soldiers—the "scope" referred to an attachment to guns—with stories about soldiers and armies and pinups.[5] Otherwise, Reid-Daly was like many senior Rhodesian military figures in that he was hired by a private security firm. In this case he was employed by Security Scouts, run by Ant White.[6] The company employed a number of former Selous Scouts. Reid-Daly resigned from Security Scouts after he talked about "smelly gooks" in a speech at Rand Afrikaans University. "No gook talk here," proclaimed the *Sunday Times*.[7] He then joined another firm and perhaps another before he was hired by Security Specialists International, which then hired many former Rhodesian Selous Scouts and a few former Rhodesian SAS, possibly on Reid-Daly's recommendation.[8] In 1981 Security Specialists International was awarded a contract to train the Transkei Defence Force.

The Transkei Defence Force

Transkei was the first South African homeland to be granted juridical independence in 1976. It was the culmination of the apartheid policy of "separate development," and it was an opening for Xhosa elites, however uneasy their relationship with Pretoria.[9] How Reid-Daly came to command the Transkei Defence Force is subject to some debate. Several former Rhodesian Army officers assumed that Peter Walls, who remained loyal to Reid-Daly throughout the events of 1979, recommended him.[10] Geoffrey Allen wrote a two-part exposé of the TDF in *Scope* magazine that informed Stiff's account. Allen insisted that Reid-Daly had been put up for the job by one of his benefactors, Isaac Kaye, the heir to a chain store and pharmaceutical empire and a loyal patron of Reid-Daly until his death.[11] Whether Kaye came to Reid-Daly or Reid-Daly approached him I cannot say, but Kaye was not the first wealthy businessman to take an interest in working with him (see chapter 4). In November 1980 Kaye asked Reid-Daly to join his Security Specialists, known as Double S; Kaye was the primary shareholder, and he had already appointed Erasmus as managing director. The reputation of former Rhodesian soldiers and the expanse of Kaye's other businesses seem to have been powerful bargaining chips. By April 1981 Reid-Daly had recruited seventeen former Selous Scouts and several other former Rhodesian soldiers to Transkei Security Services; two months later he signed an exceptionally generous contract. Both Allen and Stiff make much of the contract, which provided housing, school fees, and transport for children, all tax free, paid for by South Africa. A. J. Balaam, one of the first Selous Scouts to join the TDF, wrote that he "was living the life of luxury and ease" in his first few years in Umtata.¹²

The contract also gave Reid-Daly the army he always wanted. Having been promoted no higher than regimental sergeant major in the RLI, Reid-Daly only became a lieutenant colonel in the last years of the Selous Scouts, but he became a major general in the TDF and sported a "Montgomery-style beret" instead of the usual officer's cap. Erasmus was given the rank of brigadier general. The reason given for these promotions was that they would be dealing with senior South African officers and did not want to be disadvantaged by rank. A. J. Balaam put it bluntly: Reid-Daly was "paranoid" about his status in the South African Defence Force. He was also very much a dandy by military standards; as an RSM in the RLI he was notorious for checking on how closely his men shaved. And however he imagined Selous Scout pseudos would dress, he always wore "shiny boots, starched trousers, and a bush hat," as if he were on parade; "no shorts, T-shirt or vellies for him."¹³ Dress and rank were only part of the new army. He introduced new tactics and branches of the service. He hired his son to teach karate to troops, and he set up counterinsurgency practice in the forested areas of Pondoland. This was not a Kitson-inspired counterinsurgency exercise in a forest; that region had been in open revolt against the apartheid state in the late 1950s and early 1960s. The long Transkei coastline, despite its history of failed invasions, allowed him to create a navy. Transkei had never had one; its only possible port was closed by a sandbar. The only military presence there was when the TDF seconded a few soldiers to serve as lifeguards at tourist resorts. Under Reid-Daly's command there was to be a Transkei navy. He hired a man who inflated his credentials in the South African navy to command Transkei's first warship, a steel-hulled oceangoing vessel in need of repairs but a bargain from its owner, a Pretoria widow. Reid-Daly canceled the order when the so-called captain was jailed on gunrunning charges. "I will not tolerate inefficiency," he explained. For a few months he searched for amphibious vessels to buy; he gave up on the project when they proved too expensive. He also set up a Transkei Air Force with a few helicopters and one fixed-wing aircraft that were mainly used to fly the prime minister around. Reid-Daly tried to purchase two secondhand, short-haul Skyvan aircraft from Malawi. These too would have been a bargain because each plane came with a contract with Israel to train their pilots.¹⁴

Beyond the training courses and navy, the TDF did not perform to expectations in those operations for which the Selous Scouts were famous.

Between 1983 and 1984, A. J. Balaam and Bob Macenzie, an American who had served in the Rhodesian SAS before joining the TDF (see chapter 8), trained the Lesotho Liberation Army (LLA). The LLA was the armed wing of a nationalist political party whose electoral victory in 1970 was annulled by a coup. Political operatives were arrested or killed; the survivors went into exile, eventually forming the LLA in 1979. South Africa took an interest in this army as Lesotho began to move away from Pretoria and refused to ban either the ANC or the PAC.[15] In the early 1980s the TDF was tasked with training the LLA to become a liberation army that would destabilize Lesotho and perhaps the entire region. When unmarked trucks driven by white men arrived at the isolated farm MacKenzie and Balaam had chosen for training, they realized that the forty recruits were funded by South Africa. The recruits had been press-ganged and issued with insufficient clothing for cold weather. By the time the men were trained, it was winter; they managed a few ambushes, but some were arrested and some gave themselves up to the police.[16] Years later, Balaam blamed Reid-Daly, who had never understood that he was "nothing" in South Africa, "just somebody to be used" and cast aside. Balaam had served under Reid-Daly in the RLI and the Selous Scouts. It had never been an easy relationship, but they "tolerated" each other. Balaam admired Reid-Daly's loyalty to his men but was always wary of him and his loyal clique. In Transkei he realized "that the Reid-Daly of Rhodesia died in Rhodesia. . . . Now it was all about the money. . . . If it meant abusing the trust and loyalty of the men who served under him, so be it. If it meant training terrorists-cum-liberation armies instead of fighting them, so be it."[17]

Even less successful was the plan to kidnap and assassinate the president of Ciskei, Lennox Sebe. Operation Duiker was itself an operation-within-an-operation of Operation Katzen: it was tightly packaged in need-to-know intelligence that was nevertheless known to many people. Peter Stiff was one of the many who knew of it: A. J. Balaam assumed he had been invited to Umtata by Reid-Daly, who briefed him, possibly in the hopes of writing a book in the future. There were many stories, colorful and strategic, about the operation. Did it really begin in an East London pub when a "loud mouthed white man" was offered a reward for the assassination of the president's brother and rival, or was it a South African attempt to short-circuit Xhosa resistance to destabilize the region?[18] Both may be true, of course—both were reported by Peter Stiff, who may well have heard them in Transkei and South Africa—but taken together they describe the casual way the end of apartheid was played out in homeland politics. A propaganda war against the president, for example, consisted of pamphlets thrown from an airplane flying low at night over Ciskei. The planned abduction of the president, however, was a complete disaster. The twenty-two-man raiding party stormed the presidential palace at Bhisho at 3:00 AM on 10 February 1987. They were quickly routed by the presidential guard; most of the raiders escaped in waiting helicopters. By morning, evidence of TDF involvement was clear. There were two TDF vehicles left on the street, each with Transkei registration: a car rented in Port Elizabeth by Jean-Michel Desble, formerly of the French Foreign Legion, the Selous Scouts, and Craig Williamson's Long Reach and currently with the TDF; and a pickup truck that contained a briefcase with the plans for the raid and the names of its personnel.[19]

The reaction from Transkei and possibly South Africa was swift and severe. Some thought that Desble's relationship to Long Reach raised too many questions for South Africa; others thought that generals in the TDF saw this as their chance to rid themselves of corrupt advisers. Reid-Daly seems to have thought he could weather this; he had been given Transkei citizenship the previous month. He told his men they could leave if they wanted to, but he did not order them to do so. Only a few left. At the end of March, Transkei canceled the contract with Transkei Security Services, and the next day the remaining seventeen white advisers were arrested and marched through Umtata's townships before being taken to jail. No one was arrested or charged, but they were given fifteen minutes to pack up their belongings and leave the country. Reid-Daly fled to Port Elizabeth with a South African Police escort. He then returned to serving in figurehead positions in private security firms.[20]

How did this happen? It is possible to argue, as Timothy Gibbs does, that the "interlocking insurgencies of the Cold War era" brought Reid-Daly to Transkei, where he was able to "reshape" the most tractable parts of the army, but he could not manage local politics. It is also possible to argue, as A. J. Balaam did, that in Transkei Reid-Daly believed the legend of the Selous Scouts. Once free of the control of the Rhodesian Army hierarchy, "he ran amok."[21] The only journalist to write about the TDF, Geoffrey Allen, considered Reid-Daly washed up and corrupt. Reid-Daly threatened to sue *Scope*, and much to Allen's chagrin, the magazine paid him ZAR15,000 to drop the case. Peter Stiff was outraged. Although *Scope* was a "girlie" magazine, "as a matter of journalistic ethics they should have stared him out."[22] A few years later Reid-Daly sued Stiff for defamation of character because of Stiff's description of his role with the Transkei Defence Force;

Stiff settled out of court on the condition of silence for what was said to be ZAR3 million.²³

Fighting, Writing, and Suing

These were not Reid-Daly's first lawsuits, of course, nor was this the first time he sued Peter Stiff. His earlier lawsuits against Stiff and Galago were over who wrote *Top Secret War*. According to the first of these lawsuits, it was not clear how much of *Top Secret War* was Reid-Daly's work. The first and last chapters and parts of the penultimate chapter were written by Stiff—the shift in voice is obvious to even a casual reader—but all the operations described in Reid-Daly's manuscript appear in the book, with language and idioms intact. Stiff thought it always rankled Reid-Daly that he was not listed as sole author.²⁴ Nevertheless, the collaborative effort helped create a postwar vision of Rhodesian military might, depicting regiments and soldiers who achieved far more in recollection than they did in the 1970s. The operational history in *Top Secret War* was complicated, as befits pseudo operations. The text itself was designed to be read as a dictated memoir, with short paragraphs and many ellipses as if these were the words of a man reflecting on his past. The text also had drama, humor, and stereotypes. There are scenes of blacked-up white Scouts revealing their blond hair to unsuspecting guerrillas ("Take off your hat, Winston"), of white and African Selous Scouts overjoyed to see that they both had survived a contact or operation, and of insurgents turned in prison and in the bush. White Selous Scouts as a group tended to be portrayed as rugged fourteen-year-olds, shouting at FRELIMO troops during operations in Mozambique and making jokes to each other about farts, genitals, and women's urine, but African Selous Scouts tend to be portrayed as larger-than-life soldiers, loyal and courageous. There was Corporal Hamale, who refused to leave the guerrilla gang he had trained even when he was compromised—"they are my men," he explained—and the injured Lance Corporal Burundu, who demanded an artificial leg so he could return to operations.²⁵

After the success of *Top Secret War*, Stiff wanted to publish a pictorial history of the Selous Scouts. Reid-Daly's original benefactors were not interested, so Stiff produced and published the book on his own. His main sources were the interviews he had done in connection with the 1982 publication, and documents made available to him by Reid-Daly and many other Rhodesians. *A Pictorial Account* was published in 1984; it sold at least as well as *Top Secret War*.²⁶ In 1988 Gideon Henry Erasmus sued Galago, insisting that the bulk of the text came from the book whose copyright he held. The participants' testimony and the judgment are instructive. Reid-Daly, for example, explained that he wrote the book to tell the story of the Selous Scouts—"in a subjective way"—and "to engender some finance." He invented dialogue so as better to portray "the average Selous Scout, the way he talks, the way he lived." Sometimes he "exaggerated or embellished the true story" to make it a better one, but he selected the operations he described and the order in which they appeared in the book. Reid-Daly took great care to change the names of African Selous Scouts still in Zimbabwe, to protect them from reprisals. An expert witness for Galago pronounced the writing style "racy," making liberal use of army slang and military jargon.²⁷

So was *Pictorial Account* the same text as *Top Secret War*? If it was, the muddy waters of authorship spread between Reid-Daly, Munnion, and Stiff and probably a few more Selous Scouts became even more opaque: there is no single or identifiable authorial voice. The court noted that "there is no copyright in ideas or thoughts or facts." Copyright lies in how ideas or thoughts or facts are expressed. Galago argued that *Pictorial Account* was unlike *Top Secret War* in writing: it had less detail, less dialogue, and less background material. The prose was "more coherent, grammatical, and complete," and it did not rely on ellipses. The judges were not impressed. These were cosmetic differences, they insisted. Comparing twelve chapters in both texts, they saw "what is in effect an abridged version of *Top Secret War*." There could be no case, as Stiff's lawyer had argued, that these similarities were "house style." Stiff had "availed himself unlawfully of a great deal of the skill and industry that went into the writing of *Top Secret War*," which was why Erasmus and not Stiff had the copyright. *Pictorial Account* represented an infringement of copyright.²⁸ Galago appealed, but lost. Galago was liquidated and began publishing as Lemur but continued to use the Galago imprint, an illegality about which authorities appeared to have been unconcerned.

In 1999 Reid-Daly, having been given or purchased the copyright for the text of *Selous Scouts: Top Secret War*, produced a memoir that was barely revised from it. Published by Covos-Day, *Pamwe Chete: The Legend of the Selous Scouts* contains most of the text of the 1982 book and all the maps. Covos-Day had been founded a few years earlier by Chris Cocks, author and editor, and a British lawyer (Day); it published children's books and reprinted Cocks's war memoirs. It reprinted many Rhodesian war memoirs that had been privately published. Cocks jumped at the chance to publish Reid-Daly.[29] He believed this was a different book. There were small changes, as we have seen, and anecdotes and a chapter aimed at South African readers. There are no ellipses and no sense that this was ever a dictated memoir. The publication information page at the front of the book lists a first publication as *Selous Scouts: Top Secret War* (1982), but Stiff's name is not included anywhere. The seventeen maps that appeared in *Top Secret War*, drawn by and copyrighted to Frances Lategan, later Frances Stiff, and licensed for reproduction only in Galago books, were reprinted in the 1999 Covos-Day edition without attribution or permission. Frances Stiff sued Reid-Daly and Covos-Day for infringement of copyright in a lawsuit that complicated the already byzantine authorship of *Top Secret War* and raised questions that are critical to the study and use of war memoirs: What exactly is the authority that comes from having been in war?

On Being There

Could memories be copyrighted? Is the fact of having been in war a property, shaped by time and place in a language specific to both, but owned by a former combatant? Did being an eyewitness to events or a landscape allow for more legal control over distribution of an image than being a draftsman did? Reid-Daly denied copying the maps. His first line of defense was that the maps were not original to Lategan, but that he, along with the former Scouts Clive Warren and Chris Gough, drew the maps and gave them to Galago.[30] He claimed to have had access to the maps drawn before and after various operations, in many cases drawn by or with the aid of the men who had been on those operations. Frances Stiff testified that she drew the maps herself, using a variety of sources. In the map that became the basis for many other maps, for example, she used the Rhodesian land tenure map; she used a grid to make the map smaller and in doing so introduced a few errors, including leaving out the extended tip of Lake Kariba. When she sent the map to the printer, she omitted several place-names so the map didn't look cluttered.

All this made her the "author" of the work, the judge said: for work to be original and requiring copyright, it had to have been created and not simply reproduced. When Frances Stiff compared her original map with the one in *Pamwe Chete*, she found it to be identical, down to the errors and omissions, which indicated that map had been scanned into a computer and then published. Several maps of external operations were identical to those in the 1982 text as well. Many of these maps were of the eastern border of Rhodesia and Mozambique. Since each one was hand-drawn, towns and roads were not in the same place on each map. These different positions appeared in the relevant maps in *Pamwe Chete*. A few maps had several towns in the wrong places, but they were published in *Pamwe Chete* without correction. The 1982 publication also contained an organizational chart—an "organogram"—of ZIPRA/ZAPU that appeared in a chapter written entirely by Peter Stiff. The original version of this had his handwritten instructions to the printer on it, but the printer had mistaken "commissar" for "commissioner" and used the latter term. The same chart appeared in *Pamwe Chete*, with a man called "commissioner."

The defense—which was in fact two defenses—by Reid-Daly and Covos-Day was by and large feeble. The judge complained that most of the defense testimony was from former Selous Scouts who were loyal to their former commander and present-day employer: when he first testified, Warren referred to Reid-Daly as the "boss." Loyalty did not mean consistency, however. Several former Selous Scouts said they had met with the Stiffs to discuss maps and drawings. Others testified that they had drawn the maps themselves. Clive Warren, for example, had been a trainee electrician before joining the Selous Scouts; he had taken a technical drawing course at school. When he came to South Africa, he worked in Reid-Daly's security firm in Secunda, guarding SASOL. Reid-Daly, then in Transkei, asked him to assist with maps and drawings that "Joe Public" could understand; Warren used a debriefing map as his guide and used SASOL's equipment to reduce them. He gave them to Chris Gough for corrections, which he entered on a new map. Warren said he left out place-names because he was pressed for time. Reid-Daly supported Warren's testimony, insisting that the maps were based on Rhodesian Army maps he had brought from South Africa. These were the maps he gave to Stiff when Galago asked for maps, however. Winston Hart—the same blacked-up Winston who could remove his hat and show his blond hair to insurgents—was Special Branch liaison to the Selous Scouts. He said he had met with the Stiffs at Reid-Daly's request but could not really explain how much input he had in making the maps or charts. He certainly did not draw the maps.

None of this, the judge noted, detracted from the Stiffs' claim that the maps and diagrams originated with them. Reid-Daly and Covos-Day then fired their lawyer and hired another. As befits this story, the defendants' account of the maps and charts then changed. Former Selous Scouts contradicted each other and their earlier testimony. Reid-Daly now claimed that he gave "updated" debriefing maps to Warren and Gough, which they used to make "composite" maps. Although it was not clear that these were ever debriefing maps, Reid-Daly explained the errors in the published maps by suggesting that an overburdened clerk in Salisbury in 1980 had omitted some place-names. Timothy Bax (see chapter 8) was a former Selous Scout who had served in the 5 Reconnaissance Regiment in Phalaborwa until he resigned to work for Reid-Daly in Secunda. He testified that he had given the maps to Warren and Gough, but Gough testified that he had "sourced" the information for various maps before drawing them. Warren could not identify any of the sources he used for his maps. In what the judge called an "astounding attempt" to explain why his drawing of Lake Kariba was identical to Frances Stiff's, he produced his source, a Shell road map published before Lake Kariba was created. The date on which the maps were given to Stiff was disputed: Gough said he had given the maps to Stiff early in 1982, although Stiff maintained he had received them in June 1981. Reid-Daly presented his appointment book to corroborate Gough's testimony. The entry that was to prove when he gave the maps to Stiff was written in a form that did not appear anywhere else in his dairy. The judge clearly thought it was added much later—"an attempt at self-corroboration," he wrote—and further doubted its veracity because Reid-Daly could not explain what had happened to the original maps prepared by Warren and Gough.

The judge found for Galago. There was no fine, but the legal fees—ZAR150,000—destroyed Covos-Day.[31] The company was bankrupted; Day resigned to become the legal counsel for Greenpeace, and Cocks lost his house and his car.[32] Shortly after the trial, both Stiff and Reid-Daly announced they were planning more lawsuits, for infringement of more copyrights by Stiff and for plagiarism and defamation of character by Reid-Daly. Peter Stiff complained to journalists that "Reid-Daly has one hell of a reputation as a soldier, but suddenly he believes he should have a big reputation as an author."[33] Reid-Daly's reputation as a soldier won out, apparently, as Stiff settled out of court in his defamation of character lawsuit.

If nothing else, the made-up diary entry should have exiled Ron Reid-Daly and his many memoirs to the land of James Frey. It did not. All the lawsuits over who owned which words and which photographs and which maps seem to have solidified the legend of the Selous Scouts, if not the narrative: the story—I use the term with great care—of blacked-up white men fooling guerrillas trained in Bulgaria or Libya remained the same. The contests were not about what was true but who profited from the story. We have already seen contests over what the Selous Scouts did and how well they did it, but none of these was by Stiff, who believed in the power of the regiment in a way that only some of its operators did. Perhaps more important, these court cases revealed with great clarity that Ron Reid-Daly was not the author of these books. Instead, he was kind of a literary creation, first by former comrade and commander Peter Walls, then by his benefactors, and finally by at least one ghostwriter and then a coauthor. It is entirely possible that he did not write the relatively few additions to *Pamwe Chete* on his own. It is also very likely that Reid-Daly or Munnion or Stiff or some combination of the three (at least) lied, or made up more than a diary entry.[34] I do not think any of this is a problem. On the contrary, I think knowing how malleable and absorbent Reid-Daly's authorship was and how extensive Peter Stiff's was allows a more critical and more engaged reading of the Selous Scouts material here and in the previous two chapters, precisely because it is not one man's war story.

6 "EVERY SELF-RESPECTING TERRORIST HAS AN AK-47"

Guerrilla Weapons and Rhodesian Imaginations

General Peter Walls, commander in chief of the Rhodesian forces, was convinced that ZANLA was sending teenage auxiliaries to the assembly points mandated by the cease-fire agreement signed in London in December 1979. Had ZANLA sent real fighters, they would have been armed with automatic weapons. Instead, it sent men who carried stick grenades or obsolete weapons. Yet as commander in chief Walls would have seen the reports on the bombing raids on training camps in Mozambique in which he learned most guerrillas initially trained with wooden guns; he would have read the interrogation reports in which many cadres complained that they did not always have access to any guns at all, let alone automatic ones. Walls had already shown himself to be nearly hysterical over the cease-fire. He had talked Margaret Thatcher into giving him direct access to the newly appointed governor, Lord Christopher Soames, undermining the cease-fire agreement, and he was to make a series of intransigent demands before threatening a coup over the results of the 1980s election.[1] None of this fully explains his distress at the weapons men took into assembly points, although it is very likely that he imagined that making a case for the best guerrilla fighters abroad in the land would allow him to unleash the Rhodesian Army. Even so, why did he make one kind of weapon the synecdoche of one side in this war?

Guns of War

Why indeed? In the thoughtful introduction to his study of guns in nineteenth-century Central Africa, Giacomo Macola observes that most histories of guns are histories of efficacy, how efficiently a weapon kills or wounds. Such scholarship has often ignored the ways that guns, perhaps more than other technologies, become dense with long-lasting meanings and cultural attributes. Each weapon and its possibilities contain expectations of expertise and the weight of gender and age.[2] This is Tim O'Brien's point in the story "The Things They Carried," in which the weight of guns becomes equivalent to the emotional weight of letters from home. In the case of the Kalashnikov automatic rifle, its importance was bundled into its history. At the end of World War II, most nations understood that their infantries would change in the atomic age. The USSR, however, had a greater belief and interest in infantries than the other Allied powers did and soon developed a new kind of shooting with which Soviet infantries would be transformed. The AK became a storied invention: a wounded infantryman (Kalashnikov), whose talents are promoted and praised, develops an automatic assault rifle that is better than anything that came before. The AK—the 47 referred to the year of the final design—was a staple of Soviet aid starting in 1950; the pattern was given to the Chinese in 1955.[3]

Other militaries, including that of the United States, were reluctant to develop new kinds of rifles, let alone automatic ones. Lightweight rifles, whether or not they were capable of automatic fire, made infantries more mobile. They allowed for airborne infantries—a critical factor when soldiers were moved around the countryside by helicopters. Automatic rifles did not make soldiers better marksmen. Indeed, they were never intended to be accurate in the sense of hitting a specific target. Instead, automatic weapons were to produce "area fire," spraying an area with rapid, lethal fire: anyone in the path of this fire would be hit, but if the path was too high, or obstructed in any way, the fire still served its purpose by keeping the enemy from advancing. Automatic weapons gave infantry greater range, so they could engage an enemy they could not see; they could pin down enemy troops while their own troops advanced. Area fire was a way of thinking about guns that confronted and contradicted American traditions of marksmanship, but it became a necessity of Cold War wars, when the US Army faced AK-47s in Korea and Vietnam, although it maintained that long-range aimed fire was best for Europe.[4] The Rhodesian Army, however, was slow to acknowledge the importance of automatic weapons. Indeed, it relied on a US special forces publication on guerrilla warfare to identify the Soviet-made automatic weapons found cached in the country in 1966.[5]

It was the automatic nature of the AK that gave it so much authority. Many authors tended to crow about its six-hundred-round-per-minute rate of fire, but that figure is unreasonable: any serious burst of automatic fire requires changing magazines, and this slows the rate of fire considerably. What was important about automatic weapons was not the number of bullets a gun could fire, but who controlled that fire and to what end. Automatic rifles represented both an innovation and a problem for militaries. Unlike the machine gun, which provided the firepower of forty infantry in a fixed space, automatic rifles dispersed shooting; they undermined command and control. Riflemen had always been difficult to control, even after intensive drill; they could open and cease fire as they chose; they were sometimes erratic, sometimes distracted, and sometimes excited. Once armed with lightweight, efficient, automatic weapons that allowed for more firepower from fewer infantry, soldiers were freed from centralized command, as effective fire could come from anywhere.[6] Biometrics were put to work to prove this was efficient in wartime, that effective fire was more important than accurate fire. An analysis of three million casualties in the two world wars found that it was the degree of exposure to fire that inflicted wounds; aimed fire did not influence the manner in which the enemy was shot.[7] At the same time, no one could be sure that his automatic fire had killed an insurgent; dispersed shooting meant dispersed killing. The idea of a confirmed kill, a death for which an individual soldier was responsible (see chapter 1), emerged precisely for this reason.

Did this change the nature of this war? Contrary to the Rhodesian "won every battle" narrative, this was not a shooting war. Tony Ballinger, an officer in the Rhodesia Regiment, described his routine as one of "patrol, ambush, patrol. Annoy the locals, burn things down."[8] The result was gains neither in territory nor in popular support; instead, security forces sought to capture or kill guerrillas. Aside from trying to ambush the patrols tracking them, most guerrilla gangs were not trying to engage security forces at all. After 1974 the Rhodesian Army often claimed that when guerrillas did stand and fight, it was because they thought the security forces were a patrol of the other guerrilla army.[9] Guerrillas were trained to withdraw, and for most of the 1970s it did not seem that everyone in the Rhodesian forces was eager to shoot either. By 1977, when the Rhodesian government announced eventual majority rule, many white soldiers complained that they did not know what they were fighting for, and simply did not fire their weapons.[10]

AKs and FNs

However infrequently security forces and guerrillas shot, the weapons with which they shot became a way to talk about skills and loyalties. Both guerrilla armies had AK-47s, but not nearly as many as Rhodesian authors imagined. Until 1973 the Rhodesian Army issued national servicemen the British self-loading rifle (SLR). It was then replaced by the Belgian-made FN, NATO's rifle of choice sold by a range of European networks that violated UN sanctions, or its knockoff copy, the South African R3. The FN never really took hold in facts and fictions about Rhodesian security forces, but the AK-47 became quite literally the sign of both guerrilla armies. Thus the back cover of a novel about a Coloured Rhodesian soldier who is captured and turned by ZIPRA reads, "His FN is replaced by an AK-47."[11] And AKs were everywhere. There was the favorite urban legend among white Rhodesians of the gardener and the lawnmower and the eventual discovery of an AK-47 (see chapter 2). A fictional foreign-born priest who supported guerrillas—a favorite wartime trope in policy and prose—was found to be hiding "two AKs, seven grenades, four thousand rounds of 7.62mm ammunition, and an RPG launcher" in his mission. The rifles bore his fingerprints.[12] Rhodesia's supporters could only imagine how Africans would use the gun. In Robin Moore's eventually published war novel (see chapter 8), an American nun looks after a wounded guerrilla. She asks if he needs anything. "Just my AK-47 so I can go out and kill white people," he replies.[13]

White soldiers seemed to have found different meanings in the guns they were issued. David Pike had an honors degree in Latin and ancient Greek when he was called up in 1971. He was trained on the SLR, about which he was lyrical. It was "a handsome weapon of black steel so beautifully tempered that the muzzle rang like a silver bell when flicked with a fingernail." It was not automatic, but it recocked itself after every shot so that a soldier could keep firing so long as he could squeeze the trigger. The SLR had a long range—up to six hundred yards—but was heavier than the FN or the AK.[14] The SLR was in use throughout the war, issued to the Territorial Army whenever FNs were not available. Tony Ballinger owned rifles years before his national service. He was nevertheless stirred by his first visit to the regimental armory. "I loved the smell," he wrote, "oiled gun metal, grease and a faint odour of cordite and explosives."[15] Brian Jackson, SAS, loved the R3, even though its fiberglass stock had to be sprayed with Rhodesian camouflage to keep it from shining in sunlight, because it was accurate at long range. He nevertheless believed that "the AK-47 is probably the best assault weapon ever made."[16]

The FN and the AK were studied and lauded in great detail by Rhodesian troops. The best descriptions of both weapons is in the writings of two national servicemen in the RLI, Chris Cocks and Angus Shaw. Both men wrote at length about both weapons, especially the FN. It had two rates of fire. It could be shot as a repeating rifle or as a fully automatic weapon. The Rhodesian Army frowned on automatic fire; it wasted too much ammunition, and when on automatic the gun tended to pull upward and was difficult to control. Besides, when FNs were in constant use, as they were in Rhodesia after 1976, they tended to jam when fired on automatic. As a rule, the heavier the gun, the easier it is to keep it low when firing. The better marksmen in the RLI fitted their FNs with telescopic sights or a device that hid the gun's flash; these added weight to the muzzle to keep it low, but they still used their weapons as single-shot rifles.[17] The FN weighed almost ten pounds loaded—about the same as the AK-47—but the FN's twenty-round magazines weighed about the same (just over one pound) as the AK's thirty-round magazines, so for every fifteen pounds a Rhodesian soldier carried, a guerrilla carried ten. Guerrillas carried as many magazines as were available rather than a set amount; Rhodesian soldiers were frequently unwilling to carry as many magazines as required on patrol.[18] So, when a white sergeant in a novel by a Rhodesian Regiment veteran solemnly removes extra ammunition from his pack, saying, "If I can't kill him with forty rounds . . . I deserve to lose," he was making his pack even lighter than the five magazines carried by soldiers experienced in evading regulations.[19] By the mid-1970s some army units began to follow the BSAP's long-standing practice of training cadets with flashlights rather than pistols. Switching the flashlight on with the motion of a finger patterned the reflex to fire before men were exposed to the noise of the gun. This was in part designed as a way to control flinching, and in part designed as a way for soldiers to practice without ammunition. The security forces were generally asked to conserve ammunition; the infantry were trained to shoot at targets rather than spraying fire.[20] Even then, a number of white Rhodesian young men claimed that their weapons training was irrelevant: they had been taught to shoot by their fathers and were excellent marksmen years before their national service.[21] But the young white men in the Rhodesian forces learned to use the FN quickly.

The FN, not unlike the United States' M16 a decade earlier, was a test of drill and discipline.[22] The FN was a sophisticated, "temperamental" weapon; it required special care. Former national servicemen boasted that they were trained to assemble and disassemble the rifle blindfolded, to replace the magazine in thirty-five seconds ("harder than it sounds"), and to practice allowing the cocking mechanism to release itself; too much pressure could cause the gun to jam.[23] Rhodesian soldiers rarely criticized the rifle; when they did it was because it did its work too well. Jeremy Hall, an RLI commando, complained that a guerrilla killed by a high-velocity FN round died at once. His comrades moved on. But a man shot by an Eastern Bloc weapon sustained injuries that required the attention of three or four men who would otherwise be returning fire.[24]

The AK, however, was a gun anyone could use; that was a large part—perhaps the largest part—of its importance. The AK was supposedly so easy to use that it required no adjustments in the weapon or cartridges. It had few movable parts and was said to be easy to maintain. Many said it was superior for bush warfare because its barrel was shorter than that of the FN; it did not get snagged in branches and vines. Its stock was retractable when made of metal, fixed when made of wood or plastic; guerrillas preferred the plastic stocks because weapons were frequently cached underground. It had a curved "banana" magazine, which made it instantly identifiable; the magazine carried thirty rounds. In terms of firing, the AK-47 was the opposite of the FN: the first downward click on the AK firing selector was for automatic fire; the second was for repeating single shots. When the gun was fired on automatic, the blowback raised the barrel so that shots went high.[25] Guerrillas, according to Rhodesian soldiers, tended to spray automatic fire in any surprise encounter. Rhodesian officers often assumed that guerrilla commanders encouraged wasting ammunition through extravagant bursts of automatic fire; they cheerfully recounted the exceptional number of spent cartridges found after contacts—400 here, 150 fired at one doorway somewhere else. But 400 cartridges meant that a patrol of ten, nine of whom carried automatic weapons, fired a total of eleven magazines: it may have been a sloppy strategy or gross disobedience, but it was not extravagant bursts of fire. Rank-and-file guerrillas claimed they often fired on automatic because in the bush it was rare to get a clear shot.[26] Even so, guerrillas were completely dependent on the supply of ammunition to the front.[27]

The AK, however well suited it might have been to bush warfare, was a donated weapon. It was foreign made and brought to Africa whole: no assembly was required, and no experts were necessary to explain how it was to be used. The story of the lawnmower is a case in point: the rifle, like the lawnmower of Rhodesian suburban lore, could be disassembled and cleaned in a way that proved that alien technologies could be mastered. Historians of technology have disagreed about what constitutes such mastery. Daniel Headrick has argued that those technologies that arrived ready to use, like radios or automatic weapons, became popular almost at once: their everyday use was more important than their internal workings or their place of origin. Clapperton Mavhunga has argued that the very off-the-shelf nature of these technologies made them easy to domesticate. Technology transfer was made to meet the complexities of local needs, as nineteenth-century bullet casings and discarded food tins were remade as bowls and spearheads.[28] Rhodesian authors reflected these arguments. Peter Stiff's war novel contains a predictable description of guerrillas' weapon caches—"countless tons of arms and equipment," plus radios and medical supplies—and the "explosives Africans could not possibly understand." Another author of another novel describes a guerrilla holding "two small grenade mines" charged with a plastic explosive he knows nothing about "except that it smelt of almonds."[29] Kevin Thomas, however, called the donated weapons he cataloged—"the AK-47 assault rifle, the RPD machine gun, and the RPG7 anti-tank weapon"—"organic firepower," elemental weapons that were part of the landscape. These were the weapons ZIPRA and ZANLA carried into battle; they matched anything Rhodesian soldiers carried.[30] But for most Rhodesian authors the AK was in "the tradition of Russian weapon: rugged, dependable and cheap," effective even after long periods without cleaning or lubrication.[31] It was so simple that illiterate peasants could operate it to great effect. The simplicity and the power of the AK underscores the question I want to ask of Peter Walls: If the AK-47 was a cheap, simple, donated weapon that required almost no training to use, why did the Rhodesian general insist that it was the mark of experienced, disciplined guerrillas?

African Shooting

Walls was not alone in his vision of skilled guerrillas fighting with sophisticated weapons. Guerrilla shooting and fire discipline were described with near reverence in many contact reports. (These were detailed summaries of each incident in which fire was exchanged with guerrillas; each one passed through the chain of command from subunit commanders to brigadiers, each of whom commented from a somewhat different vantage point.)

ZANLA, trained in guerrilla warfare, never sought out battles and were especially skilled at withdrawing: gunners would cover their comrades' escape with "accurate and effective fire." Returning fire on a riverbank, three guerrillas walked slowly, "in a most disciplined manner with one firing and the other two moving." Delaying parties fired on advancing troops from four hundred meters away. Subunit commanders frequently noted the degree of "aggressiveness, accurate fire, and orderly drills in withdrawing" demonstrated by guerrillas. The same officers did not think black Rhodesian soldiers were as skilled. One complained that if an RAR Special Company had "displayed the same degree of firing ability as the terrs, the terrs would not have made it."[32] Published materials were no less admiring. Guerrilla guns were kept in good condition, their fire was "extremely accurate" and "landed right on target." Guerrillas followed orders and maintained "total control" over their ambushes.[33] In contrast, novels and memoirs by and about guerrillas report men putting their weapons on automatic, in great frustration, and "firing blindly"; they wrote of their losing familiarity with weapons in the inactive years of 1976–77. In their postwar writings, at least, guerrillas did not boast of accurate fire or extraordinary skills.

What is most important here is that guerrillas were almost always said to be better shots than the RAR, even though the RAR was the most experienced infantry battalion in the country by the 1960s. In 1974 a second RAR battalion was formed, followed by a third in 1977 and a fourth in 1978. 4RAR never saw action as a battalion but were immediately integrated into white reserve units of the Rhodesia Regiment (RR); 3RAR were given increasing extended postings with independent companies of the RR.[34] RAR officers praised the regiment's training. David Caute, reporting for *The Observer* in 1978, watched a passing-out parade of RAR with a white officer, who told him, "The day a group of terrorists pass out like that will be the day I'll start to worry."[35] Nevertheless, officers seemed to think that training with guns did not make skilled soldiers: race did. Officers claimed that African soldiers fired high when they were "excited." At the same time, the Rhodesian Intelligence Corps, biologists, and PhD candidates in the humanities tasked to analyze situation reports from the war found the reverse to be true: by every possible measure, 1RAR was the most effective unit in the Rhodesian Army. They had the best performance in operational areas: the most kills and the fewest unit deaths. 1RAR had one hundred kills before the RLI did. The 2RAR ranked third, only slightly less effective than 1RLI.[36] In the annual all-forces service shooting competition, the RAR fielded two teams of four men each.[37]

After the war, white officers joked that the only RAR fire that killed guerrillas was that of the troop commander "because he was white" or that of the platoon sergeant major "because he had fifteen or twenty years of experience behind him."³⁸ Such ideas seeped into other branches of the security forces. A young Rhodesian Air Force pilot, a man who had not had much contact with any infantry unit, black or white, claimed that the RAR "were good reliable blokes but their operating was pretty shit."³⁹ Both 1RAR and 2RAR received scant praise in Rhodesian Army contact reports. In the 1960s there were frequent complaints that RAR ran away from contacts or got lost on patrol.⁴⁰ In the 1970s RAR shooting was often described as "ineffectual," "poor," and "dismal."⁴¹ RAR patrols "showed a distinct lack of aggression"; their firing was "not good enough" and "not up to standard," and they "hit the ground as soon as shooting started." One patrol disregarded clear orders and shot a guerrilla as he tried to surrender, another did not heed whispered commands to begin firing, and another initiated fire without orders, and even then "it was haphazard and not aimed."⁴² Officers in the 2RAR, whether in their diaries or in fiction, complained about "mediocre shooting" by the few men who actually fired their weapons in a contact.⁴³

Where does this leave me, or Peter Walls? If the weapon is simple and has no real aimed fire, how do we understand Rhodesians' praise for guerrilla shooting? Is the question one of vocabularies, that praise for soldiering is expressed in the words for accuracy whether or not they apply, or is it what Bill Nasson has called the bizarre combination of nuance and contradiction in which Africans' use of firearms is so frequently described?⁴⁴ The idea that the enemies of European expansion were good shots while African allies were poor shooters had been a commonplace trope of South African wars in the nineteenth century. Then, however, the idea was fueled in part by demands that all Africans be disarmed in peacetime. Such a residue of conquest could not be easily bundled with twentieth-century ideas about Africans and their weapons. As white officers (and authors) sought to explain Africans' relationships to how they fought—substances that turned bullets to water, mystical weapons, and so-called cultural weapons that were also cheap weapons, spears, and machetes—contradiction may have seemed like the most logical explanation.⁴⁵ The problem of this chapter is how to write history with that nuance and contradiction: how to understand Rhodesians' belief in the power and efficacious use of donated weapons, whatever guerrillas said about their soldiering and whatever the qualities loyal Africans brought to this war. The idea that African enemies were good shots remained a way of talking about Africans fighting against Rhodesia, even though it is impossible to have a concept of accurate fire with automatic weapons. It also became a way to talk about the provenance of guerrilla weapons and the intimate ties that linked AKs and other weapons to Moscow or China. Even in the early years of the war, it was commonplace to describe guerrillas as having a power and precision that was shaped by global forces. A white farmer told a reporter for the *Daily Telegraph* that "these chaps are using highly sophisticated weapons. I would call it Mao Mao rather than Mau Mau."[46]

Of Mao and Training Camps

Did guerrillas make the same fuss over AKs that Rhodesian authors did? To what extent did that particular weapon mark seasoned "self-respecting" guerrillas? Rhodesians believed that Africans' knowledge of guns was irrefutable proof of guerrilla training; it is not clear how much value Africans placed on that training. Special Branch was condescending about guerrilla training in the 1960s. Reports claimed that men trained in Algeria would be unlikely to carry out an ambush "in the textbook manner." Men trained in African camps were not even expected to follow the textbook. They were instructed, for example, to make a smoke grenade with the powder of twelve dried chilies, twenty-four match heads, sand, and petrol. Special Branch belittled ZANU's camps in Tanzania, where instruction "lacked the sophistication of the course held in Russia or Red China." Nevertheless, ZANLA recruits heard lectures "by one of their own kind in their own language and this may have compensated for the lack of specialized instruction."[47]

When guerrillas were an imaginary, and before the first armed guerrillas entered the country, some Rhodesian novelists described guerrillas as drug-crazed urban youth incapable of covering their tracks in the bush. Others described militias quickly organized by white farmers that could easily defeat well-armed "Pan-African" rebels because "it's not the guns, gentlemen, it's the men behind the guns."[48] After 1967 and 1968—after the first guerrilla incursions into Rhodesia—two novels marked a transformation in their descriptions of African guerrilla training. One was by a former policeman, the other by a Bulawayo prosecutor. Their texts listed what a guerrilla recruit learned in Moscow (or Peking) above and beyond firing and cleaning machine guns, and above and beyond the imaginings of Rhodesian Special Branch: "how to make explosives and how to blow up bridges and buildings and railway lines, how to tap telephones, use radio, how to use trick cameras and invisible ink."[49] It is not altogether clear that guerrillas prized their training, however. The guerrillas captured and interrogated between 1966 and 1968 described an almost hands-off training in Tanzania, where recruits had to prepare their own food and supervise their own exercise before instructors showed up at 9:00 AM. In the morning they received weapons training in which they were allowed to fire five rounds each; in the afternoon they heard lectures on map reading.[50] The earliest first-person accounts of guerrilla training in Russia seemed sensible, if uninspired. Men were trained in command and control, compass reading, and first aid. They learned how to assemble and disassemble rifles and were given target practice at various distances. After a few weeks they were divided into small groups, each of which received specialized training in weapons, radio and Morse code, explosives, and tactics, so they could return to Africa and train others.[51] Rhodesian officers, however, seemed unwilling to believe that guerrillas might have had limited training with guns. When a captured ZAPU described his Russian target practice—five rounds with an AK, ten rounds with an automatic pistol—it was "suspected that he fired considerably more rounds than he cared to admit."[52] More than a decade later, when surveillance of ZAPU's Kafwambila camp in Zambia revealed no armory and no weapons training, no one thought ordnance was in short supply. Instead, it was assumed that guerrillas took target practice in the bush nearby.[53]

The fact of Russia, rather than target practice therein, captured the imagination of Rhodesian authors, authorities, and foreign journalists. The ZANLA recruits trained in Ghana in 1964 and Egypt in 1965 went largely unnoticed.[54] Training in Russia, or China, was a powerful trope in Rhodesian fiction: novelists imagined guerrillas falling in love with Chinese instructors, or with Russian instructors, or carrying Mao's Little Red Book with them on patrol in Central Africa.[55] But only ZAPU sent men to Eastern Europe for training after about 1970, and then only seasoned cadres. These men recalled their time there with great fondness: they found Russians unpretentious and East Germans warm.[56] In the late 1970s journalists tried to discover if the ZIPRA they met had really been to Russia: if they could not speak with certainty about the climate or the language, even sympathetic journalists like David Caute assumed they had not actually been there. "Russia was the glamorous, important place to have been, a mark of selection."[57] For guerrillas, however, Russian and Chinese training had multiple meanings in the early 1970s, especially after many ZIPRA had defected to ZANLA. In many writings about guerrillas it became commonplace for ZANLA to recall ZAPU Russian training—whether their own or not—with contempt. Russians believed in "confrontational, pitched-battle" warfare that had nothing to do with the realities of their struggle in Africa, they complained, apparently to anyone who would listen. The same men had nothing but praise for their training in China, although it is not clear that any ZANLA went there after 1968 or 1969: starting in 1970 the Chinese began to send instructors to ZANLA's camps in Tanzania. Nevertheless, several ZANLA in exile gave astounding descriptions of being trained in China, where, among other things, they said they had been taken to the caves of Hunan, so they would understand the importance of history and ideology.[58]

ZANLA trained as a guerrilla army, at least in theory. According to captured guerrillas, their training camps in Tanzania in the early 1970s were chronically short of guns. There were not enough guns with which to train recruits, and automatic weapons were kept in the local police station at night, not in the camp. Much of their weapons training was by demonstration, sometimes with AKs and sometimes with old British World War II guns. The rest of the time the Chinese instructors showed them how to use bayonets and knives in hand-to-hand combat. This was followed by refresher courses, and drill, designed to combat boredom and boost morale rather than give everyone experience with guns.[59] These instructors were a staple of Rhodesian fiction, sometimes urging caution and sometimes insisting on foolhardy attacks.[60] There were even fewer guns in ZANLA's camps in Mozambique. When Keith Nell, SAS, was charged with training surrendered ZANLA into security force auxiliaries, he soon realized most of them had received almost no weapons training (see chapter 9).[61]

What constituted guerrilla training in the camps of Mozambique? Most young male recruits spent entire afternoons reciting the names of all the parts of a submachine gun, "like school children," each standing when called upon and shouting, "Barrel, piston, cover, hand grip, chamber . . . ." After weeks of such training, men were finally "heading for the gun." They were instructed to make wooden replicas of AKs. Most cadres trained with wooden replicas until they were sent back into Rhodesia—thinking, as at least one cadre did, that they had been transformed into agile, armed, combat-ready militants—but they traveled unarmed: FRELIMO did not want armed groups in the countryside.[62] ZANLA were only issued guns when they entered Rhodesia. Once there, ZANLA men were told that a gun was to be used "on the enemy and for the protection of the masses," and never turned on one's comrades.[63] ZANLA women were told, "A gun is not an object for you to use as an instrument of showing off, neither is it a certificate that you are equal to men comrades. A gun is only for killing the fascist soldiers . . . and the eradication of racial discrimination."[64] As late as the mid-1970s, however, not every ZANLA, male or female, on every patrol carried a gun. Many in the rank and file carried Soviet- and Czech-made Simonev single-shot rifles, often with only a few clips of ammunition, but most carried land mines and stick grenades. Only officers carried Tokarev pistols, which became a favorite souvenir for Rhodesian troops and a few guerrillas.[65] ZANLA began to receive large numbers of automatic weapons from the USSR in early 1978, and only then were they able to replace the older weapons they had given the rank and file.[66]

Indeed, Wilfred Mhanda hardly mentioned guns when he wrote about his time as a ZANLA military instructor in Kongwa and Mgagao camps in Tanzania in 1971–73. Like other officers, he had been trained in weapons and shooting by Chinese instructors through interpreters. A few, including Mhanda, were singled out to be trained as instructors; his specialty was "curved fire artillery." Beyond that there was an emphasis on physical fitness, mainly runs. There was also a night school, in which Mhanda taught reading and writing, because recruits needed basic literacy and numeracy to infiltrate Rhodesia.[67] Although Agrippah Mutambara, a ZANLA commander, claimed his men were trained with guns in Tembwe camp in Mozambique beginning in 1975, he insisted that the mark of a well-trained guerrilla was not his ability to shoot but the calluses formed on his knees and elbows as he learned to crawl to evade detection. Recruits were lectured on the characteristics of each weapon, after which they were issued AK-47s. "The feel of a real gun, and not the wooden replicas we had been accustomed to . . . caused great excitement among the trainees," who only then were taught to crawl while holding the rifle and how to crawl or roll to a new position as they fired. There was also extensive target practice: it was "critical" that cadres learned to shoot accurately at both still and moving targets so they could conserve their "meagre supply of ammunition."[68] Most ZANLA rank and file—at least those who wrote novels or talked to white men who did—did not think they had mastered automatic weapons. They described spraying automatic weapon fire as an act of desperation, not strategy. One ZANLA patrol ignored their commander's order to hold their fire, but fired with such long bursts of their AKs that they had to switch magazines and soon ran out of ammunition.

Another patrol shot "wildly" when driven into an ambush by circling helicopters.⁶⁹

Whether or not ZIPRA was trained as a conventional army, it too was often short of guns. Many cadres were trained in Rhodesia and Zambia by comrades who had been trained abroad; more often than not they trained without guns.⁷⁰ A very few ZIPRA trained on heavy artillery and antiaircraft guns, because "if we were going to train everybody on such a gun ... who would be fighting, because it is going to take some time for one to know the technicalities of such guns."⁷¹ Most rank-and-file ZIPRA, however well-trained and disciplined they thought themselves to be, did not have regular experience handling the weapons they would shoot. There were not many AKs available to recruits in the 1960s and early 1970s, and when there were, there was not always enough ammunition for serious target practice.⁷² Such practice was often fraught. A recruit might be given ten cartridges for a Serminov rifle. If he missed the target with all ten, he might be accused of being a Rhodesian agent sent to sabotage ZIPRA. If he hit the target, he might be accused of being a Selous Scout sent to infiltrate ZIPRA and undermine the struggle.⁷³ Most of the time cadres were taught by demonstration, which may have been preferable.

Such stories of target practice may have been part of the body of wartime gun stories told by guerrillas. One such story may have been Mutambara's list of the weaponry his men took on patrol in September 1976: AK-47s, hand grenades, bazookas—both Russian and Chinese—and mortars and their bombs.⁷⁴ Others were the "propaganda" bullets used in the camps of Mozambique that "burst" several times after being fired. There were stories that, during a battle, some ZANLA dug their automatic rifles into the hillside and left them firing as they fled. Many stories circulated through liberation movements in Tanzania. In one, the South African Pan-African Congress planned to receive a shipment of arms that would be cached on the banks of the Limpopo. When they dug up the boxes, they found a few pistols, no ammunition, and a large supply of sedatives. There was a note telling them to sell the drugs and buy arms with the profits.⁷⁵

Guerrillas, whatever stories they heard and repeated, were not so certain that their training made them skilled and sophisticated. Rank-and-file ZIPRA recalled their first contacts with perhaps more awe than pride. One man admitted that he "never believed" his gun would really work. But once under fire, he overcame his fear and switched his rifle to automatic and killed two white soldiers: "After that I became brave."⁷⁶ ZIPRA were justly proud of their training abroad, their firepower, and their possession and mastery of sophisticated weapons, but these were part and parcel of political parties and political loyalties; they were not necessarily identified with the world of foreign places and ideas. The Special Branch who scorned ZANLA's Tanzanian camps, where men were trained "by one of their own kind, in their own language," articulated this very point, that guerrillas loved these technologies and their skills to manage them in large part because they were provided by Africans, at home. A ZIPRA veteran told Jocelyn Alexander and JoAnn McGregor that going for military training was his "first time to board an aeroplane and I felt, Oh! ZAPU is great!"[77] In their own writings no guerrillas seemed to think that what was great about the weapon was that it was Soviet made. It's possible that the AK, available in many more countries than those in which it was manufactured, was a truly global weapon; its users may have been ignored any sense of its place of origin.

Weapons More Sophisticated Than AKs

If automatic rifles were unmoored from the nations that provided them to guerrillas, land mines and antiaircraft artillery were linked to their place of origin. ZAPU was funded primarily by the USSR, although Joshua Nkomo was a prodigious fundraiser and took money from all possible sources. The joke was he could have breakfast in Moscow, lunch in London, and dinner in Washington.[78] Partly for that reason ZAPU's army in Zambia was larger and better armed than that of Zambia, a fact that was a constant source of tension between ZAPU and the Zambian government. Zambia's Rhodesian-born minister of home affairs tried to control—or, failing that, to monitor—the ordnance donated to ZIPRA. This did not work, of course, but he did pressure ZIPRA into keeping their guns in Zambian armories, which meant that ZIPRA trained there could only practice with automatic weapons when Zambians allowed them to. To maintain a supply of sophisticated weapons and artillery, ZIPRA commanders constantly moved their tanks and antiaircraft missiles around the country or out of it altogether. By their own accounts, ZIPRA did not want Zambia to know the extent of the sophisticated weapons they had. But such Zambian ignorance seems unlikely, since ZIPRA propaganda routinely announced the destruction of planes and tanks on the ground in Rhodesia, and ZANU officials in Zambia regularly complained that the Russians "showered" ZIPRA with tanks.[79]

The years 1978 and 1979 were a period of Soviet largesse, probably because of their successful militarization of Ethiopia. In Southern Matabeleland in 1978, rocket-propelled grenades (RPGS) were in widespread use by ZIPRA.[80] RPGS are lighter than AKs but more expensive to manufacture and more complicated to operate. Most famously, ZIPRA had Soviet surface-to-air missiles, the Strella 7, with which gangs claimed to shoot down two civilian aircraft. In the various Rhodesian accounts of the Viscount disasters (see chapter 2), ZIPRA's access to such weapons was almost as important as how they used them. Indeed, there was widespread Rhodesian outrage after a nervous Nkomo, trying to conceal the kinds of weapons his army now had, told a BBC interviewer that his cadres brought the first plane down with "sticks and stones."[81]

My point here is not to make Peter Walls even more of a straw man than I have already done in this chapter. Instead, I want to frame his insistence that real guerrillas carry AK-47s with the well-known rumor that he was the target of the second Strella 7 surface-to-air missile (see chapter 2). Did he believe that the AK-47 was a commonplace, not-very-sophisticated weapon—at least, not when compared with other weapons guerrillas had. The Viscount disasters—and the bombing raids that were Rhodesia's retaliation—occupied an important but fleeting space in Rhodesia's military history: they were proof of African savagery, even as majority rule was on the table. That was the kind of contradiction Bill Nasson described; as such it brought renewed weight to ideas about Africans and their weapons. This was the weight that became manifest in the heavier weapons and various antiaircraft that both ZANLA and ZIPRA took to the assembly points—or had them brought in by the same teenage auxiliaries Walls claimed were already in the camps—in preparation for possible attacks by air.[82] After the war, the heavy weapons outside the country figured in another plotted coup: in mid-1980 factions in the Zambian Defence Force managed to divert some of ZIPRA's weaponry to their arsenals as it was being shipped to Zimbabwe.[83] Years later, however, ZIPRA intelligence was to doubt its reliance on heavy weapons with the logic of conventional warfare. While ZIPRA had enough mortars and skilled cadres to assault a garrison, they did not have enough trained infantry in Rhodesia to press home the advantages these weapons gave them.[84]

Wooden Guns and Noisy Guns

Most ZANLA commanders and almost all of its high command considered training with wooden replicas of guns to be poor training. It is not altogether clear why. The object of drill is to condition soldiers to perform, to continue shooting when exhausted, under fire, or injured; drill makes sure that soldiers, however fatigued, shoot at their enemies and not at their comrades. Automatic weapons, and the nature of area fire, were well-suited to training done by demonstration, as in ZIPRA and ZANLA camps. Wooden guns were a reliable way to accustom cadres to the weight of automatic rifles. Nevertheless, the ZANLA high command had grave reservations about men who had trained with wooden replicas. They may have learned this disdain from their Red Army instructors who recalled their own disastrous training with wooden guns in 1939, or it may have been based on the records of killed and wounded that ZANLA struggled to maintain.[85] When ZANLA officers needed its best soldiers, either to hunt down mutineers in 1975 or to form the short-lived Zimbabwe Peoples' Army, they took men from their camps in Tanzania, who had trained with more guns than were available to cadres trained in Mozambique.[86]

What does this mean for my understanding of Rhodesian imaginaries? How do the wooden-gun-toting guerrillas become the men carrying new AKs, proficient in blowing up bridges, trick cameras, and invisible ink in the eyes of the white men who had been crack shots long before their national service? There are exceptions of course—as in the novel in which guerrillas favor bayonets because they are bloodier, or the former RLI befriended by Alexandra Fuller who insisted that guerrillas couldn't shoot straight[87]—but overall, most war memoirs and novels make the same point: that guerrillas were well trained and equipped in the art of war, while guerrillas complained they were not. Why? Surely there was a strong desire on the part of Rhodesians, intensified by settler myths, to have a worthy enemy, but did that worth require invisible ink and trick cameras? On the whole, security forces gained respect for the two armies and their fighting skills throughout the 1970s. A 1977 lecture to RLI concluded with a list of what guerrillas were not: invisible, invincible, as well trained and well equipped and as intelligent "as you are."[88] Guerrillas, however, did not think themselves badly trained or poor soldiers. Their frequent complaints and uncertainties about their fire discipline (that they went on automatic too often, too late, too thoughtlessly) suggest that they were trained to have much better fire discipline than they managed during contacts.

Why do some Africans shoot accurately and some dismally? The reasons could not be racial; Rhodesian authors found no physiological reasons Africans could not shoot; instead, Rhodesian African soldiers could not shoot straight because of the technological constraints of their cultures and histories. Lt. Col. Ron Reid-Daly, who wrote contemptuously of the

Rhodesian Army's ideas about African soldiers, was shocked by the "abysmally poor standard of shooting" in the RAR. It was "a quite incredible experience" for someone like himself, "who had spent almost his entire service with European troops, to witness for the first time, the unbelievably appalling standard of musketry of the volunteer African soldiers," even though they were experienced soldiers. There was nothing wrong with African eyesight, he insisted: Africans had better eyesight than the average white Rhodesian and had much better peripheral vision, especially when on patrol. African shooting, Reid-Daly surmised, had nothing to do with innate African qualities but "something to do with the gun itself, which was a much more alien weapon to an African than it was to a European." Something, most likely the noise of firing, gave Africans "an ingrained fear of the weapon," and they could not control their "natural flinching reaction." None of this was natural, wrote Reid-Daly. The best African shootists he had ever seen were the Portuguese Flechas, who were trained specifically to become accustomed to the sound of automatic fire.[89] Reid-Daly was not alone. Former RAR officers interviewed in 2005 claimed that their African troops couldn't "shoot very straight." Again, this was because of African culture and history, nothing else. Africans had limited encounters with guns and had not seen enough movies or television to be familiar with guns, so they were unprepared for the weapons' kick or noise.[90] There seemed to be no other reason that guerrillas were good shots than that they had trained in Russia or China.

The problem of loyalist African shooting was said to be particularly acute as the RAR expanded in wartime. If any explanation was given for poor RAR shooting, it was guerrilla conduct. In 1978 an RAR officer patiently explained why his men did not fire on guerrillas leaving a mission school. It was known that the guerrillas frequented the girls' dormitory on weekends, and the soldiers did not want to risk shooting civilians or children, so they held their fire.[91] Africans' kinship with other Africans was only half the discursive battle, however; the other half was Africans' kinship with Rhodesian whites, how it was constituted and how it cleaved. Whatever the statistics about their effectiveness, the RAR could never quite become the equal of white soldiers, but this was not because of race. It was because of culture, history, and exposure to technology. RAR could be made into good soldiers, perhaps not as good as whites but at least as good as the guerrillas they fought. The most romantic, and technologically aware, version of this is from a novel by Alan Thrush, formerly an officer in 2RAR. Rhodesia's "rugged, rain-soaked beauty" was "the birthplace of the enemy, and of the RAR." How, then, could white men, born in hospitals, well fed and well served by indoor plumbing, who only saw the bush "with detached interest" from "the shelter of their parents' car," fight on the same side as Africans, men who "lived easily among the wild animals of the bush" and who bore the "physical rigours of the war very easily indeed"? How indeed? It required training whites to have the physical stamina of Africans, rather than training Africans in the sophisticated ways of whites.[92] This was why all Selous Scouts, black and white, were required to take a training course in living off the land that was to make white men like Africans (see chapter 4). Africans had a natural advantage.[93]

The noise of the gun, indoor plumbing, and ease of living in the bush challenge ideas about martial races in this racially charged liberation struggle.[94] It's not that Rhodesians did not believe that Ndebele were Zulu warriors but that they insisted that being of a martial race had no place in modern war. "The Shona," I was told again and again, were better soldiers than the martial Ndebele because they were not accustomed to harsh discipline. Ndebele codes of discipline were so harsh and embodied that ordinary military discipline did not matter: What was three days in the brig to them?[95] But the challenge seems to hit the proverbial brick wall: If white ideas about African shooting were not about race, what were they about? Let me return again to Peter Walls and suggest that these ideas may flow from the barrel of one specific gun, not from ideas about race or skills specific to races. Daniel Headrick has argued that the complexity of nineteenth-century technology encouraged racist thinking: as tools and machines became more complex, they required specialists to operate them; natives were unable to participate in the mechanics of domination.[96] In this liberation war, the simplicity and portability of automatic weapons may have discouraged racist ideas about guerrilla shooting. For Rhodesians, the FN was a white man's gun, "temperamental," in need of special sights and weights to improve it. Every Rhodesian knew the FN was hard to use, but there were no cultural reasons why white soldiers could not learn to do so: all they needed was frequent drill and target practice.[97] What was important for Rhodesian thinking about the AK—thinking that began to take shape in the late 1960s—was twofold. First, it was a donated weapon, proof of guerrillas' access to the evil spaces of the Kremlin and Hunan. Second, it could be used on arrival; no specialists were required to show cadres how to use them. The internationalism of the weapon was linked to ideas about how easy it was to use.

But how can I explain that the noise of the gun might have terrified Africans who fought for Rhodesia but not those who had crossed borders to go to Mozambique, Zambia, or Russia? Did these men lose their fear of guns and their technology-deprived histories simply by changing, or even asserting, a political loyalty? Absolutely. While the Africans who fought for Rhodesia flinched, the Africans who traveled, in body or in spirit, to Moscow and Mozambique did not; they became the cosmopolitans who had learned to manage sophisticated weapons. It did not matter if the most iconic of these weapons required no special skills to operate it. But if such men turned, and fought for Rhodesia, as did many in the Selous Scouts, they returned to their old poor shooting ways.[98] When RAR defected and joined guerrillas, they became much more skilled at soldiering: they led attacks that shot down helicopters, or they gave commandos their best firefight of the war.[99]

Guns were only one weapon of this war. Rhodesia had another imaginary, one born of technological mastery and indoor plumbing and hard science. Biological and chemical weapons became a staple of postwar writing in the mid-1980s and have been promoted as a specialized and successful form of counterinsurgency.

7 "A PLASTIC BAG FULL OF CHOLERA"

Rhodesia and Biological and Chemical Weapons

During this war, guerrillas firmly believed that Rhodesian security forces were poisoning them. Poisons were a well-known means of harming people in Central African systems of thought; while few guerrillas would have doubted the possibility that a jealous neighbor or an angry wife might poison them, wartime poisoning by Rhodesians was different. Rhodesians had weaponized sickness in a way friends and family did not: it was political, not personal. After the war, Rhodesians wrote about their various biological and chemical warfare schemes, in descriptions that often became more elaborate and fanciful as time went on. In this chapter I am not asking about the Rhodesian arsenal of chemical and biological weapons. I am asking instead how ideas about such weapons took hold among guerrillas and soldiers alike, and how guerrillas' and soldiers' ideas about such weapons shaped each other.

This chapter, then, requires two frames. The first consists of accusations of the use of biological and chemical weapons in twentieth-century wars. These accusations took many forms. As the Japanese invaded China in 1936–37, for example, they claimed Chinese troops polluted wells with bacteria as they retreated. Chinese civilians later avoided the Japanese army's cholera vaccinations, insisting that the injections were lethal. In 1952, on the border of China and North Korea, Chinese reported American aircraft dropping cardboard boxes filled with live insects and soybean stalks. A few weeks later a railway worker saw a large number of black beetles on the tracks and later became ill and died. A medical examination of the beetles revealed they contained anthrax bacteria. As Biafra fought a losing war for its independence from Nigeria in the mid-1960s, rumors circulated that cooks loyal to Nigeria were poisoning university students. Later it was said that British food aid was in fact poisoned: Nigeria had been advised that this was the quickest way to end the succession. Biafrans rejected the food. When Rhodesians introduced Depo-Provera in the 1970s, many Africans claimed it was designed to sterilize them. Indeed, majority-ruled Zimbabwe banned the contraceptive in 1981.[1] In war-torn Rhodesia guerrillas claimed their food had been poisoned by villagers, who were forced to do so by security forces; they claimed that uniforms and boots had been soaked in various poisons by Rhodesian soldiers desperate to kill them; and they claimed anthrax and cholera were introduced into specific areas.[2] A decade later, in the Horn of Africa, many Somalis believed that Americans dropped chemicals that would cause gunmen to faint, so that US soldiers could be come by helicopters to disarm militias.[3]

Do these stories accurately describe policies, or do they describe a causal agent of a disease? Wartime afflictions do not always have clear-cut etiologies. For example, Anglo-American researchers studying Gulf War syndrome could not identify any single cause. No pollutant appeared in sufficient quantities to make soldiers sick. The syndrome seemed to originate in the cluster of chemicals, vaccines, and medications given to soldiers and with the chemicals to which they were exposed. Moreover, the anticipation of exposure to biological and chemical weapons created an intense level of anxiety very much like that of post-traumatic stress disorders. But even a commonplace diagnosis like post-traumatic stress disorder applies a medical label to a range of physical and emotional conditions that oversimplify and perhaps overdetermine symptoms and causes.[4]

The second frame is once again about place. Indeed, what is the place of locality in widespread ideas and accusations about biological and chemical weapons? How do I write about illness and death as if they were counterinsurgency strategies, not widely held beliefs? This chapter underscores the specificity of Rhodesia and the specificity of the evidence in the historiography of biological and chemical weapons. This evidence contains specifically local accusations: poisoned underwear, poisoned boreholes, and spirit mediums who claimed to afflict a population that Rhodesians authors would later confess to have sickened themsevles. And perhaps more than any other, this chapter underscores the place of published evidence in this historiography; in many cases contemporary observers saw illness and nausea and death they could not fully identify and contextualize. Later they read some now-it-can-be-told memoir of Rhodesian war practices and realized that the physical conditions they saw were the result of Rhodesian biological and chemical warfare. I have nothing against reading and what can be learned and deduced from texts, but in this chapter I am concerned that in these instances the Rhodesian literature serves to close off other possibilities and other explanations.

This is what I mean: Glen Cross's exceptionally thorough 2017 book pulls together a great deal of information to show that Rhodesia used chemical agents extensively but in small quantities and with rudimentary delivery systems. These "poisons" were not apparent to medical personnel at the time. For example, doctors in Harari Hospital (now Harare Central Hospital) detected chemical poisoning in the 1970s but did not connect it to the security forces. At around the same time, hospital staff in Bulawayo detected "intentional" thallium contamination of canned beef but never investigated the source of the poison. A young American doctor working in Mozambique in the late 1970s saw many young, fit ZANLA whose symptoms resembled the recently identified hemorrhagic fevers (Marburg, Ebola), but he soon discovered they were caused by the blood thinner warfarin. He had no idea what the source of this poison was. Years later, however, the American doctor read Ken Flower's account of the clever, covert operations with which Rhodesia fought its war; he realized that Rhodesian soldiers or mercenaries had supplied guerrillas with uniforms soaked in warfarin.[5]

This chapter is about Rhodesian war writing and the possibilities that literature denies. Put simply, when young men exhibited symptoms of organophosphate poisoning, how could doctors tell if they were guerrillas targeted in counterinsurgency operations or if they were farmworkers who were not issued protective clothing? Shocking as thallium in canned beef was, how could even the most experienced medical personnel know if it had been placed there intentionally or by sloppy production techniques? In the training camps of Mozambique in the late 1970s, ZANLA was intensely divided. Were those young, fit men poisoned by Rhodesians or by dissident factions in the guerrilla struggle? Warfarin—commonly used as rat poison—was available in any village store; anyone could buy it, and anyone with access to a comrade's food or drink or uniform could administer it. How much warfarin was needed to kill fifteen guerrillas? Was it enough to soak a uniform in blood thinner once, or did it have to be repeated again and again in the camps? However uniforms were adulterated, was it possible to target specific guerrillas, or did poisoners have to be satisfied with killing whoever wore the treated uniforms? To be sure, Rhodesians wanted ZANLA dead, and they bombed guerrilla camps in Mozambique to accomplish that. Was poisoning a handful of guerrillas here and there an effective counterinsurgency strategy? If it was a strategy, was it the desperate act of a beleaguered nation, as both Cross and I have been told, a strategy directed from above and carried out by willing chemists, professors, and Territorials?[6] Or was it the work of a handful of dedicated but unsupervised Special Branch, men who knew the districts in which they operated and how pesticides worked? There is another possibility, one I will elaborate later in this chapter: that poisonings were an African idiom of harming, and the debates and accusations about poisonings percolated into the lore of Rhodesian security forces.

The evidence in this chapter, like evidence for biological and chemical warfare in many places, is very contradictory when it is not sketchy or frayed around the edges. The existence of unsupervised security forces, operating over a large area, complicates this chapter just as it complicated the war. More important, perhaps, is that the either/or narrative, the conventional history of white racists versus African nationalists, broke down in the later years of this war. The question of who was fighting for which cause against which soldiers was never well defined for long. ZANLA and ZIPRA, despite forming a Patriotic Front with which to negotiate, were at odds with each other and with the newly formed Special Branch–inflected armies of Bishop Abel Muzorewa and Reverend Ndabaningini Sithole (see chapter 9). ZANLA and ZIPRA fought against the Rhodesian security forces, and sometimes against Muzorewa's private army and more often against Sithole's, as did the Rhodesian special forces tasked with training security force auxiliaries. All of these armies were factionalized in the extreme.[7]

Ken Flower's Confessions

What did Flower write that convinced a young physician that the men he saw dying from overdoses of blood thinner were killed by Rhodesian agents? *Serving Secretly* was the earliest and perhaps the most influential of now-it-can-be-told books that described Rhodesian biological and chemical weapons. Chemical warfare saddened him, Flower wrote, because it revealed the ways that war brought out the worst in so many men. One such man was the Rev. Arthur Kanodareka, a Muzorewa supporter whose story throws Rhodesian accounts of poisoning into high relief. Ken Flower was sorry to report that the CIO compromised Kanodareka, who then supplied poisoned uniforms to young men who were being sent to guerrilla training camps. Many hundreds of recruits would die "a slow death in the African bush" from this "diabolically successful" operation. In a rather convoluted passage Flower insisted that this operation was so successful Kanodareka had to be killed, as he was likely to be found out sooner or later.[8] Rhodesian soldiers, including those writing about the evils of the security forces a few years later, believed that Kanodareka was one of many agents who sold the poisoned jeans to greedy shopkeepers who sold them, killing villagers and not insurgents. Some thought Kanodareka was actually working for the UANC, poisoning guerrillas in the Patriotic Front, but after he joined the militant, anti-Muzorewa wing of the party he was murdered, shot many times on an isolated road.[9] Although Flower claimed Kanodareka's murder was a successful Rhodesian operation, it was not clear if he was killed by the UANC or Rhodesian Special Branch, or by pro-Muzorewa elements in Special Branch or Special Branch in UANC, nor is it clear that his death was intended to keep a poisoning operation secret or to punish UANC dissidents.

What is not clear is central to this chapter. Even as canonical an account of poisoned uniforms as Flower's has different versions and ragged edges. Most published accounts of poisoned food or clothes border on the anecdotal: this or that Rhodesian solider was told not to touch a batch of clothing, or was warned against taking painkillers from the dispensary at a ZANLA camp, or heard that a few guerrillas died in agony after swallowing something tainted by the Rhodesian war effort. Flower indicated that the sole purpose of poisoned uniforms was to kill guerrilla recruits: if fewer men crossed the border, fewer men could fight Rhodesia. Later authors insisted that the purpose of chemical weapons and poisons was to sow distrust between guerrillas and the civilian villagers on whom they depended for food, clothing, and security: men who saw their comrades die would retaliate. Certainly the documents provided to Peter Stiff by Henry Wolhunter, Special Branch, who, along with his wife, prepared the chemicals at Bindura, make this claim. These documents were reproduced in a war memoir by Jim Parker, a police reservist who claimed to be Special Branch and was attached to the Selous Scouts for much of the war. At the end of a list of distributed materials—sixteen packets of biscuits to Beitbridge, thirty-four sets of clothing to Mount Darwin, and so on—was a note indicating that the murder of tribespeople by guerrillas in the areas where the goods were distributed "is on the increase."[10] This motivation rested on a highly idealized picture of guerrilla-civilian relations in the late 1970s. In many parts of the country, guerrillas were already tense and coercive; poisons could make them more violent, as we will see, but no less coercive.[11]

Rhodesia's chemical weapons program may have remained the stuff of memoirs had it not been for the anthrax letter attacks that occurred in the United States in 2001. In a series of steps that I can only imagine, FBI agents interviewed Michael ("Mac") McGuiness about Rhodesia's chemical weapon program, Z Desk. McGuiness had been a police superintendent when he began the program at the Selous Scouts fort at Bindura. He provided a coherent history of Rhodesian chemical warfare, with names and places and techniques, although other policemen interviewed by Cross called the program amateurish, relying solely on chemicals off the shelf. This was deliberate, they said: the chemical weapons were easily available in any farm supply store; they could be purchased in bulk without importing anything or arousing international suspicion.[12] Besides, after 1977, Rhodesia's domestic markets were saturated, so anyone who invented a better mousetrap or a new rodent poison might well have offered it to the military.

According to Cross, Rhodesia's chemical and biological warfare program began in 1976 and lasted until 1979, when the war was brought to a negotiated end. It was staffed by national servicemen and Territorials. Or was it? Were young conscripts and reservists on their third call-up the right men to mix hazardous chemicals? The security forces were hardly a monolith without struggles over authority and claims to knowledge. Those struggles did not end when the war ended. In a series of letters to the editor of South Africa's *Sunday Times*, McGuiness complained that Parker was never a fully attested member of Special Branch, but a police reservist. Parker did not respond, but his publisher, Peter Stiff, did. Stiff himself was former BSAP and knew McGuiness well, but he had hours of taped interviews between Parker and McGuiness, which indicated to him, at least, that McGuiness accepted Parker's status as a subordinate, even if he was a reservist and not a regular policeman.[13] Once again, we see a published account of this war (and its crimes) becoming a source of debate and contention.

The Problem with Poisons

Chemical and biological weapons are illegal. They are considered immoral: they are not soldierly, they are "dirty," as if other weapons might be "clean." One of the phrases that first got me thinking that this was a worthwhile line of inquiry was a passage from a Rhodesian wartime novel, the incomprehensible plot of which takes place in Rhodesia, South Africa, Biafra, and a fictionalized island nation off the West African coast. Somewhere in the story the Rhodesian paid assassin representing currency interests tells another assassin who works for the Rhodesian government, "Your lot would want to spread anthrax over his toothbrush or slip some fungus into his socks. We still kill like gentlemen."[14]

The use of chemical weapons in World War I so shocked Europe that they were banned, although not so much that they were not used in Palestine in 1918 and Iraq in the 1920s.[15] The conventional wisdom holds that in the decade after World War I there was a military disincentive to develop more and better chemical weapons: it was simply too costly to develop weapons that might never be used.[16] Such wisdom is wrong, however. Chemical weapons were researched and developed in peacetime, but they were developed to kill insects. Killing insects did not raise ethical issues and could proceed with government funds but without fear of reproach. Edmund Russell's point that improved pesticides allowed chemical warfare to find "a niche in civilian life" is critical to the arguments in this chapter. "If pest control was the civilianized form of chemical warfare, then chemical warfare was the militarized form of pest control." Using pesticides as weapons of war, however, required moving people into a specific, nonhuman category; the enemy was equated with pests. This was not a metaphor, Russell argues, but an act: "Saying people were pests was different from saying they were pets; these terms implied different ways of treating people."[17] Pets—not human but tamed and domesticated by humans—occupied some of the most intimate spaces in the Rhodesian war effort (see chapters 2, 3, and 9), but pests were to be eradicated.

Clapperton Mavhunga has taken Russell's arguments further than anyone else. Writing with many of the sources I use here, he argues that Rhodesian whites thought of black Zimbabweans as pests, as vermin, as bodies that were appropriate to kill with the same chemicals used against insects and rodents.[18] His analysis gives a disturbing depth to the anecdotes Russell provides as amusing, such as when Japanese troops on Iwo Jima believed the planes spraying gray clouds of DDT to protect American soldiers from malaria were spewing a kind of poison gas.[19] Together, Russell and Mavhunga remind us that most wartime poisons were in fact insecticides or rodenticides, including the most common ones in this chapter, parathion (an organophosphate insecticide), thallium (used in Rhodesia to kill baboons that raided farms), or blood thinners like warfarin (a common rat poison).

In this section I want to challenge both Russell and Mavhunga on two key issues. First, if the chemical weapons of Rhodesia's arsenal were commonplace pesticides, how could a guerrilla determine whether he was sick because of Rhodesian actions or because he had visited a farm where pesticides were used? Second, pests may not be the only animalization at play in this literature. Writings about Rhodesian chemical weapons have a studious intimacy about them and suggest another example of something we see often in this book, of the domestication of Africans (see chapters 2 and 3), of Africans treated like pets. There is a pride in intimate knowledge in the sources I cite—the items of clothing poisoned were those Africans liked best, the poisoned underwear, and the intimate knowledge of the frequency of African bowel movements that was required to know how much to poison basic foodstuffs.

There is a larger problem with chemical and biological weapons: they are inefficient. Poison gas caused 2 percent of military deaths and injuries in World War I. Glenn Cross describes Rhodesian poisoning activities in two weeks of November 1977: 365 pieces of clothing and eighty-five cans of meat were contaminated, as well as many other items, including canned peas, toothpaste, brandy, medicines, and cigarettes. The number of guerrillas who died from poisoning in this period was seventy-seven.[20] My point is not that this number is too great or too small—presumably everyone who produced figures on dead guerrillas had reason to exaggerate—but was it worth the effort? Could the funds used for poisons and recanning meats have been better spent on bullets? And could the men at z Desk be sure the poisoning was done by Rhodesian agents using Rhodesian poisons and not African witches using local herbs?

Other Possibilities

Whatever the efficiency of chemical weapons, poisons resonated with the peoples of South Central Africa, where African systems of healing and harming are largely systems of ingestion or of substances rubbed on the skin. Which substance is medicine and which one is poison does not depend on the substance—as in warfarin—but on the intent of the provider and how much was ingested. "Intent" is not necessarily the domain of the living, however. For the most part, the spirits of ancestors guide everyday life; they dispense advice, warnings, gifts, and punishments all the time. As one healer told me, the living act out the wishes of the dead. Ancestors determine human actions, and humans are praised or punished by them. In 1995 and 1997 I was repeatedly told that men under forty-five were dying from HIV/AIDS because ancestors were furious that guerrillas sought their help during the war but did not show the proper fealty after that. It was not a disease but a "punishment."[21]

Not every dead Zimbabwean becomes an ancestor, however. Without the proper burial rites, spirits wander in the void, tormenting the living. Thus the spirits of the thousands of war dead still buried outside the country, in common graves, were critically important in the first years of Zimbabwean independence. Few guerrillas were praised as highly as the men who stayed behind in Mozambique or Zambia to bring the bodies back: they had to find the graves and retrieve the remains without disturbing the remains of other fallen comrades.[22] A reburial with the proper rituals could make a dead man an ancestor. Ancestors' spirits possess individuals who become their mediums; all mediums can heal, but not all healers are mediums. Mediums' contact with ancestors is a key element in the diagnosis of an ailment; that contact also helps them find the herbs that can remedy an affliction. If mediums kill to avenge a death or to punish, they are acting on behalf of the dead; they are not malevolent. Witches—who either become witches because they are exceptionally jealous or are possessed by the spirit of an animal—harm willfully and out of envy and anger. They are malevolent and most often kill by poison.[23] Perhaps for that reason, poisoning is an assumed risk of everyday life. Any African who feared for his life could reasonably assume he would be poisoned, and those who did not took precautions—such as drinking or eating first when serving—to avoid any blame for subsequent illnesses.[24]

If a guerrilla became ill, or watched a comrade die, how could he know who was responsible? Was it a jealous comrade, a bitter wife, or a Rhodesian agent, or was he suffering for something his family had done years before? Whatever the medical tests and whatever the context, it was not always clear if a death was caused by Rhodesian poison or by poison demanded by ancestors or a poison administered by a witch. JoAnn McGregor's research on ZAPU in Dandanda in Northern Matabeland in 1977–78 underscores these questions as she shows how guerrillas negotiated the difference between poisonings that were counterinsurgency operations and poisonings by witches. These were not always exclusive categories; many people believed that witches had a role in Rhodesian poisonings. There were "poisoning rings," groups of women who were given clothing poisoned by Rhodesians to give to guerrillas; some were given poison to put in guerrillas' food. Two of these women were members of the ZAPU women's committee. One confessed to being a Rhodesian agent, but others did not: one threatened the comrades who executed her; blackbirds flew out of the corpse of another. Many people McGregor spoke to did not see any contradiction between witchcraft and biochemical warfare, but guerrilla commanders did. One commander had read about the Algerian war, in which the French used chemicals to kill guerrillas. He spoke about this with his comrades and then surmised that "perhaps there was a secret weapon used by the Rhodesians to kill us and . . . in such a way as to cause mistrust between us and the locals." If Rhodesians used chemical weapons, witches should be left alone. They "have been with us since the beginning" and were not an appropriate target for military action.[25]

What's a historian to do with this? On the ground, the line between witches and Rhodesian agents was at best blurred and permeable, while in Salisbury and various Selous Scout forts, there were no witches, only scientists and unpretentious empiricism. An anonymous document from a South African policeman attached to the BSAP before 1975 reported that he was asked to collect fecal matter from a guerrilla camp and send it to Pretoria for analysis. Cross assumed this was to see if the men had been poisoned. One finding of such tests was that Africans evacuated their bowels twice a day and Europeans only once; hence the dosage of thallium had to be doubled to kill an African.[26] A book about the Rhodesian assassin Taffy Brice (nom de print of Taffy Bryce) reports a preference for thallium, a heavy metal poison commonly used to kill rodents and baboons. When the hit man meets with an agricultural chemist—Sam Roberts, perhaps a pseudonym and pseudo-profession for Robert Symington, professor of anatomy at the University College of Rhodesia, who was said to develop wartime poisons—who supplies poisons for various agencies of the Rhodesian military, the chemist wants to know if he plans to kill an African or a white man. Bristling at such a grossly racialized question, Brice asks, "Does it matter?" The chemist explained that with some poisons race and culture did matter: "Africans need twice as much to constitute a fatal dose than does a white. A white man moves his bowels only twice a day, while an African goes three or four times." The chemist had first learned about thallium and difference when he was asked to "doctor" some sacks of maize meal in a farm store that, according to military intelligence, a group of guerrillas were about to raid. When guerrillas raided the store, they took the food, burned the store, and returned to their base in Mozambique. They died six days later—twice the time it would have taken the poison to kill a white man.[27]

If men died six days later in another country, does the attribution of a specific death or deaths to Rhodesian poison assume too much? Can it be a confirmed kill? The medical cause of death is not always straightforward; it can be a matter of context and suspicion. Ian Hacking's remarks on how doctors explain the seemingly inexplicable death of a two-month-old in a crib are important here. Whether the death is considered sudden infant death syndrome or child abuse depends on what is known about the parents, the context, and the categories and experiences the physician brings to his or her medical practice.[28] The literature that straddles occupational and environmental health makes this point as well. In Martha Balshem's study of cancer in an industrial, largely Polish neighborhood of Philadelphia, heavy smokers disregarded medical opinion and educational campaigns and insisted that the high rates of cancer among them were due to pollution and the chemicals with which many adults, and cancer victims, worked. At least one widow struggled for months to have her husband's death certificate altered so that his twenty-odd years of smoking cigarettes was not given as the sole cause of his death from lung cancer. She blamed his death on the explosion three years earlier in the chemical plant in which he worked.[29]

Balshem's book makes a strong case for competing epistemologies, two very different but very accurate modes of explanation that explain the same medical condition. But are there different ways of explaining the same contamination? Was processed meat poisoned by sloppy factory procedures or by successful counterinsurgency protocols? In 1977, for example, fourteen local people died in Matabeleland after eating Liebig's processed meat that had been canned in the factory nearby. Everyone on the ground accused Rhodesians of having poisoned the meat; Special Branch knew that McGuinness had poisoned one case. Government doctors analyzed the meat and found traces of "bubonic plague bacteria" in some cans. Liebig's sent a team from Britain to inspect the factory; they found unhygienic conditions and fired more than a hundred workers.[30] Neither insurgency nor counterinsurgency could keep ideas about poison from spilling over into ideas about African hygiene and sanitation, ideas about Africans and their inability to maintain standards so important to Europeans.[31]

Both an unhealthy workplace and anthrax on a toothbrush reveal the most significant problem in the deployment of chemical and biological weapons, namely, what is the delivery mechanism? A sloppy meat-processing plant would be too unreliable to weaponize in wartime. A poisoned toothbrush might work well for an assassination, and a village woman might be careful to use a packet of poison only for the food she cooks for guerrillas, but what if a state wanted to hit a broader target in a way that was not so very broad as to kill civilians and allies? Could Rhodesian security forces poison a well and be sure no white person would drink from it? Could a shopkeeper be given poisoned clothing or tainted tinned meats and keep his promise not to sell them to loyal civilians?

Poisoned Food

Guerrillas relied on peasant support in the war. The ideal was that guerrillas' food was prepared for them by the villagers they had convinced of the legitimacy of their cause; the less than ideal way of obtaining food involved coercion and threats of violence. When guerrillas were on patrol in the Rhodesian countryside, they might be able to tell a teenage auxiliary— *mujiba*—to taste their food, but for the most part they were at the mercy of the villagers who cooked their food. One old man told me that poisoning food was simply too big a risk for anyone to take. If guerrillas were poisoned by a meal, they would retaliate against the villagers who prepared it.[32] Retaliation worked both ways, however. Guerrillas' dependence on villagers' food made them easy targets for locals who disagreed with their cause or their conduct. I was told that Rhodesian soldiers would tell the village women that the war was already lost; they gave them "packets of poison" to add to the food they prepared for guerrillas. Many women used the packets: some knew they contained poison and some did not.[33] There are graphic and powerful descriptions of this in postwar writings. Martinus Daneel recounts a story in which a commander is warned by a spirit that his men are in danger. When an old man came to dish out food to the patrol instead of sending his daughters, the commander realizes that the food is poisoned. One comrade had already eaten the food; the rest threw it on the ground because of the ancestor's warning. When the comrades confronted the old man, he confessed. He had two cousins in the Rhodesian Army, and they gave him the poison he put in the guerrillas' food.[34] In one postwar novel, a guerrilla eats poisoned food. He is very sick, but he survives, after which he and his comrades debate whether or not he was intentionally poisoned. Another man recounts how as a child he almost died from eating mushrooms his mother had picked: "Obviously my mother didn't mean to kill us. It's difficult to decide if this case was accidental or intentional." When the guerrillas questioned the woman who cooked the food, she admitted that her son was in the Rhodesian police, and that he had given her a packet of dried, poisonous mushrooms, which she saved to cook for guerrillas.[35]

These accounts raise two questions. First, who knew which mushrooms were poisonous and which were not? There were African herbalists in the Rhodesian Army; healers repeatedly told me that these were the men who identified noxious mushrooms and made poisons for food. All poisons have antidotes, I was told: "There is nothing that is done by someone that cannot be cured." Thus, when guerrillas died, one medium insisted, it was not because poisons were so lethal but because healers were away from their home areas and did not know which plants and herbs could reverse the effects of a poison. Second—and much harder to answer with any certainty—is who administered the poison? Most of the men and women I spoke to in 1995 and 1997 thought that Rhodesians and their agents asked villagers to poison guerrillas' food, but they also claimed that guerrillas sometimes poisoned each other: "a comrade would poison another to get his post" or to get rid of a political enemy. Some said that guerrillas, and the mediums who guided them, were responsible for most food poisonings: this was one of the ways ZIPRA and ZANLA fought each other. Others said it was the food Rhodesians provided guerrillas.[36] In a small area of Gutu South, for example, eleven of thirty-two dead guerrillas brought from Mozambique for reburial died from poisoned food.[37] Were these eleven guerrillas killed by Z Desk, or an ambitious comrade, or a witch?

How do questions of mushrooms, intent, and healers' knowledge of local flora fit with the mealie (corn)meal "doctored" by "Sam Roberts"? Of all possible foodstuffs, why was maize meal, a staple of rural African diets, selected for poison? Yes, Rhodesians could be sure guerrillas would eat it, but so would everyone else. How could Rhodesians be sure that weaponizing a staple starch would not harm civilians and Africans loyal to the regime? Were there no more cosmopolitan foods that guerrillas might prefer? Guerrillas certainly thought so. Guerrilla patrols carried canned meats whenever they could. ZANLA reported that some cans of "Leox" (Liebig's) contained poisons; sometimes these were dropped from airplanes on areas where guerrillas were sighted, sometimes they were put on sale in shops. ZANLA had evidence this was a Rhodesian plot not just against guerrillas but against all Africans: in 1978 "anti-poisons" were withdrawn from hospitals and clinics in Manicaland in Eastern Zimbabwe.[38]

Rhodesian accounts of poisoning did offer African guerrillas more choices than mealies, however "low tech" McGuiness admitted his operation was. Warfarin was mixed with maize meal, and thallium was injected into canned meats with a "micro-needle." Sometimes poisons were ground into powder and mixed with processed meat and repacked in new tins, and sometimes cigarette tips were poisoned with a variety of insecticides—all by national servicemen.[39] I have my doubts about this. I have been told that Rhodesian mothers complained about the stripteases and pornographic films shown in depot.[40] Did no mother or father write to protest their sons' handling poisons? Besides, how well did any of this work? How long did it take to poison meat in cans? Wouldn't it be simpler to make a hole in the can and let bacteria contaminate the contents? Re-tinning is possible with the right equipment at the right heat, but given the consideration for African men's bowel movements, how many poisoned tins could be produced in a week to be worth the effort? How many guerrilla deaths resulted from how many man-hours of work with microneedles and pressure cookers?

Not many. Ed Bird was Special Branch in Beitbridge, Southern Matabeland, beginning in 1976. He had long suspected that a local grocery and mine were supplying food to guerrillas "for protection": the grocery van left food at the mine, which was then handed over to a ZANLA detachment. When Bird learned of McGuiness's operation at Bindura, he realized he had a way to deliver poisoned items to guerrillas without arousing their suspicion. Bird requested a slow-acting poison, which Henry Wolhunter—who later provided much of the documentation of Z Desk to Peter Stiff—delivered. There were Dr Strong 500 capsules, said to increase sexual potency, "which terrorists craved," tins of bully beef, and sachets of Eno's Liver Salts, a favored cure for hangovers, and various items of clothes tainted with a heavy metal poison as well as untainted colas, bread, and cigarettes. Bird's plan was to truck these to meet the grocery van on its rounds. The African Special Branch who posed as the driver explained that he was a guerrilla who had just stolen these goods, which should be delivered to the guerrillas camped nearby. He himself was needed elsewhere. The goods were delivered to twelve guerrillas, including the detachment commander, who celebrated their good fortune at once. In a few hours three guerrillas became violently ill and died. The detachment commander clearly understood they had been poisoned: he shepherded his men back to their camp, where they purged themselves with saltwater to induce vomiting. Two of the village women who stayed in the camp died in the night; by morning, four guerrillas and two women had died. This did not cause a rift between the villagers and guerrillas, however. On the contrary, the surviving guerrillas and villagers attacked the drivers of the next grocery van when it next came and forced them to eat the remaining food. They did not die, and after a few hours they were bayoneted. One survived to tell the story.[41]

It was indeed a good story, and it may have been told many times before it appeared in print. But as wartime strategy, at best it suggests a local Special Branch unsupervised with fungible budgets. At worst, it was a waste of time and resources. As counterinsurgency it was a dismal failure: instead of the success of a few clever men against many guerrillas, this was the deployment of many resources and man-hours to kill four guerrillas and two camp followers.

Did guerrillas anticipate being poisoned? Clearly they did, if they knew how to make a purge from ingredients at hand while on patrol in the countryside. Many commanders had teenage mujibas taste their food before they themselves would eat it. New recruits to ZANLA camps in Mozambique in 1976 were stripped naked; their clothes were taken away, and they were forced to jump for perhaps five hundred meters to dislodge any concealed packets of poison they carried.[42] Beyond the camps, and on patrol in Rhodesia, did guerrillas suspect poisoning? Rumors of poisoned food are not simply wartime rumors but are narratives that cause comrades and civilians alike to avoid places and people.[43] Poisoned tinned meats or adulterated alcohol might well kill, but they might also lead guerrillas to avoid those brands and the merchants who sold them.

Poison Pills

Pills are a dangerous delivery system for poisons. On the one hand, it is easy enough to contaminate any medicine that is in tablet form. On the other, it is almost impossible to be sure that only guerrillas will take the doctored aspirin or iron supplement. Or if guerrillas did take the tainted tablets, how many would they need to take to get sick? Poisoning the right guerrillas at the right time took considerable effort and involved at least two branches of the security forces. John Cronin took his men to the ZANLA infirmary a few hours after the Rhodesian Army raid on Chimoio in 1977. The noise of the raid gave them headaches. He found new boxes of aspirin, everyone took a few, only to be told by angry Special Branch that the room should have been cordoned off. Some of the pills contained a fast-acting poison as it was thought that ZANLA would return in a few days to take whatever medical supplies were left. Special Branch "poisoned random samples" of painkillers and put them back in their boxes.[44] The same year a pathologist in a Bulawayo hospital blamed thallium poisoning on contaminated Jection pills, a popular laxative made locally.[45] If a laxative was popular, would guerrillas and their supporters even be a plurality of its users? Besides, if thallium was flushed from the body with every movement of African bowels, was a laxative the best pill to use as a poison?

For all the anecdotes, the most effective poisoning of pills was in the form of medical supplies. However well-funded and well-armed ZANLA was after 1978, the number of recruits increased dramatically; they were often sent into Rhodesia with very little training. ZIPRA called them "seven-day wonders." Ian Linden described the "poorly trained, under-equipped" youth who fought in the rural areas in mid-1978 as "nervous wrecks." When they came to sympathetic mission stations, they demanded tranquilizers from the dispensary, or drink, before they asked for food.[46] Africans who worked in chemists' shops or laboratories were particularly vulnerable: there were constant demands for drugs or syringes, and many of the men so employed sent their families to the capital. They themselves were routinely searched by security forces for extra bottles of pills.[47] In interrogation, captured guerrillas talked constantly about the shortage of medicines. Among the contaminated items in one of the lists Wolhunter gave Peter Stiff were medical supplies, including three bottles of arsenic, thirty-two bottles of penicillin, one bottle of chloroquine, two of vitamin B, and one of milk of magnesia. The "results" were seventy-nine "confirmed" guerrilla dead.[48] Such a list of medications could be used as easily for healing as for harming; the straight line linking a list of products to confirmed guerrilla deaths is hard to credit. Indeed, it was the curative properties of these medicines that generated the most detailed stories. In April 1978, a white farmer informed Ed Bird of guerrillas based in the area. No one knew their exact location, so military action was not feasible, but the comrades had compromised the farm foreman who provided food and medical supplies for them. Bird hatched a plan to attack the guerrillas: the foreman would supply goods prepared by Special Branch, including a two-hundred-pound sack of mealie meal that was untouched. Knowing the rumors in the district, Bird assumed that guerrillas would avoid the mealie meal and not question the contents of a sealed container of medical products, which contained patent medicines treated with thallium. Indeed, after a weekend of drinking beer, thirty hungover guerrillas helped themselves to vitamins, Eno's Liver Salts, and Dr Strong 500 capsules. Within a few days, the men sickened and many died. Bird believed this was because they continued to treat themselves with the tainted medicine that made them sick in the first place.[49]

Poisoned Clothes

Anyone could poison food, but poisoning clothes seems to have captured the imagination of guerrillas, scholars, and Rhodesian authors with particular force. The journalists who flocked to Zimbabwe in April 1980 were baffled by guerrillas' stories of poisoned uniforms. In 1997 I was repeatedly told that more guerrillas died from wearing poisoned clothes than from eating poisoned food.[50] There was something ingenious and mendacious about poisoning clothing. As counterinsurgency, it was an operation that required considerable organization and means of distribution. Perhaps because of the effort it required, many guerrillas considered poisoned clothes the most effective of Rhodesia's counterinsurgency tactics.[51] Over the years I have been told the number of guerrillas killed by poisoned uniforms was anywhere from a few hundred to thousands. ZANLA's official list of war dead attributes only sixty-nine deaths to poisoned clothes; I have been told the number of ZIPRA fatalities was in the thousands. However many or few guerrilla deaths were due to poisoned uniforms, there was a chronic stomach ailment among war veterans attributed to having worn poisoned uniforms.[52] The stomach ailment raises another question, however: Were poisoned uniforms lethal or just unhealthy?

Did poisoning uniforms work as well as Ken Flower said it did? An officer in Rhodesian military intelligence officer told me there were no poisoned uniforms, but there had been a plan to use poisoned underwear against guerrillas. The poison was absorbed quickly and thus was very effective, but the underwear did not always get to guerrillas. Shopkeepers sold it to whomever wanted to buy it; the plan ended up killing the wrong people.[53] Henrik Ellert told a similar story, in which poisoned clothes operations were abruptly stopped in early 1978 because of reports of widespread civilian deaths with the symptoms of poisoned clothes. A secret inquiry soon discovered that the shopkeepers and agents on whom Special Branch relied to make sure the poisoned garments went to guerrillas and guerrillas alone not only grossly exaggerated guerrillas' demand for certain items but often had no relationships with guerrillas and simply took advantage of the opportunity to sell clothes they had not purchased. No one was sure if the shopkeepers knew the clothing was poisoned, but the number of civilian deaths so outraged the police commissioner that Special Branch was ordered to abandon the program.[54]

Once again, we see evidence so diverse that it requires examination. Do the different versions prove the secrecy of Z Desk or do they show that so little was known about the program that all descriptions were anecdotal and partial? Or were there many such programs, bootstrap operations that were sinecures for chemists who could not export their new pesticides? Or are these social and literary constructions, well-known stories told by guerrillas and white soldiers alike as first-person narratives? Take Taffy Brice. In a book by Peter Stiff that has been reprinted three times, Brice takes credit for high-profile assassinations in both ZANLA and ZIPRA. He was skilled at planting bombs, in cars and in the mail. Whatever my doubts about Brice's talents, he was storied. In retirement in Britain he was interviewed for a popular book on chemical warfare published in 1999. He showed off his expertise on poisons: his favorite was ricin, which took three days to be fatal. In that respect it was like thallium, which he claimed had to be taken orally. (He did not mention the frequency of bowel movements.) He regaled his interviewer with the story of his plan to assassinate Robert Mugabe in London during the constitutional talks of 1979. Although the assassination was called off at the last minute, it forms the conclusion of Peter Stiff's accounts of Brice's expertise with explosives. In the book first published in 1985, Brice placed a Claymore land mine in a briefcase. He knew where he would place it and chose the briefcase with care. The detonator required ball bearings, and he explained to the clerk that he needed dozens of packets for an "electronic game" he was making. Years later, when he was being interviewed in London, he described how he planned to kill Mugabe with a ricin-tipped bullet. To make sure the ricin stayed in Mugabe's body long enough for it to be lethal, he modified the head of the bullet so it would explode in the body. It is not clear why he thought the bullet alone was not enough.[55]

Why do these two modes of called-off assassination attempts matter? To return to the Equiano test, are two modes of assassination the same as two birthplaces? Is Brice a more or less accomplished assassin because he told two stories? It is hard to credit a political reason for his telling a new story: Mugabe was alive and in power in 1985 and in 1999. But in the manner of Equiano scholarship, what do these two stories, taken together, suggest? In the 1985 book, poisons were not Brice's weapon of choice. They were lethal and interesting to learn about, but they were no substitute for a well-placed bomb. In 1999 he claimed to have used poisons for what would have been the highest-profile assassination of them all. Does this reveal another issue altogether, that chemical weapons are a recent addition to Rhodesian war stories, an awful boast that describes the postwar nation but not the war-torn one?

Poisoned bullets seemed to be postwar, but poisoned clothing was a wartime complaint. There are the anecdotal accounts I discussed earlier; some are backed by science, some by military authorities, but most tell a similar story, of chemists and Special Branch preparing poisons and getting them into clothes, of convoluted ways of getting them onto guerrilla bodies, of guerrillas dying in pain and terror. There was the description favored by South Africa's Project Coast, that perhaps a dozen times during 1977, twenty-five-gallon tins of "a foul smelling liquid" were delivered to McGuiness at Bindura. The chemicals were then poured onto large sheets of tin and dried in the sun. Once dried, the chemicals were odorless. The flakes were pounded into a powder using a mortar and pestle. The powder was brushed onto clothes or mixed with processed meats. Other policemen told Cross that clothing was dipped in a solution of parathion and then dried. Twenty-five hundred pairs of contaminated underwear and an equal number of T-shirts were processed and distributed to the field.[56] How many guerrillas had to die for the security forces to recoup the investment of time and energy of pulverizing three hundred gallons of poison and the cost of twenty-five hundred pairs of underwear? When John Cronin happened upon stacks of shirts and trousers in the Special Branch compound in Mount Darwin, he was told they had "crystalized pesticides" sewn into their linings. Because there were store owners working for Rhodesia who would "make sure the right people get these things," these would cause guerrillas to die, bleeding from every orifice, in a few days.[57] Who did the sewing?

Poisoned clothes and their delivery worked like clockwork, according to Peter Stiff and his authors. "Sam Roberts" received several hundred pairs of underwear and T-shirts from Special Branch and soaked them in parathion. These were then sent to farm stores that were thought to be future guerrilla targets. The owners were told not to sell these clothes but to put them on high shelves. When these stores were raided, guerrilla took the clothes and burned the building, so it worked perfectly: guerrillas died from poisoning and civilians were spared.[58] A cattle rancher learned that his farmworkers were collaborating with guerrillas. He waited until the guerrillas approached him, as Special Branch said they would. They told him the district was a transit point for guerrillas moving north, and they needed money for food and clothes. The rancher, following Special Branch, suggested that he provide food and clothes to the guerrillas, which would save them time and money. The guerrillas agreed. The clothes were contaminated, but by the time the poison in the new denims had worked its way into the bloodstream, there was no treatment available. Special Branch assumed the men died a slow and painful death. After a few months, the guerrillas ceased contact with the rancher. Special Branch did not seem overly curious as to why: perhaps they moved on, or succumbed to the poisons themselves.[59]

Did guerrillas really not know what was making them so sick? Did they not think that clothes could contain poisons? Pesticide poisoning was a persistent occupational health problem among farmworkers in Rhodesia well before the 1970s: men who carried spraying equipment on their backs and those who handled and distributed pesticides were at the greatest risk.[60] Farmworkers knew the symptoms of exposure to organophosphates; it is likely that others had heard of them as well. Were any guerrillas surprised to learn that clothes might contain poisons? Did they ask if sudden, painful deaths might be due to poisoned clothes and not Rhodesian counterinsurgents or witches? Did guerrillas not wash the clothes that might be the source of affliction? For all the investigation on the frequency of African bowel movements, Rhodesian security forces seemed unconcerned about how often Africans washed their clothes. There were stories that claimed guerrillas, or the local women in their camps, did not wash their clothes at all. Unlikely as these stories were, taken together they imagined Africans' naive greed that made even seasoned guerrillas impatient for new clothes and thus vulnerable to this particular chemical weapon: they took whatever clothes were free and did not wash them even when they caused pain or irritation. A former BSAP told Glen Cross that he had heard of a "'double hit,'" in which a patrol returning to Mozambique had been supplied with poisoned clothing. When they arrived at their base camp, "the older hands pulled rank and took the clothing to wear themselves" without even bothering to have someone wash them.[61] A Canadian doctor working in Chiweshe District in 1978 saw a sudden influx of patients with organophosphate poisoning. The only thing they had in common was putting on the underwear they found in plastic bags in the hills. Although they washed these items, one woman "was killed by a bra, a man by a pair of shorts." The doctor knew that farmworkers in the district often mixed pesticides with their bare hands and that their clothing often became contaminated, but he had never seen symptoms so severe.[62] These accounts do not describe vermin, but pets. There's something homey and trusting here, beyond the intimacy of undergarments; the descriptions are like those of the greedy dogs that don't know when to stop eating, the innocent creatures that did not fear caches of clothing left on hillsides in plastic bags during a war.[63]

There's another question: Did every African believe that every item of poisoned clothing was an act of counterinsurgency, or came from Rhodesian sources? One wartime study indicates that clothing poisoned with pesticides was sometimes sold by itinerant vendors; many of the men who became sickest were those who had suffered organophosphate poisoning earlier, probably as farmworkers. Organophosphates, however absorbed and for whatever reason, remain in the body long after initial exposure. New exposure—either from new clothes drenched in insecticide or from old clothes that were never fully cleansed of insecticide—can bring the symptoms back rapidly.[64] Farmworkers who had been previously exposed to parathion were especially susceptible to relapses if they came into contact with the substance; they exhibited all the symptoms of being poisoned. All this raises still another question: Did the fatal clothing came from Rhodesian intelligence, pilfering farmworkers, itinerant traders, or all of these?

Africans spoke of more imaginative poisonings than were possible with shirts and underwear. The men and women I spoke to in 1995 knew about poisoned uniforms, but they wanted to tell me about poisoned gum boots. White soldiers gave gum boots to comrades; these had a poisonous powder in them—on the inside, not the outside. Comrades would first develop foot sores and were unable to walk; I was told that many eventually died. Others said the powder simply immobilized men, causing sores on their feet that made it necessary for them to sit without walking for weeks. Although Rhodesians used the poison, the powder was an African medicine, and anyone afflicted by it could be cured by a healer who knew which herbs to use.[65]

Anthrax and "a Plastic Bag Full of Cholera"

The largest recorded outbreak of anthrax in humans occurred between November 1978 and October 1980 in Zimbabwe. There were almost 11,000 human cases, 182 human deaths, and perhaps 10,000 cattle deaths. The onset of the disease was rapid: there had been 2 reported cases of anthrax in all of Rhodesia in 1978, and 4,002 in 1979. More important perhaps was that the epidemic spread over a larger area than most anthrax epidemics do, and lasted longer as well.[66] All this has led many medical authorities to maintain that this anthrax epidemic was the result of Rhodesian biological warfare. Whether or not this particular disease was part of Rhodesia's wartime arsenal, it was part of its wartime political imagination, so it is possible to look at anthrax in scientific writing, white writing, and mediums' accounts.

Meryl Nass, an American physician working in Zimbabwe in the late 1980s, believed the epidemic was deliberate. She arrived at this conclusion through a process of elimination—and after reading Ellert's *Rhodesian Front War*. Rhodesia had one of the world's lowest anthrax rates in the 1960s, so the precipitous increase in the number of human and animal cases aroused suspicion. Anthrax spreads by cattle eating spores, not through contact with insects or ticks, which do not transmit enough blood to spread the disease. Thus, the epidemic could not be blamed on guerrillas' antidipping campaigns or the breakdown of veterinary services during the war, although African farmers may have been unwilling to ask government veterinarians to treat their sick cattle. Humans cannot contract anthrax from butchering or eating infected cattle. Moreover, there was no clear-cut explanation for why the epidemic occurred where it did. The data on the spread of anthrax, mainly from research conducted in the United States, indicated that the disease might take on epizootic proportions in areas with a history of anthrax outbreaks, but areas with no history of anthrax tended to have only sporadic and mild epidemics of the disease. All of this, Nass argued, indicated that anthrax was a Rhodesian biological weapon. The United States, England, and Japan had weaponized anthrax during World War II; it could have been available to Rhodesian scientists at any time, and it could have been deployed as part of the increased militarization of the war in 1979. The intensification of the war meant the increased immiseration of local populations and the evisceration of medical and veterinary services available to that population.[67] This, Glenn Cross wrote, led to the anthrax epidemic; it was not a deliberate act by Rhodesian forces.[68]

Nass wrote before Rhodesian tell-all memoirs told all. In one such memoir Jim Parker provided less than detailed accounts of spreading anthrax and cholera. He seems to have heard of Nass's writings, at least, but he did not address her medical reasoning. A doctor—whom McGuiness disparaged as a gynecologist without the training to weaponize anthrax successfully—based at the Selous Scouts fort told Parker that the Selous Scouts and the SAS had "deployed anthrax spores" to attack African-owned cattle in Matabeleland in 1979. This was to limit the food that an invading ZIPRA army could forage. According to Parker, these spores were for a strain of anthrax that was not contagious to humans, unless they ate the meat of infected cattle; then they would sicken and die. Cattle on white-owned farms were not at risk from these spores because white farmers had access to veterinary services. The disease spread through the province—and to Africans—because of stock theft, the unregulated movement of stolen cattle, and the sale and consumption of contaminated meat.[69] Why would Parker make these claims about anthrax? Did he really believe Rhodesian biological weapons harmed only Africans and their cattle? Did he actually believe that cattle on white-owned farms would not contract anthrax? It is possible that biological weapons were deployed with mediocre intelligence and limited forethought. It is also possible that Parker was writing for another audience altogether, one that wanted to read about the invincibility of white Rhodesia, the "won-every-battle mantra" told as a story about cattle and their diseases.

The former guerrillas in western Zimbabwe interviewed by Jocelyn Alexander, JoAnn McGregor, and Terence Ranger firmly believed Rhodesia used biological weapons but may have overestimated the subtlety of the security forces. Many Africans recalled seeing airplanes drop "white powder" on pastures and cleared land; they believed this caused anthrax and other diseases. A few people said they saw Rhodesian soldiers sprinkle "small pills" into dams; these "killed the fish and poisoned cattle, which then became bearers of anthrax." Others thought the disease was spread by ticks, now out of control because African cattle were not dipped, or resulted from the pollution caused by gunfire and smoke. The idea that anthrax was spread through the pollution of wartime is not implausible; long-dormant anthrax spores may well have been loosened from the earth by land mine explosions. Guerrilla commanders had more sophisticated ideas about Rhodesian counterinsurgency, however. Several thought that cattle on white-owned, commercial farms had been deliberately infected with anthrax, so that if the cattle were stolen by guerrillas the disease would spread to Africans. One man imagined what Rhodesians imagined about guerrillas: "They suspected we could kill the animals and give the meat to freedom fighters," so they infected the cattle with anthrax, in order to give the disease to guerrillas.[70]

Parker dismissed rumors that Ndebele ZIPRA had poisoned cattle. He quoted a BSAC administrator from 1896 as proof: Ndebele were pastoralists who measured prestige and wealth in cattle. They would have done nothing to harm cattle.[71] In 1979 did white men love their cattle any less than Ndebele did? Were the young men who learned to track from Africans, on the farms of their childhood or as police or in the game department, really willing to risk the lives of livestock? I have been told that no white youth brought up on a farm, or in the presence of someone who was, would ever poison a well.⁷² African mediums, however, had no such scruples. The spirit mediums I spoke to in 1997 did not have any doubts about what, and who, caused anthrax during the war: they did. Mediums brought anthrax as a punishment after guerrillas had failed to perform the proper rituals—or any rituals at all—after they asked mediums for their support. The disease was a punishment for certain districts. I asked how this was possible given the wide area affected by anthrax. "Mediums don't need to be near someone to cure them or to harm them," I was told. Different mediums have different powers; "there are grades of mediums like grades of tobacco," was the explanation. During the war mediums gave comrades warnings about what they should do; "guerillas were warned," one medium said. I asked if the anthrax the mediums brought was to kill people or cattle. "Cattle," one medium said, "but some greedy people ate these cattle and they got anthrax and they died."⁷³

Poisoning water was another issue altogether, but not always a credible one. Jim Parker described the various attempts by security forces to limit guerrillas' access to water during the drought of 1975–76. Soldiers poisoned water pans near the Mozambique border in the southeast of the country. They used an organophosphate (Supermix DFF) so powerful it would kill animals and humans. It also had a terrible smell, so soldiers did not think anyone would drink it, but then, its purpose was not to kill guerrillas entering the country, but to limit their access to water so that their routes and itineraries would be limited. To this end internal affairs sabotaged boreholes that guerrilla gangs had previously used. The watering holes necessary for the local population were left untouched; security forces patrolled these watering holes "regularly" so as to ambush any guerrillas who might use them. When the drought broke in 1976, there was enough standing water in the pans that guerrillas had a choice of routes into Rhodesia.⁷⁴

Cholera raises another set of questions. It is a bacterial infection caused by contaminated water; it is a disease of social dislocation, of refugee camps and makeshift fortifications. If any biological weapon seems beside the point, it is cholera. Yet Rhodesians claimed they spread the disease by contaminating water supplies. These accounts involve more stories of Africans' bowels and their difficulty keeping imported technologies clean and working, both critical issues in this chapter. Parker describes a Selous Scouts team that infiltrated Mozambique just over the border with Rhodesia in order to empty "several phials" of cholera bacteria into the water tank at Malverna, which supplied the FRELIMO garrison there. There had been a very sophisticated water-pumping system in place under the Portuguese, but FRELIMO had failed to maintain it, he wrote. Cholera "involves the entire bowel": its symptoms are profuse diarrhea, vomiting, muscle cramps, and dehydration. It kills rapidly. It spread rapidly wherever there was "poor hygiene control," and infected soldiers spread the disease to rural areas.[75] Selous Scouts or SAS teams introduced cholera bacteria into water supplies on both sides of the Rhodesia-Mozambique border, sometimes making RLI patrols sick. One FRELIMO garrison that housed ZANLA personnel reported two hundred deaths from contaminated water.[76] But there were rivers near the border from which no cases of cholera were reported, despite the best efforts of the Rhodesian Army. This was later explained by the habits of guerrilla hygiene: the men who bathed there did not swallow enough water to become sick. A Rhodesian operative told an American investigator that he had taken "a plastic bag full of cholera" to poison the westernmost watering hole in Mozambique, which would be ZANLA's last staging area before entering Rhodesia. The operative stabbed the bag with a knife and then tossed it and the knife into the water. "Hundreds" of people and animals died from cholera, although guerrillas eventually learned to avoid this watering hole.[77]

Ian Martinez was a CIA analyst who later practiced law. It is not clear how he came to write about Rhodesia's chemical and biological weapons program or how he found the Rhodesian operatives who insisted on anonymity before being quoted, but he was more concerned with the question of redress than most authors who have written about biological weapons. He suggested a course of action familiar to many Rhodesian soldiers and their editors, the lawsuit. He had been told that ZIPRA poisoned ZANLA and vice versa, which meant white Zimbabweans could no longer be blamed for wartime atrocities. Martinez believed that the fact that there had been no official inquiry and no truth commission into these poisonings proved that these were the actions of guerrillas, not desperate whites. This did not mean that war veterans and ordinary Zimbabweans should not be compensated for sickness and death; they just had to look to other countries and bodies for legal solutions to crimes committed against them. They could do this by using another country as a legal forum. He provided the names of the laws with which such suits could be joined.[78]

Lawsuits or not, Z Desk or not, chemical and biological weapons were stories told in exact numbers. Whether 25 gallons and 325 pairs of underwear and 77 dead or 7 dead or 11 dead—it wasn't as many as the thousands Flower boasted about, but it gave a degree of scientific clarity to stories, many of which seem to have been told in barrooms and officers' clubs years before they appeared in print. These numbers do not make accounts of chemical weapons any more or less true, nor do they make the weapons any more or less efficient, but they were offered as details that proved men had been there—in the laboratory if not the battlefield—and that their recollections carried weight (see chapter 2). If they appropriated the work of mediums and witches, so be it: more often than not they were less interested in African deaths than they were in seeking to reinforce ideas about African hygiene and habits. Numbers became increasingly important in the last years of this war, as chapter 9 will argue: counterinsurgency was best lauded in the number of kills and the matériel required to reach those.

8 "WILL TRAVEL WORLDWIDE. YOU PAY EXPENSES"

Foreign Soldiers in the Rhodesian Army

If there is a tension in this book between the historian of the war and the reader of wartime writing, it is most pronounced in this chapter, which begins with a frame and a question. The frame, of course, is the war. Whenever it began—1967, or 1968, or 1973—hardly matters. By the early 1970s, especially after the failed attempts to settle the conflict, there was a sense in and out of the country that however romantic and brave the heirs of the pioneers were, they were left alone to suffer an inevitable defeat.[1] It was a war in a specific place of a specific people, but not so many people that when the war intensified it could be fought without massive conscription and onerous reserve duties. The war brought questions of Rhodesia's white population to the fore in new and powerful ways: the question of how the country could generate the manpower with which to go to war was framed by that of who would fight for Rhodesia.

The question is about nationality. Who was Rhodesian and who was a foreigner were not straightforward questions. Most of the relatively few white Rhodesians left their options open; many had taken dual or even triple citizenship in federal times. After UDI and the illegal status of Rhodesia, being Rhodesian was a matter of residence, whatever passport someone carried and whatever passport he or she gave customs officials in Europe or North America. For many Britons or men and women from former colonies and the white Commonwealth and South Africa, Rhodesia was port of call, a place called home they were prepared to leave if need be. Perhaps one of the best examples is Major John Anderson, who was born in South Africa of British parents. He had served in the British Army and was sent to Southern Rhodesia to train troops there during World War II, after which he returned to Britain. In 1957 Anderson returned to Southern Rhodesia to join the army of the Central African Federation; when the federation dissolved, he became chief of staff of the army in Southern Rhodesia. In 1965 he was forced to resign after stating his opposition to Rhodesian independence. Whether he was a British citizen, a Rhodesian citizen, or a South African citizen (or some combination of the three) hardly matters. What does matter is that he had a home in Britain to which he returned after he resigned.[2] There were many like him, men and women whose belonging was unsettled before they came to Central Africa; men and women who could change from being Rhodesian or British or South African at a moment's notice. As the war in Rhodesia went on, the reverse became true. Karl Greenberg was born in Britain but brought up in Rhodesia. He went to London when he graduated from high school in 1976. He hated it and applied to the BSAP, knowing that it paid the passage of British recruits. The BSAP, however, wrote back telling him he had attested when he was sixteen and would be considered a deserter if he did not return at once. Greenberg was baffled: he left Rhodesia a British citizen, but he had to return to Rhodesia to join its police.[3]

Anderson's and Greenberg's were only two of the many complicated lives and itineraries that problematized what "foreign" meant in 1960s and 1970s Rhodesia. There was a relatively large Greek population that came in the late 1920s; many retained Greek nationality. There were four thousand Afrikaaners, few of whom carried South Africa passports. None of this mattered until Rhodesia became a republic in 1970 and the difference between citizen and resident became concrete, but it begs another question: Were second-generation Greek residents of Rhodesia Greek or Rhodesian? Before 1965, Rhodesian statisticians divided and subdivided the white population. Who was born in the country, who was born in the United Kingdom or in South Africa, were all categorized and counted. There were debates about Sephardic Jews from the Isle of Rhodes, a group that constituted the largest Jewish population until after World War II: Were they to be counted as Jews or Greeks? After 1965 there was a shift against disaggregating the white population. Until Rhodesia became a republic in 1970, national service was based on residence, not citizenship.[4] White residents, whatever passports they carried, were added to the number of white people in the country. Citizens of white Commonwealth countries and South Africa were not easily thought of as foreign because they shared ties of empire and history and the fantasy that they had subdued native races. There is a fictional character who, like the author, was born in Kenya, lived in Australia, and came to fight for Rhodesia. Why did he come to fight African nationalists? "My parents were killed by Mau Mau when I was a kid. It has nothing to do with politics. It's a personal thing."[5] It was Americans in the Rhodesian forces who everyone found truly foreign: they had no personal and certainly no historical reason to be there.

How, then, do I study the place of foreign soldiers in this war? None of the journalists I quote often in this book had more than a passing interest in foreign soldiers fighting for Rhodesia. Concerns about Americans fighting for Rhodesia, and the meaning thereof, fell to two distinct venues: authors with an almost reflexive support for liberation movements in Southern Africa, and authors who were against such movements, especially if the suppression of those movements was one in which white American youths could participate. The best known of Rhodesia's authorial supporters were *Soldier of Fortune* magazine and the novels of Robin Moore, albeit not his best-known novels, *The French Connection* and *The Green Berets*. In 1976 Moore abandoned the novel he was working on because General William Yarborough—the model for the hero of *The Green Berets*—suggested he write about Rhodesia. He thought this would be more exciting than his current book project and "easy to plot."[6] *Soldier of Fortune* and Moore's writings stand in stark contrast to most of the wartime writings—both academic and journalistic—of the 1970s and 1980s, which were not without a certain predictability: the US government approved or even supported American soldiers fighting for Rhodesia. *Soldier of Fortune* and Moore insisted the opposite was true. All these accounts, as well as archives and my field notes, constitute the sources for this chapter.

Soldiers without Borders

Given my two frames, what would constitute a mercenary in Rhodesia in the 1970s? For Rhodesian-born soldiers, it was anyone who came from another country to fight. Angus Shaw was scathing, writing that if these men "went around looking for other peoples' nasty little wars to fight in," they were the same as mercenaries. "It wasn't their war." Rhodesian-born Jake Harper-Ronald, who left the British Army to return to Rhodesia to join the SAS, thought otherwise; they had "come along for the ride."[7] Both followed the canonical legal and anecdotal definition of mercenaries, which has remained fairly constant for centuries: the mercenary is foreign; he did not belong to the place for which he fought. Until the end of the eighteenth century, most states and warring entities used mercenary forces; it was only after the French Revolution that citizen armies became the norm in Europe, but even then, the French Foreign Legion was founded in 1831 to allow foreigners in the French military. Armies were schools for the nation; they turned men into citizens. Citizen armies weren't necessarily better armies than mercenary ones, but they demonstrated the authority of the state over its citizens. They also gave those armies the moral authority of the nation. Mercenaries were not of much interest until the era of decolonization and its aftermath, when they were seen as the opposite of national armies, men without patriotism, loyalty, or discipline. The epitome of such mercenaries was the force raised by Col. Mike Hoare—whom we will meet again—in the Congo in 1960 and 1964: literally hired guns, thugs paid to do a violent job. Hoare was his own best publicist, demonstrating how many publications he could eke out of several marginally successful military assignments. The 1960s were the era of African independence: what may have been most important about mercenaries was not their pathology but their mission. In Congo and in Biafra mercenaries were white men hired to fight African separatism. Mercenaries opposed some idealized will of the people and certainly the idea of a unified nation-state. Thirty and forty years later, mercenaries have been rehabilitated by the private contractors—Sandline, Executive Outcomes, Blackwater—deployed starting in the 1990s. Not only was their use increasingly widespread, but they were reckoned to be considerably more successful than 1960s mercenaries were; they supported states, not secessionist regimes. The hiring of these companies, however, suggests another kind of instability for the states that employ them, that these are governments that are unable both to monopolize violence and to protect their citizens within their borders.[8] All of this, however, presupposes an uncontested notion of a state. What about states that are contested, such as Rhodesia, or imagined, such as the nations that armies of national liberation struggle for?

None of this explains why anyone would find being a mercenary a good idea, or why it might be worthwhile to go "along for the ride." Mercenaries of the postcolonial era might be desperate characters, but they could think of themselves as *Soldier of Fortune* imagined its readers: "Professional adventurers." Mercenaries were perfect antiheroes, men who were willing to risk their lives for causes advertised in the personal columns of newspapers.[9] Or so they imagined. John Early was a graduate student in 1975 when he was recruited to fight with Holden Roberto's FNLA in Angola. He never learned the name of anyone who contacted him or how they got his number: there were phone calls and money orders in the mail and a polygraph administered by a Mr. Smith and a Mr. Jones. Nevertheless, Early went to Kinshasa. Only then did he find the operation risky and amateurish, so he flew to Johannesburg and contacted a friend in the Rhodesian forces.[10] Peter McAleese, former SAS, worked on an oil rig; he had been jailed several times for domestic violence. He began his circuitous path to Rhodesia after answering an advertisement in the *Evening Standard* in 1975. He signed a contract to fight with the FNLA, but not before he attended a recruitment meeting in which he found the organizer self-important and the other men who answered the ad ridiculous: some claimed to be Mossad or CIA, another boasted that had had flown gliders into Dien Bien Phu but had the year of the battle wrong, and an eighteen-year-old Briton insisted he had fought with FRELIMO against the Portuguese.[11] McAleese did not exaggerate. In 1975 the CIA was horrified to learn that the British recruiters it had hired to find mercenaries for the FNLA supplied them with more than one hundred men, few of whom had any military experience. Two were street sweepers. A half-dozen Americans joined these mercenaries in Kinshasa, including grandstanding publicity seekers.[12] Were good mercenaries or foreign soldiers so hard to find in the first years after the war in Vietnam, or had the art of mercenary recruitment lost some of its professionalism? Richard Woodley answered ads for mercenaries from *Soldier of Fortune* and found that most of them were scams, as eager—and as able—to sell young adventurers certificates of service as they were to send them to Angola.[13]

Why would foreign men come and enlist in the Rhodesian Army? Many of the men who came in the late 1960s left soon after. It is impossible to make generalizations about why they left, but a few complained to their fellows that there wasn't enough war going on. By the mid-1970s there was enough of a war for several foreign servicemen. Mike Borlace had been about to sign on to the sultan of Oman's air force when casual conversation in a London pub made him interested in the Rhodesian Air Force. He had heard good things about the country from pilots who trained there during World War II.[14] John Alan Coey resigned from the US Marine Corps to go and fight for Rhodesia in 1972. He saw his mission as a Christian one, fighting communism and internationalism as was no longer possible to do in the United States: this was as important as converting Africans. He never found Rhodesia to be the anticommunist beacon he had hoped for—"The University of Rhodesia is no better than Ohio State University in third-rate liberal and Marxist teaching"—but he decided to stay in the hopes that he could someday right the situation.[15] He was killed in action in 1975, trying to save others.¹⁶ John Cronin loved the Marine Corps, but peacetime maneuvers bored him. He went to Rhodesia in August 1976, eager to enlist.¹⁷ And there was Bob MacKenzie, a Vietnam veteran and arguably the only US soldier with a genuine, if tenuous, CIA tie: his father-in-law had been the acting deputy director of the agency in 1962. He fought with the SAS but is perhaps most famous for his genuine mercenary activities after he left Rhodesia: in 1980 he went to South Africa, joining first the Transkei Defence Force and then Executive Outcomes. As part of its operations in Sierra Leone, he was put in charge of the Gurkha Security Group; he was killed on patrol and according to most accounts eaten by young rebels there as well.¹⁸ MacKenzie was the only American soldier I have ever heard described as a "brilliant soldier," a "quiet American" who "got on with the job."¹⁹ There was the fictional commando for whom fighting for Rhodesia was "a personal thing," and there were the fictional American soldiers championed by Robin Moore. I will return to Moore's troubled time in Rhodesia later in this chapter, but let me quote two phrases taken from his novel that was eventually self-published in 1991. In two separate scenes, two US citizens desire to be Rhodesians. One introduces himself to an army recruiter in Salisbury by saying, "I may sound like an American, but I'm a Rhodesian." The other, an American fighting with the Rhodesian forces, ponders returning to the United States: "To tell you the truth I feel more like a Rhodesian than an American."²⁰

Can someone belong to a nation because they feel like it? Can someone announce he is Rhodesian a day or two after arriving in the country? On the one hand, why shouldn't a country that imagined its own independence have soldiers who imagined they belonged there? Soldiers who pitched up for a few years and then left were not so different from much of the civilian white population. If wars of national liberation do not require nationals to fight them, as Erik Kennes and Miles Larmer argue for Angola, why should anyone think counterinsurgency should be the work of citizens alone?²¹ On the other hand, this is more than a little strange, that someone can claim nationality based on broad, possibly even opaque, emotions. Is belonging to a country a matter of wishing it were so, of approving of politics and a way of life, a state of mind rather than a legal category? I do not want to credit Moore's fiction with more realism than it had, but he brings something about the idea of foreign soldiers in the Rhodesian Army to the fore: the idea that the state represented something more than an outdated struggle against African nationalism. For supporters of UDI, foreign soldiers proved there was something desirable about white rule in 1970s Africa in and of itself; for opponents of Rhodesian independence, this proved that the racism of the regime appealed to US citizens and their government.

Whatever the individual reasons that made men want to fight for Rhodesia, there were not enough to make a military difference, but there is a literature written by Americanists that insisted that the US government approved of these men. Between 1975 and 1980 the number of Americans fighting in Southern African armies proved one thing, these authors asserted: that the United States did not enforce the laws that could have curtailed it, and this was proof of tacit acceptance if not outright support. According to this literature, without the backing of intelligence organizations in Western capitals, Rhodesia would have had no foreign soldiers and thus no ability to withstand African nationalists.[22]

The Location of Foreigners

Foreign soldiers, mercenary or not, may have been more useful to talk about than to fight with; their discursive and descriptive power was far greater than their impact on the conduct of the war. Mercenaries were thought to be everywhere. Taking her lunch by the hotel pool, Jan Morris saw a group of tanned young men, stripped to their shorts, speaking Taal: "Some were probably mercenaries."[23] It is almost impossible to tell how many foreign soldiers fought for Rhodesia given the range of figures and the myriad reasons to exaggerate or minimize them. It is also impossible to tell if the reported figures, exaggerated or minimized as they might be, are for a year, a few years, or for all the years Rhodesia was at war, which could be 1968–80 or perhaps 1974–80 or 1976–80. Newspapers bandied about figures that did not make much sense: 40 percent of the Rhodesian Army was foreign born, the London *Sunday Times* reported, a figure that was reasonable in a country where perhaps 60 percent of adults were born in other countries. There was a figure of two thousand Britons in the Rhodesian forces, but what did that mean? Were these men born in the United Kingdom? Were they men who carried British passports? Did they think of themselves as British subjects even when they got their call-up notices, or had they come from Britain specifically to fight for Rhodesia? Some obviously did just that, but the figures for British volunteers were equally hard to follow. The *Sunday Telegraph* reported that seventy recently demobilized Britons had gone to Rhodesia in two months of 1976, out of the twenty thousand men who left the British forces every year. The *Sunday*

Times reported that there were eight hundred mercenaries in the Rhodesian Army, and that five potential mercenaries wrote every day, although it did not clarify if these were business days or every day of the year.[24] There was the issue of pay. The Rhodesian Army insisted that foreign soldiers were paid and taxed at local rates, but authors struggled to show how Rhodesia nevertheless created a mercenary force. Salaries were reported and compared without much attention to rank or bonuses or family allowances.[25] Calling taxes "local" was perhaps an oversimplification: Rhodesian income tax was graduated, so that a bachelor was taxed at a higher rate than was a father of four earning the same income.[26]

Still, how many foreign soldiers fought for Rhodesia? Leaving out all the men with dual citizenship and omitting those who were foreign nationals resident in Rhodesia, how many men came from another country to join the security forces? Former Rhodesian generals have scoffed at me when I asked if there were fifteen hundred foreigners in the Rhodesian Army or if four hundred Americans served in the RLI, as I had read. There were a thousand regulars in the RLI, far and away the largest all-white infantry unit in the country: there was no way it was 40 percent American. It was more likely there were two or three Americans in each command, perhaps a few dozen total. Including Americans in the SAS and the Selous Scouts, at any given time there were perhaps one hundred Americans serving in Rhodesia between 1976 and 1980. An American volunteer agreed. Other sources put the number of Americans at four hundred.[27] Many deserted, however. A. J. Venter, a South African journalist—he often wrote for *Soldier of Fortune*, sometimes about Bob MacKenzie—wrote that perhaps half of the Americans who had joined the Rhodesian Army left before their contracts ended.[28]

The Rhodesian Army did not publicize any version of these numbers. For military manpower boards, Americans, Britons, Irishmen, and Australians allowed for occasional but welcome opportunities to juggle the national servicemen who had to be released early to go to universities abroad with reluctant reservists.[29] Foreign soldiers were literally placeholders, not nearly as well regarded as their supporters believed; foreign soldiers lamented that regulars and national servicemen despised them. Americans sometimes deserted before their contracts were up, going to Botswana or simply going home for a visit and never returning. They saw the cause as lost, not worth dying for.[30] For all the assertions that the RLI had hundreds of Americans, foreign soldiers in that regiment complained bitterly about the "tyrannical, arbitrary, and capricious treatment" they received from base staff and soldiers. This was a constant grievance in the 1977 survey of soldiers' morale.[31] Rhodesia's SAS, storied as it was, had a rate of desertion by foreign nationals unparalleled by other squadrons; two Britons complained that there was not enough action to hold their interest and signed on with a group going to fight with Phalangists in Lebanon.[32]

What of the Rhodesian state and its ability to hire or at least attract foreign soldiers? The Rhodesian Army, which had every reason to dissemble, seemed baffled that anyone would accuse it of using mercenaries. It also seemed baffled about how it might find them. In 1970 the Operations Coordinating Council (OCC), the decision-making body for the security forces, complained that all it knew about the recruitment of foreign soldiers was from "casual sources," especially gossip from hotel bars. There were stories that a Rhodesian colonel had secured a contract with the Cambodian government to train small groups of mercenaries who would soon arrive in Salisbury, and there were rumors that a British-born Rhodesian resident and former Congo mercenary was recruiting mercenaries. Was this the same man who was an ex-mercenary who came in 1964 and now worked in a mine? No one seemed to know, but one or both of these men frequently went to Cambodia, where, according to casual sources in Bulawayo, whatever force one or both men was raising "ran into difficulties."[33] Even formal recruiting trips seemed poorly planned. In February and March 1974, before there was any real crisis in manpower for the security forces, Lt. Nick Lamprecht, Rhodesia's long-serving recruitment officer, and K. C. Chalmers of the ministry of foreign affairs went to New Zealand and Australia to recruit officers for the Rhodesian forces. On arriving in New Zealand, they learned that the country had a manpower shortage of its own, and they left the next morning. After a week in Australia they found twenty interested men, but all of them were concerned that Rhodesian Army pay was between 50 and 60 percent less than what the Australia paid at any rank. Lamprecht tried to impress on them the low cost of living in Rhodesia. Travel costs posed another problem: Rhodesia may have sought foreign soldiers, but it did not want to spend foreign exchange on them. Recruits were asked to pay their own way, to be refunded in Rhodesia. (Because Australia maintained sanctions against Rhodesia, the ticketing was to be from Sydney to Malawi.) Those who could not afford to do this were given tickets purchased on South African Airways purchased in Salisbury, but by 1977 the cost of reimbursing volunteers was such that the OCC recommended the practice be discontinued. Sanctions made even the most successful recruitment trips difficult, so Chalmers suggested Rhodesia to advertise for officers in Australian newspapers.[34]

After 1974, however, recruitment shifted. Portuguese rule had ended in Mozambique and Angola, and African soldiers who had fought with Portugal were suddenly, if not eagerly, available; such men not only would lessen the burden of war on white citizens but also could be paid less than white soldiers. Less than two months after the Carnation Revolution in Portugal, the OCC met to consider taking in *flechas* from Mozambique.[35] Ten flechas had already crossed the border and had been assigned to mixed-race units, and ninety more wanted to come. It was decided that they come as refugees, to be screened by Special Branch.[36]

A year later, however, readily available white soldiers were not such a bargain. In 1976 former Portuguese officials who maintained contact with Rhodesian forces offered two thousand white soldiers who had fought with UNITA in Angola. These men were eager to join the Rhodesian Army and be under Rhodesian command, although if things changed they would want to be released to join an anti-FRELIMO movement in Mozambique. The OCC was dismissive: What could these men do? They didn't speak English, and even if they worked for internal affairs guarding protected villages, there were not enough weapons available to arm all of them.[37] Between 1976 and 1977 there were many offers of foreign soldiers. Col. Mike Hoare wrote proposing an international brigade for Rhodesia. This would be extremely useful if Cubans and Russians became involved in the conflict. Hoare planned to model this force on the French Foreign Legion and raise it in Europe and Miami himself. It was to be characterized by "severe discipline"; its men were to be motivated by anticommunism and not monetary rewards. Its men would perhaps speak French. Hoare insisted that this regiment would be nothing like "the mercenary soldier of recent times," but again, the OCC was not convinced. Any international brigade raised by Hoare would be called a mercenary force.[38] In 1977 the exiled King Lekka of Albania, who had been at Sandhurst with several Rhodesian officers, personally inquired if Rhodesia would be willing to train officers and NCOs and then a company and eventually a battalion of Albanians who would form an expeditionary force to retake his kingdom. The king would send as many English-speaking men as he could find, and once trained these men would be available to fight for Rhodesia, paid at local rates. Rhodesia made no formal response.[39]

The Rhodesian Army did accept almost two hundred Frenchmen in 1976. Whether or not they were former Legionnaires or paratroopers became an issue of some debate, but whatever they had been, French intelligence agents wanted them out of Djibouti right away. Getting them to Rhodesia was regarded as an achievement by Rhodesia's CIO, and no one else.[40] They formed an independent company of the Rhodesia Regiment and stumbled through villages, with great brutality and assaults on local women. They were returned to Cranborne Barracks for retraining, but most left the country.[41]

Mail-Order Mercenaries

How did foreign men come to join the Rhodesian Army if they weren't veterans of Portuguese colonial wars or adventurous Australians? Newspaper and magazine advertisements began to replace personal visits as the war intensified after 1976. *Soldier of Fortune* interviewed Lamprecht in the spring of 1977, ostensibly because young men had been writing to the magazine asking about military service in Rhodesia. It was a thinly disguised advertisement, in which Lamprecht explained that Rhodesia needed fit young men, preferably without military experience, who could be trained to join Rhodesian infantry units. The Rhodesian Army was as willing to take men without military training as it was to take veterans. Veterans had their own ideas about how to fight wars, and the Rhodesian Army did not necessarily want more soldiers; it was keen to bring in men who could be trained as medics or given guard duty on farms. Lamprecht and his staff read the letters of inquiry carefully, since many of the young men who wrote were "obviously nuts." Those who were not nuts would receive recruitment packets and would be asked to supply a host of documents; Lamprecht would give his most serious attention to the men who made the effort of having documents notarized. A successful applicant would be given an appointment with rank and would be reimbursed for the cost of travel to Rhodesia. Lamprecht challenged anyone to find a mercenary in the Rhodesian forces. Everyone joined the army under the same conditions, for the same pay, with the same equipment.[42]

This did not mean that race was not a factor. A West German man advertised for "safari guides" with military experience before he was arrested in 1977.[43] Andre Dennison, former SAS and British Army regular who had served in Malawi and Ulster, answered the same kind of personal advertisement that Peter McAleese did, which sought former commandos, SAS, and paratroopers seeking "interesting work abroad." The ad was placed by John (some said Tony) Banks, formerly British Army, who sought men to mount raids from Zambia into Rhodesia. The pay was very good and the life insurance policy generous, but he warned the men that the work involved "fighting for blacks against whites." Dennison reported this to Peter Hosking, then director of Rhodesian military intelligence and soon to command 2RAR; he offered to infiltrate the group. He did, and helped select men, but Banks's sponsor withdrew. Dennison then took up a commission in the 2RAR.[44] On the ground, however, the Rhodesian Army policed itself, at least in ways to talk about race. When an amicable American soldier was photographed in the *Bulawayo Chronicle* with swastika armbands, he was deported the next day.[45] When Tim Bax—born in East Africa, brought up in Canada—joined the Selous Scouts, Reid-Daly questioned his ability to work with African troops.[46] Indeed, the only Selous Scout I know of who did not praise African Selous Scouts was the American John Early: they were good, he wrote, but "not nearly as dependable as the average white soldier is."[47]

There were many contingencies that brought foreign men to Rhodesia. McAleese had no money after his time with the FNLA; he planned to go to Paris and join the French Foreign Legion. Once there he met a journalist he had known in Kinshasa, who suggested he go to Rhodesia instead: he liked fighting and Rhodesians had a war.[48] Timothy Bax was working as a draftsman in South Africa when he went on holiday in Rhodesia. His car broke down, and he could not afford to repair it, he told his drinking companions in a Salisbury bar; he couldn't get a job because he only had a two-week visitor's permit. One of them had a solution: Bax could join the Rhodesian Army for a year or two. The drinking companion knew Major Lamprecht well and said he could easily arrange for a residence permit if Bax enlisted.[49] There were the men written up in *Soldier of Fortune*, innocents who came for a holiday and decided to stay, then and there—"Rhodesia is safer to move around in than California"—or the young engineer who lost his return airfare in the casinos of Victoria Falls and stayed to work in road construction.[50] Fighting for Rhodesia was a job, probably a good one for professional soldiers like Dennison and McAleese, and almost as good for the tourists and gamblers, but it was nothing close to a belief in the country or a commitment to its cause as Rhodesia's supporters imagined.

"Professional Adventurers"

But what of the young men with some sense of place, or politics, or a sense of adventure beyond automobile repairs? How did they get to Major Lamprecht? *Soldier of Fortune* was said to provide a steady stream of volunteers. Some placed ads, such as "Individual seeks employment in high risk situation. Eight years military experience. Can travel anywhere. College educated. 150 IQ. Familiar with small arms and armor, ex-racing driver." "Ex-army vet. Viet 65–66. 2/7 Cav. 31 yrs old, seeks job as merc or security. Combat experience. Good physical condition. Will travel worldwide. You pay expenses." Would-be recruiters placed ads in shooting magazines; one read, "The Rhodesian Army offers excitement and adventure. I know. I've been there. Young Americans of European ancestry write to me for free details pertaining to recruiting."[51] Some men claimed to have been impressed by the several articles about Rhodesia that regularly appeared in *Soldier of Fortune* after 1977. Its editor was Lt. Robert K. Brown, a US Army veteran, a self-proclaimed veteran of the Bay of Pigs invasion, and a great cheerleader for any kind of war. He was not a recruiter, he insisted: that was illegal, and even if it was not, there were too many steps along the way—first month's pay, life insurance, transport—to justify the risk if funding fell through. Brown regarded the men who advertised as recruiters in his magazine as complete frauds, for which there was ample evidence. Most of these advertisers seemed more attentive to popular culture than they were to African or American politics. Many had heard stories of thousands of crisp, new US dollars piled up in hotel rooms in Kinshasa, but mercenaries were recruited for Angola years after the CIA's reported largesse. One recruiter insisted he was being paid by a foreign entity he was not allowed to name, and another claimed that the Congress for Racial Equality (CORE) in New York was actively recruiting mercenaries.[52]

Factions of the Rhodesian Army considered Brown unscrupulous, however; some officers claimed he charged Americans $10,000 for information about joining the Rhodesian security forces: contact with him should be handled "with extreme caution."[53] Nevertheless, Brown first went to Rhodesia in 1977, where he met three foreign soldiers serving in the RLI. "For obvious reasons," he gave each one a nom de guerre, and they gave him formulaic stories in return: one left the US Army because of its lax discipline and drugs; another had been in the Marines and the French Foreign Legion and joined the Rhodesian Army as soon as he learned about the war; and the third, a Scotsman, simply did not enjoy civilian life. Over beers they told him that the RLI was 30 to 40 percent "foreigner." The previous year, however, Brown had told a journalist that there were fifty to one hundred Americans in the Rhodesian Army, a handful of Americans in Angola, and a dozen in the French Foreign Legion, "and that's about it."[54] Over the next two years Brown published several stories about the war in Rhodesia, taking great pains to not discuss those Americans who came to protect white people or stop the onslaught of black nationalism. He wrote instead about the taciturn Vietnam veteran or the innovative American soldier he met there. He praised units rather than the Americans in them, especially Rhodesia's mounted regiment and its armored car unit. It is impossible to tell if these articles prompted Americans to volunteer—an American did say he thought the Rhodesian war romantic; it had a cavalry[55]—or if Lamprecht or someone else read the personal ads, but Americans did volunteer for reasons that had a great deal to do with race, as everyone but Brown reported. David Caute wrote of two Americans he and Christopher Hitchens met at one of the pool parties Robin Moore gave every weekend: one came because after Vietnam and Angola, "we can't afford to lose any more countries," while another—serving in the unit that guarded white-owned farms—said he "didn't care about those rich guys with their farms.... I'm fighting because they are white, and the white man is running out all over."[56]

In contrast, Brown wrote about Americans fighting in Rhodesia as if he was a chaperone introducing debutantes; he described going to war in a far-off land as an adventure, "like bungee jumping," a Rhodesian Army officer told me.[57] Brown was proud of all of them—including a few who had enlisted for less political reasons than Bax—whether or not they came after reading an article or two in *Soldier of Fortune*. Darrel Winkler was an American volunteer, a Vietnam veteran who served in the Armored Car Regiment; he had come to Rhodesia through a series of chance encounters. He in turn looked after men like "Reb," a musician from California who wanted to fight communists somewhere. Rejected by the US Army for his eyesight, he wrote to Lamprecht after he read an article on the Rhodesian Armored Car Regiment ("The Black Devils") in *Soldier of Fortune*. In Rhodesia he found his way to Winkler, who helped him enlist. He then followed Winkler when he was given a command in the 2RAR, which Brown claimed was because the government didn't want an American in charge of the ARC, "the most powerful regiment in the country." Rhodesian military intelligence did not trust Winkler, however. He claimed to have had experience with armor and asked to be put in the ARC. He had none; soldiers and officers soon became very suspicious of him, thinking he was a CIA plant.[58] Brown's most detailed description about how young men might get to and be employed in security work in Rhodesia was from August 1979, a few months before the end of the war. Brown's article recruited men for the Guard Force: they would guard white-owned farms, sometimes stopping stock theft and possibly capturing a guerrilla. The work was domesticated for a reason: young men had to be weaned from the wars in their heads. "Rhodesia is not the Alamo and you are not Davy Crockett," he wrote, admonishing recruits that they should not come if what they wanted to do was shoot black people. Instead, he advised his readers on courtesy, dress, and which bars in which cities would yield employment contacts. Airfare was not reimbursed, but farm guards earned about US$550 per month. There was the possibility of a small bonus for capturing cattle thieves, and Brown thought it necessary to dangle the reward for capturing a guerrilla or guerrilla weapons in front of his readers. As of late 1978, however, this reward had only been available to men deputized as bounty hunters.[59]

The progressive North American authors who wrote about American soldiers in Rhodesia were less concerned with personal stories than they were with the connections that brought these men to Central Africa. It was an era of belief in an overarching American power, expressed in weird and wonderful flowcharts that showed the state department, the department of justice, and the CIA all working to send mercenaries to Rhodesia via *Soldier of Fortune* and various "para military marketing" companies in the United States. The state department and the department of justice both facilitated mercenaries going to Rhodesia and covered up their role in doing so. The proof was in the articles on Rhodesia in *Soldier of Fortune* and in newspaper accounts of Rhodesians recruiting British pilots in Iran.[60]

Richard Lobban's 1978 article saw American foreign policy behind every American soldier in Rhodesia. Because he relied mainly on newspaper accounts, his evidence tends to be about men who died, or deserted, or who made it their business to be available to the press either in the United States or Rhodesia, including Major Mike Williams, whom we will meet again.[61] Ward Churchill's 1980 article was much more detailed, citing the laws US arms dealers and soldiers were violating in Southern Africa. He wrote extensively about Brown and his biography, making much of his earnings as a mercenary recruiter. He reproduced some of the ads from young men seeking mercenary work "anywhere in the world, if you pay transportation."[62] These form the genealogy of Gerald Horne's encyclopedic chapter on foreign soldiers in the Rhodesian Army. Horne's research was comprehensive. He wrote at length about John Murphy, said to be the man who introduced American slang to the Selous Scouts ("fire 'em up"), who also had murky ties to the US and South African governments. Murphy left Rhodesia, returned to the United States, and from there joined the South Africa Defence Force, "an example of the close ties that existed between the US military and the military forces of Rhodesia and South Africa." If any further proof was needed, General Magnus Malan had spent years at Fort Leavenworth in Kansas, where he helped formulate the hearts and minds program in Southeast Asia.[63] And there was Bob MacKenzie, who became a mercenary even if he wasn't one when he was in Rhodesia. Murphy and MacKenzie were both Vietnam veterans, well regarded by Rhodesian officers; they did not seek out journalists. Two Americans did: Major Mike Williams and John Early, who, in addition to his cloak-and-dagger recruitment to the world of African wars, claimed to have revolutionized parachuting in the Rhodesian Army. He tried but failed to democratize the Selous Scouts, although he wrote that the unit had killed more guerrillas than the entire Rhodesian Army combined had done. Early provided one of the most charitable descriptions of Peter Walls I have read, in which Walls told Murphy and Early—alone among foreign soldiers—that there would be a cease-fire and elections in a few months. The Selous Scouts would be disbanded, and the two might not want to stay on.[64]

Early and Williams were dismissive of Africans' ability to be soldiers, whether they were guerrillas or security forces. A vignette about Williams in a 1979 book about American mercenaries begins with his telling the story of Africans and their inability to use imported technologies. Having just laid a Russian-made land mine in a dirt road, the guerrillas remembered they had been told to tamp down the covering soil, to conceal the mine. The guerrillas joined hands and began jumping up and down on the mound of earth: they were all killed in the resulting explosion.[65] The portrait of African guerrillas in these writings and those of Robin Moore represents a separate trend from the genealogies of *Top Secret War* in which Africans might have weaknesses but were worthy foes, with new and sophisticated equipment. However easily they were fooled by empty slogans or false promises of education, African insurgents were not fools. For the Williamses and the Earlys and Moores of this war, they were.

Crippled Eagles

Robin Moore was a better amanuensis for American soldiers in Rhodesia than Robert Brown was. Although Moore had never been a soldier, he had gone through special forces training to write *The Green Berets*, and in the mid-1970s he had somewhat less problematic credentials than Brown. He also had his own money and could set up shop in Rhodesia. Excited by the prospect of researching and writing about the country, Moore hired an assistant, former CIA agent Verne Gillespie, whom he paid $2,000 per month, to make arrangements for him. Moore arrived in Salisbury in August 1976, less than two months after Henry Kissinger's visit to the region, amid the planning of the Geneva conference in October. Rhodesia, Moore learned when Gillespie met him at the airport, was eager for good publicity or at least an end to bad publicity; Moore claimed he could access the world of television news on behalf of Rhodesia. Gillespie's partner, Lin, worked for Rhodesian television; she was able to arrange meetings for Moore in which he suggested ways for the overseas press to be "harnessed."[66] Unable to go on patrols with the army as he had done in Vietnam, he offered himself to several officials: he could meet with visiting journalists and help them see what was really happening. To this end he offered to publicize photos of guerrilla violence for "psychological warfare." Most of all he wanted to interview Americans fighting for Rhodesia as research for his novel. In February 1977 he bought a house, which he called the "Unofficial US Embassy." He called himself "the Ambassador," willing to serve until such time as President Carter lifted sanctions, recognized Rhodesia, and appointed a career diplomat with experience in Africa. Moore and Gillespie sought out American soldiers. Moore had already met a few, and they told others about him, and within a few weeks he began to host an open house with free hot dogs, hamburgers, beer, and whiskey by the pool and tennis court every Saturday for Americans fighting for—or doing doctoral research in—Rhodesia. Moore called this the "Embassy of Goodwill." He and Gillespie would talk to the young men about where they came from and how much they cared about Rhodesia's freedom; they offered advice on personal and financial matters. It was, Ross Baughman wrote, "a cross between Rick's Café and a USO hospitality center for mercenaries."[67]

These soldiers were the Crippled Eagles, the Americans crippled by the harassment, or potential harassment, of the US government. It was an emblem on the front door of "the embassy," as Moore asked everyone to call it, an American eagle with one crippled wing on a red, white, and blue shield, crossed by an FN rifle and a white quill pen. The crippled, bandaged wing signified US harassment of the Americans who fought for Rhodesia, the FN was the standard-issue weapon of Rhodesian forces, and the quill "signifies the truth now being told about this war against Communism in Rhodesia."[68] Moore soon began to market this: there were also Crippled Eagle T-shirts, tie tacks, key rings, and sew-on patches—all eventually advertised in *Soldier of Fortune*—as well as the forthcoming novel.[69] Within the year, Moore produced a nonfiction book, aimed at US readers to show black Americans there was nothing racist about Rhodesia and that sanctions should be lifted at once. The book, which was based on Rhodesian government publications, concluded with twelve vignettes of foreigners fighting for Rhodesia.

"Foreign" was an elastic term for Moore—Was the Irishman who settled in Rhodesia in 1957 Irish or Rhodesian?—but "American" was not. Americans fighting for Rhodesia were appalled by US policy toward Rhodesia, and most of them, perhaps coincidentally, wanted Andrew Young, Carter's ambassador to the UN, to come and see for himself that the fight here was not about race. Most of these men were combat veterans in their thirties; a younger man came because he could not stand by while the rest of the world abandoned Rhodesia to communism, which he hated. One said he wanted to protect Anglo-Saxons as well. When asked if they were mercenaries, they all scoffed: mercenaries would be making a lot more money.[70] One of the Americans so profiled was a frequent guest at "the embassy." Mike Williams was the oldest American serving in the Rhodesian Army. A former Congo mercenary, Moore wrote that he was given a commission a few months after he arrived in Rhodesia in 1976. His assignment was difficult and dangerous, the command of a Protection Company (read: Coloured) at Rutenga, guarding the railroad. Coloured troops required discipline—"You rule them, don't let them rule you"—and he believed that Rhodesians thought an American, with perhaps a less gentlemanly approach to soldiering, could command them best.[71] Within a year he was second in command of Rhodesia's mounted (and all-white) regiment, the Grey's Scouts, formed in 1975.[72]

All these men—the Crippled Eagles and the British volunteers and the men who imagined mercenary work glamorous and those who came on holiday and just stayed—raise questions of motivation. Why did these young and not so young men join a foreign army? Was anticommunism or racism their sole motivation? Even if someone imagined that fighting for a minority government in Africa a decade after decolonization had nothing to do with race, how can we understand going to fight for Rhodesia so it wouldn't be another Angola or Vietnam but not another Ethiopia? What explains the imagined power and authority of the US ambassador to the UN, or even of the UN?[73] These questions are not about Rhodesia: the only thing that was specific to Rhodesia that was part of the foreign soldiers' stories was that Rhodesia had loyalist African soldiers and the war was therefore not about race. Perhaps all mercenaries know little about where they are fighting, but in this case these men steadfastly maintained they were not mercenaries, they were paid and taxed as white Rhodesians were. What seems to make these foreign soldiers distinctive is the country they claimed to know the most about, the country whose power was overestimated time and time again: the United States. Rhodesian generals and military intelligence understood this; they knew these volunteers did not "worry" about the cause, and in turn military commanders "didn't worry about motivation": foreigners could not know about growing up with Africans.[74]

Most of the literature I cite in this chapter was produced in the 1970s, an era in which the CIA seemed all-powerful and behind every assassination and coup. This was perhaps an oversimplification of the Cold War, a vision of superpower intervention without much attention to internal struggles in African politics. What this literature ignores is that by 1976, Rhodesia's war effort was less about preserving white rule than it was about keeping guerrillas at bay until an end to the war—on terms favorable to whites—could be negotiated. I am not, however, arguing that these authors should have done more research; I want to take their ignorance seriously. Let me take up a point Ashis Nandy made more than twenty years ago, which is that there are indeed people without history. They are not backward tribesmen or isolated populations, but people who have a concrete idea of the world and understand it to be constructed by events radically different from the those most of us know. They have historians and historical consciousness, they have historical specifics and historical contingencies, but they have a different past and a different way of arriving at that past.[75] I will return to this point in the next three sections, which describe the conflicts over what is seen.

A Photographer's Poses

Shortly after the 1977 book was published, Moore's world in Rhodesia unraveled. His offer to vet foreign journalists for Rhodesia had gone terribly wrong. Ross Baughman, a newly arrived Associated Press photojournalist, had sought him out almost on arrival. Baughman had begun his career by infiltrating a Nazi group in a small Ohio town and publishing stories about its activities, including a murder; he joked that he practiced "kamikaze journalism"—high-risk, short-term interventions rather long-term investigations. Rhodesia was his first overseas assignment. He wanted to get closer to the war, and he saw Moore as his point of entry, although no one in the Associated Press office in Salisbury knew him or knew much about him. Baughman phoned Moore mentioning a mutual acquaintance, which got him in the door. Moore seemed taken with Baughman—he had him photograph the official opening of "the embassy"—and he took him to visit army bases and to watch passing-out parades that were not nearly as exclusive as Moore claimed. One weekend by the pool Moore introduced Baughman to Mike Williams "with enthusiasm," and Baughman pounced. It was easy, he wrote, to convince Williams to allow Baughman to come on patrol. Were the bad press and worldwide disdain for the Rhodesian Army a problem for Williams and his men, Baughman asked? If no one understood the cause, and the dedication of Rhodesian forces, perhaps it was because no one knew about it. Baughman offered to show them. Take me on patrol, he promised, and he would explain everything. Williams was convinced; he was so eager that he did not contact his immediate superior but went to the officer who was in charge of permission, the deputy of Major Don Stannard of Salisbury Special Branch.[76]

Baughman trained briefly with the BSAP. He went on patrol with the Grey's Scouts in the west of the country. He wore an army uniform, he was on horseback—the Grey's Scouts gave him the Western saddle he requested—and he was armed. There was not enough manpower to babysit him in a contact, he was told: he would have to be able to defend himself. Baughman was thrilled. He wanted to be close to action and was willing to be armed and in uniform to have a kind of access no other journalist had. This would not interfere with his work because he did not require dozens of rolls of film for hundreds of photographs. He had a strong sense of composition, he wrote. He had studied great paintings and photographs, and he knew what he was looking for, which made it easier to find.[77] Baughman saw many of the activities he was looking for. At "a desolate, forlorn school" in rural Lupane, soldiers beat students only slightly younger than they were; they put a noose around the neck of one youth. A popular teacher—and Muzorewa supporter—and his wife were tortured; Baughman unwittingly supplied one of the instruments. A few days later he watched Grey's Scouts "softening up" their prisoners. Men were forced to stay in stress positions for perhaps forty-five minutes. When one man collapsed, he was taken behind a building and told to be silent as a soldier fired a shot into the ground; another collapsed shortly after that, and he too was taken behind the building. Before a shot was fired, two men at the end of the line began crying, saying they would talk.[78]

8.1 An African youth stands with a rope tied around his neck. Two Grey's Scouts ride behind him. Lupane, Rhodesia, September 1977. Photo by J. Ross Baughman, courtesy of AP Photo.

8.2 A Rhodesian soldier holds African villagers at gunpoint, forcing them to hold a push-up position, in Kikidoo, Rhodesia, 17 September 1977. Photo by J. Ross Baughman, courtesy of AP Photo.

After two weeks Baughman was asked to return to Salisbury. He was not sure who gave the order, but he assumed it was someone in intelligence who was wary of a journalist's unrestricted access to a war zone. He was told this was to clarify his credentials, but he understood that it was about checking his photographs. Baughman hid three of his twelve rolls of film and managed to overexpose most of the others before handing them over to Special Branch. The three he kept were "dynamite. This is my testimony." He planned to leave for South Africa as soon as he could, but in the few days before he left he was followed and harassed. On Friday he got phone calls every few hours throughout the night. Each time, there was silence followed by a hang-up. On Saturday there was another call with the sound he eventually recognized as that of a magazine being clipped into an automatic pistol. There was one call Sunday afternoon, in which the gun was fired. Was this Williams or Gillespie, or have they handed it over to PsyAc, he wondered?[79]

When he gave the photos to the AP office in Johannesburg, he was told to send them and accompanying text to New York for final approval. He grudgingly knew why. He may have violated Rhodesia's official secrets act. However elastic this was for journalists, Baughman understood that he had jeopardized the position of those who worked in Salisbury: they might not be deported, but they could be constrained in their ability to report on anything the military did. When the photographs were finally published, it was without his byline; the story reminded readers that guerrillas committed atrocities as well. Even so, the photographs won the Robert Capra Award from the Overseas Press Club. Shortly thereafter, Mike Williams was forced to resign his commission. He returned to the United States and soon appeared on a network morning television program in which he denounced the photographs as staged and insisted that Baughman encouraged the torture. The award was withdrawn because so much about them was in doubt. Shortly after that the photos won a Pulitzer Prize.[80]

That was Baughman's story. It was well enough known to other journalists that David Caute published a short version of it in 1983.[81] Major Mike Williams told another one, as told to and perhaps aided by Robin Moore, in which he was convinced the Rhodesian government blamed the Baughman incident on him: he was told to resign his commission in large part for "inviting Ross Baughman to the bush."[82] In his journals Moore believed he was set up with Baughman by Verne Gillespie, at least indirectly. Gillespie claimed Moore owed him money and had taken over his Salisbury house and was renting out the rooms to make money. This debt may not have been salary, but the trust fund set up in the United States for the Crippled Eagles, which was in Gillespie's name. Once the debt was settled, Moore could have his house back. Moore was more concerned about Baughman, however; he hoped to counter the photographer's stories in the book about Mike Williams, which he thought was going to be "a winner."[83] In that version, Baughman came to Moore's house one weekend. Williams and Moore were wary of him, especially when he asked to go on patrol with the Grey's Scouts. Williams told him he would have to go through proper channels. He was surprised when Baughman got permission, but soon learned this was not because of any potential propaganda value to his photographs but because Stannard wanted his girlfriend, a South African national, to get a job with the Associated Press in Salisbury. Stannard was an easy man for men in and around the military to blame (see chapter 4), possibly because he inflated his importance to those same men.

Williams was convinced Baughman would "screw us over if he can," so he sent him out with a nineteen-year-old troop commander to find a bus robber. This is where Baughman first proved to be trouble: not satisfied with seeing the prisoner restrained on the ground, he first kicked him and then heated a beer bottle with his cigarette lighter and burned the man's chest. Nevertheless, Williams allowed Baughman to accompany him so he could get combat footage, although Baughman shied away from any contact. Instead, he promoted violence in order to photograph it. When a prisoner tried to escape, Baughman shouted, "Shoot him! Shoot him!" When Williams was out on patrol, Baughman talked the members of a call sign into getting a few Africans to pose in a push-up position, as if this was interrogation. Later he persuaded one of the young national servicemen to put a noose around a suspect's neck. He even took a photo of his nineteen-year-old handler holding a baton while an African lay on the ground nearby. These were the Pulitzer Prize–winning photos, the publication of which forced Williams to resign from the Rhodesian Army.[84] A recent history of the Grey's Scouts called Williams's account "made up of inaccuracies and nonsense." He was a cowboy. He carried a Colt 45, and he liked to enter a kraal and pull his horse to a sharp halt, often causing him to fall off his mount. A captain in his command said he let Baughman "hoodwink" him, but the photographs were only one reason he was removed. He had shot two Coloured soldiers in the Rhodesian Defence Unit, thinking they had broken the curfew, "and for general incompetence." Although the author did not talk to any Grey's Scout who was an eyewitness to the events Baughman described, some thought the photos were staged or doctored. Others could not see what the problem was. As the regiment's riding instructor said, a guerrilla "in a prone position being interrogated at gun point . . . is of course, as everyone knows, the only sensible and safe way to question an enemy."[85]

Between Baughman's account and the regimental history, there is much that was not sensible, however. Even in an army with young national servicemen, Williams's mention of nineteen-year-olds is telling. The Grey's Scouts were young—Baughman was struck by how young they were—and somewhat casual: one called-up farmer rode his one-eyed farm mare on operations.[86] Baughman describes the frustration of national servicemen who wanted the romance of a cavalry on rugged terrain but did not have working equipment, like radios.[87] These were the young and angry soldiers Bruce Moore-King called "edgy and irritable" as they dragged bedsprings out of African huts during barely supervised interrogations.[88] Were they assigned to patrol isolated schools and villages because various JOCs thought they were best served patrolling teenagers, or were they particularly violent with youths their own age?

There are two more interpretations of the photos. The first came from the discussions, public and private, about why the Overseas Press Club had "unresolved questions" about the authenticity of the pictures. According to a member of the prize committee, these questions involved the context in which they were taken, not just of a war but the conduct of a war photographer. First, what was Baughman's relationship to the army, and was he a participant in the events he photographed? The answer was no: he went on patrol as an accredited AP photojournalist. Once, when soldiers built a fire in front of a suspect's house, he carried a metal box spring and put it on the fire in the yard. He thought soldiers were destroying the man's property, but instead they were heating the box springs to make his wife lie on them and answer questions. He said he had no idea this would happen. Second, did Baughman wear a uniform and carry a gun? He did. This was a condition of his going on patrol. Experienced photojournalists were taken aback. When photographers and correspondents are armed, they undermine the protection of noncombatants in the Geneva Convention: "You cannot shoot pictures and shoot people at the same time." Third, were Baughman's pictures taken on an "authentic mission"? Were they posed? Did Baughman's presence precipitate overzealousness by these Grey's Scouts? Baughman insisted that these were the most candid of the pictures he took in Rhodesia: in a rare defense of the Rhodesian soldiers, he said it was "inconceivable" that they would have beaten people and burned villages for his sake. Some of the jurors for the prize went further: How can you tell if a photo is posed or unposed?[89]

Indeed, how can one tell? War photographs are usually staged in some way. Even before Mathew Brady and his associates took photographs in the Civil War, a British photographer rearranged cannonballs on a Crimean road to provide a sense of the drama and danger of war. Twentieth-century war photographs were taken with more mobile technologies than were available in the 1860s, but some were still staged. Was the photo of a Spanish soldier reeling from a gunshot to his head—the photo that made Robert Capra famous—an action photograph or one taken when the photographer was on simulated battle maneuvers? Capra never provided documentation to prove the man was killed by enemy fire, but its importance may not be when it was taken but how it captured the moment of death. The famous photograph of US Marines planting the flag on Mount Suribachi was not staged but it was a repeat of an earlier flag raising. The battle was over, the photographer supplied a larger flag, and the Marines who raised it struggled against the wind, not the enemy, to do so. Nevertheless, the photo is a candid picture of Marines raising a flag after a battle.[90] Does this make the image staged, or less authentic than a picture taken in the heat of battle? If an image is composed, or taken with a larger flag than the original one, is it a simulation? And if an event is staged, isn't the photographer nevertheless an eyewitness?

Staging photographs with soldiers is not wholly straightforward; they have an interest in a certain portrait of themselves in war. By the mid-1970s these young men had grown up with the technology of cameras, as they had with guns. Even if they themselves did not take pictures, they understood the import of posing for a photograph; they too had ideas about composition and their place within an image. Did a young Scout place a noose around a teenager's neck for the camera or for his commanding officer? That may be Baughman's most composed photograph with the mounted Grey's Scouts as the frame. The prisoners in stress positions raise other questions altogether. Mike Williams insisted that Baughman asked troopers to pose five Africans—not prisoners—in the push-up position for his most famous photo. Did these men volunteer? Were they paid? Williams doesn't say. If the men were prisoners, how did Baughman or any other individual soldier get the prisoners to pose? In a powerful essay on the Abu Ghraib photographs, Errol Morris argues that prisoners could be posed because they were hooded: the power of the image of the man on the box with loose wires attached to his hands is that the prisoner doesn't see the deception; he thinks the threat is immediate, while we see the cruelty and the cynicism.[91] But can five prisoners, eyes wide open, be posed? What threat of brute force greater than what they endured while posing would make the prisoners comply? How long did it take Baughman to pose the photograph? Did the men ask for special treatment if they posed willingly? Even if the photo was not posed, its composition suggests it was staged, but not in terms of its violence but in that it appears that one man with a gun controls five frightened prisoners. Was the man with the gun that fearsome, or do we need to look at what is outside the frame: in the lower left-hand side of the photograph we see the top of a shoulder in shadow; the fabric below the epaulette is rumpled. Whether posed or not, the shoulder tells us that there is more going on in this photo than the single soldier and his pistol. Indeed, who guarded the prisoners when a man was taken away and a gun was fired? One of Baughman's most ardent defenders in the world of photography prizes wrote that the "Pulitzer pictures speak for themselves," but they do not.[92] Instead, they suggest possibilities far more violent and terrifying than the image portrays.

Crippled Eagles: The Novel

Moore returned to Rhodesia only once, in April 1979: as president of the Rhodesia America Society, he came to observe the election. He felt unwelcomed by Rhodesian officials. On his first night back in the hotel bar he got "a limp handshake" from a cabinet minister who had welcomed him to his office two years earlier. Moore thought this was because Lin, Gillespie's partner, was sleeping with him.[93] Moore did not abandon Rhodesia or his writing projects about the country, however. A year earlier he had written in his journal, "I've got too much time and effort invested in Rhodesia and I feel I can continue to be of help, it's just a question of how." To this end he met with Rob Brown of *Soldier of Fortune* to ask him to run stories about Moore's operations in Rhodesia and to plug Crippled Eagles paraphernalia, especially T-shirts.[94]

Moore's investment in Rhodesia did not go unnoticed by the US government, which had joined the British government in trying to organize a negotiated end to the war and some semblance of majority rule. Moore was a fierce critic of President Carter's policies toward Rhodesia. While he disparaged Kissinger's "threats" against Americans fighting for Rhodesia, he approved of Americans fighting for Israel, Moore seemed unaware that

Kissinger's machinations on behalf of Gerald Ford had created the opening for Carter's policies.[95] Moore reserved his greatest vitriol for Andrew Young, whom he described in racist terms as often as possible and as publicly as possible, without any understanding of how Young's interventions followed Britain's lead.[96] According to confidential White House memos leaked to Washington columnist Jack Anderson, Moore was the first American in a decade investigated by the treasury department for violating sanctions against Rhodesia. According to Anderson, federal investigators subpoenaed the accounts of Moore's sometime literary agent and the marketing group of which Moore was the principle shareholder. Moore invited one of Anderson's reporters to join him at a meeting with the New York office of Foreign Assets Control during which Moore asked why he was being investigated. Why did the government wait until after his pro-Rhodesia book was published rather than investigating him when he first traveled to Rhodesia? Carter's representative joked that the government sometimes took a while to get moving. Moore then asked if the investigation was retaliation for his criticisms of Andrew Young, to which Carter's representative said that was "absurd."[97] No charges were brought against Moore.

Moore had been planning his novel about American soldiers fighting for Rhodesia since his first visit there. Gambling at a casino in Victoria Falls, he noted that all the dealers were white women, and he quickly thought through a plotline in which an American soldier on leave falls in love with a "girl dealer."[98] As he wrote, he talked to editors at McGraw-Hill about publishing the book.[99] But "because of the unorthodox way I operate," he decided to use McGraw-Hill as a backup. Moore had what he called "tax shelter books," texts published by companies extensively subsidized by Moore, in the form of both loans to the press and investments in the finished book. This was not so much a tax dodge as a way to make sure that the expenses Moore incurred writing and publishing a book would offset most of the taxes he would have to pay on a best seller. The publisher he used most often for these books was Condor, which was very much in his debt by 1980.[100]

Moore finished *Crippled Eagles* in March 1980. It was loosely based on the lives of the American soldiers Gillespie had interviewed at "the embassy" and a few men who remained in contact with Moore after they returned to the United States. Moore left no stereotype unturned: guerrillas wanted to go shoot white people, white nuns sympathetic to the nationalist cause slept with guerrillas, missionaries refused to leave their stations, and

Rhodesians assured Americans that theirs was not a race war. He knew the book would be controversial; he decided to make it a tax shelter book rather than send it to a commercial press. By the end of July, however, he was worried that Condor required more and more of his loans to stay afloat.[101] The solution was to set up a new press, Jennifer Publishing Company in Miami, founded in June 1980, which published *Crippled Eagles*.[102] The copy I have is an advance copy, with no ISBN, no cover design, and no blurbs except for "Soon to be a major motion picture" on the back cover. By September 1980 Jennifer changed its name to Condor Publishing Company.

In September 1980 Moore brought several hundred of these advance copies to a *Soldier of Fortune* convention at which he was a featured speaker. Rob Brown and Mike Williams were there. Moore began by talking about the breakdown of discipline in the US Army, which he claimed began in Vietnam with black soldiers fragging their officers. He repeated a phrase he claimed to have coined in Vietnam, "What's the big deal about killing a gook?" Moore said he knew that Andrew Young and the third world members of the UN were upset by his support for Rhodesia. He described how the treasury department accused him of violating foreign asset regulations by transferring funds to Rhodesia, and how he became so angry he had blurted out, "You wouldn't have me here if I hadn't made the president's pet coon mad at me." Just in case anyone at the convention was confused about whom he meant, he said, "I was of course referring to Andrew Young." Brown of *Soldier of Fortune* was horrified, and Mike Williams refused to speak to him.[103]

Moore was still carrying around advance copies of *Crippled Eagles* in March 1981, but the book was not published until 1991, and then by Affiliated Writers of America as *The White Tribe*. Affiliated Writers of America offered Avon the paperback rights, but nothing came of that.[104] Moore was not a man who overlooked government interference in his activities, and while he seemed to have hinted that the government stopped the publication of *Crippled Eagles*, I think it is more likely that he understood that this was not the right time for his novel.

Africa and the People without History

Robin Moore died in February 2008. In 2009 *Soldier of Fortune* published an article that accused him of working for the CIA to bring white rule in Rhodesia to an untimely end. It began with a quote from Col. Mike Hoare to prove that the CIA—"once the world's greatest intelligence-gathering service and a major tool in American administration"—had given up on Africa in 1977. President Jimmy Carter and Andrew Young (of course) began to undermine Rhodesia's war effort and worked to install the "life-long Marxist" Robert Mugabe in a one-party state. To do this, Carter and Young created a massive sting operation in Rhodesia with Moore and Gillespie at its helm. "The embassy," with its weekends of hot dogs and hamburgers for American soldiers, was set up not for R & R but to learn more about these soldiers, to publicize the Rhodesian cause and provide Moore with material for his novel. Gillespie asked these young men for personal information that he said would be used for press releases for their hometown newspapers. He taped conversations with American soldiers so he could send them to "friendly" radio stations, but Joseph C. Smith, the author of the article and a Vietnam veteran, knew the tapes would go to CIA headquarters and beyond. More troubling was that on one weekend, there were perhaps half a dozen photographers who took soldiers' pictures from every angle. Smith knew he had been "made"; indeed, when he returned to the United States, no security firm with a connection to the US government would hire him. He was willing to concede that Moore might have been a pawn in a larger game. He quoted a letter Moore wrote to General Yarborough—the man who got him interested in Rhodesia in the first place—saying he was no match for Carter and Young and "the adder in my own fruit basket, Vernon Gillespie," who was taking orders from Carter's CIA. Smith wrote that many Crippled Eagles had wanted to take Gillespie out on a patrol and shoot him, but Moore understood the ramifications of such an act; he refused to give the go-ahead.[105]

Moore's literary estate responded at once. The letter was signed by his wife and sent by his lawyer. but it was in all likelihood written by Henry Newkirk, Moore's longtime assistant. The *Soldier of Fortune* article was offensive and defamatory, the letter said, and could have a detrimental effect on the future income of Moore's trust and the sales of his already published books and his as yet unpublished memoirs, especially among readers in the "Special Forces community." If there was no immediate retraction, Moore's estate would sue the author and the magazine that published it. Newkirk refuted every point, writing that Moore went to Rhodesia as an author inspired by General Yarborough, not as a government agent, that he had no idea Gillespie was a CIA plant, and that the sole purpose of "the embassy" was to give American soldiers a home away from home. If these men were questioned at all, it was not done there. In fact, Moore continually warned

Americans fighting for Rhodesia not to give their real names to anyone because of US government reprisals for their participation in a foreign army. Moore had never allowed foreign press in "the embassy." The only photographer he allowed in was Ross Baughman, who deceived him and Major Mike Williams. Moore had been told that Gillespie had orders to get him, Moore, out of the country or to kill him, but no one who read Moore's 1977 book would "ever suggest that Robin was involved in a CIA plot to put a communist terrorist in power in Rhodesia."[106]

How do I understand this? Is this just another lawsuit in the world of Rhodesian publishing lawsuits, or is this litigation by people without history? It is not simply that these men do not seem to know much about the history of decolonization, or guerrilla war, or the none-too-clear-cut alliances within a region; they seem oblivious to current events. It appears that the last thirty years might have had no impact on their thinking; otherwise, they might have realized that Rhodesia was on the ropes by 1977 or that Robert Mugabe wasn't such a Marxist after all. Yes, these people have a different history from the one I know, one that rests firmly on the importance of a few hundred American soldiers and an overwhelming sense of American power. This isn't a mythical history of Rhodesia's anticommunism and its downfall, but it is a mythologized history of America and Americans. The specifics of Rhodesia's history do not seem to matter in these accounts. These men could fight for Rhodesia because the CIA approved of their mission, or they could be harassed for doing so because the CIA disapproved of it; it was the agency's global reach that held these histories together, rather than anything to do with events on the African continent. And this may not be as outlandish—the pun is deliberate—as it sounds. Foreign soldiers and mercenaries may add another, internationalized layer to the imaginary of states' war making that is contested and struggled over.

9 "WHAT INTERESTS DO YOU HAVE?"

Security Force Auxiliaries and the Limits of Counterinsurgency

In the last years of the war, Rhodesia did not have enough soldiers—white and black—to fight a war or even maintain a cease-fire. Territorial forces were stretched to their limit, and many men did not respond to call-up notices or report for reserve duty. When Chris Cocks was a Police Anti-Terrorist Unit (PATU) stick leader in 1979, he realized that each eight-man stick was in practice five men at the most. Some reservists were away or were sick, and some "just plain didn't feel like it."[1] The legend of the Selous Scouts proved to be just a legend—one of which the army had grown tired—and the promise that small groups could outsmart a guerrilla juggernaut seemed increasingly unlikely. A fictional intelligence officer tells a group of high-ranking officers that Rhodesia was in danger of losing the war "because we can't kill the enemy as fast and he can replace his casualties. At the end of the day, gentlemen, it's a battle of numbers."[2] After 1977 Rhodesian security forces required more and more soldiers, even if they were guerrillas.

SFAs

Security force auxiliaries (SFAs) were in theory composed of surrendered guerrillas who came on side to fight for one of two parties of the internal settlement. One was Rev. Ndabaningini Sithole's ZANU, so called to invoke his early leadership of the party and to distinguish it from ZANU(PF), the other Bishop Abel Muzorewa's UANC, which was a political party with no history of an army in exile or anywhere else. Without question, SFAs were the most reviled unit in the Rhodesian Army. The men who trained them were often contemptuous of their soldiering skills, and as we shall see, they were not always unhappy when SFAs were killed. The villagers interviewed by Jocelyn Alexander and Joann McGregor remembered how much "rougher" SFAs were than regular units of the Rhodesian Army; they attacked people and their property because of greed and ambition, not military strategy. They were "untrained people excited by carrying guns," proud to be seen armed and "eating canned beef and baked beans."[3]

The deployment of SFAs in 1978 and 1979 was said to predict an awful future. It was "the beginning of civil war in Rhodesia," an African MP told parliament.[4] ZAPU insisted that the real reason SFAs were brought into the war was to prove that civil war in Zimbabwe was "inevitable," that "if left alone, the Africans would kill each other."[5] SFAs were accused of various massacres in 1978 and 1979—attacks on missions and civilians—and their violence and indiscipline were noteworthy during the elections of 1979 and 1980. By then, however, both had become the private armies denounced by human rights groups and nationalists in exile. SFAs were despised on the ground. In 2006 I was told that people in one district did not support the Movement for Democratic Change because so many of its local officers had been SFAs.[6] Only Joshua Chakawa's 2015 doctoral dissertation argues that SFAs were legitimate army, with ideologies, discipline, and commitments.[7] Even the most neutral authors considered them to be a good idea that was not executed with any care or forethought. SFAs tended to be unruly and ham-fisted in counterinsurgency operations, acting in ways that the "lessons from" literature insists must be avoided at all cost: such actions would alienate local people and drive them into guerrillas' arms. But such lessons rest on a belief that villagers' loyalties are either/or, that they become steadfast in reaction. Rhodesia's SFAs were abroad in the land in 1978 and 1979, by which time, if villagers were choosing sides, it was not for the first time. Indeed, a liaison officer with a UANC unit concluded that had SFAs been introduced two years earlier, they might have made a difference.[8]

There was much that was suspicious about SFAs. No one could say for sure if they were bona fide guerrillas willing to come on side, or if they were insurgents who surrendered because they were tired of fighting, or young men so unruly that ZANLA and ZIPRA cast them out, or urban criminals who saw these armies as a way to hone their skills. Many had been press-ganged into these armies, as were youths who had been press-ganged into ZANLA and ZIPRA, but on the whole men joined Muzorewa's or Sithole's forces much as men joined guerrilla forces: they were recruited, they believed it would make them safer, or a friend or relative—sometimes one who had been press-ganged into a unit—recruited them. Chakawa suggests that many of the guerrillas who came on side were in fact mujibas, young men who already served guerrilla armies in an auxiliary capacity.[9] The numbers of SFAs were widely disputed—Sithole once claimed he had 20,000 men he could mobilize—but by mid-1979 the Rhodesian Army claimed there were more than 8,000 UANC SFAs and slightly more than 1,500 loyal to Sithole's ZANU.[10] But the import of SFAs was not simply their numbers but their ability, as Mac McGuiness put it, to convince "tribes people" that the government should be part of any Rhodesian settlement.[11] Thus Rhodesian attempts to publicize the commitment of SFAs to the cause of the internal settlement featured Comrade Max, who wore an animal skin cap and ZANLA denims and pounded his AK on the ground as he announced, "I am the new DC in this area. I run the educational system and deal with the civil problems." He assured the television crew that he would punish anyone who tried to harm them. Twenty-one-year-old Comrade Mick Jagger was photographed with Muzorewa; Comrade Mick commanded 400 SFAs before he was jailed for intimidation shortly after the 1979 election. There was Comrade Lloyd, a ZANLA defector loyal to Sithole who trained in Uganda and who had the blessings of white farmers in his area because he kept cattle safe from guerrilla raids.[12] JOC believed that auxiliaries needed better publicity, especially overseas. Comrade Max had been overexposed. All the publicity "could be to his detriment." Indeed, Max was said to have gone to Britain shortly after the 1980 election.[13]

This chapter has two distinct concerns. The first is that of this book: I am less interested in what SFAs did than in what was written about them. I am less interested in why men came on sides, voluntarily or less so, than I am with why they were described with such contempt and outrage. While there is no doubt that the kindly, gentle turnings described in *Top Secret War* were as unlikely as they were uncommon, how do we understand even the fictive trust and admiration for the turned guerrillas in the Reid-Daly/Stiff version of the Selous Scouts and the scorn heaped on SFAs by the same authors? SFAs might have been violent in the extreme, but they were subjected to great violence by the security forces they were supposed to help. Whatever the intensification of murder and mayhem they brought to the countryside, SFAs themselves were slaughtered not just by the ZANLA and ZIPRA patrols for which they were wholly unmatched but by Rhodesian forces. The second is the untidy end of the war-in-the-place and how it upended the counterinsurgency practices Rhodesians called their own. Indeed, was a war fought with surrendered guerrillas still a guerrilla war?

If the bush war was a specific engagement with a landscape that white men learned from black men, what happens when white men teach black men what they learned from Africans? Does the specificity of this war unravel when guerrillas were trained not by men who knew the valleys and the animals of this country, but by Libyans and Ugandans?

"Utilizing Surrendered Terrorists"

The idea behind SFAS was that the political parties in the internal settlement would each have a semblance of an army that would prove to someone, somewhere, that these parties were on an equal footing with ZANU(PF) and ZAPU. It was hoped that an African head of state, however fictive his position might be, by his very existence could convince guerrillas to lay down their arms and join the new government to build a lasting peace. For Ken Flower and Rhodesia's CIO, this meant there would be fighting forces that would guarantee Sithole and Muzorewa a foothold in the countryside; they were to "politicize" the population.[14] Sithole had in fact proposed a militia of his own ever since he was ousted from ZANU's chairmanship, but it took reports by PsyAc and proposals from Special Branch to set such plans in motion.

In 1977 PsyAc circulated "The Need for the Immediate Implementation of a Safe Return Policy." Without any discussion of how it arrived at its figures, the report reprised that of Frank Kitson (see chapter 3). It listed six categories of guerrillas, the percentage of guerrilla forces each one represented, and how likely each one was to lay down its arms. There was the "dedicated hard core," men who had been trained and indoctrinated in Tanzania or Eastern Europe and were fully committed to Marxist ideologies. These constituted 25 percent of guerrilla forces: "Only the bullet will convert them." Then there were the "hardened" criminals, men who continued their crimes "under the terrorist banner." These were at most 5 percent of guerrilla forces, but they were highly motivated to remain guerrillas. They could "be bought but not converted." More promising was "the long serving workhorse," cadres who after two or three years had seen comrades killed and captured and had "started to wonder if they are really going to win." These were the men who got little in the way of praise and rewards, and "many of them would defect if they had a chance to do so." They constituted 15 percent of guerrilla forces. "The average terrorist" was even more likely to come on sides. These were the men who joined the struggle for the promise of a better life, men who were "unemployed or disgruntled," who did not necessarily understand the ideologies at play but enjoyed the power of the guns they held. These men were not really dedicated and were "susceptible to being convinced they would be better off" if they came into the fold. PsyAc estimated that these were 20 percent of guerrilla forces and that perhaps half of them could be encouraged to defect. "The school-boy adventurer" was equally likely to desert, but for other reasons. These were the young men who joined the struggle because they thought it was glamorous and that independence was near. Now they are "fertile ground for psywar counter action." Such men probably represent 20 percent of guerrilla forces, but possibly half could defect, "especially after a contact, particularly if aircraft is involved." Last was "the unwilling conformist," guerrillas who had been abducted or men who are now as disillusioned as was the schoolboy adventurer. Such men "go along with the gang" because they do not have the "gumption . . . to desert." These men constitute 15 percent of guerrilla forces, but most would desert "if they got the chance."

Even a cautious reading of this report suggested that 40 percent of guerrillas would defect in the right circumstances. The right circumstances, PsyAc made clear, were those in which guerrillas received inducements to surrender; these would not only limit guerrillas' ability to bargain but would save lives. What should those inducements be? "A safe return campaign" would include some form of amnesty, "arguments proving that majority rule has already been achieved," some rewards for weapons handed over and further rewards for information about guerrillas. This was not simply about gathering intelligence but giving these men money with which they could have a "fresh start" in life. They should be given food and clothing, and they should be told they could eventually return to their families. They should also be protected against guerrilla retaliation.[15]

Special Branch studied this report—"with more optimism than the dictates of common sense demanded," according to *Top Secret War*—and brought a plan to the Operations Coordinating Council in January 1978.[16] This was loosely based on a scheme Sithole had brought to the CIO a year earlier. In that plan, supporters would form teams that would be stationed on the routes with which ZANLA entered the country from Mozambique. These teams could vet cadres as they entered Rhodesia. Those who supported Sithole, or were willing to swear allegiance to him, would be allowed in and dispersed to various "collection points" from which they would be sent for training. The others would be turned back. Although

Sithole claimed that many of the guerrillas he met on the border wanted to stop fighting altogether, he was confident he had enough men to continue fighting on his behalf: security forces simply needed to supply them with food, clothing, and ammunition. Once the men were assembled, someone would be appointed to coordinate their training, which could be up and running in two weeks. The CIO was skeptical but saw in Sithole's contradictory evidence the possibility of an army of surrendered guerrillas. Special Branch officers joined him in his home, waiting for guerrilla delegations that never came.[17]

"A Letter to the Comrades"

If long-standing political loyalties did not induce guerrillas to surrender, what would? Rhodesia's Safe Return Program, which became SRP almost at once, was confusing. Was it a program or a policy? Did it offer some degree of amnesty, or did it require guerrillas to change sides? In mid-1977, PsyAc wanted some form of amnesty and financial rewards for weapons, especially Soviet Togarev pistols. Leaflets dropped by air in May 1977 were perhaps too aggressive to make anyone change sides. The texts scoffed at ZANLA training and weapons—"even your new weapons did not help in your cowardly firefight" a few days earlier—and reminded guerrillas of "the truth you know in each of your minds": that "you are cowards, you are badly trained."[18] A few months later, the CIO wanted more amnesty. The ministry of law and order wanted guerrillas who had committed capital crimes to be punished, but Ken Flower thought that once the "fear" of hanging or imprisonment was removed, more guerrillas would surrender. He wanted this plan implemented at once, however politically unpopular it might be, and he wanted both Sithole and Muzorewa to be allowed to bring in their own surrenders.[19] This was to make the SRP even more confusing and less supervised than it had been. Flower's plan was only implemented with earnest certainty in the run-up to the 1979 election.

Early in 1978 the men in Mozambique and Zambia condemned the amnesty offered by the SRP: it could not be taken seriously, wrote the acting president of what was left of Zimbabwe's ANC, unless the government released detainees and political prisoners. The very term was ambiguous; it did not seem to take into account that surrender implied defeat. What worried guerrillas most was that there was nothing in writing; anyone who surrendered in this "safe return" did so based on oral promises; they could be at great risk.[20] A year later, in the weeks before the 1979 election, OCC wrote back to the comrades, much to the delight of the British observers whose report reproduced two handwritten letters to the comrades. (I cannot ascertain if these were the only two or two selected from several such letters.) One was from "former commander Judahs Smoke," sent from a hospital in Fort Victoria to his comrades in the bush. Smoke described how he was seriously injured in a contact with security forces; instead of being left for dead, he was taken to the nearest hospital, where he was treated free of charge. This "proves that security forces aren't murderers as guerrilla thought." He implored the leaders of his platoon to report to the nearest security forces, as some comrades have already done. No harm came to these men; instead, they joined the security forces. "Why should you continue fighting yet we have reached our final goal?" "Stop fighting and join the interim government. Don't delay because if you don't do this before one man one vote elections of 20th April then you might not get a chance to save your lives." There was another handwritten letter, this time from Father Discipline, asking his former comrades "to forget about the war"; the letter stated it was time to rebuild the new Zimbabwe, "so come home and defend your country." General Walls issued several statements, both before and after the election, to both ZANLA and ZIPRA, asking guerrillas to surrender. They would be fed and clothed, and if they so desired they would be transferred to the interim government auxiliaries, Pfumo reVanhu, Muzorewa's army.[21] By the time Muzorewa was prime minister, there were more texts. The UANC issued a flyer titled "Come Home Your Land Awaits You," which called itself "your passport to freedom, and a new and peaceful life in Zimbabwe." All the eager guerrilla would have to do is hide his guns and ammunition, take off his uniform and put on civilian clothes, and bring the paper to any UANC office, where he would be greeted "with peace and joy." The flyer had a short form for the guerrilla to fill out "when you are safe," that asked name, age, previous occupation, and "what interests do you have?"[22]

Could the men so recruited form an army that could actually go into combat against ZANLA or ZIPRA? Special Branch thought this was possible. Some guerrillas had already been brought on side by the work of the ubiquitous Mac McGuiness, when he was Special Branch attached to the Selous Scouts. He had been in contact with officials from Sithole's ZANU and Muzorewa's UANC; he insisted he could identify those guerrillas who were, individually or in groups, ready to come on side. McGuiness had already had some success in that he found "various groups" loyal to Sithole in the northeast of the country, and groups supporting the UANC in the southeast. The actual numbers were small. McGuiness said there were twenty-nine men loyal to Sithole undergoing training in Uganda, as well as one hundred recruits held at a mining town just over the border in Botswana. McGuiness believed that only surrendered guerrillas with allegiance to Sithole or Muzorewa could be used in such an army, and that their administration, deployment, direction, and resupply had to be clandestine and "the sole prerogative of the Selous Scouts," whose experience made them "the only unit capable of such an exercise." These groups would then operate much as the Selous Scouts did, but without radio communication or direct European control.[23] It was hoped that such cadres could operate on the Mozambique border and amplify the leadership dispute in ZANLA and the poor conditions in the camps there. Surrendered ZANLA who had already infiltrated the country might be sent to fight ZIPRA in Midlands. Sithole was thrilled. He boasted to journalists that his army of surrendered guerrillas would allow him to regain control of ZANLA.[24] Muzorewa seemed bewildered by these schemes and programs until he realized that his soldiers would be shock troops to help him in the 1979 election. Indeed, the observers tasked with declaring the 1979 election free and fair were dismayed by "out of control" SFAs loyal to Muzorewa who did not stop "short of physical violence and intimidation of potential voters."[25]

The Dictators' Travelogue

Who was to fund these additional armies? Who paid for the food and clothing for these men? Complaints about how SFAs were paid occupy a larger place in this literature than anything else I've read; how guns or uniforms were purchased never involved so much passion and anguish. *Top Secret War* expressed outrage that Rhodesian government funds were used to train SFAs, for example, but other sources claim that they were paid for from afar. Jim Parker, Special Branch, insisted that South Africa had been funding Sithole for years; it was only in late 1978, and under pressure from US chrome importers, that it abandoned him for Muzorewa. Separate but ever-increasing funds came from South Africa's directorate of military intelligence to support the training of SFAs. Ken Flower brought Sithole to meet the king of Morocco, who gave Sithole $1 million because he was anti-Marxist. Peter McAleese said the sultan of Oman was another benefactor because he had seen what Marxism wrought in Zanzibar.[26] Some

SFAS were trained in Rhodesia, and then in Zimbabwe-Rhodesia, and some were trained abroad in what amounted to a tour of African dictatorships. Muammar Gaddafi trained men for Muzorewa, and Idi Amin trained an indeterminate number of men—depending on the text anywhere from twenty-nine to two hundred—for Sithole. The Anti-Apartheid Movement claimed that some guerrillas were trained in Malawi—Hastings Banda had long supported Sithole—and others were trained by the Shah of Iran's secret police before his downfall.[27] Early in 1978 some armies loyal to both Sithole and Muzorewa were said to be trained in Sudan and in what was then Zaire.[28]

Did Special Branch really ship a few hundred men out of the country, to nations that nominally sanctioned Rhodesia, and have them trained by soldiers they otherwise held in contempt? What kind of arrangements were made for such men, and what kind of training was available to them? Presumably, elements in Malawi's army were tasked with training Zimbabwean guerrillas, but who in those tumultuous years in Iran trained young African men? Was this an official operation, or did a few enterprising policemen train them during their off-hours? It seems possible that whoever brokered the occasional deals that brought British pilots to Rhodesia from the Persian Gulf or relabeled Rhodesian tobacco produce of Angola was also willing to be paid for the transport and training of SFAS; it seems less likely that any military training with reasonably new weapons or knowledge of guerrilla tactics took place.

The exceptions seem to be Libya and Uganda. It is likely that Gaddafi, perhaps even more than King Hassan of Morocco, sought to extend his own influence in Africa rather than allow for that of the USSR, but who transported UANC men to him, and where were they trained? And how and under whose auspices did Amin become involved? Henrik Ellert claimed that many of the Sithole men who trained in Uganda were survivors of the purges in ZANU in 1975 and 1976 who had made their way to Uganda.[29] This may have made political, if not geographic, sense. Amin supported as many liberation movements as would accept his support; he gave land in Bunyoro to the PLO for training. Amin had ties to Sithole going back to 1975, when he headed the OAU. Sithole and members of his high command visited Amin before and after he was removed from ZANU's leadership. Did Sithole approach Amin, or did Oscar Kambona, head of the OAU liberation committee, which channeled East European funds to guerrilla movements? Kambona was close to Amin and perhaps Sithole as well, whom he would have known from his time in Dar es Salaam when he first set up his

9.1 Idi Amin and Zimbabwe Striking Force, n.d. Courtesy of the Uganda Broadcast Corporation.

own ZANU after being ousted as party leader by Robert Mugabe the previous year.³⁰ Whatever the genealogies and connections, ZANU(PF) stalwarts insisted that Amin was Sithole's "benefactor." The line between Amin and Muzorewa and Special Branch vanished at various times in the 1970s, so it is worth asking if it was Sithole or a branch of the Rhodesian security forces that requested that Amin organize the training,?³¹

Certainly, Rhodesia had a role. In December 1977 a group of guerrillas loyal to Sithole refused to fight alongside ZIPRA in Zambia; they were arrested and flown to Uganda.³² Again, who were these men, who arrested them, and who paid for the airplane? Who clothed and fed them? Photographs from the archives of the Uganda Broadcast Corporation depict Sithole's men wearing SFA uniforms. These uniforms were a boon

9.2 Passing-out parade, Zimbabwe Striking Force, n.d. Courtesy of the Uganda Broadcast Corporation.

for beleaguered Rhodesian manufacturing and only available there, but they were hardly the denims or the East European camouflage of the Patriotic Front. Was Britain involved? The foreign office in London hosted a meeting in January 1978 between Amin and a ZANU representative to discuss training Sithole's men. A few months later, there was a report of Rhodesian guerrillas training there. A Shell executive who provided information to Britain said these men were trained by Cubans or perhaps Palestinians but not by the Ugandan army. This may not always have been the case, as the soldier inspecting the passing-out parade of Sithole's men wears a Ugandan army uniform.[33] Amin called these men the Zimbabwe Striking Force—he was partial to the term "strike force"—but what kind of training and what kind of access to guerrilla weapons were available in Uganda in 1978?³⁴ Did Rhodesia supply guns as well as uniforms and airfare?

In June 1978 Stephen Macharaga, ZANU's former press secretary and a former probation officer in Luton, reported that forty-eight men had returned from Uganda to Rhodesia in a Rhodesian military aircraft.³⁵ Several authors insisted they were flown back with Air Trans-Africa, Rhodesia's sanction-busting airline, flying over Tanzanian airspace at night.³⁶ Once back in the country, Sithole's SFAs seem to have had individual sponsors. David Caute wrote of a white rancher, Bob Gawler, who bankrolled Comrade Lloyd, loyal to Sithole and trained in Uganda, to protect his cattle. The district commissioner approved of this, presumably with the knowledge that a few years earlier in other districts white farmers had created African militias to guard their livestock.³⁷ Did those white farmers have contacts who could arrange for SFAs to be shipped to Uganda and points north? I will return to Sithole's men trained in Uganda later; their itinerary and demise encapsulates this chapter, and many issues in this book.

Operation Favour

How were SFAs trained if they did not go to Uganda or Libya? In March 1978, as the army debated more and more call-ups, there were very few surrendered guerrillas. Several generals were concerned that even those few had not seen action; others were relieved as it was not at all clear that the army could manage a larger number of surrendered guerrillas. The RAR, at least, would have nothing to do with them.³⁸ However many surrendered guerrillas there were—and no one thought there were many—were left to the Selous Scouts to be constrained and trained. This was Operation Favour. Much of what was to constitute training was firmly in the Selous Scouts' wheelhouse: the first farms designated as SFA training camps were "frozen," with no other security forces allowed in; Selous Scouts disguised as guerrillas would arrive, pretending to be guerrillas who had already surrendered and supported the internal settlement. As surrendered guerrillas, the Selous Scouts could round up villagers and exhort them to support Muzorewa in all-night pungwes. They could forcefully insist to whichever guerrillas they encountered that it was time to change sides. How were these Selous Scouts to exhort villagers? They were to promote the internal settlement with the narrative that peace and black rule had been achieved. Each Selous Scout was to have a passable cover story in the sense of Frank Kitson's cover stories. Their efforts failed. Was this because there was no peace, or because no one believed it? Did the Selous Scouts tell the stories found in the PsyAc report, and did they present themselves as schoolboy adventurers or long-suffering workhorses? Or did they, as former guerrillas who had already come on side, have their own stories? For experienced Selous Scouts, all of this should have been straightforward: the only difference between this and their earlier operations was that they were infiltrating guerrilla gangs not to hunt them down but to convince them to join them in the fight. In many places, Selous Scouts seem to have managed this, at least throughout 1978, and with as much self-confidence as informed their earlier operations: Comrade Max, for example, was a Selous Scout liaison officer to UANC SFAs; he was said to have been a turned guerrilla who outlived his usefulness and had been tasked with making tea at the fort for at least a year. Farther west, near Gokwe, Sithole's SFAs were accused of poaching elephants and of taking visiting SADF hunting with them.[39]

Operation Favour has been left out of official Selous Scout history, however, and it is absent from almost all the secondary material that relies on *Top Secret War*. Operation Favour does not appear in the copious list of operations in either *Top Secret War* or *Pamwe Chete*, and in the recent collection *Selous Scouts: The Men Speak*, no one spoke of that operation. So what did the Selous Scouts say they did? *Top Secret War* was crystal clear about who was to do what kind of fighting and where: the Selous Scouts were to train the men who were, or pretended to be, former guerrillas, but they were to do so by pretending to be members of another unit and not the "dreaded skuz'apo." Indeed, Selous Scouts trainers had to slow down their instruction in guerrilla tactics; if they demonstrated their expertise, the men being trained to pretend to be guerrillas would realize they were being trained by men who had successfully pretended to be guerrillas. *Top Secret War* insisted that this was a waste of the talents of specialized personnel and a waste of Rhodesian government money. The "so-called auxiliary terrorist[s]" were to be "re-trained and imbued with enthusiasm for their new duties." They would then be set up in *"frozen* areas" in which the newly pretend surrendered guerrillas could "minister to the tribal people there in much the same way they had been doing all along when working for ZANLA or ZIPRA."[40] So were these men, trained by Selous Scouts pretending to be another regiment, really surrendered guerrillas, or were they men pretending to be surrendered guerrillas? And what kind of training would serve the needs and keep the focus of surrendered guerrillas and unemployed urban youths?

How do I understand the role of the Selous Scouts in Operation Favour? Did they do what they said they did or what other authors said they did? The different accounts are not a problem, I think. Historians always deal in contradictory sources, always sift evidence and calibrate analyses to figure out who we think is right. We base our decisions on what we have come to expect from different authors, and why we think one or two might dissemble when others would not. Given the concerns in this book, is it enough to read what *Top Secret War* said the Selous Scouts did with SFAs? Reading that text, I have to ask, How big a problem was it that the Selous Scouts did not admit to being Selous Scouts when they trained SFAs? How seriously do I have to address the layers of masquerade and pretense that inform the Selous Scouts' own account of training of SFAs? They were intense, even by the standards of blacked-up pseudos. But were all the masquerade and pretense necessary? If men were really surrendered guerrillas, presumably they would not need a lot of instruction in guerrilla weapons and tactics. If they were in fact unemployed urban youths, would they have cared who trained them or have been wary of instructors who were at ease with guerrilla tactics? What then were the Selous Scouts pretending about? Did they fear discovery? What would have happened if surrendered guerrillas, men who agreed to fight for the internal settlement, found out the "dreaded skuz'apo" were within range?

Was this masquerade part and parcel of keeping counterinsurgency counter, of keeping the pretend world at the fore? Were secrecy and deception essential to the war effort? Was it necessary to perform secrecy and subterfuge everywhere? Apparently, it was. Keith Nell, SAS seconded to Special Branch to train SFAs, described an interrogation with two captured ZANLA in early 1979. They had been sent to him because he knew the camp they had been in in Zambia; his knowledge of detail could be used to confirm or deny their stories. He was pleased about the assignment because he thought it would give him an edge with Special Branch. The captives were straightforward in their information; they were senior guerrillas who had trained in Libya and Tanzania, but their descriptions of camps and movements made Nell suspicious. He took them to a shooting range, where it became clear they had not been trained with guns at all; they missed the targets altogether. Their knowledge of explosives was minimal beyond laying land mines. Nell's report to his commanding officer was that these were low-ranking guerrillas, and not the senior hard core they claimed to be. His supervisor roared with laughter: of course these men weren't high-ranking guerrillas, he said. They were "nobodies" the CIO used to get their "spying buddies into SB to see what we're up to."[41] Was this the intelligence war—or the intelligence war-in-the-head—fought for no other reason in 1979 than to show the expertise of this or that unit?

Did the SFAs in the camps really not figure out who was training them? Joshua Chakawa interviewed men who boasted that they had been trained by Selous Scouts who were turned guerrillas who had been trained in Mozambique, including a Comrade Max. There was no subterfuge.[42] Barry Stranack, a Selous Scout, assumed that many surrendered guerrillas were ZANLA sent to gather intelligence on the SFA project. He was the sole trainer; he was so suspicious of the former guerrillas that he would go to sleep in one place for a few hours and then move to another to avoid attack.[43] Jim Parker described several attacks on Selous Scouts trainers in these camps. If the SFAs did not know who they were, would they have been more or less aggressive? And what caused the attacks? An unannounced helicopter landing in one case and a gun discharged by accident in another, aggression and confusion at a roadblock, a shooting and a camp riot that could only be diffused by UANC officials, and a land mine on the road Muzorewa was to travel. All of these were characterized as misunderstandings, events and responses for which there was a perfectly adequate explanation. But were these misunderstandings about not knowing who was who or of knowing who was who? For example, there is a story from *Top Secret War* about a white Selous Scout who drove to a newly established camp at sunset, unannounced. He thought the man who tried to block his entrance was ZANLA: he wore denims and was fully armed. The Selous Scout shot the man on sight. This caused a riot at the camp, where white and black Selous Scouts were threatened with almost every weapon in the camp because a white soldier had killed one of their own—not because the shooter was a Selous Scout. Even a member of the interim government—"a former and apparently reformed terrorist"—had difficulty convincing the men that the shooting had been an accident.[44] What was the place of understanding and misunderstanding when guerrillas were both acting as guerrillas and learning to become new kinds of guerrillas from a regiment normally tasked with masquerading as guerrillas but now masquerading as a less flamboyant unit?

By late 1978 SFA training was handed over to the Special Branch, with considerably less make-believe. Keith Nell told Martin, a captured guerrilla, that he would be sent to a bush camp where there were many of his comrades who now supported Muzorewa. Many of these men were from his area and had "common interest" with him. "The plan is to re-train and equip you with firearms so you can go home and fight these ZIPRA thugs."

Nell explained that the camp was on a well-established guerrilla infiltration route "because you comrades need training to be prepared for an attack by fighters at any moment."[45] Special Branch employed its own auxiliaries to train former guerrillas, usually men from the security forces who were not attested policemen but paid well above normal police salaries. This work attracted several foreign soldiers almost at once: these men, including Peter McAleese, lost their "gunner's pay," a thirty-three-dollar monthly combat bonus no longer available to foreign nationals. As more and more men—not necessarily surrendered guerrillas—arrived in the training camps daily, a decidedly not neutral BSAP took over more and more of their training. By January 1979 preparations for the April election had begun, and several Special Branch claimed that the police were now Muzorewa supporters.[46]

Training SFAs

The training of SFAs seems to have been haphazard, without formal protocols or procedures. The men interviewed by Chakawa maintained that the men recruited in late 1977 and 1978 were trained for between three and eight months. They were not always well-equipped: they told Chakawa it could take as long as two months to be outfitted with guerrilla weapons. By late 1978 and throughout most of 1979, SFAs' training was rushed—sometimes as short as a month, but more often three months. The shorter training periods consisted of target practice, assembling and dismantling guns in the morning, with lectures in the afternoon on guerrillas' political ideology and how to gather intelligence about guerrillas.[47] Nevertheless, when security forces visited these camps, they were "horrified" to see SFAs practicing Warsaw Pact drills and singing chimurenga songs.[48] Whatever they sang, by mid-1979 there was a general sense in the country that badly trained SFAs were everywhere. There were more attacks on training personnel in the camps; one white officer was shot in the back. Eighty-eight UANC SFAs were detained for refusing to obey orders at the end of June. A week later there was a mutiny and attempt on a white officer's life at the SFA camp at Mrewa. By late August 1979 more than 1,200 ZANU SFAs had been detained. There were 209 held in Gwelo alone in connection with eighteen murders, numerous rapes, and cases of extortion. Another 150 were in Chikurubi Prison.[49]

Peter McAleese did not believe SFAs were trained with fully operable weapons. Rhodesians so distrusted them, he wrote, that they "often gave them AK bullets with only a couple of grains in the charge, in case they went on a rampage." McAleese may have taken the job for the money, but he was impressed by the one hundred UANC auxiliaries trained in Libya he was in charge of. They were "keen, enthusiastic, and their leadership intelligent," albeit tainted by an obedience to party dogma. These men were put in charge of a protected village—Keep Three—where they did a very good job. They kept the village clean, made note of malnourished children, and reported any suspicious comings and goings. Several months later, in December 1979, McAleese was asked to train a new group of auxiliaries. McAleese's description of the unruly men he made into trackers was to shape future accounts of SFA training and comportment. This group was in marked contrast to the first: the men wore an assortment of track suits, brightly colored shirts and knee socks, and jeans and hats of every color and shape; half the men, he complained, wore mirrored sunglasses. He soon learned that Special Branch had rounded up "every unemployed freeloader" and every unenthusiastic surrendered guerrilla in the region and sent them to McAleese. He managed to raid the quartermaster's stores to get the men outfitted, and Mac McGuiness found them helmets that had been used by the police at a nearby nickel mine. Two months later, McAleese had fifty SFAs ready to be deployed.[50] Henrik Ellert trained a group of SFAs in Midlands in 1979: within two months they had reopened several schools and a clinic in a village and restored a cattle-dipping service.[51]

Keith Nell was tasked with training a group of SFAs to track down the ZIPRA who had shot down a civilian aircraft in 1978. The success of his unit has been contested (see chapter 2) but by his own account owed much to Martin, the cautious young guerrilla who not only came on side but identified which police constables sympathized with ZAPU. Nell had what I can only call a Kitsonian relationship to Martin, with whom he worked closely and to whom he could not bring himself to say goodbye, so powerful were his emotions. As an instructor Nell knew that discipline did not follow from the granting of amnesty, and that the isolated camp was "not the parade ground at Sandhurst," but he was furious when he saw these men "swaggering around with bootlaces undone" and weapons balanced casually on their shoulders. Others wore red bandannas rolled on their foreheads, "several neck chains and a cigarette dangling from the lips, believing that their appearances made them ultra fearsome and extra cool." The instructors of his group were so inept that they injured twelve SFAs in their first shooting exercises.[52]

Descriptions of men who didn't even try to look or act like soldiers were honed in a recent memoir by Lindsay O'Brien, a New Zealander who had left the Rhodesian police to do farm security. It was boring work, and when he was offered a vaguely defined job for twice his police salary on a month-to-month contract, he jumped at the opportunity. The job was training auxiliaries. O'Brien did not expect many surrendered guerrillas and was in fact sanguine about whom he would have to train. If the government paid unemployed African youth, he reckoned, they would be out of "ZANLA's reach." He was, however, discouraged when he met his first UANC group—scores of Africans wearing blue denim and carrying AK-47 rifles, "milling aimlessly around." Far from being surrendered guerrillas, these were young men "dragged out" of urban townships. Only one of the 150 had ever been a guerrilla. The men had received rudimentary military training "conducted with questionable discipline." Again, they wore cheap denims and "struck arrogant poses with their AK-47s," hiding behind sunglasses with cigarettes dangling from their lips. They were like "black James Deans," he wrote, but clothed, fed, and armed by the Rhodesian taxpayer. There was a general grumbling about the pay SFAs received, which in theory was R$30 a month during training and R$40 a month when deployed—with bonuses, it could be as much as R$200 a month—which may have contributed to their unpopularity.[53] The men trained by Lindsay O'Brien, however, were rarely paid; he joked that the men who robbed buses were the entrepreneurs of the group. O'Brien was one of several authors who assumed that when a ragged patrol returned to camp unarmed, they had sold their weapons to ZANLA and had not been ambushed as they claimed.[54] Auxiliaries were a boon for local manufacturers, who supplied cheap clothing, canvas bandoleers, wool blankets, and green towels and provided kickbacks to the white liaison officers who ordered the equipment. O'Brien could not get over the raggedness of the auxiliaries, that they went on patrol like football fans leaving a game. He wrote that these men loved the prestige of imagining themselves to be former guerrillas, bringing peace to the land "sprinkled with the occasional bank robbery." The one genuine former guerrilla, Albert, who had been in Khami Prison for ten years before becoming an auxiliary, had no interest in fighting. Instead, he was keen to provide food to local villagers, as a key to win their hearts and minds; sacks of mealie meal were proof of goodwill. (It may be noteworthy that villagers did not seem to think the mealies were poisoned.) O'Brien's intelligence soon learned that the mealie meal was quickly handed over to ZANLA. He pleaded with Albert to stop handing out food, but Albert insisted: eventually the villagers would understand the auxiliaries had only their welfare at heart. "They will switch allegiances, you'll see," he said. They would switch right back, O'Brien replied, when ZANLA murdered a few.[55]

Killing SFAs

Two things stand out in this section: first, the stories of SFAs killed in groups, either in their training camps after rioting or in a first deployment because of their incompetence, are always reported with specific numbers: 183, 178, 500; second, the delight of security forces in describing these killings. When 41 men trained by the Selous Scouts were killed three days after they arrived in Wedza, Basil Moss, their commander, radioed Reid-Daly. "I don't know whether to classify this as good news or bad news," he began. When he interviewed survivors, however, he realized that the circumstances of the killings had great potential. The survivors described how two of their number—according to *Top Secret War*, either looking for food or looking for women—had gone off on their own; they were captured by or joined with a ZANLA patrol. The leader of the patrol demanded a meeting with the auxiliaries, or the two new members of the patrol suggested it; in any event, the auxiliaries led the ZANLA patrol to their comrades. A few managed to run away, but in all 41 SFAs were shot on the spot. To Moss, this seemed like an opportunity to use SFAs as "live bait." SFAs could enter an area; an isolated auxiliary or two could find, or be captured by, genuine guerrillas. The SFAs could then tell the ZANLA gang where the rest of his comrades were, so that the remaining SFAs, or the Selous Scouts who were masquerading as SFAs, could massacre them.[56]

Compare this with Captain Hamale, the African Selous Scout who refused to leave the ZANLA gang he had trained even though he was compromised. He did not want to kill them, however suspicious they might be. "They are my men," he said. "I trained them." Killing the men, Reid-Daly soon realized, might drive Hamale to ZANLA ("think of the havoc he could cause"), so it was arranged to have the entire gang, including Hamale, captured and turned, a few at a time. By the time everyone was turned, Hamale could reveal himself and enhance his status. Hamale was relieved that his men would survive and did everything he could to make the turning successful.[57] Why was it so important to save Hamale's ZANLA and not Muzorewa's former ZANLA? Why were the men who had never been guerrillas expendable when a ZANLA gang was not?

While I know of no Captain Hamale stories beyond the one in *Top Secret War*, there are many stories, and many published versions of stories, in which newly trained or clueless SFAs were killed before they went to war. Some did not survive camp discipline, some were killed in riots or as punishment for having rioted, and others were killed in their first deployment. Peter McAleese, for example, boasted that he once refused orders to kill an unarmed captive. He was keen to kill in a firefight, he said, but he would never kill in cold blood (see chapter 1). He did not, however, reflect on a story he repeated in which two hundred surrendered ZANLA guerrillas ran riot in a camp, threatening their white training officers and digging defensive bunkers. Special Branch had no patience for this, McAleese reported: a liaison officer, known to this group, came to the camp and issued the former guerrillas "smart, red baseball caps." The next day fire force attacked; armed RLI stormed through the camp while an Alouette K-Car hovered above, blasting 20mm cannon at anyone wearing a red baseball cap. McAleese—the man who wrote several pages about his emotions after his first kill (see chapter 1)—was pleased: "In all 178 stroppy ZANU PF died."[58] The question is not one of who can kill with impunity, I submit, but of who can claim they can kill with impunity.

Take the 100—or 200, 90, or 50—men loyal to Sithole trained in Uganda. Uganda was happy to see them leave, according to Ellert, as their work in Idi Amin's most notorious security organization had become an "embarrassment" for Amin. In April 1978 Rhodesia's CIO sent a freighter from Rhodesia's sanctions-busting airline to return these men to Rhodesia. Sent to an isolated farm for training, the men soon began unauthorized patrols in the countryside, looting, burning, and raping as they demanded villagers tell them the whereabouts of guerrillas. Within a few days, a Rhodesian Army patrol attacked and killed them all. Ken Flower was relieved: their deaths were listed as "'terrorist' deaths but they were prophylactic killings intended to save the lives of countless civilians."[59]

Sithole's men were deemed problematic everywhere. In early 1979 in Gokwe liaison officers reported that they terrorized villagers to get them to support his ZANU; they no longer followed orders from security force personnel. They had begun to cache their weapons as well. No one thought they could be disciplined, so the security forces sought to withdraw them from the operational area.[60] Were these the same Sithole men massacred in Gokwe in July 1979? There are many accounts of a massacre or massacres of SFAs loyal to Sithole during that month. Parker insists these were "a diehard group of some 200 Sithole men" who had been trained in Uganda, who raped and robbed their way around the district. Parker claimed they had to be eliminated in preparation for the February 1980 elections, but no elections had been announced. In July 1979 it would have been very difficult to predict a timetable for a cease-fire and election.[61] The tension, if any more was needed, was that the Commonwealth Heads of State were about to meet in Lusaka, without the still unrecognized Zimbabwe-Rhodesia. That the meeting would issue a communiqué that became the basis for Lancaster House conference and the agreements it reached would have been very difficult to predict. According to Parker, a "top secret plan" was devised to disarm these men. The SFAs were told that a high-ranking Sithole politician was coming to address them and that they would be paid at the same time. They were to assemble on the camp's airstrip. A large force of 10 Rhodesia Regiment had surrounded the airstrip, and two eleven-ton Mercedes trucks with canvas flaps were driven onto the airstrip. The canvas flaps were drawn back to reveal each truck carrying no Sithole supporters but two manned machine guns. A spokesman shouted over a loud hailer that the SFAs were to lay down their weapons; they did not, and the machine gunners opened fire. Even those who tried to escape were shot by Rhodesia Regiment troops. All were killed.[62]

Was this the same massacre listed in a hobbyist's compilation of Rhodesian Air Force air strikes in which there is a minimal listing of a fire force operation against an auxiliary mutiny on 21–22 July 1979, in which 183 auxiliaries were killed?[63] Was this the same massacre reported in the press a few weeks later? Fay Chung, ZANU(PF), attributed the killings—of 183—to Muzorewa, who was both prime minister and minister of defence: he wanted to defeat Sithole once and for all. The deaths were the result of "crossfire." Survivors had different ideas about what happened. One told *The Guardian* that the men were sent to the airstrip, where they would be given NATO weapons and taught how to communicate with aircraft. They were told to come unarmed; otherwise they would make the pilots nervous. They were fired on, and those who tried to escape were shot by ground troops; one said helicopters pursued them into the bush.[64] The *Washington Post* quoted other survivors who told other stories. These too said the men were asked to disarm when government planes flew overhead. They laid down their weapons, and the pilots fired on them. One said the number of dead was closer to 300; forty-three troop carriers were brought to the area. An African farmer said he was "arrested" by security forces and forced, along with several other men, to help pile the dead into two trucks. He counted 160 bodies. The bodies were then thrown into a big pit that was set on fire. Two survivors described the attack on their camp, ten miles away, by soldiers using five helicopters and four troop carriers. They said another 58 Sithole supporters were killed at a camp near the Mozambique border.[65]

Whatever the numbers, and however they are parsed, this is a lot of men killed—easily more than the number of men trained in Uganda—by soldiers on whose side they supposedly fought at a time of intense manpower shortages. That they were without discipline or that they terrorized the countryside is not a wholly satisfactory explanation. Were all these killings necessary? Was there no space left in the country's prisons? These killings are like those attributed to chemical weapons (see chapter 7): the numbers are surprisingly specific and the killings are described with such enthusiasm and specificity. Let me take a term from Stuart Mark's work on sport hunting in the United States. When animals are called semidomesticated, they have lost their autonomy in that they do not hunt for themselves; they are fed and sheltered. Examples of semidomesticated animals are lions in private hunting parks in Southern Africa and quail in private estates in North America. These are animals that are available to be killed; they can be "flushed out" by guns or dogs or people; they can be the "live bait" of the Selous Scouts operations in Wedza or the "prophylactic killing" of the CIO.[66] In this way, Sithole's men in Gokwe were characterized as wild, untrustworthy animals that could not be let out of their enclosures.[67]

The problem with semidomesticates, or any hunting metaphor, however well it describes these killings, is that it makes war irrelevant. What is important here is how these killings constitute part of a war effort, however botched or desperate, and how the different numbers and details of the events of July 1979 reflect on the conduct of that war. First of all, if men do go to war to kill (see chapter 1), would the perpetrators of this massacre be satisfied with the bland description of numbers and trucks? Would no perpetrator recall these events with pride? Second, the deaths seem to stand in numerical isolation. The most we learn about any of the dead is that they were loyal to Sithole or, far less often, Muzorewa. Are there no records of these deaths? Drew Faust's work on the American Civil War describes men giving detailed instructions for who should be notified if they were killed. Other soldiers, who had the basic literacy to write their names unaided, wrote lists of the dead, sometimes to curry favor with officials and sometimes to show off their writing skills.[68] Surrendered guerrillas or petty criminals must have asked some friend or accomplice, somewhere, to notify their families if they died. The young urban Africans, so decried by SFA liaison officers, would have been able to read and write; they may have written letters home or made lists of fallen comrades. Did their relatives never ask what happened to their sons and nephews? Did they not seek compensation?[69] Third, what happened to the bodies? If they were thrown onto trucks and then into pits by farmers threatened with arrest and worse, were those men tormented by the spirits of the dead treated thusly? Identities were more than names in Central Africa. In Lupane in 1998, former guerrillas were baffled by the construction of a tomb of an unknown soldier. How could someone be unknown, they wanted to know.? Who was this man, and where was he from?[70] If several hundred SFAs had been killed by helicopter fire, would not ZANLA and ZIPRA have used this as a reason to refuse going to assembly points a few months later?

The Limits of Counterinsurgency

When I began writing this chapter, I was troubled by how exact these numbers were. As I wrote, I began to realize I was distracted by the 178 red baseball caps, that the exact numbers were not a problem to be solved but an example of the way counterinsurgency was described. Body counts have historically been a way of talking about success in guerrilla war. Beginning with the Korean War, body counts could measure success when no territory was taken and no villages were pacified.[71] The idea of accurate body counts proved something meaningful about the success of counterinsurgency operations, even when those operations were designed to gather intelligence, not kill the enemy. An American serving in the Selous Scouts was impressed with how Rhodesia reckoned body counts. "Unlike Americans in Vietnam, Rhodesians didn't consider a guerrilla a guerrilla unless a weapon was found with his body." Special Branch verified the number of enemy dead with exceptional rigor, he wrote. If eleven men dressed as guerrillas were killed and only ten weapons were found, the body count was ten.[72] In conventional wars body counts take on other meanings. American generals fighting in the Persian Gulf—and in the shadow of Vietnam—wanted to avoid body counts at all costs. Counting enemy corpses got in the way of appreciating the technologies that rained death from the sky. Soldiers, however, understood that the number of their own dead was sacred, numbers that should be reported with reverence, an accounting categorically different from the order of battle enumerating trucks and tanks.[73]

But what should I make of the exact numbers of SFAs killed? These numbers are exact, and they almost stand alone, even if no one can agree on how many of Sithole's men were sent to Uganda or how many were killed in Gokwe a year later. Addressing and interrogating these numbers brings me into the territory of Rigoberta Menchú, and questions about the massacres she described (see chapter 2), about who killed and who was killed and how. In Gokwe in July 1979 there was perhaps a fire force operation killing 183, or 178 wearing baseball caps, or the 200 shot in Parker's account, or the 300 that survivors thought a more accurate number. The numbers are shocking, but the amounts of personnel and equipment—Alouettes, Mercedes trucks, machine guns, airplanes—are even more striking even if they are exaggerated or underestimated. Did survivors count the number of troop carriers or airplanes or machine guns while being fired on? Did they talk about it among themselves later? Did they use exact numbers to make their stories more dramatic and credible? Were the survivors' stories like those told in Menchú's carefully and socially constructed accounts, combining memories and imaginaries of being tricked to their own execution, of being chased into the bush by helicopter fire? But what of the soldiers' accounts? What am I to make of the boasts of cleverness and command, of dispensing red baseball caps and eleven-ton Mercedes trucks and unimaginable firepower to eliminate fewer than two hundred mutineers? Did security forces use exact numbers to make their stories more dramatic and credible?

There is another question, one that comes directly out of the debates about Menchu's story: Does the actual number of Mercedes trucks, or Alouettes, or of soldiers, matter? In terms of this book, the answer is a resounding yes because counterinsurgency is about small groups and single individuals—T. E. Lawrence, or Frank Kitson, or Ron Reid-Daly—and its conduct is a matter of exact numbers and proportions: a counterinsurgency unit should have a ratio to insurgent forces. Nowhere is this clearer than in the "lessons from" literature (see chapter 3). "Successful" counterinsurgencies—Malaya or El Salvador—should have a ratio of ten security forces to one insurgent. Because Rhodesia's ratio was probably less than one to one, it could rely on smaller units that gathered intelligence. This generated its own set of numbers. Thus, the Selous Scouts operated in eight-man sections, a number chosen by the Rhodesian Army "precisely because this was the size of the typical insurgent unit." By 1978 the Selous Scouts were credited with giving intelligence that led to 68 percent of all enemy kills.[74] John Early, an American serving with the regiment, went further: "The Selous Scouts alone had killed or captured more enemy than the entire army."[75] There were the inevitable tallies of the dead in various raids, and the Selous Scouts' postwar glee at comparing the UNHCR's numbers of dead and wounded at Nyadzonya—"exactly half"—with the number reported by ZANLA.[76] Did accounts of killing 178, or 200, or 300 SFAS offer another version of this, that Rhodesia did not need these hundreds of auxiliaries, even though their slaying required many soldiers?

But why kill men you trained, men who were broadly on your side? Even if numbers are exaggerated and some massacres made up, this is not a sound military strategy. If there was no overall policy to defeat the enemy, if there were at best competing ideas about how to position Rhodesia and Zimbabwe-Rhodesia in future negotiations, what was the role of auxiliaries other than to show the white population that the guerrilla war was winding down? If the war was to end by driving ZANLA and ZIPRA from host countries, did auxiliaries serve any other purpose than being expendable? And by mid-1979 were counterinsurgency operatives less concerned with victories than they were engaged in protecting their own expertise? Separate from poaching and ivory-running operations—which were all white anyway—the Selous Scouts had constructed a specific kind of African Selous Scout (see chapter 4) that was undermined by unruly SFAs. Where the killing of hapless or violent or Sithole-supporting SFAs made sense was in promoting an ideal of counterinsurgency, the "dreaded skuz'apo." The elite units who defined themselves with great and exclusive clarity as small, skilled groups that were so specialized and elite that former guerrillas or urban toughs who had learned their ways had to be contained and eliminated.

For the army at large, these stories from the last years of the war threw too much into high relief. Killing the enemy was not a practice recounted with anecdotes and exact numbers, but killing men trained to fight alongside security forces was.

CONCLUSIONS

For most of the many years I've been working with this material, I did not think I'd write a book about it. It's not that I had misgivings about writing a book about white soldiers fighting against African nationalism, but that it seemed to be a project that was too episodic, too disjointed to be a monograph. Indeed, three chapters are revised from articles written more than a decade ago about topics that caught my eye, rather than a desire to answer a specific question. I'm not sure I can say what exactly made me realize this material could be a book, but it had to do less with the politics of my subject matter than with the processes of writing history, and the questions of evidence that were at play therein. The questions that are so basic to social history but also to studies of war are those of experience, however troubling the term might be: What was it like to be there? How did soldiers describe being there years after the conflict was over? As I began to read and reread these memoirs, and as more memoirs were published, and revised and published again in this century, it struck me that this was a body of literature that offered a glimpse of soldiers' actions—and reactions to other soldiers' descriptions thereof—that gave me a history of this war that turned out to be broader and more political than anything I originally thought I'd write. Many narrow, personal accounts raised big questions.

The most important of these questions—but not necessarily the first one I asked—was that of Rhodesia's overall strategy. Did the country and its security forces have a clear idea of military victory in mind? Just as there were shifts in the official rationale for the war—defending minority rule, fighting communism, defending a specific and limited form of minority rule or defending an even more limited form of majority rule—there were shifts in its goals. While many tendencies in the security forces wanted to vanquish guerrilla armies once and for all, government and military officers imagined a negotiated settlement in which Rhodesian military strength would guarantee some form of minority rule or at least significant protection for whites.

But if majority rule was even on the table, what were the military goals? By the mid-1970s, regular soldiers and national servicemen complained that they did not know what they were fighting for. Many insisted they were being held back, that the war effort was not aggressive. For me, writing about this war in what Leonard Smith has called a won/lost battle narrative seemed beside the point: it could not accommodate the ambiguities and sometime exhaustion of command and control.[1] For that reason, I have not spent much time in this book debating scholars who have argued about who won and who lost and why. Much of what those authors wrote went beyond the "won-every-battle" mantra, but not necessarily with great subtlety. Many of these scholars' texts claimed that Rhodesia lost because it had no support from Western powers or lost in spite of covert support from Western powers, or that Rhodesia lost because guerrillas had Russian support or Chinese support or support from Christian groups in Europe.[2]

In this book I am concerned with soldiers' understanding of the war and their experiences therein, how they described the war, how and what they debated about it, and the extent of their frequent and often litigious disagreements. All of this answered questions larger than the ones I had originally asked. These memoirs, taken together, suggested that counterinsurgency and small intelligence-gathering groups tracking guerrillas in the bush might have been more successful as a story than they were as a practice. These memoirs revealed that "turned" guerrillas did not always turn for long, that they were often biding their time until they could rejoin their comrades in Mozambique or Zambia. Reading these memoirs led me to doubt some of the more elaborate schemes of chemical and biological warfare. These descriptions were of some of the most inefficient strategies imaginable, and they often seemed to be postwar embellishments of African ideas about harming that took hold in the security forces.

There were other questions, of course, not the least of which was that of pseudo gangs. Did those white men really think they could pass as Africans? Did the young men who demanded to be seen as descendants of pioneers believe they could successfully mimic Africans? The answer was actually yes and no, but the more important question was what did being like an African mean to young men who were as proud of their tracking skills as they were of fighting to keep government in "responsible hands"? Any interrogation of this masquerade, whether it was real or imagined, raised the larger question of race in this war. Were black and white binaries—signaled by the two names of the country—or were they shorthand for political loyalties? Was this a war between blacks and whites, in which whites pretending to be black and blacks fighting for Rhodesia made it even more complicated than I thought, or was this about ideology and competing nationalist visions that happened to be articulated by blacks and whites? All these questions were problematic, however. Black and white might be opposites, but they were at best a messy binary. Yes, whites fought against Africans, often with other Africans, but just as there was a seepage of vocabulary ("mombies," for example) and language ("Your Shona is better than mine!"), there was the idealized childhood of Rhodesian soldiers—even those who were born in Britain—who learned the ways of the wild from Africans. This was bushcraft, a knowledge of place that was raced at its core. Africans were not to be looked down upon, but learned from: their knowledge could be appropriated, but as most Rhodesian memoirists would tell you, appropriated knowledge was never as good as that of Africans. This did not mean national servicemen believed Africans deserved full political representation; it meant that Africans' knowledge was the means to tame the land whites claimed for themselves. It was this notion of taming—and not, perhaps, more nebulous ideas of conquest or suppression—that made literal subservience come to the fore in this war. The forms of domination white soldiers sought were decidedly intimate. Ideas about racial domination were bundled into ideas about domesticity—not just in the hearth and home and the guerrillas who became expert at making tea, but in service and domestic work, as in the "tame" terrorists brought on side by the Selous Scouts or the government of Zimbabwe-Rhodesia. Race turned out to be really complicated; it was the category of superior knowledge of flora and fauna and that of loyal subservience. Was this why so many SFAs were so readily killed? Was their knowledge of the Rhodesian wild compromised by training in Uganda or Iran? Were Sithole's men so untamed and wild that they had to be killed by the hundreds?

Nevertheless, this was not a war fought by rugged young white men against undisciplined black men who were wild and untamed. If Africans crossed the border to train in the camps of Mozambique and Tanzania, they were assumed to be better trained with better guns and more elaborate subterfuge than they themselves said they were. Moreover, they had weapons—most often new weapons—that were proof of a transnational network of support and expertise. Africans changed with place, not time.

It was bushcraft and the ways of the wild learned best from Africans that changed with time, to accommodate the Rhodesian war effort. White soldiers had to learn to track guerrillas and to learn how guerrillas covered their tracks, how they marched when they were tired, and how they tended wounded men. Wartime training included knowledge of African food preferences, learning the frequency of African bowel movements, and knowing which patent medicines guerrillas found most efficacious and which accessories of dress were in fashion at which time.

If white men could masquerade as black men, however briefly, could black men pretend to be white, ever? The set of skills Africans could learn to be like whites was decidedly limited, and most often limited to household chores. Again, we see black and white as a messy and uneven binary: pseudo only worked one way. Black men could not pretend to be white men, but white men could pretend to be white Rhodesians. But if a white American could feel like a Rhodesian or if an Australian could come to fight guerrillas for personal reasons, what did it mean to have been born in the country? Was whiteness at work in the Rhodesian imaginary? I have argued elsewhere that whiteness had a very specific meaning in the British Empire. In many colonies "white" was a vague and ambiguous term that referred to a constellation of physical and cultural traits that joined a debate as to whether or not white bodies could live in Africa or Asia. This question was thrown into high relief with the decolonization of settler colonies.[3] The participation of the American men who told David Caute and Christopher Hitchens that they had come to Rhodesia because the "white man is running out all over" was a special kind of response. Rhodesia was a place for whites that was worth traipsing around the globe for. On the ground, however, the idea of a unified white condition was risible. Rhodesian-born soldiers, like Angus Shaw, were contemptuous of the foreigners who came to fight with them. "It wasn't their war." They "went around looking for other peoples' nasty little wars to fight in."[4] A generalized condition of whiteness had limits, as Ian Smith noted when he realized South Africa was willing to sacrifice Rhodesia for security on its northern border. "When the crunch comes," he wrote in his memoirs, "blacks will stand together but with the white people dog starts eating dog."[5] Moreover, a global whiteness seems to have been irrelevant for many white Rhodesian men, wherever they were born and wherever they grew up. The fictions of childhood associations with Africans became a way to claim an attachment to Africa. As their belonging to the country was challenged, tropes of land and belonging quickened.[6]

These war memoirs are one of the forms that quickening took. Along with Rhodesian war novels, they are a genre of experience, of history, and of a profound link to a place that was not always grounded in an author's biography. These texts are categorically different from the "won-every-battle" mantra and stand in sharp contrast to that of Rhodesia's line in the sand, the place where white men said, "So far and no further!"[7] They express doubts and misgivings and disobedience even as they depict good shooting, successful contacts, and the comradery of army life. These memoirs do more than add pranks and hesitation to the literature of Rhodesian intransigence and courage; they complicate the "lessons from" genre of military expertise. Even without these memoirs, there is something humbling about small groups gathering intelligence studying the kinds of hatbands guerrillas liked best and which patent medicines cured impotence. Taken together, these memoirs suggest that there were limits to the Rhodesian and perhaps any white nationalist project, limits most clearly legible in the tension between fighting and writing. In their writings, whites wanted African servants not only good at making and serving tea but tamed from their former selves, but those were not the goals for which they fought. But in fighting that war, white soldiers—even those who wanted a more aggressive army, even those who wanted more Africans in that army—did not take all orders as a given, nor did they obey all commands. This was the tension of men who boasted about the killing of hundreds of men trained by security forces in mid-1979 just as they joked about Rhobabwe. These were men who understood they were fighting for a negotiated settlement and who could not fully envision a future in a country governed by Africans.

NOTES

Notes to Chapter 1

1 Godwin, *Mukiwa*, 321, 325.
2 Indeed, see Wood, *So Far and No Further!*
3 Nasson, *Boer War*, 285–300.
4 Blight, *Race and Reunion*.
5 Chennells, "Rhodesian Discourse, Rhodesian Novels," in Bhebe and Ranger, *Society in Zimbabwe's Liberation War*, 2:102–29. For the rising itself, the large body of literature is very skillfully summarized by Ndlovu-Gatsheni, "Mapping Cultural and Colonial Encounters."
6 Southern Rhodesian farmers, at least, sought a federation without any irony at all: "The copper mines could pay for the development of the whole area, the same as coal mines did in Britain and gold in South Africa." Carl Herbert Fox, Salisbury, 7 November 1973, National Archives of Zimbabwe [hereafter cited as NAZ] /ORAL/FO2.
7 See Leys, *European Politics in Southern Rhodesia*; Blake, *History of Rhodesia*; Murphy, *Party Politics and Decolonization*; and Mlambo, "From the Second World War."
8 See White, *Unpopular Sovereignty*, 68–104.
9 Ranger, *"Are We Not Also Men?"*; Wood, *So Far and No Further!*; Murphy, "'Intricate and Distasteful Subject,'" 764–65; Watts, *Rhodesia's Unilateral Declaration of Independence*, 62–63.
10 This summary is from White, *Assassination of Herbert Chitepo*, 16–18.
11 Shubin, *Hot Cold War*, 151–75; Mazarire, "ZANU's External Networks," 83–106; Dabengwa, "Relations between ZAPU and the USSR," 215–19. For township violence, see Scarnecchia, *Urban Roots of Democracy*.
12 Martin and Johnson, *Struggle for Zimbabwe*, 73–85; Macmillan, *Lusaka Years*, 39–90; Davis, *ANC's War against Apartheid*, 58–84.
13 White, *Assassination of Herbert Chitepo*, 18–24; Martin and Johnson, *Chitepo Assassination*, 79–81; Chung, *Re-living the Second Chimurenga*, 85–106.
14 See, for example, Mhanda, *Dzino*.
15 See I. D. Smith, *Great Betrayal*.
16 White, *Unpopular Sovereignty*, 233–50.
17 White, *Unpopular Sovereignty*, 255–76.

18 Mlambo, *White Immigration into Rhodesia*, 1–2, 5, 11–12; Brownell, *Collapse of Rhodesia*, 3–4, 72–79.
19 Bolze and Ravan, *More Life with UDI*, 141; author's field notes, Bulawayo, 10 July 1999. Louis Bolze came to Southern Rhodesia from South Africa in 1955 to work for the railway. In 1964 he set up a publishing company and book clubs to buy what he published. In 1966 he worked with a local illustrator to produce a cartoon history of UDI.
20 Hughes, *Whiteness in Zimbabwe*; Pilossof, *Unbearable Whiteness of Being*.
21 Author's field notes, Barton-on-Sea, 31 July 2003; Binda, *Masoja*; Stewart, *Rhodesian African Rifles*.
22 Bond, *Incredibles*, 10–11; Binda, *Saints*, 22–23; Binda, *Rhodesia*, 148–52; Hoare, *Mercenary*, 66–67.
23 The most famous example is Eugene de Kock. See de Kock, *Long Night's Damage*, 58–60; Jansen, *Eugene de Kock*, 47–64.
24 Commanders' Secretariat, Operations Coordinating Committee [OCC], Minutes, 20 April and 2 July 1974, Rhodesian Army Association Papers [hereafter cited as RAA], British Empire and Commonwealth Museum, Bristol; RAA/2001/86/026(A)/157.
25 Seirlis, "Undoing the United Front?," 80; Bond, *Incredibles*, 10–16; Chris Cocks, *Fireforce*, 111.
26 BSAP HQ, Salisbury, to Comops, Utilization of Manpower, 22 August 1977; Guard Force HQ, Salisbury to Comops HQ, Re: Sixty Days In–Thirty Days Out Call-up, 23 August 1977, RAA/2001/086/147/927.
27 Caute, *Under the Skin*, 135–37; Brownell, *Collapse of Rhodesia*, 82; Godwin and Hancock, *"Rhodesians Never Die,"* 88, 113, 135, 158–59, 254; Alexandre Binda, *Rhodesia Regiment*, 192, 228; Anti-Apartheid Movement, *Fireforce Exposed*, 8; Cilliers, *Counter-insurgency in Rhodesia*, 43–44; Commanders' Secretariat, Operations Coordinating Committee, Minutes, 29 April 1976, RAA/2001/086/241/159, Joint Operating Command Minutes, 26 June 1978, RAA/2001/086/015/892; Secretary for Law and Order, Usage of 50–60 Age Group, 9 March 1979, RAA/2001/086/147/927.
28 Rousseau, "Counter-revolutionary Warfare," 1343–61.
29 See Lan, *Guns and Rain*; Reno, *Warfare in Independent Africa*.
30 Shaw, *Kadaya*, 26.
31 Hynes, *Soldier's Tale*, 77.
32 J. Morris, *Destinations*, 127–28.
33 Croukamp, *Only My Friends*, 149.
34 Gledhill, *One Commando*, 46.
35 I am grateful to Steve Davis for suggesting this line of analysis.
36 Hull, *Absolute Destruction*, 44–66.
37 White, *Unpopular Sovereignty*, 276–79.
38 White, *Unpopular Sovereignty*, 302–7. The quotation is from Lemon, *Never Quite a Soldier*, 261.

39 Godwin, *Mukiwa*, 208; Doke, *First Born*, 75.
40 Intelligence Reports, casual sources, 27 May 1976, RAA/2001/086/050/1001.
41 Army Counter Intelligence, Consolidated report from Main JOCs [Joint Operational Command] on State of Morale in the Territorial Army, typescript, 5 May 1977, RAA/2001/086/263/997; Wylie, *Dead Leaves*, 39.
42 Consolidated Report on the State of Morale in the Territorial Army, 5 May 1977, RAA/2001/086/263/997.
43 Army Counter Intelligence, Morale throughout the Rhodesian Army, typescript, 1 June 1977; Army Counter Intelligence, interim report on Morale throughout the Units of the Rhodesian Army, typescript, 14 June 1977; Army Counter Intelligence, interview with half of C Squadron at Old Cranborne Barracks, RAA/2001/086/263/997. RAR, in contrast, wanted a pay review at once and home loans; many African regulars suggested that if African, Coloured, and white troops went through basic training together, the army would be much more efficient. Secret, carbon, n.d., but with July 1977 material, probably by Military Intelligence, African soldier morale, RAA/2001/086/263/997.
44 Onslow and Berry, "*Why Did You Fight*," 15. For happy white farmers, see Palmer, "Land Reform in Zimbabwe, 1980-1990," 163-81.
45 The canonical versions of this are Cocks, *Fireforce*, 7-8, and Godwin, *Mukiwa*, 207-9. The quotation is from Coltart, *Struggle Continues*, 53.
46 See White, *Unpopular Sovereignty*, 177-205.
47 Officer commanding, CID, to Commander of the Army, Deserters, 19 January 1977, RAA 2001/086/047/141.
48 Morris, *Destinations*, 127.
49 Wylie, *Dead Leaves*, 39.
50 For colonial soldiers, see Mann, *Native Sons*, 33-41; Moyd, *Violent Intermediaries*, 2-3. For guerrillas and RAR, see White, "'Whoever Saw a Country?,'" 619-31.
51 Fulton, *Into the Vortex*.
52 Dower, *War without Mercy*. New technologies made it easier to dehumanize enemies: a thermal image provided a less troubling target than a face. See Grossman, *On Killing*, 186-92.
53 Bourke, *Intimate History of Killing*, 28-30, 45, 79.
54 Sassoon, *Memoirs of an Infantry*, 12-13.
55 Browning, *Ordinary Men*.
56 D. Hoffman, *War Machines*, 55-56.
57 Cocks, *Fireforce*, 46.
58 Croukamp, *Only My Friends*, 149. The innocence of animals is a frequent observation in Rhodesian war memoirs. See, for example, Hall, *Weep for Africa*, 282-84.
59 MacLeish, *Making War at Fort Hood*, 121-22. For men about to retire, a diagnosis of PTSD may speed up access to medical care, but for men who continued in the service the diagnosis would stand in the way of promotion.
60 Baines, *South Africa's "Border War*," 82.

61 McAleese, *No Mean Soldier*, 7–8. In his barely revised memoir, McAleese amended the sentence to read: "I was a very aggressive young man and I had found an arena that I could sublimate this aggression." McAleese, *Beyond No Mean Soldier*, 18.
62 S. L. A. Marshall, *Men against Fire*; Strachan, "Training, Morale, and Modern War," 211–27.
63 Terrorist Training Camps: Tanzania, 7 May 1974, and Security Report: Interrogation of Captured ZANLA Terrorist Maxwell Mushonga, 29 August 1974, RAA/2001/086/809/143/3.
64 These quotations are from three former RLI, two of whom became professional authors: Cocks, *Fireforce*, 15–18; Shaw, *Kandaya*, 33–35; and Balaam, *Bush War Operator*, 132–33. Shaw told me he went to war with a notebook, recording every rumor he heard. Author's field notes, Harare, 5 July 2001.
65 Browning, *Ordinary Men*, 59, 62.
66 McAleese, *No Mean Soldier*, 156–57.
67 Balaam, *Bush War Operator*, 98–99.
68 L. Smith, *Embattled Self*, 95–100.
69 McGregor, *Crossing the Zambezi*, 146–47. An American researcher in Rhodesia in the 1970s was told that Rhodesian forces used the crocodile farm near Lake Kariba (see chapter 4) to introduce crocodiles to the lake to keep ZIPRA from crossing. Author's field notes, Gainesville, 19 March 2004.
70 Stiff, *Rain Goddess*, 207–10.
71 Meadows, *Sand in the Wind*, 318–19, 510–12.
72 R. Early, *Time of Madness*, 209–11, 262–66. Shortly after I published an earlier version of chapter 6 in 2009, I received an email from a former RAR officer. "Dear Luise," he wrote. "You are wrong about African shooting. I was in greater danger of being killed by falling branches."
73 Walsh, *Mampara*, 56–57.
74 Lunderstedt, *Forever Boys*, 115–16.
75 Shaw, *Kandaya*, 81–82.
76 Wylie, *Dead Leaves*, 128.
77 L. Smith, *Between Mutiny and Obedience*.
78 Refusal to Parade at Depot, 11 October 1973, RAA/2001/086/047/141.
79 The white officer was Andre Dennison (see chapter 8). Wood, *War Diaries of Andre Dennison*, 334n; author's field notes, Pretoria, 10 April 2014.
80 Twagira, "'The Men Have Come,'" 813–32.
81 Caute, *Under the Skin*, 364.
82 Caute, *Under the Skin*, 346.
83 Col. J. C. Kok, Plakkertjies Gerbruik in Rhodesie se Stryd Teen Terroriste, South African Police Archives, Pretoria, 30–6/1/49; Robin Wright, "Propaganda: The Other Rhodesian War," Alicia Patterson Foundation, mimeo., 1976, Sterling Memorial Library, Yale University, African Collection Group 605/Box 45/797; Scully, *Exit Rhodesia*, 72. David Caute reported television ads: for "the ladies" a

middle-aged woman in a BSAP uniform was shown holding a document. "Girls," the voice-over intoned, "if it says Confidential, it means Confidential." The version for men was a "manly" "Keep your trap shut." Caute, *Under the Skin*, 330.
84 Almost a quarter of the text of one book is devoted to practical jokes and pranks. C. Warren, *Stick Leader RLI*.
85 Rhodesia Broadcasting Corporation, *Broadcasting in the Seventies*, 8.

Notes to Chapter 2

1 Foucault, "What Is an Author?," 206–22. When I went over my notes to begin this book, I was struck by how many former soldiers talked about these books, recommending some and dismissing others For a paraphrase of the beginning of the film *Patton*, see Gledhill, *One Commando*, 46. For a citation to my work, see Parker, *Assignment Selous Scouts*, 292.
2 Barlow, *Executive Outcomes*, 522.
3 Appiah, "Is the Post- in Postmodernism?," 336–57.
4 Jal, *War Child*, 7, 178–79.
5 Fuller, *Scribbling the Cat*, 253.
6 Margery Perham, "Foreword," xi.
7 J. G. Davies, *Hold My Hand I'm Dying*, 30.
8 Barnett and Njama, *Mau Mau from Within*. Barnett's dissertation was a study of the guerrilla forces in central Kenya, completed in 1963. Barnett set up the Liberation Support Movement in Richmond, British Columbia (where he taught), which published "Life Histories from the Revolution." Although several of these life histories were published well into the early 1970s, the three Mau Mau life histories are at least as interesting as Njama in that the men interviewed did not have a stable Mau Mau narrative in which to locate themselves. One boasts of his cleverness working as a police informer as his cover.
9 Okello, *Revolution in Zanzibar*.
10 Grimstad, "Zanzibar," 146.
11 Odinga, *Not Yet Uhuru*, xii.
12 Davis, "Struggle History and Self-Help," 174.
13 Couser, *Memoir*, 22–23.
14 Foucault, "What Is an Author?"
15 Clough, *Mau Mau Memoirs*, 16–21.
16 Willis, "Two Lives of Mpamizo," 319–32.
17 Carretta, "Olaudah Equiano or Gustavus Vassa," 96–105; *Equiano the African*; and "Methodology in the Making," 172–9.
18 Byrd, "Eboe, Country, Nation," 123–48; Sweet, "Mistaken Identities?," 279–306.
19 Stoll, *Rigoberta Menchú and the Story*, 181–83; Arias, "Rigoberta Menchú's History," and "Arturo Taracena Breaks His Silence," 3–28, 82–98. I owe much of my thinking about testimony to L. Smith, *Embattled Self*, 195–97.

20 Burgos-Debray, *I, Rigoberta Menchú*; Stoll, *Between Two Armies*; Warren, "Telling Truths," 198–218.
21 Burgos-Debray, *I, Rigoberta Menchú*, 186; Stoll, *Rigoberta Menchú and the Story*, 70–88.
22 Burgos, "How I Became," ix–xvii.
23 Dane Llano, "I, Rigoberta Menchú?," 96–101.
24 Couser, *Memoir*, 84–86.
25 Aznárez, "Rigoberta Menchú," interview with Rigoberta Menchú in Arias, *Rigoberta Menchú Controversy*, 110, 113, 113.
26 Dahmen, "Construction of," 115–30; Rak, "Memoir, Truthiness," 83–85.
27 Borst, "Managing the Crisis," 148–76.
28 Hynes, *Soldiers' Tale*, 1.
29 L. Smith, *Embattled Self*, 198.
30 Fussell, *Great War and Modern Memory*, 310.
31 O'Brien, *Things They Carried*, 82.
32 Hynes, *Soldiers' Tale*, 75.
33 L. Smith, *Embattled Self*, 21.
34 Van der Byl is quoted in many places; see White, *Unpopular Sovereignty*, 29–30; Shaw, *Kandaya*, 26.
35 Fussell, *Great War and Modern Memory*, 155–79; Hynes, *Soldiers' Tale*, 31–33; L. Smith, *Embattled Self*, 148.
36 Hynes, *Soldiers' Tale*, 77–80; see also Fussell quoting Robert Graves, *Great War and Modern Memory*, 205.
37 Hynes, *Soldiers' Tale*, 165–76.
38 Hynes, *Soldiers' Tale*, 206.
39 Baines, *South Africa's "Border War,"* 14–22, 34–49.
40 De Kock, *Long Night's Damage*; Gobodo-Madikizela, *Human Being Died That Night*; Jansen, *Eugene de Kock*. For a detailed discussion of interviewing a professional interrogator, see Coetzee, *Written under the Skin*.
41 L. Smith, *Embattled Self*, 13, 148–49.
42 Whitlock, *Soft Weapons*, 5–8, 106–10.
43 Whitlock, *Soft Weapons*, 72.
44 Lamb, *House of Stone*.
45 Stiff, *See You in November*; Flower, *Serving Secretly*; White, *Assassination of Herbert Chitepo*, 86–87.
46 Cocks, *Fireforce*, 7. Some version of this story appears in other memoirs and novels. See Godwin, *Mukiwa*, 208; Doke, *First Born*, 74–75; and White, "Civic Virtue, Young Men," 103–21.
47 Cocks, *Fireforce*, 110–11.
48 Cocks, *Survival Course*, 54. This was reissued by 30 Degrees South in 2008 as *Out of Action*.
49 Personal communication, 12 May 2017.

50 Godwin, *Mukiwa*, 208; Doke, *First Born*; Conrad K., *In the Shadow*, 200. For a summary, see White, *Unpopular Sovereignty*, 187.
51 Moore-King, *White Man, Black War*, 52–56.
52 Baughman, *Angle*, ch. 6.
53 McAleese, *No Mean Soldier*, 86.
54 Cronin, *The Bleed*, ch. 7; Cross, *Dirty War*, 115–16.
55 Nyathi and Hoffman, *Tomorrow Is Built Today*, 34–35; Nell, *Viscount Down*, 19–49; Pringle, *Green Leader*, 60–91; *Murder in the Zambezi*; Luise White, "'Deafening Silence,'" 111–26.
56 Caute, *Under the Skin*, 309–11; Nell, *Viscount Down*, 352–61; Pringle, *Green Leader*, 96–97.
57 Wessels, *Handful of Hard Men*, 185–88.
58 Alp, *Uncomfortable Truth*.
59 Godwin, *Mukiwa*, 300–301; author's field notes, Durban, 6 August 2001; Johannesburg, 20 August 2004.
60 For a description of the panic and anxious recriminations within a patrol when innocent curfew breakers were shot, see Moore-King, *White Man, Black War*, 45–50.
61 Shaw, *Kandaya*, 81–82; author's field notes, Harare, 5 July 2001.
62 Hynes, *Soldiers' Tale*, 3–4.
63 Stiff, *Selous Scouts: A Pictorial Account*, 170–71.
64 Harper-Ronald, *Sunday, Bloody Sunday*, front matter.
65 Author's field notes, Germinston, 14 April 2014.
66 Moylan, *See You Back*, 25.
67 Stranack, *Demand a Brave Heart*, 76. Spelling may be the lowest form of literary analysis, but bad spelling may offer some insight into just how oral some of these texts are and how slow security agents were to learn about African politics. In 1962, South African authorities arrested the Africans, including ANC leaders and a few informers who met at a guerrilla training school in the Western Cape. The police doing the interrogations did not necessarily know what guerrillas did and what their training might require. One policeman learned of a pamphlet about Xastro's Xuba, writing the title of a pamphlet as though it was Xhosa. In the transcription of the testimony of another informer, "guerrillas" is written "gorillas." Davis, *The ANC's War against Apartheid*, 38. In South Africa, guerrillas now working for the South African police were called askaris, from a Swahili word that comes from Arabic, meaning someone armed. The word seems to have been first coined by guerrillas: MK trained in Tanzania, and before Swahili newspapers came up with the literal translation for "fighter," men being trained to use arms would have heard the Swahili word. But as late as 1988, interrogators and prosecutors could not spell the word. One spelled it s-c-a-r-e, saying he thought it was English. The prosecutor could not spell it either, saying it was a-s-c-a-r-i-s, or perhaps it ended with e-s. Security files from Maputo reported that Jacob Xuma

and Albie Sachs both lived on Julius Ngere Avenue, surprising as it is that they did not know the name of the president of Tanzania, Julius Nyerere. Dlamini, *Askari*, 35, 124.

68 Of a large literature, one edited collection stands out; see Hansen, *African Encounters with Domesticity*.
69 Comaroff and Comaroff, "Home-Made Hegemony," 37–74; Hunt, "Colonial Fairy Tales," 143–71.
70 Reid-Daly as told to Stiff, *Top Secret War*, 66, 94–95, 224–25; Reid-Daly, *Pamwe Chete*, 472. The actual authorship of *Selous Scouts: Top Secret War* is so opaque and contested (see chapter 5) that I am citing it by its subtitle only.
71 Thomas, *Shadows in an African Twilight*, 177–81.
72 Cocks, *Fireforce*, 57,
73 Atkins, *Once upon a White Man*, 79–80.
74 Trethowan, *Delta Scout*, 167.
75 Ballinger, *Walk against the Stream*, 156.
76 Reid-Daly, *Top Secret War*, 372.
77 Ballinger, *Walk against the Stream*, 277.
78 Reid-Daly, *Top Secret War,* 147.
79 Taylor, *Lost in Africa*; Shaw, *Kandaya*, 3–8; Cocks, *Fireforce*, 62–63; Cocks, *Survival Course*, 123; Stiff, *See You in November*, 309.
80 Godwin, *Mukiwa*, 301–2.
81 Holmes, *Acts of War*, 360–65; Fussell, *Great War and Modern Memory*, 189–90.
82 Lessing, *African Laughter,* xi–xii. Lessing lists "honkey" for whites not as derived from American slang but as indigenous "because whites talk through their noses, say Africans."
83 Bond, *Incredibles*, 151–54.
84 S. Smith, *Ginette*, 121–22.
85 A novel about a Coloured Rhodesian soldier who defects to ZIPRA is written in the first person entirely in Taal. Hotz, *Muzukuru*. Angus Shaw, former RLI, wrote a novel in which several chapters are largely in Taal. See Shaw, *Kandaya*.
86 I am grateful to Keith Breckenridge for this explanation. Personal communication, 22 July 2018.
87 The South African Jeremy Hall, who served with the RLI, glosses the derivation of "frantan" from "fry and tan." I find this a reach. Hall, *Weep for Africa*, 14.
88 Howard, "United States Marine Corps Slang," 188–94; Dower, *War without Mercy*, 162–63; Burke, *Camp All-American*, 111, 246n; Stiff, *Warfare by Other Means*, 131; White, "'Whoever Saw a Country?,'" 619–31; for going Asiatic, see Sledge, *With the Old*; author's field notes, Pretoria, 22 May 2008; 10 April 2014; 4 June 2015. The South African epithet "kaffir" only took hold in Rhodesia in irony. In the 1970s Rhodesians used the word "kaffir" to depict qualities separate from race, as when the right-wing politician expressed relief at the failed settlement

with Britain in 1972: "The black kaffirs have saved us from the white kaffirs." Niesewand, *In Camera*, 18.
89 Which is not to say Hollywood did not have place in the war-in-the-head. When pro-government forces were under siege in the mutinies of 1981, they first called their makeshift fort the Alamo. They quickly corrected themselves and called it Rourke's Drift. White, "'Whoever Saw a Country?,'" 626.
90 Caute, *Under the Skin*, 288–89.
91 Caute, *Under the Skin*, 288–89.

Notes to Chapter 3

Some of the material in chapter 3 first appeared in Luise White, "Precarious Conditions: A Note on Counter-Insurgency in Africa after 1945," *Gender and History* 16, no. 3 (2004): 603–25.

1 My main inspirations for this paragraph are Marshall, "Imperial Nostalgia," 233–56, and Porch, *Counterinsurgency*, but see Hoffman, Taw, and Arnold, *Lessons for Contemporary Counterinsurgencies*; Nagl, *Learning to Eat Soup*; Mumford, *Counter-insurgency Myth*; S. Jones, *Waging Insurgent Warfare*.
2 Hoffman, Taw, and Arnold, *Lessons for Contemporary Counter-insurgencies*, 31.
3 John Hickman, in Pittaway, *Selous Scouts*, 17–19; Thomas, *Shadows in an African Twilight*, 159.
4 Hoffman, Taw, and Arnold, *Lessons for Contemporary Counter-insurgencies*; Nagl, *Learning to Eat Soup*, 91–95; Gregorian, "'Jungle Bashing' in Malaya," 338–59.
5 Kitson, *Low Intensity Operations*, 29–33, 122–26, and *Bunch of Five*, 65; Nagl, *Learning to Eat Soup*, 66–68.
6 J. G. Davies, *Hold My Hand I'm Dying*, 30.
7 Mitchell, *Africa Vortex*, 1–4; Gledhill, *One Commando*, 9–13.
8 Pittaway, *Selous Scouts*, 19.
9 Flower's notes, 1957, quoted in Anderson and Ellert, *Brutal State of Affairs*, 177–78; Flower, *Serving Secretly*, 9–10, 114. For the contradictions of Flower, see White, *Assassination of Herbert Chitepo*, 34.
10 Oginga Odinga, then minister of home affairs, claimed to have taken the heat for deporting Henderson from independent Kenya. Africans did not understand why he and the white police commissioner remained in positions of authority. Kenyatta saw this as an opportunity to make Odinga seem antiwhite: he asked him to deport Henderson, which "brought the wrath of British expatriate circles on my head, as though I had acted independently." Odinga, *Not Yet Uhuru*, 277. Daniel Branch told a more complicated story, in which the United States was worried about growing Chinese influence on Odinga, and Britain was worried that Britons would soon be removed from Kenya's security forces. Neither Americans nor Britons believed that the deportation of Henderson was

Kenyatta's idea, but that Odinga was flexing his muscles as minister for home affairs. Branch, *Kenya*, 42–43. Another version is that this was all a performance. The British needed a mole in Rhodesia and arranged the firing of Henderson so that he would have the necessary gravitas in Rhodesian circles to be welcomed there. Author's field notes, Cambridge, 17 June 2011.

11 Kitson, *Bunch of Five*, 33.
12 Kitson, *Gangs and Counter-gangs*, 73–75, 125–26.
13 Henderson, *Man Hunt in Kenya*, 37.
14 Kitson, *Gangs and Counter-gangs*, 126; Kitson, *Bunch of Five*, 42–46; D. Smith, *My Enemy, My Friend*, 254–70.
15 Henderson, *Man Hunt in Kenya*, 70–71.
16 Kitson, *Gangs and Counter-gangs*, 126–27.
17 *Top Secret War*, 25–29, 33–36.
18 Reid-Daly, *Pamwe Chete*, 58–59.
19 Thomas, *Shadows in an African Twilight*, 171, 205–7; Wood, *Counter-Strike from the Sky*, 96–98; Record of meeting on fire force tactics, 18 May 1977, RAA/2001/086/010/869.
20 Croukamp, *Only My Friends*, 181, 220.
21 Balaam, *Bush War Operator*, 101–5, 118–19.
22 Anderson, *Histories of the Hanged*. Writing about Sierra Leone, Paul Richards noted that wars fought with inexpensive weapons like machetes are bloodier but no more brutal than wars fought with laser-guided weapons. They are not bloodthirsty or barbaric, but they are cheap. Richards, *Fighting for the Rain Forest*, xx.
23 Some of what passed for conventional was problematic in the extreme. A mid-1974 proposal suggested that captured guerrillas be used to clear roads of land mines by "forcing them to drive in vehicles over roads in advance of military vehicles." Generals were horrified. If this became common, it would "provide adverse publicity for Rhodesia." Moreover, any guerrilla who knew the location of land mines could bypass them without arousing suspicion, endangering security forces. Joint Planning Staff to Security Council, OCC, Report on Counter-measures to Landmining in Rhodesia, 14 May 1974, RAA/2001/086/237/143.
24 *Top Secret War*, 100–103.
25 Cilliers, *Counter-insurgency in Rhodesia*, 127–28.
26 *Top Secret War*, 103–6.
27 *Top Secret War*, 104.
28 C (Rhodesian) Squadron, Special Air Service Regiment, Combat Manual, reprinted in *African Combat*, 161.
29 Thursh, *Of Land and Spirits*, 233–34.
30 Quoted in Pringle, *Dingo Firestorm*, loc. 1493–94.
31 Parker, *Assignment Selous Scouts*, 135–36.
32 Cilliers, *Counter-Insurgency in Rhodesia*, 127–28; Martin and Johnson, *Struggle for Zimbabwe*, 281–82.

33 *Top Secret War*, 105; Reid-Daly, *Pamwe Chete*, 472.
34 Mumford, *Counter-insurgency Myth*, 111–12.
35 Dlamini, *Askari*, 40–46.
36 *Top Secret War*, 88.
37 Thomas, *Shadows in an African Twilight*, 166–65, 176–77, 183–93.
38 Bird, *Special Branch War*, 55–64; *Top Secret War*, 123–25.
39 Parker, *Assignment Selous Scouts*, 143–46.
40 *Top Secret War*, 373–84. See also Stiff, *Taming the Landmine*.
41 International Defence and Aid Fund, Story of Elliot Sibanda, Misc. research material and documentation relating to a proposed but unpublished book on political prisoners, 1980, NAZ/IDAF/MS591/14.
42 Ryan, *Those Who Dared*, 83–85.
43 International Defence and Aid Fund, Story of Martin Gutu, NAZ/IDAF/MS591/14.
44 Kitson, *Gangs and Counter-gangs*, 83–84. Kitson told a less adventurous story in *Bunch of Five*. There was no pretending to be an Indian, but the realization that "if we disguised ourselves with face blacking and wigs and put some yellow dye in our eyes, we could pass as Africans in the dark and accompany our teams" (35).
45 Brubaker, *Trans*, 93.
46 S. Smith, *Ginette*, 53.
47 J. Morris, *Conundrum*, 117–22.
48 Stiff, *See You in November*, 134.
49 Wood, *War Diaries of Andre Dennison*, 267; Balaam. *Bush War Operator*, 93.
50 Kitson, *Gangs and Counter-gangs*, 183.
51 Godwin, *Mukiwa*, 284; see also McAleese, *No Mean Soldier*, 185–86.
52 *Top Secret War*, 66, 94–95; Reid-Daly, *Pamwe Chete*, 65, 93–94; Thomas, *Shadows in an African Twilight*, 161, 164. Over the years, I have been told who the man who bathed in gentian violet was. Author's field notes, passim, but see Harper-Ronald, *Sunday, Bloody Sunday*, 176.
53 *Top Secret War*, 95.
54 Balaam, *Bush War Operator*, 45, 101, 108; French, *Shadows of a Forgotten Past*, 58.
55 Military Intelligence Directorate, *Soldiers Handbook of Shona Customs*, mimeo, Salisbury, 1974, Graham Child Papers, Smathers Library, University of Florida.
56 Balaam, *Bush War Operator*, 45, 63; Croukamp, *Only My Friends*, 181–82; Thomas, *Shadows in an African Twilight*, 161–65, 208–12.
57 Thomas, *Shadows in an African Twilight*, ch. 6.
58 Morris, *Conundrum*, 110–11.
59 Harper-Ronald, *Sunday, Bloody Sunday*, 182–83; Ballinger, *Walk against the Stream*, 122–23.
60 Thomas, *Shadows in an African Twilight*, 159, 176–77.
61 *Top Secret War*, 126–27.
62 Cilliers, *Counter-insurgency in Rhodesia*, 132, makes it clear the figure was for 1978; but see Hoffman, Taw, and Arnold, *Lessons for Contemporary Counter-insurgencies*, 33; Pittaway, *Selous Scouts*, 4.

63 Author's field notes, Krugersdorp, 21 July 2017; Moorcraft and McLaughlin, *Rhodesian War*, 53; French, *Shadows of a Forgotten Past*, 58; Balaam, *Bush War Operator*, 126.
64 Author's field notes, Pretoria, 10 April 2014; Johannesburg, 14 April 2014.
65 *Top Secret War*, 224–25; Reid-Daly, *Pamwe Chete*, 259–60, 473.
66 *Top Secret War*, 236–37.

Notes to Chapter 4

1 M/C, Special Branch, Gewanda, to M/C, Special Branch, Beitbridge, 8 April 1971, RAA/2001/086/49/175.
2 Carney, *Whispering Death*, 66, 94.
3 Carney, *Whispering Death*, 122.
4 Ginzburg, *Clues, Myths*, 102–3.
5 Mavhunga, *Transient Workspaces*, 47–48.
6 The parks department did use older trackers—African men in their sixties—to slow the pace, so that younger men could track for longer periods. Author's field notes, 4 August 2006.
7 Trethowan, *Delta Scout*, 159. In the world after Tim O'Brien, I don't have a problem writing about fiction and nonfiction in the same frame.
8 Keith Meadows's fictional aged tracker, Kashili, could find where weapons were cached. Meadows, *Sand in the Wind*, 282–83.
9 Kamongo, *Shadows in the Sand*, 37–38.
10 Mutambara, *The Rebel in Me*, 64–65, 78–79; see also Samupindi, *Pawns*, 90–91.
11 Davis, *Hold My Hand I'm Dying*, 121–23.
12 Tredger, *From Rhodesia to Mugabe's Zimbabwe*, 16.
13 A Coy, 5RR, February 1978, Operation Hurricane, Contact Reports RAA/2001/086/027/1337.
14 2RAR, September 1976; 4 (Indep) Coy RAR, January 1978; C Coy, 2RAR, March 1979; Contact reports, Operation Repulse, RAA2001/086/142/1336.
15 Contact report, SAS, February 1974, Operation Hurricane, reports 8/73 to 12/75, RAA/2001/086/213/1139.
16 "African Soldiers Morale," typescript, secret, probably July 1977, RAA/2001/086/263/997.
17 Balaam, *Bush War Operator*, xvi–xix; Croukamp, *Only My Friends*, 22; I. Smith, *Bush Pig District Cop*, 71; Thomas, *Shadows in an African Twilight*, 19–21; Stranack, *Demand a Brave Heart*, 417; Wessels, *Handful of Hard Men*, 183.
18 White Rhodesian soldiers were contemptuous of whites ignorant of the wild: the most common complaints I heard about the fifteen hundred South African Police who worked with the Rhodesian Army in the early 1970s were that they were "urban" and unable to deal with life in the bush.
19 Fulton, *Into the Vortex*, 91.

20 Wylie, *Dead Leaves*, 147.
21 Taylor, *Lost in Africa*, 15.
22 Bax, *Three Sips of Gin*, 131, 135–36.
23 Trethowan, *Delta Scout*, 158–59.
24 Thomas, *Shadows in an African Twilight*, 117–18.
25 F. Martin, *James and the Duck*, 135.
26 Allan Savory, interview with author, Albuquerque, 13–14 June 2016. Not everyone thought local trackers excelled in their own environment. The storied assassin Taffy Bryce did not believe that African trackers were superior to whites in any way. This wasn't ideology, he explained, but fact: primitives were backward, while twentieth-century whites were modern. He first realized this working with Americans in Thailand in the 1960s; locals could not do effective reconnaissance. "Uneducated and primitive" people, he learned, were fine in their own areas, "but once they are moved to another patch of jungle, maybe only a few kilometers away, their tracking abilities drop off" dramatically. Well-trained white soldiers, whether European or American, "always" turned out to be "much better trackers" than Thais, Malays, or Africans. After all, the modern, Western soldier had an improved standard of education; he was a better soldier than his grandfather, so why should anyone think that an uneducated primitive would be as good? Stiff, *See You in November*, 53.
27 There was no Rhodesian game department. The Department of National Parks and Wildlife Management was created in 1964; it was routinely called "Game" or "Parks" by the men it employed.
28 C. R. A. Savory, Bulawayo, to Army HQ, Salisbury, Guerilla [*sic*] Anti-Terrorist Unit, 17 October 1967, RAA/2001/086/054/197; for trackers in the game department, see Tredger, *From Rhodesia to Mugabe's Zimbabwe*, 43–44; author's field notes, Harare, 2 August 2006; Savory, interview.
29 Minute Sheet, Summary of Discussion with Savory, 22 December 1967; Lt. Col. O. D. Mathews to Lt. C. R. A. Savory, Tracker Combat Team, 15 January 1968, RAA/2001/086/054/197.
30 Capt. Allan Savory, "Tracking in the Rhodesian Army," 83–91; Allan Savory, interview.
31 Savory, "Tracking in the Rhodesian Army," 83–91.
32 Savory, "Tracking in the Rhodesian Army"; Savory, interview.
33 Savory, "Tracking in the Rhodesian Army"; Savory, interview; Grainger, *Don't Die in the Bundu*. This book went through nine printings that I know about. The draft manuscript contained tracking information that would have compromised tracking teams; when Savory complained about this, the publisher removed it. Reid-Daly, *Staying Alive*.
34 Scott-Donelan, "Tracker Combat Unit," 92–103; Thomas, *Shadows in an African Twilight*, ch. 5.
35 Sanderson, *Intake 131*, diary entry for 10 August 1973, Kindle.
36 *Top Secret War*, 31–35; Reid-Daly, *Pamwe Chete*, 22–24; Harper-Ronald, *Sunday, Bloody Sunday*, 181–83.

37 Thomas, *Shadows in an African Twilight*, 161–68.
38 Todd Leedy, Munya Munochiveyi, and various dictionaries helped me with this.
39 *Top Secret War*, 74, 66, 67, 82; Reid-Daly, *Pamwe Chete*, 68, 74–75. Guerrillas were taught the same thing. Agrippah Mutambara told the new ZANLA he trained that if they knew the environment they could conceal themselves from the enemy, but the environment was like a "tame ass. Friend or foe alike can ride it without resistance." Mutambara, *Rebel in Me*, 79.
40 Stranack, *Demand a Brave Heart*, 434.
41 Balaam, *Bush War Operator*, 63–78.
42 *Top Secret War*, 94; Reid-Daly, *Pamwe Chete*, 93. Long hair was not encouraged; see Croukamp, *Only My Friends*, 186.
43 Thomas, *Shadows in an African Twilight*, 190–92.
44 Balaam, *Bush War Operator*, 82.
45 Wessels, *Handful of Hard Men*, 69–70.
46 Bax, *Three Sips of Gin*, 208.
47 Stranack, *Demand a Brave Heart*, 434, 470–71.
48 French, *Shadows of a Forgotten Past*, 73–76.
49 Walsh, *Mampara*, 46–47.
50 Shaw, *Kandaya*, 122–24.
51 Bax, *Three Sips of Gin*, 133.
52 Baughman, *Angle*, loc. 1122.
53 Wessels, *Handful of Hard Men*, 73.
54 Thomas, *Shadows in an African Twilight*, 170–72.
55 ZIPRA Tactics Papers, 23 May 1977, RAA/2001/086/010/869.
56 Supt. Isemonger, BSAP IIQ, Salisbury, Terrorist Tactics lecture notes, 28 June 1977, RAA/2001/086/010/869; Jackson, *Hot and Cold*, 25.
57 Jackson, *Hot and Cold*, 25; Cocks, *Fireforce*, 136–38; Hall, *Weep for Africa*, 203; author's field notes, Pretoria, 4 June 2015; Savory, interview.
58 *Top Secret War*, 198–216; Hoffman, Taw, and Arnold, *Lessons for Contemporary Counterinsurgencies*, 89; Pittaway, *Selous Scouts*, 383, claims there were eighty Selous Scouts against eight hundred ZANLA. The one Selous Scouts accidentally left behind had once farmed in the area and had the local knowledge to find his way back to Rhodesia, where he was accosted because he was wearing a FRELIMO uniform: a good day for everyone. For a somewhat different view from an operative, see Balaam, *Bush War Operator*, 115–20.
59 Author's field notes, Pretoria, 10 April 2014.
60 Author's field notes, Pretoria, 10 April 2014; Army Counter Intelligence, Morale throughout the Rhodesian Army, 5 July 1977, RAA/2001/086/263/997.
61 Author's field notes, Pretoria, 10 April 2014; 4 June 2015; Krugersdorp, 21 July 2017.
62 Taylor, *Lost in Africa*, 115.

63 *Top Secret War*, 255–59; Reid-Daly, *Pamwe Chete*, 291–96; Reid-Daly, "Summing Up," 520; author's field notes, Pretoria, 10 April 2014.
64 Selous Scouts Training Troop, Training Wing, Basic Tracking April 1977; *African Combat*, 129–31.
65 c (Rhodesian) Squadron, 22 Special Air Service Regiment, Combat Manual; *African Combat*, 161.
66 Author's field notes, Harare, 2 August 2006; Pretoria, 10 April 2014; Johannesburg, 14 April 2014.
67 Thomas, *Shadows in an African Twilight*, 63–64; Taylor, *Lost in Africa*, 76–77; Tredger, *From Rhodesia to Mugabe's Zimbabwe*, 22–24.
68 Breytenbach, *Eden's Exiles*, 261–65, 289–95.
69 Meadows, *Sand in the Wind*, 249–53, 280–82.
70 Thomas, *Shadows in an African Twilight*, 66–67; Taylor, *Lost in Africa*, 55–56, 77.
71 Author's field notes, Harare, 2 August 2006; Pretoria, 10 April 2014; 21 July 2017; Johannesburg, 14 April 2014.
72 Croukamp, *Only My Friends*, 387–88; Thomas, *Shadows in an African Twilight*, 278–79, 282–84; for funerals, see Bax, *Three Sips of Gin*, 249–53.
73 *Top Secret War*, 349–50.
74 Croukamp, *Only My Friends*, 388–89.
75 Thomas, *Shadows in an African Twilight*, 281–83.
76 Author's field notes, Pretoria, 10 April 2014; Thomas, *Shadows in an African Twilight*, 289–90.
77 Thomas, *Shadows in an African Twilight*, 291.
78 Author's field notes, Krugersdorp, 21 July 1917; Cape Town, 25 July 2017; Acer, *Spy*, 195–96; "Ex-Soldier Is Named as Palme's Assassin," *The Independent*, 29 May 1996.
79 Author's field notes, Pretoria, 10 April 2014; 18 July 2017; *Top Secret War*, 421–22.
80 Godwin and Hancock, "*Rhodesians Never Die*," 241–42, 367n; Stiff, *Warfare by Other Means*, 131; author's field notes, Pretoria, 28, 29 July 2004; 10 April 2014.
81 *Reid-Daly v. Hickman and Others*, December 23, 1980. Zimbabwe Appellate Division, 1981 (2) SA 315 (ZA). I am grateful to Meryl Federl of the Johannesburg Society of Advocates for this judgment.
82 *Top Secret War*, 423.
83 "Reid-Daly was a good leader who had, on many occasions, put his cock on the block in support of the men under his command." Balaam, *Bush War Operator*, 170.

Notes to Chapter 5

1 Author's field notes, Germinston, 14 April 2014.
2 It is hard to imagine why Munnion was not an appropriate ghost, and his disdain for Rhodesia's leadership matched Reid-Daly's. The chapter titles—"Winds of

Flatulence," "Armageddon in the Armpit," and "Why You Unshot?" to name but three—in Munnion's memoir of his years as an Africa correspondent suggest his familiarity with the genre that was to become Rhodesian war memoirs. See Munnion, *Banana Sunday*.
3 Stiff, *Warfare by Other Means*, 132.
4 Author's field notes, Germinston, 14 April 2014. According to World Cat, 116 libraries worldwide have one or more copies of *Selous Scouts: Top Secret War*, 59 libraries have *The Selous Scouts: A Pictorial Account*, and 17 libraries have copies of *Pamwe Chete*.
5 "How us army boys loved that South African magazine, with scantily-clad women covering most pages." Ballinger, *Walk against the Stream*, 251.
6 "South Africa: The Security Line-Up," *Africa Confidential* 28, no. 12 (June 1987): 1–4.
7 Stiff, *Warfare by Other Means*, 131.
8 Geoffrey Allen, "The Ducking and Diving That Led to Transkei's Downfall," pt. 1, *Scope*, 20 May 1988, 29; Stiff, *Warfare by Other Means*, 131. The double s in the initials of these companies was a reference to the Selous Scouts.
9 Southall, *South Africa's Transkei*; Gibbs, *Mandela's Kinsmen*.
10 Author's field notes, Pretoria, 10 April 2014.
11 Author's field notes, Johannesburg, 14 April 2014.
12 Balaam, *Bush War Operator*, 127. "Vellies" are *veldskoens*, canvas or hide shoes, easily repaired with any kind of sole, supposedly favored by ZAPU and pseudos; see White, "Students, ZAPU and Special Branch," 1289–303.
13 Allen, "Ducking and Diving," 28–34; Stranack, *Demand a Brave Heart*, 90–92; Balaam, *Bush War Operator*, 47, 170, 239; author's field notes, Krugersdorp, 21 July 2017.
14 "South Africa: Homeland Hell," *Africa Confidential* 25, no. 21 (17 October 1984): 4–5; Allen, "Ducking and Diving," 28–34; author's field notes, Krugersdorp, 21 July 2017.
15 "South Africa: The ANC Debate," *Africa Confidential* 24, no. 14 (6 July 1983): 3–4; Stiff, *Warfare by Other Means*, 141; Pherudi, "Lesotho Liberation Army (LLA)," 266–77.
16 Stiff, *Warfare by Other Means*, 142–43; Balaam, *Bush War Operator*, 173–99.
17 Balaam, *Bush War Operator*, 171.
18 Stiff, *Warfare by Other Means*, 223; Balaam, *Bush War Operator*, 214.
19 Geoffrey Allen, "Corrupt to the Core: The Ducking and Diving That Led to Transkei's Downfall," *Scope*, 3 June 1988: 29–34; Stiff, *Warfare by Other Means*, 226–35; Balaam, *Bush War Operator*, 217–18; author's field notes, Krugersdorp, 21 July 2017.
20 Allen, "Corrupt to the Core," 33–34; Stiff, *Warfare by Other Means*, 235–39; Balaam, *Bush War Operator*, 240–43; author's field notes, Krugersdorp, 21 July, 2017.
21 Gibbs, *Mandela's Kinsmen*, 133; Balaam, *Bush War Operator*, 47.

22 Stiff, *Warfare by Other Means*, 137.
23 Author's field notes, Barberton, 14 April 2014; Balaam, *Bush War Operator*, 214.
24 Author's field notes, Germinston, 14 April 2014.
25 *Top Secret War*, 94, 127, 147, 204, 237, 319.
26 Author's field notes, Johannesburg, 2 August 1997.
27 *Gideon Henry Erasmus v. Galago and Peter Stiff*, Appellate Division, Supreme Court of South Africa, 30 September 1988.
28 *Galago Publishers (Pty) and another v. Erasmus* [1989], 1 All SA 431(A).
29 Author's field notes, Germinston, 14 April 2014; Barberton, 24 April 2014.
30 The defendants also claimed that the copyright belonged to Galago, not Frances Stiff, which the judge dismissed immediately. Although Mrs. Stiff was a director of Galago at the time she drew the maps, she had no legal relationship to Stiff beyond marriage, so whatever copyright he had in published work belonged to him and hers to her. *Frances Florina Stiff v. Ronald Frances Reid-Daly and Covos Trading*, Witwatersrand Division, High Court of South Africa, May 2004.
31 *Frances Florina Stiff v. Ronald Frances Reid-Daly and Covos Trading*.
32 Author's field notes, Barberton, 24 April 2014. A decade later Cocks began a new publishing house, 30 Degrees South, which collapsed in 2014. By then a British publisher of military history, Helion, began to publish Rhodesian war memoirs.
33 "Selous Scout Loses His Way Using Enemy's Maps," *Sunday Times* [Johannesburg], 22 May 2004, 3.
34 When I first met Peter Stiff, I told him that I thought that a man who falsified a diary entry might not be an accurate chronicler of his own military exploits. Stiff answered, "Tell me about it." Author's field notes, Johannesburg, 30 August 2004.

Notes to Chapter 6

Some of the material in chapter 6 was published as "'Heading for the Gun': Skills and Sophistication in an African Guerrilla War," *Comparative Studies in Society and History* 51, no. 3 (2009): 236–59.

1 Quoted in Renwick, *Unconventional Diplomacy in Southern Africa*, 78; Soames, Salisbury to FCO, 9 January 1980, The National Archives, Kew, Britain [hereafter cited as TNA]/PREM19/342; White, *Unpopular Sovereignty*, 278–80, 301–6.
2 Macola, *The Gun in Central Africa*, 8–17.
3 Chivers, *The Gun*, 179–81, 191–95, 211–17.
4 Ezell, *Great Rifle Controversy*, 164–66, 285–87; McNaugher, *The M16 Controversies*, 128–29; Chivers, *The Gun*, 217–18, 251–59.
5 ZAPU Terrorist Arms, Clothing and Equipment, 27 August 1966, Operation Grampus, Binga District, 11–18 August 1966, papers in possession of Brig. David Heppenstall.

6 Keegan, *The Face of Battle*, 232–34; see also Strachan, "Training, Morale, and Modern War," 211–27.
7 Raudzens, "War-Winning Weapons," 403–34.
8 Ballinger, *Walk against the Stream*, 236.
9 Contact reports: Operation Tangent, 1 (Indep) Coy RAR, February 1979, RAA/2001/086/027/1337.
10 Joint Operating Command, "State of Morale in the Territorial Army," consolidated report, 5 May 1977, RAA/2001/086/263/997.
11 Hotz, *Muzukuru*.
12 Early, *Time of Madness*, 109–10.
13 Hotz, *Muzukuru*; Moore, *White Tribe*, 165.
14 Pike, *My Part in the Downfall*, 27–28.
15 Ballinger, *Walk against the Stream*, 35.
16 Jackson, *Hot and Cold*, 27–28.
17 Cocks, *Fireforce*, 139–40; Shaw, *Kandaya*, 63–65.
18 Moorcraft and McLaughlin, *Chimurenga!*, 104; Pandya, *Mao Tse-tung and Chimurenga*, 103–4.
19 Hampshire, *If I Should Die*, 140; Elderkin, *Last Rhodesian Soldiers*, 128; Croukamp, *Only My Friends*, 164; Warren, *Stick Leader RLI*, 108.
20 Author's field notes, Harare, 2 August 2006; Lemon, *Never Quite a Soldier*, 132; Maj. G. R. Turner to Secretary of Defence, Salisbury, 31 December 1975, RAA/2001/086/029/1112; R. W. Tait, Secretary of Defence, Salisbury, to Army HQ, re: Procurement, 14 July 1978, RAA/2001/086/016/1101.
21 Doke, *First Born*, 34–35; Trew, *Towards the Tamarind Trees*, 86–87; Wylie, *Dead Leaves*, 10.
22 The newly developed M16, by contrast, was the weapon of the American troop buildup in Vietnam; it was resoundingly condemned by those troops for jamming after repeated firing. Although its manufacturers had recognized this problem when they tested the weapon, in the field this was not blamed on the manufacturer or design, but on young soldiers who had never been instructed in the proper cleaning of the gun. In this, unlike the FN, it was the young men who failed the needs of the weapon. McNaugher, *The M16 Controversies*, 137–42; Chivers, *The Gun*, 268–71, 299–303, 305–7.
23 O'Connell-Jones, *Amazing Grace*, 68; Sanderson, *Intake 131*, locs. 299, 853; Doke, *First Born*, 15, 35–35.
24 Hall, *Weep for Africa*, 275.
25 Shaw, *Kandaya*, 63–64.
26 McNaugher, *M16 Controversies*, 128; Hotz, *Muzukuru*, 172.
27 Parker, *Assignment Selous Scouts*, 188–89; Carney, *Whispering Death*, 137; Moorcraft and McLaughlin, *Chimurenga!*, 105–7.
28 Headrick, *Tentacles of Progress*, 12; Mavhunga, "Firearms Diffusion," 201–31; see also Rasmussen, "What Moves?," 47–73.
29 Stiff, *Rain Goddess*, 193; Early, *Time of Madness*, 110; Rayner, *Day of Chaminuka*, 34.

30 Thomas, *Shadows in an African Twilight*, 159–60.
31 Moorcraft and McLaughlin, *Chimurenga!*, 104–5.
32 Contact report, Operation Hurricane, A Coy 1RR, August 1978; A Coy, 1RAR, September 1978, RAA/2001/086/027/1337; Contact report, Operation Repulse, Fire Force Chiredzu, 2RAR, August 1976, RAA/2001/086/213/1139; Contact report, Operation Repulse, Sp Coy, 2RAR, August 1978, RAA/2001/086/142/1336. A few years earlier, the Rhodesian Army had similar praise for FRELIMO. Contact reports, Operation Hurricane, 1Cdo 1RLI, August 1973; SAS, February 1974, RAA/2001/086/213/1139.
33 Wood, *War Diaries of Andre Dennison*, 35, 146, 299; Parker, *Assignment Selous Scouts*, 143, 188, 193; Cocks, *Fireforce*, 162, 216; Gledhill, *One Commando*, 82, 117; Taylor, *Lost in Africa*, 93.
34 Moorcraft and McLaughlin, *Chimurenga!*, 45–46; Bond, *Incredibles*, 22–35; White, "Civic Virtue," 115, 118–19; Flood, "Brothers-in-Arms?," 9–11; author's field notes, Harare, 2 August 2006.
35 Caute, *Under the Skin*, 190.
36 Author's field notes, Barton-on-Sea, Hants., 31 July 2003; Pretoria, 28 and 29 July 2004; Durban, 21 July 2006; Harare 2 August 2006.
37 Fulton, *Into the Vortex*, 284.
38 Author's field notes, Barton-on-Sea, England, 31 July 2003; Flood, "Brothers-in-Arms?," 35.
39 Mark Edward Dawson, London, 1983, NAZ/ORAL/232.
40 Binda, *Masoja*, 219, 227.
41 Contact reports: Operation Repulse, C Coy, 2RR, August 1977, RAA/2001/086/181/1400; Operation Thrasher, 6 (Indep) Coy RAR, June 1978, January 1979, RAA/2001/086/008/1339.
42 Contact reports: Operation Repulse, Sp Cdo, 4 (Indep) Coy, RAR; C Coy, 2RAR, January 1978, September 1978, RAA/2001/086/181/1400; Operation Tangent, 1 (Indep) Coy, RAR, December 1978, September 1978, RAA/2001/086/142/1336; Operation Hurricane, C2 Coy, 1RR, June 1978, RAA/2001/086/027/1337; Operation Thrasher, A Coy, 4RR, November 1978, RAA/2001/096/008/1339.
43 Thrush, *Of Land and Spirits*, 318; Wood, *War Diaries of Andre Dennison*, 194, 210, 243.
44 Nasson, "'Give Him a Gun NOW,'" 191–210.
45 Storey, "Guns, Race, and Skill," 687–711, and *Guns, Race and Power*, 210–22; Ellis, "Mystical Weapons," 222–36; Hutchinson, *Nuer Dilemmas*, 103; Richards, *Fighting for the Rain Forest*, xx; Behrend, *Alice and the Holy Spirits*, 39–40, 43–45, 58–62.
46 Wilkinson, *Insurgency in Rhodesia 1957–1973*, 16. This pun does not work when it is spoken; it is very likely it was published in the country at some point.
47 Special Branch HQ, Salisbury, Memorandum: Sabotage and Military Training in Tanganyika, 7 January 1964; Terrorist Training Camp, Zimbabwe African

National Union (Z.A.N.U.), Intumbi Reefs, Tanzania, 28 November 1966; Terrorist Training Camp: Zimbabwe African Peoples Union (Z.A.P.U.): Baghari Camp, Algeria, 29 November 1966, RAA/2001/086/050/1001.

48 Brown, *When the Woods Become the Trees*, 22–23; Hoare, *Mercenary*, 21–22; Ballinger, *Call It Rhodesia*, 315.

49 Davies, *Hold My Hand I'm Dying*, 430–33; see also Chapman, *Infiltrators*, 106, 138.

50 Notes on Brief Interrogation of a Terrorist Leader, 27 August 1966, in papers relating to Operation Grampus, Binga District, 11–18 August 1966, in possession of Brig. David Heppenstall.

51 Statement of Gideon Ngoshi and Joseph Nyandoro, Francistown, 24 October 1965, Botswana National Archives [hereafter cited as BNA]/OP55/41, Refugees: Individual Cases; Statement of Tshinga Dube, Francistown, 6 December 1966, BNA/OP55/58, Peoples' Caretaker Council, ZAPU and ZANU.

52 Contact report: Operation Grampus, Annex C, Report on the Brief Interrogation of a Terrorist Leader, 27 August 1966, in the possession of Brig. David Heppenstall.

53 ZAPU Camps in Zambia: Kafwambila, 16 August 1977, RAA/2001/086/174.

54 Chimutengwede, "Formation of a Guerrilla Fighter," 491–93; Martin and Johnson, *Struggle for Zimbabwe*, 83. The Rhodesian Army was concerned that men were trained in Cuba; see Cuban Training, report from a former Cuban intelligence officer, September 1974, RAA/2001/086/009/143/2.

55 Chapman, *Infiltrators*, 107; Hartmann, *Game for Vultures*, 134–35; Stiff, *Rain Goddess*, 193; Tippette, *Mercenaries*, 156; Early, *Time of Madness*, 248–56; Ward, *Sanctions Buster*, 62–63.

56 Kempton, *Soviet Strategy toward Southern Africa*, 101–2; Alexander and McGregor, "War Stories," 89–90; Nyathi, *Tomorrow Is Built Today*, 25–27.

57 Caute, *Under the Skin*, 19–21. A few fictive guerrillas did the same; see Rayner, *Day of Chaminuka*, 13.

58 Raeburn, *We Are Everywhere*, x, 46–50, 108; Wilkinson, *Msasa*, 98. Both Raeburn and Wilkinson, a Commonwealth observer in the 1980 election, based their work on conversations with former guerrillas. Raeburn's book, however, was based on his conversations with Rhodesian exiles in London in the 1970s, men who seem keen to tell him stories, which he then rewrote as "facts presented in the language of fiction." In 1966 there were sixty guerrillas training in China, and fourteen in the USSR. Special Branch HQ, Salisbury, Military Training of African Nationalists, 7 March 1966, RAA/2001/086/1050/1001; Provincial Special Branch Officer, Salisbury to Mashonaland Provinces and PSBO, Matabeleland, Chinese Aid to Terrorist Organizations, 18 August 1970, RAA/2001/086/102/141.

59 Terrorist Training Camps, Tanzania, 7 May 1974: Interrogation of Captured ZANLA Terrorist Maxwell Mushonga (Code Name Evermore Nyasha),

RAA/2001/086/009/143; Raeburn, *We Are Everywhere*, 41; Martin and Johnson, *Struggle for Zimbabwe*, 84; Chinodya, *Harvest of Thorns*, 114–15.

60 Tippette, *Mercenaries*, 225–26; Trew, *Towards the Tamarind Trees*, 31–32, 107; Armstrong, *Operation Zambezi*, 230–31; S. Smith, *Ginette*, 79–80. For Cubans training ZANLA in explosives only, see Dibb, *Spotted Soldiers*, 32.

61 Nell, *Viscount Down*, 219–20.

62 Mazorodze, *Silent Journey from the East*, 131; Samupindi, *Pawns*, 86; Chinodya, *Harvest of Thorns*, 115–16; author's field notes, Harare, 6 August 2006.

63 Notes on briefing by Asst commander Mike Edden O/C SB, Operation Hurricane, 3 November 1976, Michael Holman materials, Borthwick Historical Institute, University of York, RSF 1; Mazorodze, *Silent Journey from the East*, 137.

64 *African Freedom Fighters Speak for Themselves: ZANLA Cadre's Experience, ZANLA Women's Detachment*, pamphlet (Toogaloo, MS: Freedom Information Service, 1975), 11, Africana Collection 605/23/426, Sterling Memorial Library, Yale University.

65 Military Intelligence Directorate, Salisbury, Tembe Training Camp, Target Dossier, 14 November 1977, RAA 2001/086/042/290; Early, *Time of Madness*, 103; Rayner, *Day of Chaminuka*, 33–34; Kanengoni, *Echoing Silences*, 21; Hotz, *Muzukuru*, 171–72; Cocks, *Fireforce*, 141; author's field notes, Harare, 6 August 2006.

66 "Rhodesia I: More Trouble inside ZANU," *Africa Confidential* 19, no. 7 (31 March 1978), 1.

67 Mhanda, *Dzino*, 32–36.

68 Mutambara, *The Rebel in Me*, 65–67.

69 Gumbo, *Guerrilla Snuff*, 33; Kanengoni, *Echoing Silences*, 32–33.

70 LSM Information Center, *Zimbabwe ZAPU*, 4–5.

71 Lovemore Chabata, Harare, 7 August 1987, NAZ/ORAL/264.

72 ZIPRA Tactic Papers, 23 May 1977, RAA/2001/086/101/869. Among the available guns were a dozen Thompson submachine guns; see Summaries of Operation Turmoil, March 1978, RAA/2001/086/002/856; Main ZAPU Weapons Armoury, July 1977, RAA/2001/086/050/101; Alexander, McGregor, and Ranger, *Violence and Memory*, 146.

73 Twala and Benard, *Mbokodo*, 32.

74 Mutambara, *Rebel in Me*, 102.

75 Samupindi, *Pawns*, 92; Chinoya, *Harvest of Thorns*, 192; Jurgens, *Many Houses of Exile*, 301.

76 Alexander and McGregor, "War Stories," 91, 93–94; see also Hotz, *Muzukuru*, 234–35.

77 Alexander and McGregor, "War Stories," 87.

78 Moorcraft, *Short Thousand Years*, 168; Martin and Johnson, *Struggle for Zimbabwe*, 287; author's field notes, Harare, 16 July 2001.

79 Author's field notes, Harare, 3 August 2006; African National Council of Zimbabwe, ZIPRA Combat Diary, May–December 1976, mimeo, London, 1977, Terence

Ranger Papers, ZIPRA/ZIPA, Rhodes House, Oxford; Moorcraft, *Short Thousand Years*, 168.
80 Bird, *Special Branch War*, 140–48.
81 Caute, *Under the Skin*, 309–11; Nell, *Viscount Down*, 352–61; Pringle, *Green Leader*, 197–99; White, "'A Deafening Silence,'" 112–14.
82 Comops. HQ, Assembly Points Sitrep, 19 February 1980, RAA/2001/086/101/159.
83 Larmer, *Musakanya Papers* and *Rethinking African Politics*, 179–80.
84 Brickhill, "Daring to Storm the Heavens," 48–72. For weapons, see Kempton, *Soviet Strategy toward Southern Africa*, 106.
85 Merridale, *Ivan's War*, 66–67; author's field notes, Harare, 6 August 2006.
86 Author's field notes, Harare, 16 July 2001; 6 August 2006; Parker, *Assignment Selous Scouts*, 133.
87 Stiff, *Rain Goddess*, 149–50, 156; Fuller, *Scribbling the Cat*, 146.
88 Spt. Michael Isemonger, BSAP HQ, Salisbury, Terrorist Tactics, 28 June 1977, RAA/2001/086/221/142.
89 *Top Secret War*, 68–69. Fletchas (Arrows) were Portuguese pseudo gangs, originally recruited in Angola in the 1960s and formed in Mozambique in 1972. By 1974 many sought refuge in Rhodesia, where they were considered an ideal group with which to start the Mozambique National Resistance Movement. Flower, *Serving Secretly*, 300–302; Operating Coordinating Committee [hereafter OCC] Minutes, 19 June 1974, 2 July 1974, RAA/2001/086/237/143.
90 Flood, "Brothers-in-Arms?," 35.
91 Contact Report: Operation Trasher, 4 (Indep) Coy RAR, July 1978, RAA/2001/086/008/1339.
92 Thursh, *Of Land and Spirits*, 156–57.
93 *Top Secret War*, 74. In a revised and expanded version of this memoir, Reid-Daly amended his description: the African "already was one, as was the enemy." Reid-Daly, *Pamwe Chete*, 68.
94 Heather Streets argues that martial races were a colonial construction that contained a softer side, "dashing" and "gallant" men who informed Victorian Britain; see Streets, *Martial Races*. Giacomo Macola argues that the idea of martial races comes in part from precolonial politics and self-definition; Macola, *Gun in Central Africa*.
95 Author's field notes, Barton-on-Sea, 31 July 2003.
96 Headrick, *Tentacles of Progress*.
97 Contact reports: Operation Sable, 3 Trp, SAS, September 1972; 1Cdo, 1RLI, October 1972, Operation Hurricane, 1Cdo, 1RLI, May 1974; 3Cdo, 1RLI, September 1975, RAA/2001/086/213/1139; Operation Hurricane, 1Cdo, 1RLI, March 1978, RAA/2001/086/027/1337; Operation Repulse, Sp Cdo, 1RLI, October 1977, RAA/2001/086/181/1400; Operation Thrasher, 1Coy, 4RR, December 1978, April 1979, RAA/2001/096/008/1339; Operation Repulse, A2 Coy, 8RR, November 1979, RAA/2001/086/035/1341. See also Wylie, *Dead Leaves*, 148–49.

98 Reid-Daly liked to boast that he commanded soldiers who had trained not only in Rhodesia but in a variety of Eastern Bloc countries (see chapter 3). *Top Secret War*, 180.
99 Warren, *Stick Leader RLI*, 196–97; author's field notes, Harare, 2 August 2006.

Notes to Chapter 7

Some of the material in chapter 7 first appeared in Luise White, "Poisoned Food, Poisoned Uniforms, and Anthrax; or, How Guerillas Die in War," *Osiris* 19 (2004): 220–33.

1   Loewenberg, "Rumors of Mass Poisoning," 131–43; Endicott and Hagerman, *United States and Biological Warfare*, 3–5; Nkpa, "Rumors of Mass Poisoning," 332–46; Ushewokunze, *Agenda for Zimbabwe*, 162–69; West, "Nationalism, Race, and Gender," 447–71; Kaler, "Threat to the Nation," 347–76.
2   See, for example, Alexander, McGregor, and Ranger, *Violence and Memory*, 144–45, 172–79.
3   Peterson, *Me against My Brother*, 61.
4   Wessely, "Ten Years On," 28–37; MacLeish, *Making War at Fort Hood*, 116–28.
5   Cross, *Dirty War*, xxvi; Epstein, "In Southern Africa, Brutality and Death," *Boston Globe*, 26 December 1987, 23; Epstein and Ferber, *Changing Planet, Changing Health*, 16–17.
6   Cross, *Dirty War*, 73; author's field notes, Harare, 5 May 2014.
7   White, "'Whoever Saw a Country?,'" 619–31; White, "Animals, Prey and Enemies," 7–21.
8   Flower, *Serving Secretly*, 137.
9   Ellert, *Rhodesian Front War*, 145; author's field notes, Pretoria, 10 April 2014. Terence Ranger was so incensed that Kanodareka was accused of poisoning guerrillas that he wrote to the publisher demanding a retraction. Author's field notes, Harare, 19 July 1995.
10 Parker, *Assignment Selous Scouts*, 163. Both Wolhunter and his wife died of cancer, which they believed was caused by handling pesticides.
11 See Kriger, *Zimbabwe's Guerrilla War*, 121–35, 152–62, 179–86; Nhongo-Simbanegavi, *For Better or Worse?*, 104–20.
12 Mavhunga, "Vermin Beings," 72–73.
13 The exchange was about a plot to assassinate Mugabe; the letters were published in May 2006. See Cross, *Dirty War*, xxxvii. Many of the former Rhodesian soldiers I've spoken to did not believe McGuiness to be wholly honest. Author's field notes, Pretoria, 4 June 2015; Krugersdorp, 17 July 2017.
14 Watson, *Conspire to Kill*, 178.
15 Douglas, "Did Britain Use Chemical Weapons?," 859–87; Sheffy, "Chemical Warfare," 803–44.

16 Price, "Genealogy of the Chemical Weapons," 73–103.
17 Russell, *War and Nature*, 66, 73.
18 Mavhunga, "Vermin Beings," 151–76.
19 Russell, *War and Nature*, 135.
20 Cross, *Dirty War*, 106.
21 Author's field notes, Harare, 7, 16, and 23 July 1995; 24 July 1997; Ranger, *Voices from the Rocks*, 195–227.
22 Author's field notes, 7 and 23 July 1995; 24 July 1997; Gumbo, *Guerrilla Snuff*, 8–9, 26; Kriger, "Politics of Creating National Heroes"; Brickhill, "Making Peace with the Past," 118–39, 163–73; Werbner, "Smoke from the Barrel," 71–102.
23 Lan, *Guns and Rain*, 36.
24 Fry, *Spirits of Protest*, 125.
25 McGregor, "Containing Violence," 131–59.
26 Cross, *Dirty War*, 101–2.
27 Stiff, *See You in November*, 308–9; Martinez, "History of the Use," 1159–79; author's field notes, Harare, 5 May 2014.
28 Hacking, *Social Construction of What?*, 143–44.
29 Balshem, *Cancer and the Community*.
30 Bird, *Special Branch War*, 136. Similarly, doctors at the African hospital at Bulawayo believed that thallium in Liebig's tins occurred in the factory, in either Rhodesia or Tanzania. Cross, *Dirty War*, 132.
31 See Davis, "Training and Deployment at Novo Catengue," 1331–32.
32 Author's field notes, Harare, 21 July 1997.
33 Author's field notes, Harare, 18 July 1997.
34 Gumbo, *Guerrilla Snuff*, 25–28.
35 Chinodya, *Harvest of Thorns*, 79–84.
36 Martinez, "History of the Use," 1173; author's field notes, Harare, 7 and 11 July 1995; 17, 18, 21, and 24 July 1997.
37 Gumbo, *Guerrilla Snuff*, 9.
38 Nhongo-Simbanegavi, *For Better or Worse?*, 89; author's field notes, Harare, 17 July 1997.
39 Cross, *Dirty War*, 103–4.
40 Author's field notes, Harare, 25 July 2004.
41 Bird, *Special Branch War*, 91–94.
42 Lovemore Chabata, Harare, 7 August 1987, National Archives of Zimbabwe [NAZ]/ORAL/264.
43 Nkpa, "Rumors of Mass Poisoning," 332–46. The American John Cronin was told that guerrillas never figured out who was poisoning them and turned on villagers: "They really believe in witchcraft." Cronin, *Bleed*, ch. 8.
44 Cronin, *Bleed*, ch. 8.
45 Cross, *Dirty War*, 132.
46 Linden, *Catholic Church and the Struggle*, 272–73.
47 Author's field notes, Harare, 18 and 21 July 1995.

48 Parker, *Assignment Selous Scouts*, 165.
49 Bird, *Special Branch War*, 136–38.
50 Author's field notes, Harare, 19 July 1995; 17, 18, 21, and 24 July 1997.
51 Brickhill, "South African Legacy," 4–11.
52 Government of Zimbabwe, *Fallen Heroes of Zimbabwe*, 6–68, passim; Ellert, *Rhodesian Front War*, 110–11; author's field notes, Harare, 18, 21, and 23 July 1997; Harare, 1 August 2001.
53 Author's field notes, Harare, 23 July 1995; Pretoria, 10 April 2014.
54 Ellert, *Rhodesian Front War*, 112.
55 Stiff, *See You in November*, 328–36; Mangold and Goldberg, *Plague Wars*, 224–27. Glen Cross thought the ricin-tipped bullet "far-fetched." Cross, *Dirty War*, 85.
56 Cross, *Dirty War*, 104–5.
57 Cronin, *The Bleed*, ch. 8.
58 Stiff, *See You in November*, 309–10.
59 Parker, *Assignment Selous Scouts*, 168–69.
60 MacKintosh et al., "Survey of Risk Factors," 41–44.
61 Cross, *Dirty War*, 105,
62 Cross, *Dirty War*, 130–31.
63 One guerrilla continued to eat food his commander insisted was poisoned. Gumbo, *Guerrilla Snuff*, 27–28.
64 Laing, "Relapses in Organo-phosphate Poisoning," 225–26; MacKintosh et al., "Survey of Risk Factors."
65 Author's field notes, Harare, 18, 21, and 24 July 1995
66 J. C. A. Davies, "Transmission of Anthrax," 47, and "Major Epidemic of Anthrax," 291–98; Nass, "Anthrax Epizootic in Zimbabwe," 198–209, and "Zimbabwe's Anthrax Epizootic," 12–18, 61. For cattle deaths, see Alexander, McGregor, and Ranger, *Violence and Memory*, n.145.
67 Nass, "Anthrax Epizootic in Zimbabwe," 200–204; see also J. C. A. Davies, "Transmission of Anthrax," 47.
68 Cross, *Dirty War*, 175–210. Many white authors blamed the spread of anthrax on guerrillas' antidipping campaigns; see Moorcraft and McLaughlin, *Chimurenga!*, 179; Caute, *Under the Skin*, 209; Lessing, *African Laughter*, 94.
69 Parker, *Assignment Selous Scouts*, 171–73; Cross, *Dirty War*, 201.
70 Alexander, McGregor, and Ranger, *Violence and Memory*, 145–46.
71 Parker, *Assignment Selous Scouts*, 172–73.
72 Author's field notes, Durban, 6 August 2006.
73 Author's field notes, Harare, 18, 24 July 1997.
74 Parker, *Assignment Selous Scouts*, 89–90.
75 Parker, *Assignment Selous Scouts*, 170–71.
76 Ellert, *Rhodesian Front War*, 112; Binda, *The Saints*, 158; Parker, *Assignment Selous Scouts*, 171.
77 Cross, *Dirty War*, 112–13.
78 Martinez, "History of the Use," 1173–74.

Notes to Chapter 8

1. To quote two journalists: "The future of white Rhodesians is not one of history's more shattering problems" (Morris, *Destinations*, 134); "War or no war, the 1970s were magic times in Africa" (Venter, *Barrel of a Gun*, 347).
2. Major John Anderson, London, 24 November 1983, NAZ/ORAL/244; Anderson, *Toe-Rags*.
3. Greenberg, *Gokwe Kid*, 7–8.
4. See White, *Unpopular Sovereignty*, 182–85, 189–92.
5. Gledhill, *One Commando*, 73.
6. Journal, 9–11 January 1976, Robin Moore Papers, Box 19/7, John Hay Library, Brown University, Providence, RI [hereafter cited as Hay/RM].
7. Shaw, *Kandaya*, 182; Harper-Ronald, *Sunday, Bloody Sunday*, 82.
8. For Congo mercenaries, see Stockwell, *In Search of Enemies*, 220–21; Gleijeses, *Conflicting Missions*, 70–75; Thompson, *Mercenaries, Pirates and Sovereigns*, 10–14, 54–59, 143–54; Singer, *Corporate Warriors*, 32–39, 226–29; Percy, *Mercenaries*, 50–55, 132–33, 170, 189–99.
9. Woodley, "Killing Time with the War Dreamers," *Esquire* 86, no. 2 (1976): 81–84. He wrote that mercenaries had "licentious magic."
10. Mallin and Brown, *Merc*, 169–72. As a rule, mercenaries seem to find jobs the same way other professional groups did: they let it be known they were looking for new work, they asked if there was an opening, and they relied on friends to recommend them. See Krott, *Save the Last Bullet*.
11. McAleese, *No Mean Solider*, 76–78.
12. Stockwell, *In Search of Enemies*, 221–26.
13. Woodley, "Killing Time," 138–40.
14. Borlace, *Spider Zero Seven*, 3.
15. Coey, *Fighting Doc*, 16.
16. Author's field notes, Pretoria, 4 June 2015.
17. Cronin, *Bleed*, ch. 6.
18. Horne, *From the Barrel of a Gun*, 249, 276–77, 360n; Singer, *Corporate Warriors*, 112; Krott, *Save the Last Bullet*, 136–40.
19. Author's field notes, Pretoria, 4 June 2015. MacKenzie told at least one visiting American that he had killed Herbert Chitepo with a bomb placed in the steering wheel of his car. Author's field notes, Gainesville, 19 March 2005.
20. Moore, *White Tribe*, 23, 185, 187.
21. Kennes and Larmer, *Katangese Gendarmes*, 99–118. South African parachute units boasted that the fall of Rhodesia in 1980 sent a pool of experienced soldiers to the SADF. See Gillmore, *Pathfinder Company*, 24–25. In 1989 South Africa's Soweto Intelligence Unit was staffed by a motley crew of former Rhodesian soldiers, other Africans, Britons, and a few Frenchmen and Seychellois. Rousseau, "Counter-revolutionary Warfare," 1343–46.

22 *Guns for Hire*; Lobban, "American Mercenaries in Rhodesia," 319–25; Churchill, "U.S. Mercenaries in Southern Africa," 21–46.
23 Morris, *Destinations*, 136.
24 "The Price White Rhodesia Is Willing to Pay . . . but the Manpower Is Running Low," *Sunday Times*, 26 November 1976, 5; Lobban, "American Mercenaries in Rhodesia," 322–23.
25 Jonathan Bloch, "Britain's Contribution to Rhodesia's War Effort," typescript, London, 29 August 1979, NAZ/IDAF/MS589/9. This was probably a memo for the Patriotic Front at the Lancaster House Conference.
26 White, *Unpopular Sovereignty*, 164.
27 Author's field notes, Barton-on-Sea, 31 July 2003; Pretoria, 4 June 2015; "A U.S. Mercenary Maimed in Rhodesia Bravely Accepts the Cost of His Calling," *People Magazine*, 23 January 1978, 14–16; Caute, *Under the Skin*, 138.
28 Venter, *Barrel of a Gun*, 338.
29 Minutes, Manpower Committee, 29 April 1977 to 29 March 1978, RAA/2001/086/241/159.
30 Lobban, "American Mercenaries in Rhodesia," 322–23.
31 Morale Survey conducted with RLI, 19 July 1977; Military Intelligence Division, summary comment, Salisbury, 1 August 1977; Army Counter Intelligence, report on interviews with half of C Squadron, SAS, 15 August 1977, RAA/2001/086/263/997. For SAS desertions, see French, *Shadows of a Forgotten Past*, 37–38; Coey, *Fighting Doc*, 37.
32 French, *Shadows of a Forgotten Past*, 37.
33 Col. John Andrew Peters, Rhodesian mercenaries, 19 August 1970, intelligence reports: casual sources, RAA/2001/086/050/1001.
34 K. C. Chalmers, Defence Manpower: Recruitment in Australasia, 20 March 1974, RAA/2001/086/221/142; OCC Minutes, 7 September 1977, RAA/2001/086/223/245.
35 These were *flechas noirs* (black arrows), who were the best-known auxiliary forces fighting for the Portuguese in Angola. They were originally Bushmen, but by the mid-1970s the term was often used to describe any Africans who fought for Portugal. It is not clear that Mozambique's flechas were any specific ethnic group, although they were regarded by some Rhodesian officers as the least gun-shy of any African soldiers. See Kennes and Larmer, *Katangese Gendarmes*, 83; *Top Secret War*, 68–69.
36 OCC, Minutes, 19 June 1974, RAA/2001/237/143.
37 Commanders' Secretariat, OCC, Minutes, 12 March 1976, RAA/2001/086/241/159.
38 Joint Planning Staff, Ministry of Defence, International Brigade, Salisbury, 13 April 1976, RAA/2001/086/227/122.
39 OCC, Minutes, 7 September 1977, RAA/2001/086/223/245; author's field notes, Pretoria, 22 May 2008.
40 Ken Flower, head of Rhodesia's Central Intelligence Organization, gloated about the close ties to his opposite number in Paris. Flower, *Serving Secretly*, 74.

41 Caute, *Under the Skin*, 107; Ellert, *Rhodesian Front War*, 130-31; author's field notes, Barton-on-Sea, Hants., 31 July 2003.
42 Robert Brown, "SOF Interview: Major Nick Lamprecht, Rhodesian Recruiting Officer," *Soldier of Fortune* 2, no. 2 (1977): 13, 61. According to David Caute, Lamprecht had only recently begun to rule out men with mental health issues; see Caute, *Under the Skin*, 107. For a less than flattering fictional description of Lamprecht (identified by name) in a novel by an American who fought for Rhodesia, see Nelson, *Shadow Tracker*, 265-68.
43 Caute, *Under the Skin*, 107.
44 Wood, *War Diaries of Andre Dennison*, 4-5.
45 Lundersted, *Forever Boys*, 67-68.
46 Bax, *Three Sips of Gin*, 232-33.
47 J. Early, "John Early: Rhodesian Adventures," 187.
48 McAleese, *Beyond No Mean Soldier*, 78-83, 103-5.
49 Bax, *Three Sips of Gin*, 111-13.
50 Terence Peter Cope, "Rhodesian Goatman: $15,000 for 480 Goats and Lots of Terrs," *Soldier of Fortune* 4, no. 2 (1979): 54-55, 88; Robert Brown, "The Black Devils: Rhodesia's Elite Armored Corps," *Soldier of Fortune* 4, no. 1 (1979): 38-43.
51 Churchill, "U.S. Mercenaries in Southern Africa," 33-34.
52 Woodley, "Killing Time," 138; Horne, *From the Barrel of a Gun*, 215. The founder of CORE, James Farmer, leveled this accusation, which may have been true or may have been part of larger struggles in African American politics. "James Farmer Quits CORE in Angola Feud," *New York Times*, 20 February 1976, digital archive. I am grateful to Brian McNamara for this reference. For the CIA in Angola, see Stockwell, *In Search of Enemies*, 223-26.
53 J. L. P. Redfern, Director of Military Intelligence, Memorandum: Recruiting: Ex-USA, Salisbury, 8 September 1976, RAA/2001/086/047/141.
54 Thomas MacGregor, "Rhodesian Cattle Keep: Drums along the Pungwa," *Soldier of Fortune* 2, no. 3 (1977): 28-31, 64-68; see also "SOF Recon: Action in Southern Africa," *Soldier of Fortune* 2, no. 2 (1977): 14-21.
55 Interview with David Crowley, Marine, Vietnam Center, Texas Tech University, Lubbock, Texas, n.d.
56 Caute, *Under the Skin*, 138.
57 Author's field notes, Pretoria, 4 June 2015.
58 Woodley, "Killing Time"; Lt. Col. R. K. Brown, *I Am* Soldier of Fortune, 128-36; author's field notes, Pretoria, 4 June 2015.
59 Robert Brown, "SOF Travel Guide to Rhodesia," *Soldier of Fortune* 4, no. 8 (1979): 38; Daryl Tucker, "Danger in the Night: SOF Staffer on Rhodesian Ranch Patrols," *Soldier of Fortune* 4, no. 8 (1979): 54-59, 65, 86-87; Combined Operations directive, payment and rewards: change in policy, irregulars, October 1978, RAA/2001/086/017/919.
60 *Guns for Hire*, 10-11, 19, 25. Pilots were expensive to train, and the RhAF lost many pilots in 1965-66 when British pilots returned home. See White, *Unpopular Sovereignty*, 112.

61 Lobban, "American Mercenaries in Rhodesia."
62 Churchill, "U.S. Mercenaries in Southern Africa."
63 Horne, *From the Barrel of a Gun*, 210.
64 J. Early, "John Early: Rhodesian Adventures," 185–87.
65 Mallin and Brown, "L. H. 'Mike' Williams: Kraals and Galloping Goffles," in *Merc*, 109.
66 Journal, 19 May 1976; 6 August 1976; 14-17 August 1976, Hay/RM/19/7.
67 Notes on trip to Rhodesia, 18 February 1977, Hay/RM/19/13; Moore, *Ambassador's Report from Rhodesia*, 2; Baughman, *Angle* ch. 6, Kindle. Dane Kennedy declined an invitation to Moore's house, offered not by a soldier but by an American Vietnam veteran who was attending the University of Rhodesia paid for by the GI Bill. Kennedy, "An Education in Empire," 102–3.
68 Moore, *Ambassador's Report from Rhodesia*, 2.
69 Journal, 29 April 1977, Hay/RM/19/7; Journal, 17 May 1978, Hay/RM/19/16.
70 Moore, *Rhodesia*, 193–238. Young received special contempt in Moore's journals, with Moore calling him as often as possible "the President's pet coon." Journal, 29 September 1980, RM/20/3.
71 Moore, *Rhodesia*, 223–30; *Major Mike*, 9–17.
72 Binda, *Equus Men*.
73 But see N. Mitchell, *Jimmy Carter in Africa*.
74 Author's field notes, Pretoria, 4 June 2015.
75 Nandy, "History's Forgotten Doubles," 44–66.
76 Baughman, *Angle*, locs. 1009, 1028–36, 1045–53, 1139–82, 1328, Kindle.
77 Baughman, *Angle*, locs. 1267, 1561, Kindle.
78 Baughman, *Angle*, locs. 1725, 1570–78, Kindle.
79 Baughman, *Angle*, locs. 1982, 2001–36, 2070, 2190–98, Kindle.
80 Baughman, *Angle*, locs. 2122–36, 2181–250, 3148, 3157–74, Kindle.
81 Caute, *Under the Skin*, 138–39.
82 Moore, *Major Mike*, 359.
83 Moore, *Ambassador's Report from Rhodesia*, 2; Journal, 31 May and 15 May 1978, Hay/RM/19/16.
84 Moore, *Major Mike*, 346–60; author's field notes, Pretoria, 10 April 2014.
85 Binda, *Equus Men*, 91–93.
86 Binda, *Equus Men*, 76; Baughman, *Angle*, loc. 1103, Kindle.
87 Baughman, *Angle*, loc. 1630, Kindle.
88 Moore-King, *White Man, Black War*, 54–56.
89 Howard Chapnick, "Behind the Pulitzer Prize Controversy," *Popular Photography* 84 (1979): 97–100, 197, 202, 208, 231.
90 Griffin, "Great War Photographs," 137–50; Morris, *Believing Is Seeing*, 3–71.
91 Morris, *Believing Is Seeing*, 74–95; see also 97–118.
92 Chapnick, "Behind the Pulitzer Prize Controversy," *Popular Photography* 84 (1979): 197.
93 Journal, 17 April 1979, Hay/RM/19/20.

94 Journal, 31 May and 17 May 1978, Hay/RM/19/16.
95 None of these "threats," of having passports withdrawn, were ever carried out, but Moore often referred to Americans fighting in the Israeli Defense Force as proof of US hypocrisy. Journal, 19 August 1976, Hay/RM/19/11.
96 White, *Unpopular Sovereignty*, 236–44; N. Mitchell, *Jimmy Carter in Africa*, 332–36.
97 "US government harassment," Hay/RM/10/10. This file contains Anderson's column "'Enemies List' Still Exists," *Washington Post*, 19 July 1978, and its publication in *The Hour* (Norwalk, CT), 27 July 1978, 3–4.
98 Journal, summing up trip to Rhodesia starting 2 February 1977, Hay/RM/19/13.
99 Journal, 7 March 1978, Hay/RM/19/15; 16 April 1979, Hay/RM/19/1.
100 Journal, 16 July 1978, Hay/RM/19/7; 14 April 1979, Hay/RM/19/20; 21 January 1980, Hay/RM/19/8.
101 Journal, 1 May 1980; 29 July 1980, Hay/RM/20/3.
102 Moore had begun working on a screenplay for *Crippled Eagles*, Hay/RM/11/14.
103 Journal, 29 September 1980, Hay/RM/20/3; for the phrase from Vietnam, see also "US government harassment," Hay/RM/10/10.
104 Journal, 16 March 1981, Hay/RM/20/5; White Tribe, Hay/RM/13/17.
105 Joseph C. Smith, "Did Jimmy Carter's CIA Sting Destroy a Cold War Ally?," *Soldier of Fortune* 34, no. 2 (2009): 14–16, 18, 20–22.
106 Rhodesia: "anti-marxist," February 2009, Hay/RM/10.

Notes to Chapter 9

1 Cocks, *Survival Course*, 11, 13.
2 Thursh, *Of Land and Spirits*, 339–40.
3 Alexander, McGregor, and Ranger, *Violence and Memory*, 151.
4 International Defence and Aid for Southern Africa, "'Private Armies' in Zimbabwe," London, IDAF, 1979.
5 ZAPU, *Private Armies: A Tragedy for Zimbabwe* (Lusaka: ZAPU, 1979), 3.
6 Frederiske, *None but Ourselves*, 257; McLaughlin, *On the Frontline*, 36; White, *Unpopular Sovereignty*, 290–91; Frank Bertram, UPAM, "Free and Fair Elections," 2 March 1980, typescript; A. Greenwell, Rhodesia Elections, 1980: Results and Report, Rhodes House, Oxford [hereafter cited as RH], Mss. Afr. S. 1748(4); author's field notes, Harare, 1 August 2006.
7 Chakawa, "Abel Muzorewa's Security Force Auxiliaries."
8 Cilliers, *Counterinsurgency in Rhodesia*, 202–14; L. O'Brien, *Bandit Mentality*, 324.
9 Chakawa, "Abel Muzorewa's Security Force Auxiliaries," 140–42, 146, 155.
10 HQ Special Forces, Salisbury, The Unification of Security Force Auxiliaries, 5 May 1979, RAA 2001/086/147/927.
11 Anderson and Ellert, *Brutal State of Affairs*, 303.

12. Caute, *Under the Skin*, 269–70; Cilliers, *Counterinsurgency in Rhodesia*, 206; Anti-Apartheid Movement, *Fireforce Exposed*, 34; Chakawa, "Abel Muzorewa's Security Force Auxiliaries," 27, 160.
13. JOC Minutes, 19 December 1978, RAA/2001/086/004/895; Parker, *Assignment Selous Scouts*, 200; Chakawa, "Abel Muzorewa's Security Force Auxiliaries," 328.
14. Flower, *Serving Secretly*, 203–4; Ellert, *Rhodesian Front War*, 179–80. The third party in the internal settlement, Chief Jeremiah Chirau's ZUPO, had a local presence at best and no army whatsoever.
15. Directorate of Psychological Operations, "The Need for the Immediate Implementation of a Safe Return Policy," 17 May 1977, RAA/2001/086/090/913.
16. *Top Secret War*, 314.
17. Anderson and Ellert, *Brutal State of Affairs*, 303.
18. Makoni Gandara Military News, 15 May 1977, mimeograph dropped by air; Correspondence with Angela Cheater, 1950s through 1970s, RH/Ranger.
19. OCC Minutes, 22 November 1977; 3 January 1978, RAA/2001/086/178/246.
20. J. H. Chinamano, Acting President, ANC, Zimbabwe, press release, 21 January 1978, Terence Ranger Papers, Clutton-Brock Correspondence, Rhodes House.
21. A Guarantee from the Commander of Combined Operations, n.d., Boyd Report, Appendix J; Former commander Judahs Smoke to Comrades, 16 February 1979, Report to the Prime Minister on the 1979 Elections in Rhodesia, Appendix K; Letter to Comrades, n.d., but filed after Smoke letter, Boyd Report, Appendix L, BNA/PREM/19/106; Chakawa, "Abel Muzorewa's Security Force Auxiliaries," 117.
22. "Come Home," n.d., Sterling Memorial Library, Yale University, Zimbabwe 1551/5/69.
23. Special Branch HQ, Proposed Scheme for Utilizing Surrendered Guerrillas in Combat Role, OCC Minutes, 24 January 1978, RAA/2001/086/178/246; Anderson and Ellert, *Brutal State of Affairs*, 299, 303.
24. OCC Minutes, 7 March 1978, RAA/2001/086/178/246; Cilliers, *Counterinsurgency in Rhodesia*, 204–6.
25. Viscount Boyd of Merton, Report to the Prime Minister on the election in Zimbabwe-Rhodesia in April 1979; John Drinkwater, QC, Report on General Election held April 1979 in Zimbabwe-Rhodesia, 3 May 1979, in Archibald Campbell, Notes and Documents of a British Observer, 1979, RH Mss. Afr. s.1761.
26. Parker, *Assignment Selous Scouts*, 195, 198; Baines, "The Arsenal of Securocracy," 12–17; Ellert, *Rhodesian Front War*, 180; Flower, *Serving Secretly*, 218–19; McAleese, *No Mean Soldier*, 165.
27. Anti-Apartheid Movement, *Fireforce Exposed*, 35. These assertions are often short on comparative politics: the Shah's secret police may have been otherwise occupied in 1978.
28. Moorcraft and McLaughlin, *Chimurenga!*, 205; Martha Honey, "Sithole and Muzorewa 'Training Guerrillas,'" *Guardian*, 17 February 1978, 5.
29. Anderson and Ellert, *Brutal State of Affairs*, 299.

30 White, *Assassination of Herbert Chitepo*, 57–59.
31 For Special Branch and Muzorewa, see White, *Unpopular Sovereignty*, 230–31.
32 Parker, *Assignment Selous Scouts*, 195.
33 Foreign Office, Uganda: Calendar of Events, 1978, TNA/FCO 32/2674; notes on conversation between A. G. Munro, GM of Shell in Uganda, and Mr. W. J. Tate, Dutch Counsul-General, 4 April 1978, TNA/FCO/31/2387. I am grateful to Mark Leopold for these references.
34 Alicia Decker, personal communication, 29 January 2018.
35 David Martin, "Sithole Guerrillas 'Fly to Amin for Training,'" *The Observer*, 13 August 1978, 3. Macharaga claimed to have headed a ZANU delegation to Uganda during which Amin gave him a message for Sithole: "Tell him to salute Smith and even say 'Yes baas.' He should do whatever he can to stay in power." I am grateful to Sara Rich Dorman for this reference.
36 Ellert, *Rhodesian Front War*, 181; Parker, *Assignment Selous Scouts*, 195.
37 Caute, *Under the Skin*, 270; Chakawa, "Abel Muzorewa's Security Force Auxiliaries," 127.
38 OCC Minutes, 7 March 1978, RAA/2001/086/178/246.
39 Caute, *Under the Skin*, 269; Ellert, *Rhodesian Front War*, 180, 190; Parker, *Assignment Selous Scouts*, 196–98, 202.
40 *Top Secret War*, 315.
41 Nell, *Viscount Down*, 273–77.
42 Chakawa, "Abel Muzorewa's Security Force Auxiliaries," 160, 170.
43 Stranack, *Demand a Brave Heart*, 412.
44 *Top Secret War*, 315–16; Parker, *Assignment Selous Scouts*, 196–97; Anderson and Ellert, *Brutal State of Affairs*, 307.
45 Nell, *Viscount Down*, 155–56.
46 McAleese, *No Mean Solider*, 159; Parker, *Assignment Selous Scouts*, 197.
47 Chakawa, "Abel Muzorewa's Security Force Auxiliaries," 154–56; OCC Minutes, discussion of SB HQ Proposed Scheme for Utilizing Surrendered Terrorists in a Combat Role, 24 January 1978, RAA/2001/086/178246.
48 Anderson and Ellert, "White Man's War," 307.
49 Author's field notes, Barton-on-Sea, 31 July 2003; National JOC Minutes, 29 June, 4 July, 23 August, 5 September 1979, RAA/2001/086/022/897.
50 McAleese, *No Mean Soldier*, 163, 176, 180, 182–83; Parker, *Assignment Selous Scouts*, 198; Chakawa, "Abel Muzorewa's Security Force Auxiliaries," 160.
51 Anderson and Ellert, *Brutal State of Affairs*, 308.
52 Nell, *Viscount Down*, 205–7, 369–70.
53 Chakawa, "Abel Muzorewa's Security Force Auxiliaries," 160; National JOC Minutes, 27 June 1979, RAA/2001/086/022/897.
54 Ellert, *Rhodesian Front War*, 190; O'Brien, *Bandit Mentality*, 306.
55 O'Brien, *Bandit Mentality*, 295, 298, 305–6.
56 *Top Secret War*, 316–17; see also Parker, *Assignment Selous Scouts*, 197.
57 *Top Secret War*, 319–20.

58 McAleese, *No Mean Soldier*, 156–57, 163. The men were Sithole's army, ZANU, not ZANU(PF). Did McAleese assume that the mutineers actually supported Mugabe's army, or did he not know the basic alliances of African nationalism?
59 Ellert, *Rhodesian Front War*, 181–82; Flower, *Serving Secretly*, 204; Parker, *Assignment Selous Scouts*, 196.
60 Anderson and Ellert, *Brutal State of Affairs*, 312.
61 Parker, *Assignment Selous Scouts*, 198; White, *Unpopular Sovereignty*, 255–59.
62 Parker, *Assignment Selous Scouts*, 198.
63 Geldenhuys, *Rhodesian Air Force*, 284.
64 Chung, *Re-living the Second Chimurenga*, 324–35, quoting *The Guardian*.
65 Jay Ross, "Survivors Term Zimbabwe-Rhodesian Killings 'Massacre,'" *Washington Post*, 18 August 1979, A11.
66 Marks, *Southern Hunting in Black and White*, 180–95; Schroeder, "Moving Targets," 8–22; White, "Animals, Prey, and Enemies," 7–21.
67 These are a different category of vulnerable persons than those described in Mavhunga, "Vermin Beings," 151–76.
68 Faust, *Republic of Suffering*, 14–20.
69 At the end of Ivan Smith's PATU novel, two policeman, one white and one African, stand amid dead bodies after a shootout in the Eastern Highlands. They cannot imagine the war will end, but the African constable fears that if guerrillas win, he and men like him will be killed. He strips off his uniform and takes another from the corpse of a guerrilla. He will cross the border, and only return "with the men of my tribe," much as it saddens him to think he will return as the enemy of his old friend. The old friend, however, promises to explain that the African policeman was captured by guerrillas and taken across the border, so that his family can get his pension. I. Smith, *Come Break a Spear*, 230–32.
70 Alexander, McGregor, and Ranger, *Violence and Memory*, 262.
71 Garner and Myers, "Body Counts and 'Success,'" 377–95; Cilliers, *Counter-insurgency in Rhodesia*, 131–32.
72 Cronin, *The Bleed*, ch. 8.
73 Norris, "Military Censorship and the Body Count," 223–45; MacLeish, *Making War at Fort Hood*, 210–12.
74 Hoffman, Taw, and Arnold, *Lessons for Contemporary Counterinsurgency*, 47–48; Cilliers, *Counter-insurgency in Rhodesia*, 132.
75 John Early, quoted in Mallin and Brown, *Merc*, 187.
76 *Top Secret War*, 216–17.

Notes to Conclusions

1 L. Smith, *Between Mutiny and Obedience*, 39–42.
2 The negotiations and cease-fire that ended the war in 1979 may muddy the issue of why the winner won, but in fact, Rhodesia did very well in the constitutional

conference and got most of the protections it wanted. Zimbabwe-Rhodesia was all but erased.
3 White, *Unpopular Sovereignty*, 34–35.
4 Caute, *Under the Skin*, 138; Shaw, *Kandaya*, 182.
5 I. D. Smith, *Great Betrayal*, 182.
6 The farm invasions of the twenty-first century have intensified these ways of expressing links to Zimbabwean soil, to the extent that it is often difficult to tease out wartime tropes; see Hughes, *Whiteness in Zimbabwe*; Pilossof, *Unbearable Whiteness of Being*.
7 For one example, see Wood, *So Far and No Further!*

BIBLIOGRAPHY

Archives

Borthwick Historical Institute, York, UK
Botswana National Archives, Gabarone. Cited as BNA.
John Hay Library, Brown University, Providence, RI. Cited as Hay/RM.
National Archives, Kew, UK. Cited as TNA.
National Archives of Zimbabwe, Harare. Cited as NAZ.
Rhodes House, Oxford, UK. Cited as RH.
Rhodesian Army Association Papers, British Empire and Commonwealth Museum, Bristol, UK (now closed). Cited as RAA.
South African Police Archives, Pretoria
Special Collections, Smathers Library, University of Florida, Gainesville
Sterling Memorial Library, Yale University, New Haven, CT

Pamphlets

Government of Zimbabwe. *Fallen Heroes of Zimbabwe*. Harare: Government Printer, 1983.
Guns for Hire: How the CIA and the US Army Recruit Mercenaries for White Rhodesia. Montreal: n.p., 1976.
International Defence and Aid for Southern Africa. *Private Armies in Zimbabwe*. London: IDAF, 1979.
Rhodesia Broadcasting Corporation. *Broadcasting in the Seventies*. Salisbury, Rhodesia: Government Printer, n.d., ca. 1971.
Silundika, George. *Zimbabwe ZAPU: Interviews in Depth 2. George Silundika*. Richmond, BC: LSM Information Center, 1974.
ZAPU. *Private Armies: A Tragedy for Zimbabwe*. Lusaka: ZAPU. 1979.

Unpublished Sources

Chakawa, Joshua. "Abel Muzorewa's Security Force Auxiliaries (SFAs) during and after the War of Liberation in Hurungwe District, Zimbabwe." PhD diss., Midlands State University, Zimbabwe, 2015.

Flood, Zoe. "Brothers-in-Arms? White and Black Soldiers in the Rhodesian Army: The Attitudes of White Soldiers towards Their Black Comrades in the 1970s Guerrilla War in Rhodesia." BA thesis, Oxford University, 2005.

Grimstad, Ann Lee. "Zanzibar: The Nine Hour Revolution." PhD diss., University of Florida, 2018.

Onslow, Sue, and Annie Berry. "*Why Did You Fight?* Narratives of Rhodesian Identity during the Insurgency 1972–1980." Final report, typescript, October 2010.

Published Books and Articles

Acer, Jonathan. *Spy: Uncovering Craig Williamson*. Auckland Park: Jacana, 2017.

African Combat: Rhodesian Security Forces: Anti-terrorist Counter Insurgency Manuals. n.p., n.d.

Alexander, Jocelyn, and JoAnn McGregor. "War Stories: Guerrilla Narratives of Zimbabwe's Liberation War." *History Workshop Journal* 57 (2004): 79–100.

Alexander, Jocelyn, JoAnn McGregor, and Terence Ranger. *Violence and Memory: One Hundred Years in the "Dark Forests" of Matabeleland*. Oxford: James Currey, 2000.

Alp, Geoffrey. *The Uncomfortable Truth: An In Depth Study into the Rhodesian Viscount Tragedies*. n.p.: Geoffrey Alp, 2019.

Anderson, Daphne. *The Toe-Rags: The Story of a Strange Upbringing in Southern Rhodesia*. London: Andre Deutsch, 1989.

Anderson, David. *Histories of the Hanged: The Dirty War in Kenya and the End of Empire*. New York: Norton, 2005.

Anderson, Dennis, and Henrik Ellert. *A Brutal State of Affairs: The Rise and Fall of Rhodesia*. Harare: Weaver, 2020.

Anti-Apartheid Movement. *Fireforce Exposed: The Rhodesian Security Forces and Their Role in Defending White Supremacy*. London: Anti-Apartheid Movement, 1979.

Appiah, Kwame Anthony. "Is the Post- in Postmodernism the Post- in Postcolonial?" *Critical Inquiry* 17, no. 2 (1991): 336–57.

Arias, Arturo. "Arturo Taracena Breaks His Silence." In Arias, *Rigoberta Menchú Controversy*, 82–98.

Arias, Arturo, ed. *The Rigoberta Menchú Controversy*. Minneapolis: University of Minnesota Press, 2001.

Arias, Arturo. "Rigoberta Menchú's History within the Guatemalan Context." In Arias, *Rigoberta Menchú Controversy*, 3–28.

Armstrong, Peter. *Operation Zambezi: The Raid into Zambia*. Salisbury, Rhodesia: Welston, 1979.

Atkins, Graham. *Once upon a White Man: A Memoir of War and Peace in Africa*. Perth: Graham Atkins, 2008.

Aznárez, Jaun Jésus. "Rigoberta Menchú: Those Who Attack Me Humiliate the Victims." Interview with Rigoberta Menchú. In Arias, *Rigoberta Menchú Controversy*, 109–17.

Baines, Gary. "The Arsenal of Securocracy: Pretoria's Provision of Arms and Aid to Salisbury, c. 1974–1980." *South African Historical Journal* 71, no. 3 (2019): 1–18.

Baines, Gary. *South Africa's "Border War."* London: Bloomsbury, 2014.

Balaam, A. J. *Bush War Operator: Memoirs of the Rhodesian Light Infantry, Selous Scouts and Beyond.* Solihull, UK: Helion, 2014.

Ballinger, Tony. *A Walk against the Stream: A National Service Officer's Story of the Bush War.* Solihull, UK: Helion, 2015.

Ballinger, W. A. *Call It Rhodesia.* London: Howard Baker, 1966.

Balshem, Martha. *Cancer and the Community: Class and Medical Authority.* Washington, DC: Smithsonian, 1993.

Barlow, Eeben. *Executive Outcomes: Against All Odds.* Alberton, South Africa: Galago, 2010.

Barnett, Donald L., and Karari Njama. *Mau Mau from Within: An Analysis of Kenya's Peasant Revolt.* New York: Monthly Review Press, 1966.

Baughman, J. Ross. *Angle: Fighting Censorship, Death Threats, Ethical Traps and a Land Mine.* n.p.: Visions, 2014. Kindle.

Bax, Timothy. *Three Sips of Gin: Dominating the Battlespace with Rhodesia's Elite Selous Scouts.* Solihull, UK: Helion, 2013.

Beah, Ishmael. *A Long Way Gone: Memoirs of a Boy Soldier.* New York: Farrar, Straus and Giroux, 2007.

Behrend, Heike. *Alice Lakwena and the Holy Spirits: War in Northern Uganda 1986–97.* Oxford: James Currey, 1999.

Bhebe, Ngwabi, and T. O. Ranger, eds. *Society in Zimbabwe's Liberation War.* Harare: University of Zimbabwe Press, 1995.

Bhebe, Ngwabi, and T. O. Ranger, eds. *Soldiers in Zimbabwe's Liberation War.* Harare: University of Zimbabwe Press, 1995.

Binda, Alexandre. *The Equus Men: Rhodesia's Mounted Infantry: The Grey's Scouts, 1896–1980.* Solihull, UK: Helion, 2015.

Binda, Alexandre. *Masoja: The History of the Rhodesian African Rifles and Its Forerunner the Rhodesia Native Regiment.* Johannesburg: 30 Degrees South, 2008.

Binda, Alexandre. *The Rhodesia Regiment: From the Boer War to the Bush War, 1899–1980.* Alberton, South Africa: Galago, 2012.

Binda, Alexandre. *The Saints: The Rhodesian Light Infantry.* Johannesburg: 30 Degrees South, 2007.

Bird, Ed. *Special Branch War: Slaughter in the Rhodesian Bush. Southern Matabeleland, 1976–1980.* Solihull, UK: Helion, 2014.

Blake, Robert. *A History of Rhodesia.* London: Eyre Methuen, 1977.

Blight, David. *Race and Reunion: The Civil War in American Memory.* Cambridge, MA: Harvard University Press, 2001.

Bolze, Louis, and Klaus Ravan. *More Life with UDI.* Bulawayo: Books of Rhodesia, 1966.

Bond, Geoffrey. *The Incredibles: The Story of 1st Battalion, the Rhodesian Light Infantry*. Salisbury, Rhodesia: Sarum, 1977.

Borlace, Mike. *Spider Zero Seven: A Life in Combat*. Leicestershire: Matador, 2018.

Borst, Allan G. "Managing the Crisis: James Frey's *A Million Little Pieces* and the Addict-Subject Confession." *Cultural Critique* 75 (2010): 148–76.

Bourke, Joanna. *An Intimate History of Killing: Face to Face Killing in 20th Century Warfare*. New York: Basic Books, 1999.

Branch, Daniel. *Kenya: Between Hope and Despair, 1963–2011*. New Haven, CT: Yale University Press, 2011.

Brennan, Bonnie, and Hanno Hardt, eds. *Picturing the Past: Media, History, and Photography*. Urbana: University of Illinois Press, 1999.

Breytenbach, Jan. *Eden's Exiles: One Soldier's Fight for Paradise*. Pretoria: Protea, 2015 [1997].

Brickhill, Jeremy. "Daring to Storm the Heavens: The Military Strategy of ZAPU, 1976–1979." In Bhebe and Ranger, *Soldiers in Zimbabwe's Liberation War*, 48–72.

Brickhill, Jeremy. "Making Peace with the Past: The Work of the Mafela Trust." In Bhebe and Ranger, *Soldiers in Zimbabwe's Liberation War*, 163–73.

Brickhill, Jeremy. "South African Legacy of Zimbabwe's Secret War." *Covert Action* 43 (1992–93): 4–41.

Brown, Robert K., Lt. Col., with Vann Spencer. *I Am Soldier of Fortune: Dancing with Devils*. Philadelphia: Casemate, 2013.

Brown, Robin. *When the Woods Become the Trees*. London: Michael Joseph, 1965.

Brownell, Josiah. *The Collapse of Rhodesia: Population Demographics and the Politics of Race*. London: I. B. Taurus, 2011.

Browning, Christopher. *Ordinary Men: Reserve Battalion 101 and the Final Solution in Poland*. New York: Harper Perennial, 1993 [1992].

Brubaker, Rogers. *Trans: Gender and Race in an Age of Unsettled Identities*. Princeton, NJ: Princeton University Press, 2016.

Burgos-Debray, Elisabeth. "How I Became Persona Non Grata." Foreword to Stoll, *Rigoberta Menchú and the Story of All Poor Guatemalans*, ix–xvii.

Burgos-Debray, Elisabeth. *I, Rigoberta Menchú: An Indian Woman of Guatemala*. Translated by Ann Wright. London: Verso, 1984.

Burke, Carole. *Camp All-American, Hanoi Jane, and the High and Tight: Gender, Folklore, and the Changing Military Culture*. Boston: Beacon, 2004.

Burton, Antoinette, and Dane Kennedy, eds. *How Empire Shaped Us*. London: Bloomsbury, 2016.

Byrd, Alexander X. "Eboe, Country, Nation, and Gustavus Vassa's 'Interesting Narrative.'" *William and Mary Quarterly* 63, no. 1 (2006): 123–48.

Carney, Daniel. *The Whispering Death*. New York: Corgi Books, 1980 [1969].

Carretta, Vincent. *Equiano the African: Biography of a Self-Made Man*. Athens: University of Georgia Press, 2005.

Carretta, Vincent. "Methodology in the Making and Reception of *Equiano*." In Lindsay and Sweet, *Biography and the Black Atlantic*, 172–91.

Carretta, Vincent. "Olaudah Equiano or Gustavus Vassa? New Light on an Eighteenth-Century Question of Identity." *Slavery and Abolition* 20, no. 3 (1993): 96–105.

Caute, David. *Under the Skin: The Death of White Rhodesia*. Evanston, IL: Northwestern University Press, 1983.

Chapman, David. *The Infiltrators*. Johannesburg: Macmillan, 1968.

Chennells, Anthony. "Rhodesian Discourse, Rhodesian Novels, and the Zimbabwe Liberation War." In Bhebe and Ranger, *Society in Zimbabwe's Liberation War*, 102–29.

Chimutengwende, Hassan. "The Formation of a Guerrilla Fighter." *The Listener* 79, no. 2038 (1968): 491–93.

Chinodya, Shimmer. *Harvest of Thorns*. Oxford: Heinemann, 1989.

Chivers, C. J. *The Gun*. New York: Simon and Schuster, 2010.

Chung, Fay. *Re-living the Second Chimurenga: Memories from Zimbabwe's Liberation Struggle*. Harare: Weaver, 2006.

Churchill, Ward. "U.S. Mercenaries in Southern Africa: The Recruiting Networks and U.S. Policy." *Africa Today* 27, no. 2 (1980): 21–46.

Cilliers, J. K. *Counter-insurgency in Rhodesia*. London: CroomHelm, 1985.

Clough, Marshall. *Mau Mau Memoirs: History, Memory, and Politics*. Boulder, CO: Lynne Rienner, 1998.

Cocks, Chris. *Fireforce: One Man's War in the Rhodesian Light Infantry*. Weltevreden Park, South Africa: Covos Day, 1997 [1988].

Cocks, Chris. *Survival Course*. Johannesburg: Covos Day, 1999.

Coetzee, Carli. *Written under the Skin: Blood and Intergenerational Memory in South Africa*. Suffolk: James Currey, 2019.

Coey, John Alan. *The Fighting Doc: The Rhodesian Bush War Diary of John Coey, KIA 19 July 1975*. Solihull, UK: Helion, 2015.

Coltart, David. *The Struggle Continues: 50 Years of Tyranny in Zimbabwe*. Auckland Park, South Africa: Jacana, 2016.

Comaroff, Jean, and John L. Comaroff. "Home-Made Hegemony: Modernity, Domesticity, and Colonialism in South Africa." In Hansen, *African Encounters with Domesticity*, 37–74.

Couser, G. Thomas. *Memoir: An Introduction*. New York: Oxford University Press, 2012.

Cronin, John R. *The Bleed: With the Marines in Vietnam, and the RLI and Selous Scouts in Rhodesia*. n.p.: published by the author, 2012.

Cross, Glenn. *Dirty War: Rhodesia and Chemical Biological Warfare 1975–1980*. Solihull, UK: Helion, 2017.

Croukamp, Dennis. *Only My Friends Call Me "Crouks."* Cape Town: Pseudo, 2006.

Dabengwa, Dumiso. "Relations between ZAPU and the USSR, 1960s–1970s: A Personal View." *Journal of Southern African Studies* 43, no. 1 (2017): 215–19.

Dahmen, Nicole Smith. "Construction of Truth and Destruction of *A Million Little Pieces*: Framing the Editorial Response to the James Frey Case." *Journalism Studies* 11, no. 1 (2010): 115–30.

Davies, J. C. A. "A Major Epidemic of Anthrax in Zimbabwe: The Spread of the Epidemic in Matabeleland, Midlands, and Mashonaland Provinces during the Period November 1979 to October 1980." *Central African Journal of Medicine* 28, no. 12 (1982): 291–98.

Davies, J. C. A. "Transmission of Anthrax." *Central African Journal of Medicine* 26, no. 10 (1980): 47.

Davies, John Gordon. *Hold My Hand I'm Dying*. London: Diamond Books, 1993 [1967].

Davis, Stephen R. *The ANC's War against Apartheid: Umkhonto wa Sizwe and the Liberation of Southern Africa*. Bloomington: Indiana University Press, 2018.

Davis, Stephen R. "Struggle History and Self-Help: The Parallel Lives of Nelson Mandela in Conventional and Figurative Biography." *African Studies* 73, no. 2 (2014): 169–91.

Davis, Steve [Stephen R.]. "Training and Deployment at Novo Catengue and the Diaries of Jack Simons, 1977–1979." *Journal of Southern African Studies* 40, no. 6 (2014): 1325–42.

de Kock, Eugene, as told to Jeremy Gordin. *A Long Night's Damage: Working for the Apartheid State*. Saxonwold, South Africa: Contra, 1998.

Dibb, C. E. *Spotted Soldiers*. Salisbury, Rhodesia: Leo Publications, 1978.

Dlamini, Jacob. *Askari: A Story of Collaboration and Betrayal in the Anti-apartheid Struggle*. Auckland Park, South Africa: Jacana, 2014.

Doke, Graham. *First Born*. Cape Town: Book, 2000.

Douglas, R. M. "Did Britain Use Chemical Weapons in Mandatory Iraq?" *Journal of Modern History* 81, no. 4 (2009): 859–87.

Dower, John. *War without Mercy: Race and Power in the Pacific War*. New York: Pantheon, 1986.

Early, John. "John Early: Rhodesian Adventures." In Mallin and Brown, *Merc*, 185–94.

Early, Robert. *A Time of Madness*. Salisbury, Rhodesia: Graham, 1977.

Elderkin, Vera. *Last Rhodesian Soldiers*. Baltimore: Publish America, 2004.

Ellert, Henrik. *The Rhodesian Front War: Counter-insurgency and Guerrilla Warfare, 1962–1980*. Gweru, Zimbabwe: Mambo, 1989.

Ellis, Stephen. "Mystical Weapons: Some Evidence from the Liberian War." *Journal of Religion in Africa* 31, no. 2 (2001): 222–36.

Endicott, Stephen, and Edward Hagerman. *The United States and Biological Warfare: Secrets from the Early Cold War and Korea*. Bloomington: Indiana University Press, 1998.

Epstein, Paul, and Dan Ferber. *Changing Planet, Changing Health: How the Climate Crisis Threatens Our Health and What We Can Do about It*. Berkeley: University of California Press, 2011.

Ezell, Edward Clinton. *The Great Rifle Controversy: The Search for the Ultimate Infantry Weapon from World War II to Vietnam*. Harrisburg, PA: Stackpole Books, 1984.

Faust, Drew Gilpin. *This Republic of Suffering: Death and the American Civil War.* New York: Vintage, 2008.

Flower, Ken. *Serving Secretly: Rhodesia's CIA Chief on Record.* Alberton, South Africa: Galago, 1987.

Foucault, Michel. "What Is an Author?" In *The Essential Works of Michel Foucault.* Vol. 2, *Aesthetics, Method, and Epistemology*, edited by James D. Faubion. Translated by Robert Hurley et al., 205–22. New York: New Press, 1998.

Frederiske, Julie. *None but Ourselves: Masses versus the Media in the Making of Zimbabwe.* Johannesburg: Ravan, 1982.

French, Paul. *Shadows of a Forgotten Past: To the Edge with the Rhodesian SAS and Selous Scouts.* Solihull, UK: Helion, 2012.

Fry, Peter. *Spirits of Protest: Spirit Mediums and the Articulation of Consensus among the Zezuru of Southern Rhodesia (Zimbabwe).* Cambridge: Cambridge University Press, 1976.

Fuller, Alexandra. *Scribbling the Cat: Travels with an African Soldier.* New York: Penguin, 2004.

Fulton, Tom. *Into the Vortex: The Journey of a Young Rhodesian Boy from Childhood to Manhood.* Cape Town: Digital Action, 2015.

Fussell, Paul. *The Great War and Modern Memory.* New York: Oxford University Press, 2000 [1975].

Garner, Scott Sigmund, and Marissa Edson Myers. "Body Counts and 'Success' in the Vietnam and Korean Wars." *Journal of Interdisciplinary History* 25, no. 3 (1995): 377–95.

Geldenhuys, Prop. *Rhodesian Air Force Operations with Airstrike Log.* Durban: Just Done Publications, 2007.

Gibbs, Timothy. *Mandela's Kinsmen: Nationalist Elites and Apartheid's First Bantustan.* Rochester, NY: Boydell and Brewer, 2017.

Gillmore, Graham. *Pathfinder Company: The Philistines.* Johannesburg: 30 Degrees South, 2010.

Ginzburg, Carlo. *Clues, Myths, and the Historical Method.* Translated by John Tedeschi and Anne Tedeschi. Baltimore: Johns Hopkins University Press, 1989.

Gledhill, Dick. *One Commando: Rhodesia's Last Years and the Guerrilla War It Never Lost.* Weltevreden Park, South Africa: Covos Day, 2001 [1997].

Gleijeses, Piero. *Conflicting Missions: Havana, Washington, and Africa, 1959–1976.* Chapel Hill: University of North Carolina Press, 2002.

Godobo-Madikizela, Pumla. *A Human Being Died That Night: Forgiving Apartheid's Chief Killer.* London: Portobello Books, 2003.

Godwin, Peter. *Mukiwa: A White Boy in Africa.* London: Macmillan, 1996.

Godwin, Peter, and Ian Hancock. *"Rhodesians Never Die": The Impact of War and Political Change on White Rhodesia, c. 1970–1980.* Harare: Baobab, 1995 [1993].

Grainger, Col. D. H. *Don't Die in the Bundu.* Cape Town: Howard Timmons, 1967.

Greenberg, Karl. *The Gokwe Kid. Dick of the Bushveld.* n.p.: published by the author, 2012.

Gregorian, Raffi. "'Jungle Bashing' in Malaya: Toward a Formal Tactical Doctrine." *Small Wars and Insurgencies* 53, no. 3 (1994): 338–59.

Griffin, Michael. "The Great War Photographs: Constructing Myths of History and Photojournalism." In Brennan and Hardt, *Picturing the Past*, 121–57.

Grossman, Lt. Col. David. *On Killing: The Psychological Cost of Learning to Kill in War and Society*. Boston: Little, Brown, 1996.

Gumbo, Mafuranhunzi [Inus Daneel]. *Guerrilla Snuff*. Harare: Baobab, 1995.

Hacking, Ian. *The Social Construction of What?* Cambridge, MA: Harvard University Press, 1999.

Hall, Jeremy. *Weep for Africa: A Rhodesian Light Infantry Paratrooper's Farewell to Innocence*. Solihull, UK: Helion, 2014.

Hampshire, Tom. *If I Should Die*. Victoria, BC: Tafford, 2005.

Hansen, Karen Tranberg, ed. *African Encounters with Domesticity*. New Brunswick, NJ: Rutgers University Press, 1992.

Harper-Ronald, Jake, as told to Greg Budd. *Sunday, Bloody Sunday: A Soldier's War in Northern Ireland, Rhodesia, Mozambique and Iraq*. Alberton, South Africa: Galago, 2009.

Hartmann, Michael. *Game for Vultures*. London: Pan Books, 1976 [1975].

Headrick, Daniel. *Tentacles of Progress: Technology Transfer and the Age of Imperialism, 1850–1940*. Oxford: Oxford University Press, 1988.

Henderson, Ian, with Philip Goodheart. *Man Hunt in Kenya*. Garden City, NY: Doubleday, 1958.

Hoare, Mike. *Mercenary*. London: Corgi Books, 1978 [1967].

Hoffman, Bruce, Jennifer Taw, and David Arnold. *Lessons for Contemporary Counterinsurgencies: Lessons from Rhodesia*. Santa Monica, CA: RAND, 1991.

Hoffman, Danny. *The War Machines: Young Men and Violence in Sierra Leone and Liberia*. Durham, NC: Duke University Press, 2011.

Holmes, Richard. *Acts of War: The Behavior of Men in Battle*. New York: Free Press, 1985.

Horne, Gerald. *From the Barrel of a Gun: The United States and the War against Zimbabwe, 1965–1980*. Chapel Hill: University of North Carolina Press, 2001.

Hotz, Paul. *Muzukuru: A Guerilla's Story*. Johannesburg: Ravan, 1990.

Hove, Mediel. "War Legacy: A Reflection on the Effects of the Rhodesian Security Forces (RSF) in South-eastern Zimbabwe during Zimbabwe's War of Liberation, 1976–1980." *Journal of African Studies and Development* 4, no. 8 (2012): 193–206.

Howard, David. "United States Marine Corps Slang." *American Speech* 31, no. 3 (1956): 188–94.

Hughes, David McDermott. *Whiteness in Zimbabwe: Race, Landscape, and the Problem of Belonging*. New York: Palgrave, 2010.

Hull, Isabel V. *Absolute Destruction: Military Culture and the Practices of War in Imperial Germany*. Ithaca, NY: Cornell University Press, 2005.

Hunt, Nancy Rose. "Colonial Fairy Tales and the Knife and Fork Doctrine in the Heart of Africa." In Hansen, *African Encounters with Domesticity*, 143–71.

Hutchinson, Sharon. *Nuer Dilemmas: Coping with Money, War and the State*. Berkeley: University of California Press, 1996.
Hynes, Samuel. *The Soldiers' Tale: Bearing Witness to Modern War*. New York: Penguin, 1997.
Jackson, Brian. *Hot and Cold: Memoirs of a Rhodesian SAS Soldier*. Wandsbeck, South Africa: Reach, 2018
Jal, Emmanuel. *War Child: A Child Soldier's Story*. New York: St. Martin's Griffin, 20109.
"James Farmer Quits CORE in Angola Feud." *New York Times*, 20 February 1976. Digital archive.
Jansen, Anemari. *Eugene de Kock: Assassin for the State*. Cape Town: Tafelberg, 2015.
Jones, Karen, Giacomo Macola, and David Welsh, eds. *A Cultural History of Firearms in the Age of Empire*. Farnham, UK: Ashgate, 2013.
Jones, Seth. *Waging Insurgent Warfare*. Oxford: Oxford University Press, 2017.
Jürgens, Richard. *The Many Houses of Exile*. Johannesburg: Covos-Day, 2000.
K., Conrad. *In the Shadow of the Tokolosh*. Chelmsford, UK: Silverling Inspired, 2010.
Kaler, Amy. "A Threat to the Nation and a Threat to the Men: The Banning of Depo-Provera in Zimbabwe in 1981." *Journal of Southern African Studies* 24, no. 2 (1998): 347–76.
Kamongo, Sisingi, and Leon Bezuidenhout. *Shadows in the Sand: A Koevet Tracker's Story of an Insurgency War*. Johannesburg: 30 Degrees South, 2011.
Kanengoni, Alexander. *Echoing Silences*. Harare: Baobab, 1997.
Kariuki, J. M. *"Mau Mau" Detainee*. London: Oxford University Press, 1963.
Keegan, John. *The Face of Battle*. Harmondsworth: Penguin, 1976.
Kempton, Daniel J. *Soviet Strategy toward Southern Africa: The National Liberation Movement Connection*. New York: Praeger, 1989.
Kennedy, Dane. "An Education in Empire." In Burton and Kennedy, *How Empire Shaped Us*, 95–106.
Kennes, Erik, and Miles Larmer. *The Katangese Gendarmes and the War in Central Africa*. Bloomington: Indiana University Press, 2016.
Kitson, Frank. *Bunch of Five*. London: Faber and Faber, 1977.
Kitson, Frank. *Gangs and Counter-gangs*. London: Barrie and Rockcliff, 1960.
Kitson, Frank. *Low Intensity Operations: Subversion, Insurgency, Peace-Keeping*. Harrisburg, PA: Stackpole Books, 1971.
Kriger, Norma J. "The Politics of Creating National Heroes: The Search for Political Legitimacy and National Heroes." In Bhebe and Ranger, *Soldiers in Zimbabwe's Liberation War*, 118–39.
Kriger, Norma J. *Zimbabwe's Guerrilla War: Peasant Voices*. Cambridge: Cambridge University Press, 1992.
Krott, Rob. *Save the Last Bullet for Yourself: A Soldier of Fortune in the Balkans and Somalia*. Philadelphia: Casemate, 2008.
Laing, R. O. "Relapses in Organo-phosphate Poisoning." *Central African Journal of Medicine* 25, no. 10 (1979): 225–30.

Lamb, Christina. *House of Stone: The True Story of a Family Divided in War Torn Zimbabwe.* London: Lawrence Hill Books, 2007.

Lan, David. *Guns and Rain: Guerrillas and Spirit Mediums in Zimbabwe.* London: James Currey, 1987 [1985].

Larmer, Miles, ed. *The Musakanya Papers: The Autobiographical Writings of Valentine Musakanya.* Lusaka: Lembani Trust, 2010.

Larmer, Miles. *Rethinking African Politics: A History of Opposition in Zambia.* Farnham, UK: Ashgate, 2011.

Lemon, David. *Never Quite a Soldier: A Policeman's War, 1971–1983.* Stroud, UK: Albida, 2000.

Lessing, Doris. *African Laughter: Four Visits to Zimbabwe.* New York: HarperCollins, 1992.

Leys, Colin. *European Politics in Southern Rhodesia.* Oxford: Clarendon, 1959.

Linden, Ian. *The Catholic Church and the Struggle for Zimbabwe.* London: Longman, 1980.

Lindsay, Lisa A., and John Sweet, eds. *Biography and the Black Atlantic.* Philadelphia: University of Pennsylvania Press, 2014.

Llano, Dane. "I, Rigoberta Menchú? The Controversy Surrounding the Mayan Activist." Translated by Wilfrido H. Corral. *Hopscotch: A Cultural Review* 1, no. 3 (1999): 96–101.

Lobban, Richard. "American Mercenaries in Rhodesia." *Journal of Southern African Affairs* 3, no. 2 (1978): 319–25.

Loewenberg, Richard D. "Rumors of Mass Poisoning in Times of Crisis." *Journal of Criminal Psychopathlogy* 5 (1943): 131–43.

Lunderstedt, Steve. *The Forever Boys: The Story of Rhodesian National Service Intake 146, June 1975–March 1977.* Kimberley, South Africa: Swiftprint, n.d.

MacKintosh, M. E., D. E. Crozier, R. Guild, M. A. Jay, G. E. Jones, G. C. Mataka, and M. P. Meyer. "A Survey of Risk Factors Associated with Organo-phosphate and Carbamate Pesticide Poisoning." *Central African Journal of Medicine* 24, no. 3 (1978): 41–44.

MacLeish, Kenneth. *Making War at Fort Hood: Life and Uncertainty in a Military Community.* Princeton, NJ: Princeton University Press, 2013.

Macmillan, Hugh. *The Lusaka Years: The ANC in Exile in Zambia.* Auckland Park, South Africa: Jacana, 2013.

Macola, Giacomo. *The Gun in Central Africa: A History of Technology and Politics.* Athens: Ohio University Press, 2016.

Mallin, Jay, and Robert K. Brown. *Merc: American Soldiers of Fortune.* New York: Macmillan, 1979.

Mangold, Tom, and Jeff Goldberg. *Plague Wars: A True Story of Biological Warfare.* New York: St. Martin's, 1999.

Mann, Gregory. *Native Sons: West African Veterans and France in the Twentieth Century.* Durham, NC: Duke University Press, 2006.

Marks, Stuart. *Southern Hunting in Black and White: Nature, History, and Ritual in a Carolina Community*. Princeton, NJ: Princeton University Press, 1991.

Marshall, Alex. "Imperial Nostalgia, the Liberal Lie, and the Perils of Postmodern Counterinsurgency." *Small Wars and Insurgencies* 21, no. 2 (2010): 233–56.

Marshall, S. L. A. *Men against Fire: The Problem of Battle Command*. Norman: University of Oklahoma Press, 2000 [1947].

Martin, David. "Sithole Guerrillas 'Fly to Amin for Training.'" *The Observer*, 13 August 1978, 3.

Martin, David, and Phyllis Johnson, *The Chitepo Assassination*. Harare: Zimbabwe Publishing House, 1985.

Martin, David, and Phyllis Johnson. *The Struggle for Zimbabwe: The Chimurenga War*. London: Faber and Faber, 1981.

Martin, Faan. *James and the Duck: Tales of the Rhodesian Bush War (1964–1980), the Memoirs of a Part-Time Trooper*. Milton Keynes, UK: Authorhouse, 2007.

Martinez, Ian. "The History of the Use of Bacteriological and Chemical Agents during Zimbabwe's Liberation War of 1965–80 by Rhodesian Forces." *Third World Quarterly* 23, no. 6 (2002): 1159–79.

Mavhunga, Clapperton Chakanetsa. "Firearms Diffusion, Exotic and Indigenous Knowledge Systems in the Lowveld Frontier, South Eastern Zimbabwe, 1870–1920." *Comparative Technology Transfer and Society* 1, no. 2 (2003): 201–31.

Mavhunga, Clapperton Chakanetsa. *Transient Workspaces: Technologies of Everyday Innovation in Zimbabwe*. Cambridge, MA: MIT Press, 2014.

Mavhunga, Clapperton Chakanetsa. "Vermin Beings: On Pestiferous Animals and Human Game." *Social Text* 29, no. 1 (2011): 151–76.

Mazarire, Gerald Chikozho. "ZANU's External Networks, 1963–79: An Appraisal." *Journal of Southern African Studies* 43, no. 1 (2017): 83–106.

Mazorodze, I. V. *Silent Journey from the East*. Harare: Zimbabwe Publishing House, 1987.

McAleese, Peter. *Beyond No Mean Soldier: The Explosive Recollections of a Special Forces Operator*. Solihull, UK: Helion, 2015.

McAleese, Peter. *No Mean Soldier: The Story of the Ultimate Professional Soldier in the SAS and Other Forces*. London: Cassell, 2000 [1993].

McGregor, JoAnn. "Containing Violence: Poisoning and Guerrilla/Civilian Relations in Memories of Zimbabwe's Liberation War." In *Trauma and Life Stories: International Perspectives*, edited by Kim Lacy Rogers and Selma Leydesdorff with Graham Dawson, 131–59. London: Routledge, 1999.

McGregor, JoAnn. *Crossing the Zambezi: The Politics of Landscape on a Central African Frontier*. London: James Currey, 2009.

McLaughlin, Janice. *On the Frontline: Catholic Missions in Zimbabwe's Liberation War*. Harare: Baobab, 1996.

McNaugher, Thomas L. *The M16 Controversies: Military Organizations and Weapons Acquisition*. New York: Praeger, 1984.

Meadows, Keith. *Sand in the Wind*. Bulawayo: Thorntree, 1997.
Merridale, Catherine. *Ivan's War: Life and Death in the Red Army, 1939–1945*. New York: Metropolitan Books, 2006.
Mhanda, Wilfred. *Dzino: Memoirs of a Freedom Fighter*. Harare: Weaver, 2011.
Mitchell, Colin. *Africa Vortex*. Cape Town: Howard Timmins, 1980.
Mitchell, Nancy. *Jimmy Carter in Africa: Race and the Cold War*. Stanford, CA: Stanford University Press, 2016.
Mlambo, A. S. "From the Second World War to UDI, 1940–65." In Raftopoulos and Mlambo, *Becoming Zimbabwe*, 75–114.
Mlambo, A. S. *White Immigration into Rhodesia: From Occupation to Federation*. Harare: University of Zimbabwe Press, 2002.
Moorcraft, Paul L. *A Short Thousand Years: The End of Rhodesia's Rebellion*. Salisbury, Rhodesia: Galaxie, 1979.
Moorcraft, Paul L., and Peter McLaughlin. *Chimurenga! The War in Rhodesia, 1963–80*. Johannesburg: Sygma/Collins, 1982. Reprinted as *The Rhodesian War: A Military History*. Barnsley, UK: Pen and Sword, 2008.
Moore, Robin. *Ambassador's Report from Rhodesia (Unofficial)*. Salisbury, Rhodesia: Irwin, 1977.
Moore, Robin. *Major Mike: Major Mike Williams as told to Robin Moore*. New York: Charter, 1978.
Moore, Robin. *Rhodesia*. New York: Condor, 1977.
Moore, Robin. *The White Tribe*. Encampment, WY: Affiliated Writers of America, 1991.
Moore-King, Bruce, *White Man, Black War*. Harare: Baobab, 1988.
Morris, Errol. *Believing Is Seeing (Observations on the Mysteries of Photography)*. New York: Penguin, 2011.
Morris, Jan. *Conundrum*. New York: New York Review of Books Classics, 2013 [1974].
Morris, Jan. *Destinations: Essays from Rolling Stone*. New York: Oxford University Press, 1982 [1980].
Moyd, Michelle R. *Violent Intermediaries: African Soldiers, Conquest, and Everyday Colonialism in German East Africa*. Athens: Ohio University Press, 2014.
Moylan, William J. *See You Back in Bright Lights*. n.p., n.d.
Mumford, Andrew. *The Counter-insurgency Myth: The British Experience of Irregular Warfare*. London: Routledge, 2012.
Munnion, Christopher. *Banana Sunday: Datelines from Africa*. Rivonia, South Africa: William Waterman, 1993.
Murphy, Philip. "'An Intricate and Distasteful Subject: Planning for the Use of Force against European Settlers in Southern Africa, 1952–65," *English Historical Review* (2006): 746–77.
Murphy, Philip. *Party Politics and Decolonization: The Conservative Party and British Colonial Policy in Tropical Africa*. Oxford: Clarendon, 1995.
Mutambara, Agrippah. *The Rebel in Me. A ZANLA Guerrilla Commander in the Rhodesian Bush War, 1975–1980*. Johannesburg: 30 Degrees South, 2014.

Nagl, John A. *Learning to Eat Soup with a Knife: Counterinsurgency Lessons from Malaya and Vietnam*. Chicago: University of Chicago Press, 2005 [2002].
Nandy, Ashis. "History's Forgotten Doubles." *History and Theory* 34, no. 2 (1994): 44–66.
Nass, Meryl. "Anthrax Epizootic in Zimbabwe, 1978–80: Due to Deliberate Spread?" *Physicians for Social Responsibility* 2, no. 4 (1992): 198–209.
Nass, Meryl. "Zimbabwe's Anthrax Epizootic." *Covert Action Quarterly* 43 (1992–93): 12–18, 61.
Nasson, Bill. *The Boer War: The Struggle for South Africa*. Stroud, UK: History Press, 2011 [2010].
Nasson, Bill. "'Give Him a Gun NOW': Soldiers but Not Quite Soldiers in South Africa's Second World War, 1939–45." In Jones, Macola, and Welsh, *Cultural History of Firearms in the Age of Empire*, 191–210.
Ndlovu-Gatsheni, Sabelo J. "Mapping Cultural and Colonial Encounters, 1880s–1930s." In Raftopoulos and Mlambo, *Becoming Zimbabwe*, 48–58.
Nell, Keith. *Viscount Down: The Complete Story of the Rhodesian Viscount Disasters as Told by a SAS Operator*. Johannesburg: Keith Nell, 2011.
Nelson, Keith. *Shadow Tracker*. Johannesburg: 30 Degrees South, 2007.
Nhongo-Simbanegavi, Josephine. *For Better or Worse? Women and ZANLA in Zimbabwe's Liberation Struggle*. Harare: Weaver, 2000.
Niesewand, Peter. *In Camera: Secret Justice in Rhodesia*. London: Weidenfeld and Nicholson, 1973.
Nkpa, Nwokocha K. U. "Rumors of Mass Poisoning in Biafra." *Public Opinion Quarterly* 4, no. 3 (1977): 332–46.
Norris, Margot. "Military Censorship and the Body Count in the Persian Gulf War." *Cultural Critique* 19 (1991): 223–45.
Nyathi, Andrew, and John Hoffman. *Tomorrow Is Built Today: Experiences of War, Colonialism, and the Struggle for Collective Co-operatives in Zimbabwe*. Harare: Anvil, 1990.
O'Brien, Lindsay. *Bandit Mentality: Hunting Insurgents in the Rhodesian Bush War: A Memoir*. Solihull, UK: Helion, 2017.
O'Brien, Tim. *The Things They Carried*. New York: Broadway Books, 1980.
O'Connell-Jones, Basil. *Amazing Grace*. Kirksville, MO: Scribbles and Scribes, 2001.
Odinga, Oginga. *Not Yet Uhuru: The Autobiography of Oginga Odinga*. London: Heinemann, 1967.
Okello, John. *Revolution in Zanzibar*. Nairobi: East African Literature Bureau, 1967.
Palmer, Robin. "Land Reform in Zimbabwe, 1980–1990." *African Affairs* 89, no. 355 (1990): 163–81.
Pandya, Paresh. *Mao Tse-tung and Chimurenga: An Investigation into ZANLA's Strategies*. Pretoria: Skotaville, 1988.
Parker, Jim. *Assignment Selous Scouts: Inside Story of a Rhodesian Special Branch Officer*. Alberton, South Africa: Galago, 2006.

Percy, Sarah. *Mercenaries: The History of a Norm in International Relations.* Oxford: Oxford University Press, 2007.

Perham, Margery. "Foreword" to J. M. Kariuki, *"Mau Mau" Detainee,* 11–24. London: Oxford University Press, 1963.

Peterson, Scott. *Me against My Brother: A War in Somalia, Sudan and Rwanda.* New York: Routledge, 2001.

Pherudi, Mokete Lawrence. "The Lesotho Liberation Army (LLA): Formation, Missions, and Schisms." *South African Historical Journal* 45, no. 1 (2001): 266–77.

Pike, David. *My Part in the Downfall: Staying Civil in the Rhodesian War.* Pietermaritzburg, South Africa: David Pike, 2009.

Pilossof, Rory. *The Unbearable Whiteness of Being: Farmers' Voices from Zimbabwe.* Harare: Weaver, 2012.

Pittaway, Jonathan, ed. *Selous Scouts: The Men Speak.* Durban: Dandy Agencies, 2015.

Porch, Douglas. *Counterinsurgency: Exposing the Myths of the New Way of War.* Cambridge: Cambridge University Press, 2013.

Price, Richard. "A Genealogy of the Chemical Weapons Taboo." *International Organization* 49, no. 1 (1995): 73–103.

"The Price White Rhodesia Is Willing to Pay . . . but Manpower Is Running Low." *Sunday Times,* 26 November 1976, 5.

Pringle, Ian. *Dingo Firestorm: The Greatest Battle of the Rhodesian Bush War.* Solihull, UK: Helion 2012. Kindle edition.

Pringle, Ian. *Green Leader: Operation Gatling, the Rhodesian Military's Response to the Viscount Tragedy.* Solihull, UK: Helion, 2015.

Pringle, Ian. *Murder in the Zambezi: The Story of the Air Rhodesia Viscounts Shot Down by Russian-Made Missiles.* n.p.: CreateSpace, 2017.

Raeburn, Michael. *We Are Everywhere: Narratives from Rhodesian Guerrillas.* New York: Random House, 1979.

Raftopoulos, Brian, and Alois Mlambo, eds. *Becoming Zimbabwe: A History from the Precolonial Period to 2008.* Harare: Weaver, 2009.

Rak, Julie. "Memoir, Truthiness, and the Power of Oprah." *Prose Studies* 34, no. 3 (2012): 224–42.

Ranger, Terence. *"Are We Not Also Men?": The Samkange Family and African Politics in Zimbabwe 1920–1964.* Portsmouth, NH: Heinemann, 1995.

Ranger, Terence. *Voices from the Rocks: Nature, Culture, and History in the Matopos Hills of Zimbabwe.* Bloomington: Indiana University Press, 1999.

Ranger, Terence. *Writing Revolt: An Engagement with African Nationalism.* Harare: Weaver, 2013.

Rasmussen, Nicholas. "What Moves When Technologies Migrate? 'Software' and Hardware in the Transfer of Biological Electron Microscopy to Postwar Australia." *Technology and Culture* 40, no. 1 (1999): 47–73.

Raudzens, George. "War-Winning Weapons: The Measurement of Technological Determinism in Military History." *Journal of Military History* 54, no. 4 (1990): 403–34.

Rayner, William. *The Day of Chaminuka*. New York: Atheneum, 1976.
Reid-Daly, Ron. *Pamwe Chete: The Legend of the Selous Scouts*. Weltevreden Park, South Africa: Covos Day, 1999.
Reid-Daly, Ron. *Staying Alive: A Southern African Survival Handbook*. Rivonia, South Africa: Ashanti, 1990.
Reid-Daly, Ron. "Summing Up." In Pittaway, *Selous Scouts*, 517–20.
Reid-Daly, Lt. Col. Ron, as told to Peter Stiff. *Selous Scouts: Top Secret War*. Alberton, South Africa: Galago, 1982.
Reno, William. *Warfare in Independent Africa*. Cambridge: Cambridge University Press, 2011.
Renwick, Robin. *Unconventional Diplomacy in Southern Africa*. New York: St. Martin's, 1997.
Richards, Paul. *Fighting for the Rain Forest: War, Youth and Resources in Sierra Leone*. Oxford: James Currey, 1996.
Roberts, R. S. "The Armed Forces and Chimurenga: Ideology and Historiography." *History of Zimbabwe* 7 (1989): 31–47.
Ross, Jay. "Survivors Term Zimbabwe-Rhodesian Killings 'Massacre.'" *Washington Post*, 18 August 1979, A11.
Rousseau, Nicky. "Counter-revolutionary Warfare: The Soweto Intelligence Unit and Southern Itineraries." *Journal of Southern African Studies* 40, no. 6 (2014): 1343–61.
Russell, Edmund. *War and Nature: Fighting Humans and Insects with Chemicals from World War I to Silent Spring*. Cambridge: Cambridge University Press, 2001.
Ryan, Andy. *Those Who Dared: The Rhodesian SAS*. Columbia, SC: published by the author, 2018.
Samupindi, Charles. *Pawns*. Harare: Baobab, 1992.
Sanderson, Sandy [I. M.]. *Intake 131: Nineteen Weeks as a Rhodesian Officer Cadet*. Cirencester, UK: Memoirs Publishing Group, 2015.
Sassoon, Siegfried. *Memoirs of an Infantry Officer*. London: Faber and Faber, 1965 [1930].
Savory, Capt. Allan. "Tracking in the Rhodesian Army." In Pittaway, *Selous Scouts*, 83–91.
Scarnecchia, Timothy. "The Anglo-American and Commonwealth Negotiations for a Zimbabwe Settlement between Geneva and Lancaster House, 1977–1979." *Journal of Imperial and Commonwealth History* 45, no. 5 (2017): 823–43.
Scarnecchia, Timothy. *The Urban Roots of Democracy and Political Violence: Harare and Highfield, 1940–1964*. Rochester, NY: Rochester University Press, 2008.
Schroeder, Richard A. "Moving Targets: The 'Canned' Hunting of Captive-Bred Lions in South Africa." *African Studies Review* 61, no. 1 (2018): 8–22.
Scott-Donelan, David. "Tracker Combat Unit." In Pittaway, *Selous Scouts*, 92–103.
Scully, Pat. *Exit Rhodesia: From UDI to Marxism*. Ladysmith, South Africa: Westcott Printing, 1984.

Seirlis, J. K. "Undoing the United Front? Coloured Soldiers in Rhodesia 1939–1980." *African Studies* 63, no. 1 (2004): 73–94.

Shaw, Angus. *Kandaya: Another Time, Another Place*. Harare: Baobab, 1993.

Sheffy, Yigal. "Chemical Warfare and the Palestine Campaign, 1916–1918." *Journal of Military History* 73, no. 3 (2009): 803–44.

Shubin, Vladimir. *The Hot Cold War: The USSR and Southern Africa*. London: Pluto, 2008.

Singer, P. W. *Corporate Warriors: The Rise of the Privatized Military Industry*. Ithaca, NY: Cornell University Press, 2003.

Sledge, E. B. *With the Old Breed at Peleliu and Okinawa*. New York: Oxford University Press, 1981.

Smith, David Lovatt. *My Enemy, My Friend*. Broadoak, UK: published by the author, 2003.

Smith, Ian Douglas. *The Great Betrayal: The Memoirs of Ian Douglas Smith*. London: Blake, 1997.

Smith, Ivan. *Bush Pig District Cop: Service in the British South African Police in the Rhodesian Conflict, 1965–1977*. Solihull, UK: Helion, 2006.

Smith, Ivan. *Come Break a Spear*. Bulawayo: Black Eagle, 1980.

Smith, Leonard V. *Between Mutiny and Obedience: The Case of the French Infantry Division during World War I*. Princeton, NJ: Princeton University Press, 1994.

Smith, Leonard V. *The Embattled Self: French Soldiers' Testimony of the Great War*. Ithaca, NY: Cornell University Press, 2007.

Smith, Sylvia Bond. *Ginette*. Bulawayo: Black Eagle, 1980.

Southall, Roger. *South Africa's Transkei: The Political Economy of an "Independent" Bantustan*. New York: Monthly Review Press, 1983.

Stewart, Michael P. *The Rhodesian African Rifles: The Growth and Adaptation of a Multicultural Regiment through the Rhodesian Bush War, 1965–1980*. n.p.: CreateSpace, 2013.

Stiff, Peter. *The Rain Goddess*. Alberton, South Africa: Galago, 1973.

Stiff, Peter. *See You in November: Rhodesia's No-Holds-Barred Intelligence War*. Alberton, South Africa: Galago, 1985.

Stiff, Peter. *Selous Scouts: A Pictorial Account*. Alberton, South Africa: Galago, 1984.

Stiff, Peter. *Taming the Landmine*. Alberton, South Africa: Galago, 1986.

Stiff, Peter. *Warfare by Other Means: South Africa in the 1980s and 1990s*. Alberton, South Africa: Galago, 2001.

Stockwell, John. *In Search of Enemies: A CIA Story*. New York: Norton, 1978.

Stoll, David. *Between Two Armies in the Ixil Towns of Guatemala*. New York: Columbia University Press, 1993.

Stoll, David. *Rigoberta Menchú and the Story of All Poor Guatemalans*. Boulder, CO: Westview, 1999.

Storey, William Kelleher. *Guns, Race and Power in Colonial South Africa*. Cambridge: Cambridge University Press, 2008.

Storey, William Kelleher. "Guns, Race and Skill in Nineteenth-Century Southern Africa." *Technology and Culture* 45 (2004): 687–711.

Strachan, Hew. "Training, Morale, and Modern War." *Journal of Contemporary History* 4, no. 2 (2006): 211–27.

Stranack, Barry. *Demand a Brave Heart: A True Story*. Durban: Pinetown Printers, 2015.

Streets, Heather. *Martial Races: The Military, Race, and Masculinity in British Imperial Culture, 1857–1914*. Manchester: Manchester University Press, 2004.

Sweet, James H. "Mistaken Identities? Olaudah Equiano, Domingo Alvares, and the Methodological Challenges of Studying the African Diaspora." *American Historical Review* 114, no. 2 (2009): 279–306.

Taylor, Stu. *Lost in Africa*. Johannesburg: 30 Degrees South, 2007.

Thomas, Kevin. *Shadows in an African Twilight: Game Ranger, Soldier, Hunter*. Cape Town: New Voices, 2008.

Thompson, Janice E. *Mercenaries, Pirates and Sovereigns: State-Building and Extraterritorial Violence in Early Modern Europe*. Princeton, NJ: Princeton University Press, 1994.

Thursh, Alan. *Of Land and Spirits*. Guernsey: Transition, 1997.

Tippette, Giles. *The Mercenaries*. New York: Dell, 1976.

Tredger, Nick. *From Rhodesia to Mugabe's Zimbabwe: Chronicles of a Game Ranger*. Alberton, South Africa: Galago, 2009.

Trethowan, Anthony. *Delta Scout: Ground Coverage Operator*. Johannesburg: 30 Degrees South, 2008.

Trew, Anthony. *Towards the Tamarind Trees*. London: Collins, 1970.

Twagira, Benjamin. "'The Men Have Come': Gender and Militarization in Kampala, 1966–86." *Gender and History* 28, no. 3 (2016): 813–32.

Twala, Mwezi, and Ed Benard. *Mbokodo: Inside MK, Mwezi Twala—A Soldier's Story*. Johannesburg: Jonathan Ball, 1994.

Ushewokunze, H. M. S. *An Agenda for Zimbabwe*. Harare: College Press, 1984.

Venter, A. J. *Barrel of a Gun: A War Correspondent's Misspent Moments in Combat*. Philadelphia: Casemate, 2010.

Venter, A. J. "Recon: Action in Southern Africa." *Soldier of Fortune* 2, no. 2 (1977): 14–21.

Walsh, Toc. *Mampara: Rhodesia Regiment Moments of Mayhem by a Moronic, Maybe Militant, Madman*. Johannesburg: 30 Degrees South, 2014.

Ward, Harvey. *Sanctions Buster*. Glasgow: William MacClellan Embryo, 1982.

Warren, Charlie. *At the Going Down of the Sun*. n.p.: BookSurge, 2006.

Warren, Charlie. *Stick Leader RLI*. Durban: Just Done Publications, 2007. First published as *At the Going Down of the Sun*. n.p.: BookSurge, 2006.

Warren, Kay B. "Telling Truths: Taking David Stoll and the Rigoberta Menchú Exposé Seriously." In Arias, *Rigoberta Menchú Controversy*, 198–218.

Watson, Jack. *Conspire to Kill*. Salisbury, Rhodesia: Penn Medos, 1976.

Watts, Carl Peter. *Rhodesia's Unilateral Declaration of Independence: An International History*. London: Palgrave, 2012.

Werbner, Richard, ed. *Memory and the Postcolony: African Anthropology and the Critique of Power*. London: Zed Books, 1998.

Werbner, Richard. "Smoke from the Barrel of the Gun: Postwars of the Dead, Memory and Reinscription in Zimbabwe." In Werbner, *Memory and the Postcolony*, 71–102.

Wessels, Hannes. *A Handful of Hard Men: The SAS and the Battle for Rhodesia*. Philadelphia: Casemate, 2015.

Wessely, Simon. "Ten Years On: What Do We Know about Gulf War Syndrome?" *Clinical Medicine* 1, no. 1 (2001): 28–37.

West, Michael O. "Nationalism, Race, and Gender: The Politics of Family Planning in Zimbabwe, 1957–1990." *Social History of Medicine* 7, no. 3 (1994): 447–71.

White, Luise. "Animals, Prey and Enemies: Hunting and Killing in an African Counter-insurgency." *Journal of Contemporary African Studies* 34, no. 1 (2016): 7–21.

White, Luise. *The Assassination of Herbert Chitepo: Texts and Politics in Zimbabwe*. Bloomington: Indiana University Press, 2003.

White, Luise. "Civic Virtue, Young Men, and the Family: Conscription in Rhodesia, 1974–1980." *International Journal of African Historical Studies* 37, no. 1 (2004): 103–21.

White, Luise. "A 'Deafening Silence' and a 'Piece of Speech': Regimes of Silence in an African Counter-insurgency." In *Truth, Silence and Violence in Emerging States: Histories of the Unspoken*, edited by Aidan Russell, 111–26. London: Routledge, 2019.

White, Luise. "Students, ZAPU and Special Branch in Francistown, 1965–1970." *Journal of Southern African Studies* 40, no. 6 (2014): 1289–1303.

White, Luise. *Unpopular Sovereignty: Rhodesian Independence and African Decolonization*. Chicago: University of Chicago Press, 2015.

White, Luise. "What Does It Take to Be a State? Sovereignty and Sanctions in Rhodesia." In *The State of Sovereignty: Territories, Laws, Populations*, edited by Douglas Howland and Luise White, 148–68. Bloomington: Indiana University Press, 2009.

White, Luise. "'Whoever Saw a Country with Four Armies?': The Battle of Bulawayo Revisited." *Journal of Southern African Studies* 33, no. 3 (2007): 619–31.

Whitlock, Gillian. *Soft Weapons: Autobiography in Transit*. Chicago: University of Chicago Press, 2007.

Wilkinson, Anthony R. *Insurgency in Rhodesia, 1957–1973: An Account and Assessment*. Adelphi Paper no. 100. London: International Institute for Strategic Studies, 1973.

Wilkinson, Peter. *Msasa*. Warksworth, New Zealand: Peter Wilkinson, 1992.

Willis, Justin. "The Two Lives of Mpamizo: Dissonance in Oral History." *History in Africa* 23 (1996): 319–32.

Wood, J. R. T. *Counter-Strike from the Sky: The Rhodesian All-Arms Fireforce in the War in the Bush, 1974–1980.* Johannesburg: 30 Degrees South, 2009.

Wood, J. R. T. *A Matter of Weeks Rather Than Months: The Impasse between Harold Wilson and Ian Smith, Sanctions, Aborted Settlements and War, 1965–1969.* Victoria, BC: Tafford, 2008.

Wood, J. R. T. *So Far and No Further! Rhodesia's Bid for Independence during the Retreat from Empire 1959–1965.* Victoria, BC: Tafford, 2005.

Wood, J. R. T. *The War Diaries of Andre Dennison.* Gibraltar: Ashanti, 1989.

Wylie, Dan. *Dead Leaves: Two Years in the Rhodesian War.* Pietermaritzburg, South Africa: University of Natal Press, 2002.

INDEX

African National Congress (ANC), 113
African National Council (ANC), 8, 202. *See also* UANC
AK-47. *See* weapons.
Americans: desertion by, 174–75; in fiction, 2–3, 124, 172; lawsuits, 195–96; numbers of, 174–75; opposition to, 181–83; in Rhodesian Army, 2, 57, 169–73, 177, 179; slang and, 56–57, 181; support for, 182–85. *See also* Brown; Central Intelligence Agency; mercenaries; Rhodesian Army; *Soldier of Fortune*
Amin, Idi, 205–8, 216. *See also* Uganda; Security Force Auxiliaries
Anderson, John, 88, 167–68
animals: Africans imagined as, 21, 147–48, 160, 217–19; hunting of, 15, 86, 94, 102, 183
anthrax, 161–4; bushcraft and, 163–64; weaponizing of, 162
Armored Car Regiment (ARC), 99, 180
Associated Press (AP), 185–86, 188, 189, 190
Atkins, Graham, 53

Balaam, A. J., 24, 78, 81, 86, 94, 99, 104, 112–13, 114
Ballinger, Tony, 53, 123, 124
Barnett, Donald, 35
Baughman, Ross, 47, 97, 183, 185–90, 196; Overseas Press Club Prize and, 188, 190–91; Pulitzer Prize and, 188, 192; war photography and, 190–91
Bax, Timothy, 95, 119, 178, 180
Beah, Ishmael, 44, 55

Biafra: Rhodesian imagination of, 3, 34, 141, 146; mercenaries in, 170
biological and chemical weapons: as cause of death, 150–51; efficiency of, 153–55; history of 146–48; insecticides and, 147; peacetime research into, 147; victims of (intended), 142, 146–48, 157; war and, 141–42, 145. *See also* anthrax; cholera; poisons
Bird, Ed, 72–73, 154–56
Borlace, Mike, 171
Bourke, Joanna, 20–25
Brown, Robert K., 179–80, 181, 182, 192, 194. *See also* Americans; mercenaries; *Soldier of Fortune*
Breytenbach, Jan, 101
Brice, Taffy, 150, 158
British South Africa Company, 2, 4
British South African Police (BSAP): history of, 12, 16, 168; poisons and, 152, 157–60; Rhodesian Army, relations with, 18, 28, 54, 60, 77, 104–5, 145, 212; tracking in, 53, 83–84, 87–89; war effort and, 83, 125, 150, 168, 186, 212. *See also* Special Branch; Godwin; P. Stiff
Burgos-Debray, Elisabeth, 38–39
bushcraft, 3, 13, 19, 25; Africans and, 23, 83–89, 100; counterinsurgency and, 83, 84, 88–90, 105; guerrilla, 100–101; local knowledge and, 86, 200; whites' skills (learned from Africans), 86–88, 224–25; whites' skills (learned from books), 85; whites' skills (learned from nature), 93. *See also* tracking; war-in-the-place

Caute, David, 27–28, 48–49, 57, 128, 131, 180, 188, 209, 225
Central African Federation, 1, 10
Central Intelligence Agency (CIA), 165, 171, 172; Americans in Rhodesia, opposition to, 181–82, 194–96; Americans in Rhodesia, support for, 181–82, 185
Central Intelligence Organization (CIO): guerrilla war and, 97, 177; memoirs and, 45, 62; poisons and, 144, 157; Security Force Auxiliaries and, 200–202, 210, 216, 218. See also Flower
Chakawa, Joshua, 198–99, 211, 212
China, 6, 71, 101–2, 130–2, 138 141, 223
Chirau, Jeremiah (Chief), 8, 257n14
Chitepo, Herbert, 5–6, 7
cholera, 142, 162–63; water supply and, 164–65
Ciskei, 113–14. See also Transkei Defence Force
Clough, Marshall, 36–37
Cocks, Chris: as author, 21, 46, 51, 53, 98, 125, 197; as editor, 116–17, 119. See also Covos-Day; lawsuits
Coey, John Alan, 171
Congress of Racial Equality (CORE), 179. See also mercenaries
counterinsurgency, 13, 26, 57; African anticipation of, 163; criticisms of, 59–60; effectiveness of, 150–51, 155; literature, "lessons from," 59–60, 220; limits of, 197, 219–21; local knowledge and, 77; manpower and, 30, 172, 197–98; Mau Mau and, 34; as misnomer, 23; pleasures of, 59–61, 75–76, 79–82; regimental rivalries in, 210–11; regular armies and, 60–61, 81, 197–98; small groups in, 10, 66–67, 210; young men and, 63. See also Kitson; pseudo gangs; Selous Scouts
Couser, Thomas, 36, 39
Covos-Day, 116–18
Criminal Investigation Department (CID). See BSAP

Crippled Eagles, 182, 183, 184, 189, 192, 195; *Crippled Eagles* (Moore), 193–94. *See also* Gillespie; Moore
Cronin, John, 155, 159, 172.
Croukamp, Dennis, 15, 21, 67, 86, 102–4

De Kock, Eugene, 44, 106
Dennison, Andre, 177, 178
Desble, Jean-Michel, 114

Early, John, 170, 178, 182, 220
Ellert, Henrik, 197, 182, 205, 213, 216
Equiano, Olaudah, 38, 46, 158.
Erasmus, Henry Gideon, 109, 110, 111, 112, 116.

Flower, Ken, 62, 165, 177; confessional writings of, 143–45, 157; Security Force Auxiliaries and, 200–202, 216; Sithole and, 204–5. *See also* Central Intelligence Organization
flechas, 138, 176
FNLA (Frente Nacional de Libertação de Angola), 47, 170–71, 178
Foucault, Michel, 32, 36
FRELIMO (Frente de Liberação Moçambique), 54, 56, 67, 98, 115, 132, 171, 176; cholera and, 164–65; trackers, 86; ZANLA and, 132; ZIPA and, 7–8,
French, Paul, 78
Frey, James, 40, 46, 119
FROLIZI (Front for the Liberation of Zimbabwe), 6, 7
Fuller, Alexandra, 33, 45, 137

Galago, 50–51, 115–19. *See also* lawsuits; F. Stiff; P. Stiff
Gillespie, Verne, 183, 188–89, 192, 193, 195–96. *See also* Americans, Crippled Eagles, Moore
Ginzburg, Carlo, 84, 89; Ginzburg-Mavhunga test, 85, 105, 108
Gledhill, Dick, 15
Godwin, Peter, 44–45, 50, 54–55, 77
Gough, Chris, 110, 117, 118

282 | INDEX

Greenberg, Karl, 168
Grey's Scouts: founding of, 14, 47; interrogations by, 186–88, 189, 190–91; patrols of, 46, 184–88. *See also* Baughman; Moore-King; Williams
guerrillas: clothes and shoes of, 50, 68, 79, 92, 97–98, 160; communist threat as, 18; domestication by Rhodesian Army, 51–53, 68–72, 224; poisoning of, 144–46, 148–61; shooting by, 121–23, 125–30, 136–40; surrender of, 200–204, 210–18; training of, 6, 24, 30, 130–37; turning of, 59–61, 63, 65, 69–74, 99; urban legends about, 50. *See also* Security Force Auxiliaries; ZANLA; ZIPA; ZIPRA
guns. *See* weapons
Gutu, Martin, 75

Hall, Jeremy, 126
Harper-Ronald, Jake, 79, 169
Hart, Winston, 80, 118
Headrick, Daniel, 127, 139
Helion, 243n32
Henderson, Ian, 34, 64–65; as Rhodesian imaginary, 62–63
Hickman, John, 62, 107
Hitchens, Christopher, 180, 225
Hoare, Mike, 170, 176, 194–95
Hoffman, Danny, 20–21
Hosking, Peter, 178
hunting, 15, 83; of semidomesticates, 218; by white children, 86, 94–95, 102, 218. *See also* animals; poaching; tracking
Hynes, Samuel, 14, 41, 42, 43, 57. *See also* memoirs; war-in-the-head

IDAF (International Defence and Aid Fund), 75, 237n41
Intaf (Internal Affairs), 71, 164 176; Guard Force, 180–81

Jackson, Brian, 123, 124
Jal, Emmanuel, 33, 44, 55
JOC (Joint Operating Command), 199

Kambona, Oscar, 205
Kanondareka, Arthur (Rev.), 144–45, 249n5
Kariuki, J. M., 34–35
Kitson, Frank, 60–61, 68, 71, 220; influence of, 68, 80, 81, 112, 200, 208–9, 213; Mau Mau and, 62–65, 75–77. *See also* counterinsurgency; Mau Mau; pseudo gangs

Lamprecht, Nick 175, 177, 178, 180, 243n42
languages: African, spoken by white soldiers, 34, 59, 62, 65, 86, 224; English, spoken by African soldiers, 67, 99–100.
lawsuits: biological and chemical weapons and, 165–66; *Frances Florina Stiff vs. Ronald Francis Reid-Daly and Covos-Day Trading*, 117–18; *Galago vs. Erasmus and others*, 116, 117; *Gideon Henry Erasmus vs. Galago and Peter Stiff*, 115–16; Moore and, 195–96; *Reid-Daly vs. John Hickman and others*, 106–7, 108; *Scope* and, 114. *See also* Covos-Day; Galago; *Pamwe Chete*
Lemur, 116. *See* Galago
Lesotho Liberation Army (LLA), 112–13
Long Reach, 106, 114

MacKenzie, Bob, 113, 123, 172, 174, 182
Maltas, John, 104, 107
Martin, Faan, 87–88
Mau Mau, 37; pseudo gangs in, 60–77; in Rhodesian imagination, 34, 61, 67–68; turning in, 63–68. *See also* counterinsurgency; Henderson; Kitson
Mavros, Patrick, 105
Mavhunga, Clapperton, 84. 127, 147; Ginzburg-Mavhunga test, 85, 105, 108
McAleese, Peter, 22–24, 204, 212–13; as mercenary, 47, 171, 177–78
McGuiness, Michael "Mac": biological and chemical weapons and, 146, 153, 154, 157, 162; Security Force Auxiliaries and, 199, 203–4, 213, 249n13. *See also* poisons; Special Branch
Meadows, Keith, 102

memoirs: African, 33–34, 37; audience for, 50; authorship of 32, 33–35, 109–11, 115–20; common stories in, 52; controversies over, 37–41, 115–17; copyright of, 32, 39, 57, 110, 116–17, 119, 243n30; fiction and, 41; ghost written, 35–36, 50–51; glossaries in, 33, 54–57; numbers in, 77, 98–99, 165–66, 210; pranks in, 28, 225, 231n84; production of, 44–45; royalties for, 39, 110; self-published, 32, 48, 51, 55, 60, 75, 94; struggles between authors of, 72–73; transgender, 60; war, 41–43, 47–48. *See also* Covos-Day; Equiano; Galago; Menchú; Frey

Menchú, Rigoberta, 40, 219, 220
mercenaries: in Angola, 170–71, 176; decolonization and, 170; definition of, 169; history of, 169–70; recruitment of, 175–78
Mhanda, Wilfred, 133
Moore, Robin, 124, 169, 172, 192–96; in Rhodesia, 178, 180, 182–84
Moore-King, Bruce, 47, 190
Morris, Jan, 14, 18, 76, 79, 173
Moss, Basil, 80, 215
MPLA (Movimento Popular de Liberação de Angola), 47, 172, 179
Mugabe, Robert, 4, 5, 8, 9, 70, 90; 1980 election, 16; planned assassination of, 158–59; ZANU and, 195, 196, 206
Murphy, John, 181–82
Mutambara, Agrippah, 85, 133
Muzorewa, Bishop Abel, 7, 8, 9, 73, 144–45, 186; president, as, 197, 198, 199, 200, 202, 203–6, 208, 211, 212, 215, 217–18

Nasson, Bill, 3, 129, 136
national service: after 1971, 11–14; before 1971, 10–11; desertion, 18; disobedience, 25–28; mixed-race population and, 11; morale in, 17–19; skills and, 19, 91; training, 23, 97–99. *See also* Rhodesian Army; Territorial Army
NDP (National Democratic Party), 4
Nell, Keith, 49, 132, 210, 211, 213

Newkirk, Henry, 195
Njama, Karari, 35
Nkomo, Joshua, 4, 5, 8, 9, 48, 70, 103, 135; Viscount tragedies and, 136–37

OAU (Organization of African Unity), 5; Liberation Committee of, 5–7, 205
O'Brien, Lindsay, 213–14
O'Brien, Tim, 41, 42, 43, 122
OCC (Operations Coordinating Committee), 175–76, 202–3
Odinga, Oginga, 36
Okello, John, 35–36

PAC (Pan-African Congress), 113, 134
Pamwe Chete (Reid-Daly), 68, 72, 116–118, 120. *See also* lawsuits
Parker, Jim, 51, 70, 73, 145, 162–64, 204, 211
Patriotic Front, 144. *See also* ZANU(PF)
PATU (Police Anti-Terrorist Unit), 197, 259n69
PCC (People's Caretaker Council), 5
peace-in-the-head, 15–17, 27
Pfumo reVanhu, 9, 212–13. *See also* Security Force Auxiliaries
Pike, David, 124
poaching, 19; bushcraft and, 105–6; RhAF and, 102; Selous Scouts and, 92, 101–6, 109; UNITA and, 102 *See also* Croukamp; Thomas
poisons: African medicine and, 148–50, 153, 163–64; boots and, 161; bullets and, 158–59; canned meat and, 153; clothes and 157–61; efficiency of, 154–55, 159; food and, 151–55; hygiene and, 151, 164–66; organophosphates, 160–61, 164; patent medicine and, 155–56; ricin, 158; thallium, 143, 150, 155; underwear and, 157, 160; uniforms and, 143, 144–45; Warfarin, 143; water and, 142, 164–65; witches and, 149–50; Z Desk and, 146, 148, 153, 154, 157, 165. *See also* Bird; Flower; McGuiness
pseudo gangs, 52, 59–61; cover stories and, 61, 68–69; domesticity in, 51–52, 71, 81–82;

guerrillas turning, 51–52, 63–65, 68, 71–75; masquerade in, 65, 75–80; origins of, 61–62; patrol and, 27, 59–60, 63, 64, 65–66, 75–77, 79, 80, 86; racial categories in, 63, 66, 76–77, 81–82, 92, 95; turned guerrillas' loyalty to, 70, 99–100. *See also* Mau Mau; Selous Scouts

PsyAc (Psychological Action), 28–29, 188, 200–201, 202, 207.

Rabie, Andre, 65–66, 92.

RAR (Rhodesian African Rifles), 17, 23, 26, 43, 65, 86, 96, 127–29, 138–40, 208; 1RAR, 128–29; 2RAR, 76, 128–29, 178, 180; effectiveness of, 128; history of, 10–12

RDR (Rhodesia Defence Regiment), 11, 184, 189

Redfern, John 102, 104, 107.

Reid-Daly, Ron, 51, 52, 53, 62, 66–67, 71, 72–73, 74, 76, 92, 103–5, 199–17, 119–20, 137–38; court martial of, 107–8; in South Africa, 106–11; in Transkei, 111–15. *See also* lawsuits; Selous Scouts

RENAMO (Resistência Nacional Moçambicana), 106. *See also* poaching; A. White

RhAF (Rhodesian Air Force), 102, 254n60

Rhodesia: belonging to, 10, 13–15,172; European population of, 10, 12–13, 167; history of, 3–12, 197–200; internal settlement, 200; isolation of, 167; nationality in, 38, 42, 167–69, 172, 184, 254n60; republic of 11; war goals of, 15–18, 51, 81, 101, 222. *See also* Rhodesian Army

Rhodesian Army: aggression of 16, 17; Americans in, 1, 57, 169–75, 177, 179, 181–84, 193; bonuses in, 12, 174, 181; command and control in, 26, 123, 131, 223; desertion, 18, 168, 174, 175, 181; disobedience, 25–26, 27, 31, 96, 139, 226; foreign soldiers, recruitment of, 171–77, 184; history of, 10–12; killing by, 20–25; kills enumerated by, 99, 157, 215–19; manpower available to, 10–13, 169, 197–202; mixed-race troops, 11, 27, 89, 176; morale of African soldiers, 81, 229n43; morale of white soldiers, 12, 16–19, 25–28, 99, 175; rates of pay, 174, 176; shoes of white soldiers, 25, 91, 98, 100, 242n12

Rhodesian Front, 4, 8, 14, 91, 162

Rhodesia Regiment, 11, 25, 53, 65, 79, 96, 123, 128, 129, 219

RLI (Rhodesian Light Infantry), 16, 51–53, 96, 97, 102, 107, 109, 111–12, 128, 164; Americans in, 174, 179; disobedience in, 98; dress of, 98; fire force, 66–67, 77, 96, 216, 217, 219; foundation of, 10; memoirs from 33, 51, 54; morale in, 16, 92; national servicemen in, 23, 33, 54, 125; slang of, 56, 96–97

Russia, 5, 71, 127, 130–32, 138; ZAPU and, 6, 48, 92, 130, 135–36. *See also* AK-47

SADF (South Africa Defence Force), 85, 101–102, 209, 252n21

SAP (South African Police), 11, 71, 101, 114, 150

SAS (Special Air Services), 23, 33, 49, 58, 75, 101; poisons and, 162, 164–65; pseudo gangs, 79, 88, 98; trackers in, 70, 86–87, 89, 95

Safe Return Policy (SRP), 74–75, 200–204. *See also* Security Force Auxiliaries

Sanger, Clyde, 34–35, 36

SASOL (South Africa Synthetic Oil Ltd), 118

Sassoon, Siegfried, 20–21

Savory, Alan, 88–91, 95, 100, 105. *See also* Tracker Combat Unit

Schollenberg, Chris, 82

Scope (magazine), 110–11, 114

Security Force Auxiliaries (SFAS), 13, 197–219; Amin and, 205–8; attitudes toward, 198–99; dress of, 213–14; Iran, training in, 205; killing of, 215–20; Libya, training in 205, 210, 212–13; mutinies by, 212, 217; private armies, as, 198; Uganda, training in 205–8; uniforms of, 206–7, 214; Zimbabwe-Rhodesia, training in, 208–15

Selous, Courtney, 14
Selous Scouts, 14, 33, 51, 58; Africans in, 93–95, 99–100, 115; cover stories in, 72, 78–80, 208–9; blacking up in, 75–78, 80; bonuses and, 81, 99; domesticating Africans and, 52–53, 68–72; expansion of, 99–100; founding of, 65–68, 92; frozen areas and, 92–93, 100–102, 208, 209; kills attributed to, 80–81; mimicry of Africans and, 93; need for African soldiers in, 81–82; Nyadzonya raid of, 98–99; poaching by, 92, 101–6, 109; race in, 52, 66, 78, 82, 94–95, 98; selection course of, 23, 86, 88, 93–94, 104–6; Security Force Auxiliaries and, 208–12, 215; tracking by, 13, 23, 30, 66–67, 88, 92, 94, 96, 100–101, 106; Training Troop of, 103–5, 107; turning guerrillas, 23, 52, 59–60, 68, 71–74, 81, 82, 199, 215; 78–80, 93. *See also* pseudo gangs; Reid-Daly
Selous Scouts: A Pictorial Account (P. Stiff), 115–16. *See also* lawsuits
Shaw, Angus, 50, 96, 125, 169, 225
shooting: African soldiers and, 127–30, 137–39; ammunition, availability of, 125–26, 133; colonial conquest and, 129–30; by guerrillas, 127, 130–40; marksmanship, 65, 122, 128, 135, 139; white soldiers and, 19, 123–26, 139. *See also* Rhodesian Army; weapons
Sibanda, Elliot, 74
Sithole, Ndabaningini (Rev.), 144; Security Force Auxiliaries and, 197–99, 200–203, 211–7, 218, 219, 221; Uganda and, 204–8; ZANU and, 5, 7, 8, 9. *See also* Security Force Auxiliaries; ZANU
skuz'apo. *See* Selous Scouts
slang, 33, 64, 79, 116, 181. *See also* memoirs
Smith, Ian, 4, 9, 10
Smith, Joseph C., 195
Smith, Leonard, 24, 27, 41, 44, 223
Soldier of Fortune (magazine), 169, 174, 183, 192, 194, 195; recruiting Americans and, 57, 170–71, 177–80, 181. *See also* Brown; Moore; lawsuits
Southern Rhodesia, 1, 4

Special Branch, 7, 27, 34, 47, 49, 76, 118, 159–60, 176, 188; fiction in, 24–25, 102; intelligence from, 130–31, 134–35; interrogations by, 26–27, 68–75; Mau Mau in, 60–64; rival units and, 146, 210–11; Security Force Auxiliaries and, 200–206, 211–13, 215–16, 219; Selous Scouts in, 65–66, 104–5, 118; weapons and, 81; Z Desk of, 47, 144–45, 148, 151, 155–57, 162. *See also* Bird; McGuiness; Nell; Stannard
SRANC (Southern Rhodesia African National Congress), 4
Stannard, Don, 105, 186
Stiff, Frances Lategan, 117, 119. *See also* lawsuits
Stiff, Peter, 50–51, 71, 73, 81; as author, 69, 110, 111–16; , 109–11, 113; lawsuits and, 114–20; poisons and, 127, 145, 146, 154, 158–59; as publisher, 109–10, 117–20. *See also* Galago; lawsuits; *Top Secret War*
Stranack, Barry, 52, 86, 94, 96, 211
Symington, Robert, 150

Taylor, Stu, 87, 99, 102
technology, 59, 138, 139–44, 191; Africans' use of, 126–27, 138, 140; European thinking about, 138–39, 191. *See also* weapons
Territorial Army, 12, 16, 89, 91, 99, 124, 144, 146, 197. *See also* national service 30 Degrees South, 243n32
Thomas, Kevin, 79, 80, 86, 95, 97, 101, 102, 104, 122, 127. *See also* poaching
Thrush, Alan, 138–39
Top Secret War (book), 51, 52, 62, 68; authorship of, 109–17; influence of, 53–54, 62, 69–71, 182, 199; Security Force Auxiliaries and, 201, 204, 209–11, 215. *See also* Covos-Day; Galago; lawsuits
Tracker Combat Unit (TCU), 89, 91–92
tracking: Africans, as learned by, 84–85; antitracking, 83–84, 85, 90–91, 96–97; deskilling of, 95–97; guerrillas and, 84, 100, 123; local knowledge and, 97; race and, 53, 93–95; in Rhodesian Army, 88–90; shoes and, 90, 91, 97–98, 100;

whites, as learned by, 86–87, 94. *See also* bushcraft; Tracker Combat Unit
Transkei, 112, 114. *See also* Transkei Defence Force
Transkei Defence Force (TDF), 110, 110–15
Tredger, Nick, 85
Trethowan, Anthony, 53

UANC (United African National Council), 7, 145, 198–99, 203–4, 205, 209, 211–14. *See also* Muzorewa; Pfumo reVanhu
UDI (Unilateral Declaration of Independence). *See* Rhodesia
Uganda, 204–8. *See also* Security Force Auxiliaries; Sithole
UNHCR (United Nations High Commission on Refugees), 220
USSR, 5, 6, 68, 72, 122, 131, 133, 135–36, 138, 140, 176, 182, 205, 223

Venter, A. J., 174
Viscount tragedies, 48–49, 58, 137

Walls, Peter, 16, 48–49, 121, 182; Reid-Daly and, 92, 107 111, 120
Walsh, Toc, 96
war-in-the-head, 14–15, 57, 211, 234n89. *See also* Hynes
war-in-the-place, 24–25, 83, 142–43, 199–200; local knowledge and, 76–77
Warren, Clive, 118
Watt, Darrell, 49, 91, 95, 97
weapons: AK-47, 121–23, 125–26, 130, 139, 182; of, 182; antiaircraft, 134, 135, 136; automatic rifles, 124, 125–27; FN, 123–26, 139, 183; landmines, 133, 135, 220, 182; Rhodesian imaginings of, 137; rocket-propelled grenades, 138; self-loading rifles, 123; Special Branch collection of, 81; surface-to-air missiles, 48–49, 136; Tokarev pistols, 132, 202; unsophisticated, 130; wooden, 136–37. *See also* shooting

White, Ant (James Anthony), 104, 105, 106, 111, 165. *See also* poaching; RENAMO; Selous Scouts
Williams, Mike, 181, 182, 184, 186, 188–90, 191, 194, 195–96. *See also* Baughman; Grey's Scouts; Moore
Williamson, Craig. *See* Long Reach
Wolhunter, Henry, 145, 154, 156
Wylie, Dan, 18

ZANLA (Zimbabwe African National Liberation Army): arms of, 132–33, 157; dress of, 57, 199; founding, 6; morale in, 132; in Mozambique, 8, 54, 67, 79, 132, 155, 165–66; Nhari mutiny, 7–8; poisonings and, 143; in Tanzania, 131, 135; training in, 5–6, 23, 66, 85, 130–35, 137
ZANU (Zimbabwe African National Union), 5–8, 73, 130, 135; Sithole and, 197, 199, 200, 203, 205, 206, 207, 208, 212, 216; Zambia, in, 5, 7, 72. *See also* ZANLA; ZANU(PF)
ZANU(PF) (Zimbabwe African National Union [Patriotic Front]), 8, 197, 200, 206, 217
ZAPU (Zimbabwe African People's Union), 5–8, 48, 75, 149; 1979 election, in, 73; March 11 Movement, 6; Patriotic Front and, 144. *See also* ZIPRA
Zimbabwe-Rhodesia: 1, 9, 16, 204–19; 1979 election, 8, 73; Lancaster House conference and, 9
Zimbabwe United People's Organization (ZUPO), 8, 257n14
ZIPRA (Zimbabwe People's Revolutionary Army), 7, 8, 24, 27, 30, 47, 48–49, 72, 74, 75, 79, 99, 102, 132, 134–35, 163; in Angola, 8; in Botswana, 74; as conventional army, 11, 134–35, 136; poisons and, 157, 165; Russia and, 131–32; Viscount and, 48–50, 196; in Zambia, 7, 8–9, 24, 49, 72, 75, 131, 162, 202, 206, 210
ZIPA (Zimbabwe People's Army), 7–8

www.ingramcontent.com/pod-product-compliance
Lightning Source LLC
Chambersburg PA
CBHW051049230426
43666CB00012B/2626